Becoming T. S. Eliot

BECOMING T. S. ELIOT

The Rhetoric of Voice and Audience in *Inventions of the March Hare*

Jayme Stayer

Johns Hopkins University Press
Baltimore

 Published 2021
Printed in the United States of America on acid-free paper
2 4 6 8 9 7 5 3 1

Johns Hopkins University Press
2715 North Charles Street
Baltimore, Maryland 21218-4363
www.press.jhu.edu

Library of Congress Cataloging-in-Publication Data
Names: Stayer, Jayme, author.
Title: Becoming T. S. Eliot : the rhetoric of voice and audience in Inventions of the March Hare / Jayme Stayer.
Description: Baltimore : Johns Hopkins University Press, 2021. | Includes bibliographical references and index.
Identifiers: LCCN 2020045436 | ISBN 9781421441030 (hardcover ; acid-free paper) | ISBN 9781421441047 (paperback ; acid-free paper) | ISBN 9781421441054 (ebook)
Subjects: LCSH: Eliot, T. S. (Thomas Stearns), 1888–1965—Criticism and interpretation. | Eliot, T. S. (Thomas Stearns), 1888–1965—Technique. | Eliot, T. S. (Thomas Stearns), 1888–1965. Inventions of the March Hare.
Classification: LCC PS3509.L43 Z8699 2021 | DDC 821/.912—dc23
LC record available at https://lccn.loc.gov/2020045436

A catalog record for this book is available from the British Library.

Johns Hopkins University Press uses environmentally friendly book materials, including recycled text paper that is composed of at least 30 percent post-consumer waste, whenever possible.

For Barry and Lauren, Nick and DeAnne

CONTENTS

ACKNOWLEDGMENTS

In his fine biography of W. H. Auden, Richard Davenport-Hines begins his otherwise generous acknowledgments with the claim "I have always had a distaste for long, diffuse, emotional acknowledgements presenting their author as the centre of a uniquely loving, supportive network of scholars and admirers." I find this prejudice odd because this is exactly what I read an acknowledgments section hoping to discover: that behind the edifice of scholarship and evidence of hard labor there is love to be found. And so, without fear of sentimentality, I gladly name here many of the people and institutions who have helped, supported, and loved me during this project.

This book was originally begun more than a decade ago as my first book, but three other books, various articles, and years of Jesuit formation kept postponing its completion. Although it is my fourth published book, it is still my first monograph, and it seems appropriate to begin by acknowledging those formative influences from as far back as college and graduate school. At the University of Notre Dame, I benefited greatly from John Matthias's famous seminar on modernist poetry, which formed many future modernist scholars. Likewise, Susan Youens—though she taught musicology rather than literature—was the first to give me an inkling of how a life devoted to scholarship and archival research might be a thrilling adventure. At the University of Toledo, I was lucky enough to take Noel Stock's final course in modernism before he retired, and I am indebted to the late Wallace Martin for his help. In endless independent studies and on my dissertation committee, Jamie Barlow and Don Bialostosky were kind and crucial influences on my intellectual development.

Thanks to family and friends with whom I stayed while writing or visiting archives: Anthony and Melanie Fathman, and Matt and Julie Somers. Many hospitable Jesuit communities also served as inns or residences, and they did so without invoking Marianne Moore's distinction: Casa de los Mártires at Universidad Centroamericana in El Salvador; the Schell House community at John Carroll University, Cleveland, Ohio; the Farm Street, Wimbledon, and Wapping communities in London; Campion Hall, Oxford University; the Boston College communities in Brighton and Chestnut Hill, Boston, Massachusetts; the Eighty-Third St. community in New York; O'Brien Jesuit Community at Marquette University, Milwaukee, Wisconsin; Arrupe House at Loyola University Chicago, Chicago, Illinois.

My graduate assistants at John Carroll University provided invaluable help on this project: Rhiannon Lathy and Sean Kirby. Ellen Kriz provided valuable feedback. I thank all of my colleagues, chairs, and deans at Escuela de Idiomas, Universidad Centroamericana in El Salvador; the late Francis Ryan, SJ, John McBratney, and Deb Rosenthal and the English Department at John Carroll University; the English Department at Loyola University Chicago. I am particularly grateful for a Grauel Fellowship granted by John Carroll University, 2015–2016, and for the Francis C. Wade Chair, Marquette University, which I occupied in spring 2018. Many thanks for the enthusiasm and care of the editorial and publishing teams at Johns Hopkins University Press—Catherine Goldstead, Juliana McCarthy, Kathryn Marguy, Hilary S. Jacqmin—and to copyeditor Carrie Watterson, designer Kathleen Lynch, and indexer Amron Gravett of Wild Clover Book Services.

Most intimately involved in my thinking about this project are numerous colleagues who have responded to parts of the manuscript or to presentations. My acknowledgment of these scholars is not meant to suggest that they are in agreement with all of my claims here, only that they have been helpful in answering inquiries, correcting errors, or providing encouragement and direction. I am grateful to Jennifer Harris; Jonathan Stott, SJ; Mark Ravizza, SJ; and lifelong interlocutor John Mauk, who offered direction or responded to parts of a draft. I am also grateful to students in my Eliot seminars at Texas A&M–Commerce, John Carroll University, Marquette University, University of London T. S. Eliot Summer School, and to my peers in Jewel Spears Brooker's seminar on the early poems at the first annual T. S. Eliot Summer School, 2009.

I am grateful to Sir Christopher Ricks for many kindnesses, and without whose edition of *Inventions of the March Hare* my work would have been impossible. Many Eliot scholars, especially my friends in the International T. S. Eliot Society, have offered thoughtful criticism on presentations or drafts. Their camaraderie and warm friendship make my own thinking about the audience for this book come alive: Ronald Schuchard, Julia Daniel, David Ayers, Lyndall Gordon, Timothy Materer, Andrew Powers, Carey Karmel, Cyrena Pondrom, Marcia Karp, William Harmon, John Morgenstern, Jim McCue, Nancy Gish, Jewel Spears Brooker, Ron Bush, A. David Moody, Suzanne W. Churchill, Vincent Sherry, Chris Buttram, Frances Dickey, Michael Coyle, John Paul Riquelme, Christopher McVey, Joyce Wexler, John Whittier-Ferguson, with special thanks to Anthony Cuda. And if David E. Chinitz is the only scholar who is pleased by this book, the work will have been worth it.

My parents, of course. And even though this volume is dedicated to my siblings and their spouses—Barry and Lauren Stayer, Nicholas and DeAnne Billett—they are hereby absolved from having to read the damn thing.

I am deeply grateful to my Jesuit superiors who have cared for me, especially Tim Kesicky, Brian Paulson, Jim Prehn, Jim Gartland, Brad Schaeffer, and Ray Guiao, who ensured that I had the time, money, and travel opportunities to pursue my research. A few of my other Jesuit brothers whose support has indirectly influenced the book's completion are Paddy Gilger, Michael Rozier, Christopher Alt, Philip Sutherland, Martin Connell, Karl Kiser, Paul Panaretos, Michael Simone, and Alejandro Olayo Méndez.

A number of archives, libraries, and librarians have been indispensable to my research on this project. I would like to thank Dr. Patricia McGuire, archivist, and Tracy Wilkinson, assistant archivist, Archive Centre, King's College, Cambridge; Jason D. Stratman, assistant librarian at the Missouri History Museum Library, St. Louis, Missouri; Alison Hinderliter, Manuscripts and Archives Librarian, and the staffs of Special Collections, and of General Collections, Newberry Library, Chicago, Illinois; Miranda Rectenwald and Sonya Rooney, archives assistants, University Archives, Department of Special Collections, Washington University in St. Louis, University Libraries, St. Louis, Missouri; Diane Pierce-Williams, archivist, Cox Library, Milton Academy, Milton, Massachusetts; the late Stephen G. Crook, Librarian, Berg Collection, New York Public Library; the staff of the Special Collections Research Center, Regenstein Library, University of Chicago, Illinois; the staff of the Firestone Library, Princeton University, Princeton, New Jersey; the staff of the Beinecke Rare Book and Manuscript Library, Yale University, New Haven, Connecticut; Ann Hudak, literature and rare books librarian, and Amber Kohl, coordinator, Hornbake Special Collections, T. S. Eliot Collection, Special Collections, University of Maryland Libraries, College Park, Maryland; Stephen Dalton, reference librarian, Boston College, School of Theology and Ministry, Chestnut Hill, Massachusetts; Adam Green and Nevin Mayer, Grasselli Library, John Carroll University Library, University Heights, Ohio; Katherine Litwin, library director, Poetry Foundation, Chicago, Illinois.

Unpublished archival material is here cited by permission of the Eliot Estate, with particular thanks to Clare Reihill of Set Copyrights Ltd. Chapter 2 contains a few paragraphs that have been reworked from "Searching for the Early Eliot: *Inventions of the March Hare*," in *A Companion to T. S. Eliot*, edited by David E. Chinitz (Wiley Blackwell 2009). Likewise, chapter 7 contains a short section that has been expanded and reworked from "I Grow Old: T. S. Eliot's 'The Love Song of J. Alfred Prufrock' and *Inventions of the March Hare* 100 Years On," in *Literature Compass* (9.4, April 2012). Both are reproduced here by permission of Wiley Blackwell. Two paragraphs in chapters 4 and 5 have been revised from "Eliot's Culture Shock: Imagining an Audience for the Paris Poems," in *T. S. Eliot, France, and The Mind of Europe*, edited by me (Cambridge Scholars Publishing, 2015); they are reproduced here by permission of Cambridge Scholars Publishing. Chapter 6, "The Short and Surprisingly Private Life of King Bolo: The Bawdy Poems and their Audiences," is a revision and expansion of an article by the same title originally published in *The T. S. Eliot Studies Annual* (2017); it is reproduced here by permission of Clemson University Press.

ABBREVIATIONS

Published Works

Facsimile	*The Waste Land: A Facsimile and Transcript of the Original Drafts*. Ed. Valerie Eliot. San Diego: Harcourt Brace Jovanovich, 1971.
Gallup	Gallup, Donald. *T. S. Eliot: A Bibliography*. Revised and extended ed. New York: Harcourt, Brace and World 1969.
Inventions	*Inventions of the March Hare.* Ed. Christopher Ricks. New York: Harcourt Brace, 1996.
Letters 1–8	*The Letters of T. S. Eliot*. Vols. 1–8: 1898–1937. Ed. Valerie Eliot et al. London: Faber, 2009–2019.
Poems 1–2	*The Poems.* Vols. 1–2. Ed. Christopher Ricks and Jim McCue. London/Baltimore: Faber and Faber / Johns Hopkins UP, 2015.
Prose 1–8	*The Complete Prose of T. S. Eliot: The Critical Edition.* Vols. 1–8: 1905–1965. Ed. Ronald Schuchard et al. Baltimore: Johns Hopkins UP, 2014–2019.

Archives

Beinecke	Beinecke Rare Book and Manuscript Library, Yale University, New Haven, Connecticut.
Berg	The Berg Collection, New York Public Library, New York, New York.
Brown	Brown University Archives, Brown University, Providence, Rhode Island.
Houghton	Houghton Library Collections, Harvard University, Cambridge, Massachusetts.
Huntington	The Huntington Library, San Marino, California.

King's	Hayward Bequest, King's College, Cambridge University, Cambridge, UK.
Maryland	Hornbake Special Collections, T. S. Eliot Collection, Special Collections, University of Maryland Libraries, College Park, Maryland.
Metropolitan	Metropolitan Opera Archives, New York, New York.
Milton	Milton Academy Archives, Milton Academy, Milton, Massachusetts.
Missouri	Missouri History Museum Library, St. Louis, Missouri.
Princeton	Special Collections, Firestone Library, Princeton University, Princeton, New Jersey.
Washington	Washington University Libraries, Department of Special Collections, St. Louis, Missouri.

Becoming T. S. Eliot

The Apprentice Alone in His Workshop

The *Inventions* Notebook

How does a young man who writes uninspired doggerel about wilting flowers transform himself—in twenty months, without coaching or mentors—into the author of "The Love Song of J. Alfred Prufrock"? In this volume, I propose to explain this staggering accomplishment, following Eliot's artistic development and tracking parallel transitions in his personal maturation. The juvenilia are written by a compliant adolescent who shows little inclination to question the domestic, cultural, or religious values he has inherited. By contrast, the poems of his early maturity are written by a roiling, divided self—enraged and poised, sarcastic and self-conscious, urbane and anguished. This process of inventing culminates in "T. S. Eliot," the poet and the man.

The seeds of this transformation started to blossom in 1909, Eliot's fourth year at Harvard, when he began experimenting with elements of French Symbolism, popular culture, slang, and colloquial speech. The result was a radical shift in his style: the genteel longing of his juvenilia suddenly gave way to ardent meditations on suffering, exuberant riffs on vaudeville themes, and sarcastic critiques of social decorum. With their wildly shifting registers, some of the poems were incoherent and unfinishable. However, a number of them were viscerally potent, crackling with nervous energy and singing with lyric intensity. Since their content and tone would have been inappropriate for his conservative milieus, the young college student bought himself a notebook for private experimentation.

A medium-sized, leather-bound affair, the notebook was thought lost for decades. Late in his life Eliot was glad to think that it had vanished. When he died in 1965, it was still mysteriously unlocatable. It turns out that the New York Public Library had secretly acquired the notebook in 1958, along with the more famous manuscripts of *The Waste Land* drafts.[1] The library waited to announce the purchases until 1968, three years after Eliot's death. Even though a few scholars were allowed to view and paraphrase its contents, quotation from the notebook was generally forbidden for decades. At long last, in 1996, Christopher Ricks edited and published the notebook under Eliot's whimsical, provisional title, *Inventions of the March Hare*. All of the notebook poems have subsequently been republished—though no longer grouped together—in the 2015 edition of *Poems*, edited by Christopher Ricks and Jim McCue.

As a result of this long-delayed publication, only a handful of the notebook poems have been in the public eye for a century. Eliot's first masterpieces, including "Preludes," "Portrait of a Lady," "Rhapsody on a Windy Night," and "The Love Song of J. Alfred Prufrock" germinated in this workshop and were first published in 1915. With the publication of the entire notebook in 1996, some forty new poems were added to the Eliot canon. The event garnered a remarkable amount of attention in the popular press, and scholars followed suit. Many fine articles and chapters ensued tracing the influences of the young Eliot's reading or exploring the poems' thematic concerns.

This study offers a new way of looking at the notebook. Rearranging the jumbled groupings of the notebook, it places the verses in the chronological order of their composition, teasing out the narratives of their making. With their sequential order restored, dozens of mini-dramas become evident: a gesture that is risked and flubbed in one poem is remedied in the next; an effect first used tentatively is trumpeted in subsequent poems. Using the tools of rhetoric, I show how the earliest poems begin as garbled performances, fumbling around in an incoherent voice and a divided understanding of audience. The unsteady apprentice at first curses and coerces his audience into the shape he desires and winces from fear at its hostile judgments. But triumphs soon appear in quick succession as the artist gains control of his materials. The awkward apprentice becomes the accomplished craftsman, shifting with trademark ease between tonal registers, masterfully constructing a sympathetic audience, and broaching such daring themes as alienation, human suffering, and the stupidity of social convention. By the end of the notebook, the speakers are whispering—conspiratorially, hesitantly, in muted pain—into the listener's ear. With the workshop poems behind him as practice pieces, Eliot steps out onto the public stage of poetry with his best work, bearing the motifs and techniques that will define his maturity.[2]

The Rhetoric of Rhetoric, Voice, Audience, and Becoming

Eliot occasionally theorized about rhetoric, voice, and audience. Of the poetic voice, he said, "I doubt whether in any real poem only one voice is audible," which suggests a rather sophisticated theory of voice as non-monologic.[3] When it comes to the poetic audience, his thinking moves in the other direction: "Real poetry comes primarily from a pressure inside us, and not from a call from an audience."[4] That he considered the pressure of audience to be irrelevant to the writing of poetry is odd. Perhaps the "call from an audience" may not have been conscious to the poet during the writing process; nonetheless, the evidence of that rhetorical pressure is easily found in all his poems.

By rhetoric, I mean the choices and processes by which an author's second self—their writing persona, as opposed to their living self—attempts to direct the interest, involvement, reactions, and judgments of the intended reader. (In Wayne Booth's terminology, which I will be relying on, the author's second self is the "implied author," and the ideal reader constructed by the text is called the "authorial audience."[5]) In my practice, rhetorical analysis takes as its starting place the three Aristotelian categories: ethos (how a text suggests a speaking identity), logos (the what and how of a text's meaning or message), and pathos (how a text constructs its audience). Such a classical formulation—suggesting a transparency of language and clarity of communication—cannot entirely suffice. Because language is opaque, human motivation contradictory, self-awareness limited, communication vexed, and persuasion uncertain, rhetoric includes a surplus of moves to preempt the opacity of language and to shore up the unpredictability of communication—and, paradoxically, the surplus of moves may also work to contradict itself and create mixed messages, short-circuiting meaning rather than shoring it up. For these reasons, rhetorical analysis will necessarily attend to these slippages and contradictions, to the gray area between signifieds and signifiers, between intention and communication.[6]

In lyric poetry, the rhetorical tasks of maneuvering, persuading, or moving are often accomplished by means of a speaker, the carrier of a voice. Admirers of Eliot's mature poetry remark that his voice seems to speak directly to the reader in the first-person confessional mode. That intimate, personal voice turns out to be an elaborately constructed artifice, one that took Eliot the length of the notebook to perfect. I do not have the space to work out a theory of the relationship between an author's identity and the speaking voice of his poems, but I will operate on an assumption that many critics will support: although a poem may clearly draw on biographical material, a speaker is still an artificial construct; it takes on different rhetorical functions than an implied author. Even where my study draws parallels between the work and the life, the distinction between the speaker of the poem and the implied author still holds.

Discussion of Eliot's early voice is such a commonplace that most critics and scholars refer to it or explain it, and references to how Eliot found his voice proliferate even in newspaper reviews of *Inventions of the March Hare*. However, systematic analysis of—or even short references to—Eliot's construction of his audience are much rarer.[7] In lyric poetry, audience is a broad concept with a range of meanings. It can refer to the addressee of the poem—a "you," singular or plural, explicitly called forth by the speaker, silently existing inside the poem. Audience can also refer to a listener or group of listeners, off to the side of this I-thou exchange, whose privilege is to overhear it. This latter category is close to, though not exactly correspondent with, the authorial audience—an idealized group whom the author desires to address or move, whose expectations are met by the speaker, and who receives or responds in the way the author intends. In some cases, audience may also include the category of anti-audience, a hostile entity invoked or mistrusted, against which the expectations of the ideal, authorial audience are contrasted.

For the poems considered in this book, my conception of audience is primarily the imaginary construct whom the speakers of the poems address or attempt to persuade. For the juvenilia, how the young poet imaginatively constructs the audience of his texts is not quite the same as how he relates to his family or teachers: the living, breathing circle of support that praises the early creations. Likewise, there is an even greater difference between the imagined audience of his notebook inventions and his Harvard clubmates, professors, and coeditors at the *Advocate*. However, all of these audiences—the imagined ones and the real ones—are still related to each other in some way, and each chapter takes up the relationship as it changes and matures. Where real audiences—Eliot's early friends and editors—have weighed in on a published or unpublished poem, I consider those realities as they help us understand the way the imagined audience is constructed by the poems. Aside from the handful of early notebook poems that were published in the Harvard *Advocate* in 1909–10, it seems that no one besides Eliot saw these inventions. It is not until several years later, when Aiken responds in a letter to "Prufrock," that we begin to hear how his contemporaries were responding to his unpublished inventions.

The push-and-pull relationship between a speaker and audience readily lends itself to an understanding of the rhetorical situation as dialogic. And it is Mikhail Bakhtin's notion of "ideological becoming" that I wish to mobilize for Eliot's development, his dual process of "becoming" an artist and a young man. As will be discussed in detail in the first chapter, the authoritative discourses of Eliot's childhood included the serious literary tradition of Longfellow and Wordsworth, the moral rectitude of Puritan New England, the civic obligation of Unitarianism, the discretion and reserve of Boston Brahminism, and the class and gender norms of domestic and educational contexts. These discourses from Eliot's childhood are not so much rejected by the developing artist as they are negotiated and intermingled with other, equally authoritative (though formally disapproved) discourses: slang, popular culture, vaudeville, and frank discussion of sexuality. In addition to these two sets of competing and interlocking discourses, there is another discourse which Eliot discovered on his own and that decisively shaped his voice. Like the Longfellow-Wordsworth tradition, it is a serious literary model, though it is found outside of the Anglo-American tradition: the obsessions and tones adopted from the French Symbolist masters. Their themes of disaffected romanticism and urban decay, and their world-weary poses of irony, sarcasm, and ennui were discourses from another world that Eliot eagerly absorbed. When these external, authoritative discourses (inherited or discovered) meld into an internally persuasive discourse in the notebook poems, Eliot no longer sounds like a teenager vaguely pining for freedom and romance. Instead, he sounds like a social critic, an explorer of consciousness. He sounds like T. S. Eliot, a fully rounded self, rather than a clump of adolescent contradictions.

This process of assimilation—the transformation of externalized, authoritative discourses into an internally persuasive discourse—is what Bakhtin terms "ideological becoming."[8] Eliot's own, later understanding of becoming is not so far from Bakhtin's. As an element of self-education, Eliot argues, "wide reading . . . is valuable because in the process of being affected by one powerful personality after another, we cease to be dominated by any one, or by any small number. The very different views of life, cohabiting in our minds, affect each other, and our own personality asserts itself and gives each a place in some arrangement peculiar to ourself."[9] Like Bakhtin's, Eliot's understanding of self-authorship describes not only artistic or intellectual development but personal, psychological maturation. For example, here is Eliot at the age of forty-seven, trying to explain how he has changed to his brother, who had accused him of insincerity: "I doubt, at this point, whether as you think a personality is necessarily revealed during the first half of his life. I don't believe that I was there to be known, during that period, as clearly as you think you knew me."[10] Since Eliot was, in "the first half of his life," still a self in the process of becoming, his brother could not have "known" him so squarely as he now claims.

Almost all critics of Eliot have acknowledged the importance of the notebook poems for understanding how the young man became an artist, though there are some who cannot look past what is often a fragmentary or confused conception in these inventions. Peter Ackroyd, for example, has argued, "The poetry he was writing at this time [1909–1910] was impaled upon its own self-consciousness, fit only to be neatly transcribed in a notebook and then forgotten."[11] That some of these poems are artistic disasters makes them no less interesting: these discarded experiments allow us to watch the construction of genius. Nor does Eliot simply write them and then forget them. As this book will show in detail, Eliot constructed his early voices and audiences out of these early experiments—a process of invention that Eliot will begin again, as if from scratch, in each new phase of his writing career, enabling him to expound upon new themes and address new audiences.

Some Textual and Dating Matters

The text upon which I rely most heavily is Sir Christopher Ricks's *Inventions of the March Hare*. My own study of the original manuscripts has enabled me to make some very minor corrections to this edition. This volume is widely available, contains a useful apparatus recording alternate readings, and groups together the poems I cite, making it more relevant to my study than the more recently published *Poems*. That Eliot "fervently" wished that his notebook of early poems would never be published is understandable, though not entirely credible.[12] That he would want the poems hidden from posterity forever is altogether unbelievable, for authors who genuinely hold such intentions have simply to build a bonfire or find the nearest trash can, which Eliot often availed himself of throughout his career.

The chronological nature of my study requires that the poems be placed in a reliable sequential order. With few exceptions, all the poems can be dated with a fair degree of accuracy. There are some textual matters that complicate our understanding of the order of the poems' composition. Ricks observes, "The poems in the Notebook are dated by Eliot, mostly in pencil and mostly (it would seem from the hand) at about the same time."[13] In the absence of information that would overturn them, Ricks wisely defers to the dates imposed by Eliot some time before the notebook was sent to John Quinn, though such deference does not solve all questions of chronology. My own dating throughout is indebted to several sources: Valerie Eliot, Pierre Leyris, Ricks's *Inventions*, and my own examination of the manuscripts at various archives.[14] In the newest edition of *Poems*, Ricks and McCue supply a comprehensive list, where available, of Eliot's own claims as to dating. Since these claims sometimes contradict each other, I have had to make a choice based on what seems most plausible given the evidence of the text. In the rare case where my dating contradicts other sources, I explain my reasoning in the notes.

Another issue bearing on the chronology of the notebook is the problem of drafting versus copying. Gallup argues—presumably on the basis of fair copy handwriting, recto usage, and the nonchronological order of the initial poems—that the notebook "was apparently used by Eliot, beginning after January and before April 1910, writing at first only on the rectos but subsequently filling in many of the blanks with later poems."[15] Gallup's earliest date for the beginning of the notebook (January 1910) postdates five of the poems that appear near the opening of the notebook. If Gallup's hypothesis is tenable, those five poems must have been drafted elsewhere and subsequently copied into the notebook. By the time Eliot began writing in the notebook then, "Nocturne" had already been published, obviating the need to gather it with the other inventions.

Such textual issues are related to another: when and for what purpose Eliot purchased the notebook. Because of the remnants of a pricing ticket that still adheres to the inside cover, the origin of the notebook is known: Proctor Brothers Co., Old Corner Bookstore, Gloucester. Even though the date of the purchase is uncertain, the city of Gloucester suggests a summer purchase, since Eliot spent his summers there at the family home, the Downs. It is a curious matter only because of a probable several-month lag between the purchase of the notebook and the beginning of his experimentation in November 1909 at Cambridge. Having received the complete set of Laforgue in early 1909, Eliot had been quietly digesting the French master in anticipation of another bout of composition. So there are at least two explanations for the acquisition of the notebook: a summer 1909 purchase in Gloucester heralding a fall outburst in Cambridge or a summer 1910 purchase intended to collect the experiments of the preceding months. Because of the fair copy handwriting of the first few pages, the latter explanation is more likely, and so I would push forward Gallup's estimate to summer 1910 as the time when the notebook begins. Those poems on the opening rectos of the notebook were copied at the same time, in the same hand and blue ink. Later poems were copied in a messier hand, and loose leaves were scattered throughout. Those later, nonchronological interpolations and the messier handwriting seen on the later pages of the notebook suggest that Eliot at first used the notebook to record finished poems and eventually came to use it as a place to invent, revise, and edit.

Although I address each poem separately and in chronological order (as far as possible), my discussions of the poems are not meant to be full *explications de texte*. I focus on the poems' rhetorical organization in order to graph Eliot's emerging sense of voice and audience. Thus, to keep this book within manageable proportions, I must necessarily slight contextual or historical issues or skate quickly over the content of a poem.

A host of critics have explained the meaning, importance, and the subsequent influence of "Prufrock" and other notebook poems. And a number of commentators have provided excellent, if general, sketches of how Eliot came to voice. By way of joining this dialogue, I want to show, in stepwise manner, how Eliot got to that point by looking at the rhetorical tools he fashioned for himself, the voices he tried out, and the audiences to whom he imagined himself speaking. To restate the question with which I began: How did an ordinary, if intelligent, boy who wrote unremarkable poems become—with no help and in record time—the author of one of the most significant and beloved poems of the twentieth century? If that question matters to you, then this book, which provides one explanation of Eliot's development, matters too.

Indebted and Well Bred

Literary Models and Authority in the Juvenilia

ON BEING INDEBTED:

A true disciple is impressed by what his master has to say, and *consequently* by his way of saying it; an imitator—I might say, a borrower—is impressed chiefly by the way the master has said it. If he manages to mimic his master well enough, he may succeed even in disguising from himself the fact that he has nothing to say.

ON BEING WELL BRED:

The standard of conduct was that which my grandfather had set; our moral judgments, our decisions between duty and self-indulgence, were taken as if, like Moses, he had brought down the tables of the Law, any deviation from which would be sinful.

—T. S. Eliot, "American Literature and the American Language"

Eliot had always been an expert borrower. Set the task of writing some poetry, the sixteen-year-old poet delivered to his English master an imitation of Ben Jonson.[1] The teacher was skeptical enough to ask the young Eliot whether he had had help from anyone else. "Surprised" by this inquiry, the student assured his teacher that the verses were "wholly unaided."[2] Surprise, unsurprisingly, was Eliot's reaction to his teacher's disbelief. For a young writer with an unconscious gift for mimicry, it would not have occurred to him that materials for writing a poem might be summoned in any other way.

When those Jonsonian stanzas appeared in an issue of the school paper, the adolescent did nothing so crass as to brag about his accomplishment, nor did he mention it to anyone in his family—Eliot had always been a model of good breeding. But his mother, herself an amateur poet, was eventually shown a copy. Eliot later recalled the electric scene in detail: "She remarked (we were walking along Beaumont Street in St. Louis) that she thought them better than anything in verse she had ever written. I knew what her verse meant to her. We did not discuss the matter further."[3] A pregnant reticence—of the New England, stiff-upper-class variety—was Eliot's reaction to his parent's commendation. For a young Boston Brahmin craving his mother's approval, no other response would have been commensurate with such maternal validation.

In Eliot's emotionally charged reminiscences of his earliest verses—one regarding his facility for adopting voices, the other concerning his deference to authority—we have two clues for examining how the poet crafted a voice and imagined an audience for his earliest work. With a skill for imitation not yet linked to an intention, his earliest voices as a poet will be overwhelmingly indebted to the literary models he has been reading, so much so that his early writing will find no signature style of its own. His juvenilia confirm the young Eliot as a fickle imitator rather than a constant disciple. And as an obedient boy with an "anxious, nervous temperament," his imagined audiences will be overburdened by their own authority, making it difficult for the dutiful youth to escape from their perceived superiority.[4] Until he stumbles upon the liberating model of French Symbolism as an undergraduate, Eliot's voice will derive from those of his literary models, and his audiences imagined as stolid authority.

Voice in a Vacuum

In critical discussions of Eliot's poetry, the earliest creations are often wholly ignored or quickly limned in an embarrassed paragraph in order to contrast them with the more interesting experiments Eliot later concocted in the notebook.[5] The widely accepted argument about these early poems focuses on voice rather than audience, and the content of that argument is that the young author's voice is swamped by its literary models. Grover Smith's work on the sources of Eliot's poetry dispatches the juvenilia as "imitative and slight."[6] Likewise, A. David Moody lists the usual Romantic suspects as early paradigms—Wordsworth, Shelley, Keats, Tennyson, FitzGerald—arguing that though the "diction is drawn from these poets," the poetry is yet "undisturbed by the young author's own direct sensations. This makes the verse not impersonal but remote and artificial, its images not original but reproductions."[7] As is typical of Eliot criticism, the focus is on finding the seeds of the distinctive voice. The "many borrowed voices are composed into one voice," Moody argues of the juvenilia, "and that voice *thinks through* the conventional images with a rare cogency."[8]

John T. Mayer's *T. S. Eliot's Silent Voices* is the only work to give sustained attention to the juvenilia. And as his title advertises, Mayer's focus is on voice. The poems, he argues of the juvenilia, "all imitate voices, well-known voices of the English literary tradition; from the very beginning, Eliot instinctively responded to voice as a carrier of attitude and made it his preferred means of portraying experience."[9] Mayer's claim that voice is a "carrier" of attitude and conveyer of experience rests on the assumption that attitude and experience exist a priori, and that voice is a means of communicating that experience. This expressionist assumption, in turn, is based on the idea that a personal self—more or less coherent and identifiable—adopts voices in order to present facets of itself. Thus, Mayer sees the juvenilia as "the disguising of the personal in the conventions of the familiar."[10]

But what if the adolescent Eliot were not a coherent self whose personal aspects could be expressed or even disguised, but instead were waiting to be created? And more importantly, what happens to our view of the early poems if, instead of hearing the voice in a vacuum, we observe how that voice is projected in the direction of an audience whom the speaker seeks to move or persuade? Eliot's tryings-on of successive voices are flustered attempts to imagine an audience who will hear him. Eliot's voice is derivative because what he has to say is so derivative of what others have said or of what his audiences expect him to say. Such rhetorical concerns of a writer (how one communicates or persuades) have their analogs in the real-life personality of a writer (how one acts in the world). The adolescent self, insufficiently sussed out into a coherent personality, can be immature and gawky because the sense of self is tied to a sense of audience and occasion. The teenager is awkward with others, not in the privacy of the bedroom.

In the criticism on Eliot's poetry, the accounts of voice that ignore audience or address pathos only haphazardly can often be illuminative without being explicative. To advert to Mayer again, he inhabits the area between biography and literary criticism in order to identify the source of the poet's voice in a personal history. In an early chapter that sets up a discussion of the juvenilia, Mayer spends considerable time describing Eliot's temperament as solitary, inhibited, distant, and polite. Detailing the contexts that shaped that temperament, Mayer identifies the effects of Unitarian ethical imperatives on the young man's choices, and he rehearses the Eliot family's expectations of duty, self-denial, and high-mindedness. As a result of such influences, Mayer concludes, "detachment, formality, and role-playing characterize the generic Eliot protagonist."[11] Such an account accurately describes the speakers of these poems, and it is probable that such writerly choices on the part of Eliot the poet are obliquely related to the temperament of Eliot the person. But to say that Eliot's speakers are distinguished by their "detachment, formality and role-playing" begs the questions of a rhetorical criticism: To whom would one speak in such poses? And what would be the speaker's intended effects on an audience?

Eliot's First Rhetorical Problem

In the young Eliot's case, the answers to these questions have to do with authority, not only as the adolescent experienced it but as the writer negotiated it. Born to a respectable family that thought highly of its New England roots, Eliot was raised and educated in environments, both domestic and public, that prized authority, reticence, and duty. That the Eliots proudly repeated their motto, "Tace et fac," was one sign of the family's consciousness of tradition and continuity: its Latin a marker of class and education, and its meaning—"Be silent and do," or in one critic's brusque translation, "Shut up and get on with it"—a reflection of the family's Puritan work ethic.[12] It is a bracing variation on the saying that children should be seen and not heard, for even adults were expected to be seen working rather than heard talking. In such an environment, a budding author would understandably bridle at the notion of being silenced. One way out of that impasse would be for Eliot to defer anxiously to the superior authority of his audience and to claim his own nascent authority lightly.

Nevertheless, as with any information about a writer's life or background, the claim that Eliot was shaped by a restrictive cultural and familial environment does no literary-critical labor yet. Such biographical data serves only as hazy suggestion unless the poet's response to such restrictions can be located in the rhetorical maneuverings of the poems themselves. Rather than identify the *model* of the poet's voice in borrowed voices from the literary canon (as many Eliotists do), and rather than identify the *source* of the poet's voice in a biographical past (as Mayer does), a rhetorical criticism seeks to identify the *function* of the voice in the rhetorical present of the poems' interventions.

All emerging writers must claim a voice and imagine an audience, and they will fail or succeed in such tasks in hundreds of different ways. Among the many options available to the young Eliot, the one he repeatedly chooses is the restraining of his own knowledge as a reaction to his readers' authority. How this young author negotiates the problem of his own and his audience's authority—in other words, how he works through his first rhetorical problem—has repercussions for how he later develops as a successful poet in the notebook. The anxiety the young writer feels regarding his audience does not disappear once he forges a distinctive voice out of Laforguean materials. In some respects, as we will see in the next chapter, his audience anxiety increases after his voice has adopted timbres and registers suited to its purposes.

When we understand the limitations of voice and audience that constrained the young poet, we will be in a better position to note how the problems that beset the juvenilia survive into the notebook poems. To dismiss the juvenilia as merely imitative or unoriginal leaves us no explanation for how the notebook poems are different from them, since at first, the notebook poems are just as imitative as the juvenilia. The only difference is that the notebook pieces are imitative of Laforgue rather than of the English Romantic models of the juvenilia.

Anxious of his own authority as a writer and even more anxious of the authority of his audience, the young poet must appropriate the credibility of others' literary styles in order to say anything at all. In contrast to the varied influences of his mature voice, the voices that the adolescent Eliot adopts are based only on serious literary models rather than the argot of St. Louis streets, the discourse of broadsheets and newspapers, or the idioms of ragtime and popular culture. Even though such low- and middlebrow voices are heard around him, he has no way of bringing them into his poetry yet, not because of how he conceives of voice but because of how he conceives of a "literary" audience and the solemnity it implies. This is the same boy who was once chastised for bringing the vulgar street slang "OK" into the house.[13] Bounded on all sides by such authority, it would not have occurred to the young Eliot to transport popular discourse into his poetry.

Anthony Cuda has claimed that in the juvenilia Eliot "had imitated the amalgam of violent spiritual energy and demotic speech that he found in late Victorian English poets like John Davidson and Lionel Johnson."[14] But Cuda gives no examples of where in the juvenilia such colloquial speech can be found, and such a claim is directly at odds with what I argue in this chapter. It is true that Eliot had read Davidson prior to encountering Laforgue, but it does not follow that Davidson's influence also preceded Laforgue's. From Arthur Symons, Ernest Dowson, John Davidson, "I got the idea," Eliot relates, "that one could write poetry in an English such as one would speak oneself. A colloquial idiom." Speaking of the "terrific impact" Davidson's poem "Thirty Bob a Week" had on him, Eliot claims that it prepared him "for initiation into the work of some of the French symbolists, such as [Laforgue], whom I came across shortly after."[15] So while Eliot had been reading Davidson and others before his encounter with Laforgue, colloquial verse, as with other popular sources, fell outside the bounds of influences he admitted into his juvenilia.

As I argue in this chapter and the next, Eliot's juvenilia remains guarded and correct. It was not until Eliot read Laforgue that roiling energies would be released into his poetry. If there is any identifiable influence of Davidson on the juvenilia, it occurs quite late, after he had read Laforgue but before his November 1909 explosion. Eliot's "Ballade of the Fox Dinner" (May 1909) does make a startling turn to the colloquial. But if there is any Davidsonian influence there, it is oblique rather than direct, as Eliot's occasional poem is witty *vers de societé* written for drunken Harvard peers, not gritty vernacular written in sympathy with the lower classes. It is likely that the young Eliot "got the idea," as he says, of writing colloquial verse from Davidson, but he was not able to turn the idea into action until the more congenial Laforgue showed him the way. Another way of approaching the influence problem would be to say that Davidson prepared him to hear Laforgue, as Eliot admits, and that Laforgue enabled him to write like Davidson.[16]

Taking the juvenilia as evidence, this chapter analyzes how the problem of the writer's voice and the audience's authority is worked out. In one poem evoking Eliot's childhood—written, admittedly, not in his youth but in the 1930s—the speaker describes mischievous Jim Jum Bears who deliberately annoy their nurse. No doubt drawing on his memories of his own Irish nurse, Annie Dunne, the author includes the coy question, "Was ever a Nurse so put about?"[17] Gordon argues that the poem reveals the "secure intimacy" of Eliot's childhood spent with his beloved caretaker. But the poem also reveals a child whose playmates are adults and a speaker whose primary concern is how the bears' play affects the adult's sense of propriety. As a fuller analysis of the juvenilia will demonstrate, even the mature Eliot's rendering of childhood bears the stamp of this old rhetorical problem: How will the grown-ups react?

If this influence persevered for so long in Eliot's memory, it is because it started so early. When Eliot was approximately six or seven, he wrote a brief illustrated essay on the life of George Washington. In a child's hand, he scrawls, "George Washington was born in a plantation. He wanted to go to sea but his mamma didn't want him to, so he took to the army."[18] Unlike the thwarted first president, Eliot would eventually escape across the sea, but at this age the boy can only note how risky ambitions are scuttled by mamma's more terrestrial plans.

Not all of Eliot's childhood poetry survives, but what we do know of the missing poetry reveals something about the boy's relationship to authority. The only evidence we have of Eliot deliberately throwing away any of his juvenilia is based on his recollection that he had produced "some very gloomy and atheistical and despairing quatrains" in the style of the *Rubáiyát* around the age of fourteen. Eliot claimed that he destroyed them, and "never showed them to anybody."[19] It is telling, again, how the potentially hostile audience figures in this reminiscence: he recalls FitzGerald, the dangerously bohemian poet who inspired his quatrains, as well as their shocking atheism and unseemly melancholy. Both the revolutionary poet and the self-indulgent pose would have been anathema to Eliot's level-headed mother, and these are the probable reasons the verses were destined for the trash can.

In large measure, the Eliot of the juvenilia is not imagining an ideal audience, he is reacting to an already existing one: the Tradition, with its sober expectations. Before Eliot constructs a more sympathetic audience, the young writer's first attempts will involve responding with slavish decorum to a tradition-minded audience, defensively preempting the hostility of a conservative public, and speaking vaguely to an ill-defined listenership.

Message, Voice, and Audience: The Rhetoric of the Poems and Stories

Before turning to a detailed analysis of the poems' meanings, voices, and audiences, a short summary of the three major elements found in the juvenilia follows.

Message (logos problems): The message the young Eliot crafts is the lackluster message of the imitator, not of the true disciple. Because in imitating—his chief concern being the manner rather than the content of his literary models—he has not realized that he does not have much to say yet. In some instances, as in "Song" ("When we came home across the hill"), where he might have discovered a richer theme, the poet seems to avoid mining deeply his own experience, fearing its implications.

Voice (ethos problems): Lacking as yet his own distinctive voice and casting about for a way to claim gingerly his own writerly authority, the voice of Eliot's juvenilia is the ventriloquized sound of serious literary authority. The speaking voice changes from poem to poem: here sounding like Tennyson, there like Jonson, there like FitzGerald. Even the wholesale adoption of another's voice does not solidify the speaking identity, because whenever the speaking voice explicitly identifies itself as "I," the identity of that pronoun is curiously unstable. The "I" paradoxically asserts itself and then shuffles uneasily in the spotlight.

Audience (pathos problems): The adolescent Eliot imagines his reader to be the typical audience of a nineteenth-century schoolboy: authoritative guides who monitor compliance with norms of class, gender, and education.[20] Within all of the genres Eliot attempts in the juvenilia (love song, graduation ode, comic narrative, sonnet), the primary move he makes is born of his audience anxiety, namely, wearing lightly the literary authority he has donned and playing up to the imagined superiority of his audience. The double hesitance engendered by the insecurity of the "I" and the dominance of the "you" troubles the imaginative construction of that audience. Yet, in spite of its supremacy, the identity of the audience is no more solid than the identity of the "I."

Audiences in Eliot's juvenilia are sometimes clearly identifiable as silent readers, but they are sometimes more closely related to the addressees of the poems, the directly addressed "you." The second person turns up regularly in Eliot's juvenilia, and its appearance usually signals various troubles with which the author is grappling. As we will see in tracking Eliot's developing sense of audience, whenever "you" is invoked in the early poetry, it is not because Eliot has decided to address an audience of whom he is certain, rather the opposite. When he loses his sense of audience, the author will often hazard a shot in the dark by invoking that audience directly—a "you" that is paradoxically conjured and undefined.

Eliot published or recited thirteen poems and stories between his final year at Smith Academy and his third year at Harvard. What follows is a timeline for those publications and a work-by-work analysis of each piece. These specific interpretations reveal the particular ways Eliot addresses, or fails to address, questions of message, voice, and audience.

The Poems, Stories, and Magazines
Works spanning Jan. 1899 (Eliot at Smith Academy, aged ten years) to May 1909 (at Harvard University, aged twenty)

Fireside and *Eliot's Floral Magazine*	written Jan.–Feb. 1899
"'The Vision of Sir Launfal,' A Christmas Study"	read in Dec. 1904[21]
"A Lyric" ("If Time and Space, as Sages say")	submitted Jan. 24, 1905
"The Birds of Prey"	published Jan. 1905
"A Fable for Feasters"	published Feb. 1905
"A Tale of a Whale"	published Apr. 1905
"The Man Who Was King"	published June 1905
"To the Class of 1905"	recited June 13, 1905
"Song" ("When we came home across the hill")	published May 24, 1907
"Song" ("If space and time, as sages say")	published June 3, 1907
"Before Morning"	published Nov. 13, 1908
"Circe's Palace"	published Nov. 25, 1908

"Song" ("The moonflower opens to the moth")	published Jan. 26, 1909
"On a Portrait"	published Jan. 26, 1909
"Ballade of the Fox Dinner"	recited May 15, 1909

Fireside *and* Eliot's Floral Magazine
Written Jan.–Feb. 1899

During the 1898–1899 school year, when Eliot began his studies at Smith Academy, its new literary magazine debuted in April under the title *Smith Academy Record.* A source of pride for the school, the magazine was a big production, involving faculty, as well as older students who served as editors, writers, and business manager. The ten-year-old Eliot was too young to take part in this project, but as preparations for the school magazine were underway, the boy launched his own literary magazine at home, *Fireside.*[22] Using his free time between terms, he manufactured fourteen or fifteen issues of *Fireside* and one issue of *Eliot's Floral Magazine* in the space of three weeks, from January 28 to February 19, 1899. Now housed in the Houghton Library, eleven issues of *Fireside* are extant; they total a whopping 176 pages—well over 200 pages if we extrapolate for the missing issues.[23] The magazines reveal a fertile imagination: serial adventure stories appear, along with jokes, gossip, local news, poems, legalese, magazine copy, and editorial commentary. The virtuosic range of styles and genres on offer show a boy wholly indebted to turn-of-the-century magazine culture, an excellent mimic who drolly imitates its generic conventions.

Eliot's young ear is attuned to dialect and jargon, and he is addicted to wordplay and verbal jokes. Up-to-the-minute slang appears: "all right"; "hot stuff"; and "rushin' a can," the latter an expression meaning to take a can or "growler" to a local bar to have it filled with beer.[24] He reproduces regional and class dialect: in an advertisement for "Higginson's Hot Hoe-cakes for Husky Hoboes," a hobo applauds pancakes that he has used as ear mufflers "for t'ree years."[25] In another piece, "The Hotpepper Letters" purports to follow a country family, the Hotpeppers, on their travels in the big city. They report their findings to the editor: "Der Edetur, / Wen we cum we se a lot of pepul on bars and whels ridin' along."[26] The young boy, who occasionally misspells, does so on purpose here—not in order to approximate the actual speech of innocent country folk but to reproduce the classed manner of ridiculing illiteracy found in magazine culture and dime novels. Verbal jokes spill from every page: one letter of support for a product is signed "Jones M.

Brown" from "Kentuckyville Arazona"—gleefully mixing up first and last names, state names and city names. With the magazine as cover, the boy who was once chastised for using the vulgar expression "OK" has found a gaping loophole for smuggling slang and frowned-upon discourses into the house.

Like any good editor of a topical magazine, the boy offers news about current events. One news item appears on the subject of "Romulas" pulling off the tail of a bull. (In 1899, Romulus was a popular—if not terribly successful—Mexican strong man and bull wrestler.[27]) One fake ad for "Gold-ine," a "Cure for drunkards," picks up on the real Keeley Company's Double Chloride of Gold Remedies for the treatment of various addictions and habits.[28] In the midst of a three-week tear, Eliot observes the start of the Philippine-American War, which had begun on February 4, 1899, and other references to the recently concluded Spanish-American War appear. And in *Fireside* number 1, under "The Theatre," the editor reports, "'By the Sad Sea Waves,' is a comedy played by Mattews & Bulger." That is the title of a real comedy, with libretto and songs by J. Sherrie Mathews and Harry Bulger, that would soon play at the Herald Square Theatre in New York from February 28, 1899, to April 4, 1899.[29] It had likely come through St. Louis in previews in January.

The young editor/writer is not only copying and parodying magazine conventions, he has mastered their joke-producing formulas. John J. Soldo has discussed how the young Eliot successfully reworks the joke of Lewis Carroll's "The Mad Gardener's Song" in which a "letter from his wife" is mistaken for an "Elephant."[30] Eliot's version:

> I thought I saw a elephant
> A-riding on a 'bus
> I looked again, and found
> Alas! 'Twas only us.[31]

He gamely attempts nine different variations on this formula. The magazine provided an outlet for the linguistic obsessions that sorely tested the patience of his older sisters. One story from Eliot family lore recalls the boy's endless punning on parents' names for their children. His sister Marian tried futilely to redirect his energy: "Tom, don't you think that vein of humor has petered out?" to which he replied, "Mr. and Mrs. Dout and Peter Dout."[32]

Another of his favorite formulas is the author or character whose name mirrors their identity in some way: two purported authors of stories are identified as Hughly Stories and Gabbee Tahkers.[33] A writer of westerns is called Dimey Novles; a traveler sports the name Mr. Globe Trotere; a hobo is called Mosly Wrags; a society lady is known as Mrs. Fatum Ritchus; a merchant of bird food and accessories calls himself Dr. Kat. More problematic, if illuminating: a "History of The Jews" is written by the awkwardly named Fulish Writers.[34] (The cover of the advertised book includes a ghastly sketch of a hook-nosed Jew.) Not nearly as inventive as Gabbee Tahkers or Mosly Wrags, this old anti-Semitic trope—one that seeks to downplay the historical influence of Jews—is another element that Eliot has learned from his environment and mimicked.

The scholar who reads these pages in the archives cannot help but notice moments of concord between the boy's obsessions and the events of the author's later life. Surely most of these elements are mere coincidence or are derived from his academy education, but collectively they add up to something else: the boy's interest in Paris;[35] his poem on a "banker's clerk";[36] the dedication of numbers 3, 6, and 7 "to my wife"; the illustrated "Flags of the World" that picture only Great Britain and America;[37] a story about an elopement and announcements of elopements;[38] a jocular illustration of cats;[39] a character named "Dr. Sweany" who deals with insomnia;[40] and his recurrent disappointment, as a theater critic, that there is "Nothing exciting," "Nothing good," "Nothing special," "No theatre."[41] The author-editor has a sense of himself as ridiculous in the eyes of others: the narrator of one story meets aliens who "looked at me as if I was mad."[42] And the boy is keenly aware of sexual and social decorum. In the conclusion of "Pretty Belle," an actress—that figure of questionable sexual morality—fears the sudden appearance of her lost father into her life. "But just then a young man named Jack Carroty, came in and kicked him out. (P. S. Of course they were married.)" We observe, as well, the young Eliot's penchant for ironic juxtaposition. Two items listed under "Gossip": "Miss Catty is an heiress to $100,000,000,000!" is immediately followed by "Mr. Mat. Hantly tuned his violin yesterday."[43] And another announcement for a book title marries love song with murder: "Frank & May: A Bloodcurdling Tale of Love." Above all in the *Fireside* series, it is the boy's outsized ambition for editorial work and literary production that mark this child as father to the man.

What is most telling about these productions is the speed and voraciousness of Eliot's absorption of journalistic and editorial conventions large and small. His mastery of many genres has been explained above. Even at the level of text and design, he has picked up a number of ideas to toy with. He has caught on to alliteration as a mnemonic function for advertising: "Dr. Pearce's Pleasent Pellets for Pink People"; of rhyming slogans: "Do you subscribe / To Fireside?"; and of graphic design: for Carter's Little Liver Pills, the small "L" of "liver" nestles inside a large "L" of "little."[44] The editor offers "Premiums" (or, in the first few issues, before he learned its spelling, "Premeums") to entice subscribers, such as a "torpedo boat."[45] He makes hay out of the serialized story and news event, especially the cliffhanger tag line "To be continued"—both as a convention to be followed (drawing out a slender story through several issues) and as an occasion for a joke. A news report of a robbery cuts off in mid-climax: "Two burglars entered the house of Mr. Block. And took—. (to be continued in our next, for want of room)." This room-squandering parenthesis is followed by an ostentatious doodad that takes up even more room.

The young Eliot revels in the journalistic practice of abbreviation: "Here is a letter from our spec'l cor'dent. Manila. June 31, 1899. All quiet here. (No spec'l reason for telegraphing.)."[46] Even though he is not yet a master of spelling, its peculiarities fascinate him, overriding his narrative urges. Language, not story, is the hero of these magazines: "The Tzar (or Czar) thinks . . ."[47] Even the absence of spelling—the use of dashes to protect or coyly suppress a person's identity—engages his parodic sense: a biography of George Washington, written by the editor is entitled and signed: "George W—— by The E——r."[48] By transporting this punctuation to where it does not belong, he calls attention to its falseness, the ridiculousness of its usage.

The aspiring editor loves the insider discourse of publishing: splattered across the very neatly printed title page is the intrusive, diagonal print of "SAMPLE COPY." Here, the ten-year old is not merely purporting to "print" a magazine for domestic consumption, he is purporting to go through all the motions that editors and printers go through to get a magazine into print, including the production of galley proofs and sample copies for the insiders: editors, advertisers, and salespeople. The only convention Eliot seems to struggle with is the editorial. The ten-year-old boy has understood that this genre is unsigned, and he knows that editorials concern themselves with momentous issues. However, he seems not to have understood that editorials are expressions of opinion, that they take a position on an issue. By contrast, the boy's editorials are merely news items. It is perhaps the only instance in this profusion of imitation that a genre's rhetorical function has escaped him. One editorial reads, "England—is going to build a railroad in China," with no further comment.[49] In a later issue, he comes closest to getting the point. The editorial reads in its entirety: "There have been many parodys on 'The White Man's Burden.'"[50] He has copied here the strong beginning and staking-out of a current topic upon which an editorial would editorialize. But by not then proceeding to opinionize, he seems to have missed the cue—although it is possible that he is parodying the genre by omitting editorial content from the editorial.

His mastery of multiple conventions, and his ability to turn them inside out, reveal how attuned he is to the expectations of his audience. There are a few moments when he turns to explicitly address them in an aside. The continuation of a story from the previous number editorializes, "(If you haven't read Chap. I you arn't in it.)."[51] And in the final chapter of "Mosly Wrags," in which the hero-hobo goes back to drinking, the narrator shifts to a moralizing "we": "When let out [of lock-up] he comenced again. But <u>we</u> shall have no more to do with him."[52]

Foreshadowing the older Eliot's zeal for publishing and editing, the boy started at the same time a second periodical, *Eliot's Floral Magazine: A Journal of Floriculture*, which sends up florid nature writing and whose more limited potential doomed it to one issue.[53] In spite of his grand ambitions for editorship, Eliot never worked as a student editor for the school magazine during his seven years at Smith. He began publishing in it only a few months before graduation: four stories and two poems in four separate issues of *Smith Academy Record.*

"A Lyric" ("If Time and Space, as Sages say")
Submitted as assignment Jan. 24, 1905; published in Smith Academy Record, *Apr. 1905*

"A Lyric" might seem to undermine the argument of this chapter: the speaking "I" of this poem confidently asserts his authority, the addressee is a clearly defined "thou" who is designated as an intimate and whose own authority is neither feared nor flattered, and the authorial audience is an unobtrusive listener.[54] The reason this poem seems not to be mired in the rhetorical anxiety that the rest of his juvenilia betrays is that the young Eliot is here so irresistibly indebted to the voice and theme of Jonson that he has adopted, without variation, the entire apparatus of the carpe diem lyric. There is no struggle to define speaker, addressee, or audience because Eliot is reproducing the petrified poses and topoi of the Jonsonian love song. Even its iambs and rhymes are obediently regular.

Two years after writing this lyric, Eliot will revise it, making subtle changes to its focus. But in this first version, the speaker is in agreement with the authority figures whom he invokes: the "Sages" who argue that time and space do not matter because they do not exist.[55] Because of the irrelevance of time and space, the speaker draws the conclusion that living a century is the same as living a day, with the second stanza serving as amplification of this line of thought. Rather than pining after immortality and mourning the passage of time, the speaker adjures the beloved to let their numbered days be "divine."

The speaker, clearly defined as a male "I," claims authority by speaking to and giving a gift to the addressee, his silent beloved, "thee." The speaker also addresses her as "Love," which is immediately followed by "we"—a pronoun that will give the young poet a significant amount of trouble in subsequent poems. Under the sign of Jonson however, the marriage of "I" and "thou" is easy: "So why, Love, should we ever pray / To live a century?" With several other references to the first-person plural throughout the poem—"we," "us," and "our"—the speaker has conceived of the addressee's identity as intimately tied to his own. This imaginative relationship of speaker to beloved, because of its poetic familiarity, is free of complication. Likewise, the authorial audience has a strictly defined role: as auditors who overhear the intimate conversation between lovers, they do not shape the drama of the dialogue. Borrowing the authority of Jonson, the speaker keeps the authorial audience in check, granting it the power to witness rather than influence. Soon, that easy concord between "I" and "thou" in Eliot's earliest verse will be destroyed by the insecurities of an uncertain "I" and a domineering "you"—breaking apart the borrowed effortlessness of Jonson's "we" for the span of the juvenilia.

"The Birds of Prey"
Published in Smith Academy Record, *Jan. 1905*

Eliot's first publication is not a poem but a story. As with the other two stories published at Smith, the young author's debut shows a reasonable sense of pacing and organization, though it is obvious that his gifts are not narrative. All three are adventure stories, and the rules of that genre serve him well enough for a framework: an introductory setup, followed by danger(s), followed by a rescue or escape in the nick of time.[56] Even with this simple formula, the young author cannot quite manage to sustain interest: one danger follows another, and the resolutions sound tired rather than contented. Each of the three stories flubs the ending; all of them sound flat, as the storyteller has no moral to draw or narrative resolution to unpack. Two of the stories end with the odd detail of exactly how long it took to reach safety: "in about two weeks from the time of setting out" ("The Man Who Was King"), and "we got ahead at about three knots an hour, and after an uneventful voyage arrived in Honolulu in three months" ("A Tale of a Whale").[57] The young Eliot capably handles some modest humor in the stories, but these endings that turn to the mundane mark his uncertainty about the genre's purpose.

That he quickly writes three adventure stories speaks to the young boy's immersion in that genre. It is a limiting one for him as a developing writer, and his poems—derivative and polite as they are—offer more interesting challenges. Whereas each poem of the juvenilia records a different voice and style with which he grapples, the three stories show no such progression. It is perhaps his lack of development in that genre that allows him to drop the adventure narrative and concentrate on poetry.

For all of the stories, each opening paragraph—that most vulnerable spot of a story, where a speaker establishes a relationship with an audience—contains a slight wobble that betrays the author's anxiety about his narrator's voice. In this first story, an opening sentence sets the scene of a vulture taking off for a flight. But the second sentence already turns away from the pose of narrator: "A hungry bird of prey does not fly about for exercise, and this one seemed to have a very definite destination."[58] By avoiding the appearance of having omniscient knowledge (the bird "seemed" to be headed somewhere definite) and by turning from a narrative voice to an ornithologist's voice, the speaker both hedges and exploits his authority. The young Eliot was an avid birdwatcher, and the momentary intrusion of the ornithologist's voice grants him space to make such observations: he trusts his knowledge of birds more than his authority as a storyteller.

"A Fable for Feasters"
Published in Smith Academy Record*, Feb. 1905*

The radical shift between "A Lyric" and "Fable for Feasters" is attributable to the difference in genre: "A Lyric" is a monologic repetition of the Jonsonian voice and of love song conventions; "Fable," on the contrary, is a dialogic exchange among three elements: the genre of ghost story, the comedic properties of metanarrative derived from *The Ingoldsby Legends*,[59] and the insouciant narrator adapted from Byron.

One month after writing "A Lyric," Eliot published in his school's periodical this comic squib on authority set in a medieval monastery. Its theme of the corrupting effects of power is explored on both the thematic and the rhetorical level: the overt battle between the ghost and the Abbot mirrors a covert struggle between the speaker's authority and the audience's. The theme of corrupt power is worked out on the narrative level, pitting a mischievous ghost against an unpleasant Abbot. In the narrative conclusion, the Abbot is punished for trying to use his power coercively against the ghost, the moral being that the ghost's pranks are no cause for being so inhospitable.

With the mischievous ghost vindicated and the hypocritical Abbot punished, the problem of corrupt power has been precariously resolved on the level of narrative. But on the level of rhetoric, a more vexed problem regarding authority and power is worked out between the speaker and the audience. As with the uneasy solution in the narrative (the ghost suffers no punishment for his pranks), the rhetorical solution that the young author achieves betrays various anxieties. The most fraught moment of the poem's narrative is also the most fraught moment of its rhetoric: both climaxes occur in the ninth stanza, where the speaker turns to address the audience. Beginning with the ghost finally breaking through the Abbot's bolted doors, the stanza quickly leaves this narrative and gives itself over to haranguing the audience:

> my statement nobody can doubt,
> Who knows the well known fact, as you do surely—
> That ghosts are fellows whom you *can't* keep out;
> It is a thing to be lamented sorely
> Such slippery folk should be allowed about,
> For often they drop in at awkward moments,
> As everybody'll know who reads this romance.[60]

There are four gestures in the direction of the audience—a "nobody," an "everybody," and two "yous"—all different in emphasis. In attempting to describe and control the power of an audience, the speaker trumps its authority by adopting an ethos of superiority: "It is a thing to be lamented sorely / Such slippery folk should be allowed about." Here are struck the plummy tones of the social commentator, the curmudgeon who is disgusted with the disintegration of social mores. The speaker has slyly obscured his fear of the audience by comically upstaging its dominance.

After five stanzas of confident speech, another pattern unfolds, this time referring to the first person:

> The menus of that time I am afraid
> I don't know much about—as well's I'm able
> I'll go through the account

There is something agitated about these repetitions. And in their extremity—I, the speaker, don't know anything; you, the audience, are all-knowing—we can detect the outlines of Eliot's first rhetorical problem: how to claim his own authority and how to negotiate that power with his audience's perceived superiority.

This problem of claiming one's authority is a typical one of juvenile psychological development, but the particular moves whereby the speaker gestures extravagantly at his audience's knowledge are inherited from his source. Consider the contrasts and commonalities between the speaker's knowledge and the audience's in the following excerpts from Richard Harris Barham's poem "The Ghost" in *The Ingoldsby Legends*:

> "There's time and place for all things," said a sage,
> (King Solomon, I think,)

> No matter!—'tis a thing that's not uncommon,
> 'Tis what we have all heard, and most have read of[61]

The young Eliot's adoption of such gestures is more than slavish imitation of his source, however, because they are related to the authority that he is working out on the levels of rhetoric and narrative. Here the young Eliot has repurposed these comedic moments of faux anxiety found in "The Ghost" to work out a genuinely interesting problem regarding his speaker's relation to authority. The speaker is caught in two contradictions: trying to present himself as ignorant while knowing more than he claims and trying to present the audience as authoritative while wishing to trump that authority. Sometimes these contradictions are skillfully turned to his own comic purposes. For example, the speaker who claims to know little of medieval menus is charmingly belied by the same speaker who confidently details the menu in a fourteen-line display of alimentary erudition, from the various beasts and fowls down to the wassail. To profess ignorance and then display one's expertise is, of course, an intentional joke, what rhetorical theorists fond of Greek terminology call apophasis—pretending to deny what is really affirmed.[62] But the speaker's false modesty is more than apophatic utterance in the service of comedy. The split identity reveals an unresolved contradiction: the speaker neither believes his own ignorance—which is why he can swerve between playing the ignorance card and the scholar card—nor does he credit his audience's ultimate authority over him. The imaginative presence of the audience is here overdrawn, so the young author ironically plays up to it: *nobody* would believe *X*, *you* certainly wouldn't, *everybody* knows *Z*. No détente seems possible in the power struggle between the mischievous speaker and the potentially inhospitable readers. As a consequence, the rhetorical resolution will require more acrobatics than the narrative solution.

That narrative trajectory ends predictably, if precariously. The unpleasant Abbot disappears, after which the monks are inspired to prayerful lives of frugal piety. This tongue-in-cheek happily-ever-after plays to the audience's sympathies: the speaker intuits that his listeners prefer the ghost's pranks to the Abbot's hypocrisy. The rhetorical conclusion is a different matter, wholly unprepared for in the concluding lines. In a telling shift to the second-person plural—its only appearance in the poem—the conclusion intrudes: "We / Got the veracious record of these doings / From an old manuscript found in the ruins." This gesture defers to a different kind of authority than either the speaker's or the audience's: the authority of primary documents as historical fact. This deus ex machina is a playful snub to the audience, for this intervention of a higher authority nullifies rather than resolves the speaker-audience power struggle. The final lines, by adverting to a hitherto unacknowledged source of authority, create an escape hatch through which the speaker eludes the problems of authority that the poem has batted back and forth. The problem of ethos is shifted right out of the poem instead of resolved within it: while this shift within the poem represents the speaker's snub to his implied audience, on another level, the author is winking at his authorial audience. One of the clearest signs that the conclusion is jury-rigged (and that the author knows it) is the atypical appearance of "we," its magical function reflected even in its comically emphatic end rhyme. This coercive "we" pretends to be a combination of you-the-reader and I-the-speaker, but it is in reality a cover for a singular "I" who has cunningly adopted the royal "we"—an "I" who has chosen to affect more authority than he is entitled to by rhetorical rights alone.

This extended analysis of a slight poem can be justified only in terms of its relevance to the larger narrative of Eliot's coming of age as a writer. For it is just this problem of his own authority, his audience's authority, and the negotiation of the two that will be a major struggle that Eliot works out in the notebook.

"A Tale of a Whale"
Published in Smith Academy Record, *Apr. 1905*

As with Eliot's first story, a moment in the first paragraph reveals the speaker's anxiety with respect to his audience and his own authority. For his opening gambit, the speaker adopts the voice of the grizzled sailor: "It was in '71, I remember, that I was on the whaling ship."[63] As the scene setting continues, unnecessarily specific details obtrude: "Although the mizzen top-gallant shrouds had been repeatedly belayed to the fore staysail, and the flying jib-boom cleared, and lashed to the monkey rail, we made no progress whatsoever." Lyndall Gordon reads this gesture as the sign of an adolescent showing off his nautical jargon.[64] True enough—but it also signals the speaker's ethos. By elaborately explaining the terms and uses of nautical gear, he mobilizes his authority as an accomplished sailor—rather than as a storyteller. Similar to his first story's switch to the discourse of ornithology, this speaker's insistence on his nautical authority is intended to shore up the narrative authority that he fears he lacks.

There is another delightful moment in which the speaker describes the efforts of his crew to rig up a mast and sails into the body of a floating whale on which they are stranded. Although they have dug a hole into the dead whale and lashed a mast to its spine, a heavy wind necessitates their bracing the mast with their bodies, a pose "which looked rather undignified," the speaker notes. Even in the face of high danger, one must mind one's manners. As with all the juvenilia, the speaker is sharply conscious of an audience that watches and judges. The story reveals a young author peculiarly alert to decorum, especially when propriety is at odds with some other, overwhelming reality.

"The Man Who Was King"
Published in Smith Academy Record, *June 1905*

Another adventure story, this tale also makes liberal use of sailors and nautical terminology. The opening paragraph uses the common framing device of relating someone else's narrative, but the young author puts this traditional gesture to odd use. The original teller of the tale is described uneasily as "famous in his own country for his genius at telling stories of his adventures at sea."[65] The catch-22 here is that one's own storytelling skill must be proved in the telling; it cannot rest on the borrowed glory of someone else's narrative genius. Eliot's attempt to arrogate that glory is another sign of his struggle to claim authority as a speaker.

It is a pity to watch the adolescent struggle so, for he can be entertaining when he is not looking over his shoulder at a judging audience. One moment in the story has the speaker describing the natives of an undiscovered island that includes "a little mob of men beating bhghons (a sort of cross between tin pan and gong) and chanting monotonously." Affecting the ethos of a little anthropologist, the narrator's reduction of the natives to a "little mob" is of a piece with the flippant parentheses that liken their ritual to the trivial shrillness of a tin pan. In another moment of the story, the narrator shifts his attention from the narrative to remark on the eventual discovery of the island; shortly after the story takes place, our narrator tells us, the French had come and "educated the natives to wear clothes on Sunday and go to church, so that now they are quite civilized and uninteresting." Robert Crawford finds in these two moments contrary vectors that reveal Eliot's genuine fascination with, as well as condescension to, indigenous cultures: "The natives are interesting," Crawford notes, "but also funny, bhghons and all."[66]

In comparing these moments of light comedy to the opening scramble for authoritative grounds, the former may appear less self-consciously rhetorical than the latter. But as Crawford has shown, Eliot has adapted such comedy from Mayne Reid's blood-and-thunder adventure stories set in exotic locales. The tension in Reid's stories derives from contrasting disgruntled civilization with exciting savagery. Eliot's co-optations of these contrasts are just as rhetorical as his attempts to negotiate authority in the opening paragraph. The difference is that the comical moments are attempts by the young author to entertain (one function of the storyteller), whereas his attempts to establish authority almost always read as anxiousness and uncertainty in the juvenilia. For the purposes of my study here, more interesting than the source is the use to which the author puts such an ideology: the assertion that the natives are now "uninteresting" because they wear clothes and go to church allows the speaker to establish a persona that is attuned to the ridiculousness—and potential comic material—of decorum and implicitly, the potential ridiculousness of his churchgoing audience.

"To the Class of 1905"
Recited June 13, 1905, at commencement exercises of Smith Academy; published as "At Graduation 1905" in Poems Written in Early Youth *(1950)*

The impossible expectations attached to the valedictory gesture are exacerbated by the poet's too-keen awareness of a living, breathing audience as opposed to the passive outlines of a public readership.[67] Trying to combine elegy, wisdom, reminiscence, and deference, the poem ends up saying very little: instead, we are left with the impression of an artificial voice of wisdom that the sixteen-year-old Eliot uncomfortably dons for the occasion and of the oppressively authoritative audience with its expectations of praise, sacrifice, and tribute.

The first of its fourteen stanzas begins:

> Standing upon the shore of all we know
> We linger for a moment doubtfully,
> Then with a song upon our lips, sail we
> Across the harbor bar—[68]

Before considering how voice and audience are constructed in this valedictory poem, first consider its opening gesture, which contrasts the certainty of the present ("Standing upon the shore of all we know") to the uncertainty of the future ("We linger for a moment, doubtfully"). The reference to "all we know" sits uncomfortably. On the one hand, it seems to acknowledge that the realm of student experience is narrow. On the other hand, the phrase "all we know"—insofar as it refers to sixteen-year-olds—can sound presumptuously grandiose. This theme is uneasily handled, because the young poet sensibly wants to acknowledge that he and his peers are not ready for the future and that their beloved school must have prepared them for that future. Thus, the opening gesture reflects this ambivalence, contrasting "know" with "doubtfully," and pitting "Standing," a stance of authority, with "linger," a stance of uncertainty. These thematic contrasts reveal the paradox in which the poem is caught: How does a sixteen-year-old speak wisely? Eliot's meager solution—perhaps the only one available to a young author trapped in such a thankless task—is to be as vague as possible and to deploy unobjectionable topoi, such as permanence and change, responsibility and expectation, nostalgia and future hopes. While genre is certainly a culprit here—has there ever been a graduation ode that was not insipid?—the vagueness of the poem is another capitulation to the authority of the audience.

Eliot's "Lyric"—composed shortly before this ode—had opened with a reference to what "Sages say." Written a few months later, the graduation ode might be seen as an attempt to imitate what sages sound like when they speak. The voice of the speaker, puffing itself up into the posture of savant, is practically choked with poeticisms: "Then with a song upon our lips, sail we / Across the harbor bar." Such earnestness is ripe for parody, and once Eliot turns his back upon such sins, the older poet will be merciless in skewering empty lyricism and sentimental stuffing. Upon finding this poem in later life, Eliot would not be able to resist mocking the delusions of his younger self. Turning over the typescript to John Hayward, his bibliographer, Eliot wrote sardonically in the bomb-strafed England of 1943, "I hope you will be impressed by the pathos of the hopes which I expressed for the twentieth century and for the future of a day school which was dissolved for lack of pupils a few years later."[69]

At the time of the poem's composition, however, such sentiments are the only tropes available to a shy, bookish student who is suddenly given a stage upon which to speak. Hiding behind a puffed-up voice is one defense the young poet has chosen for this moment of public challenge. The second defense he chooses is to present a speaker who is the plural embodiment of his graduating class rather than an individual—a standard expectation for such an ode. In this poem of fourteen stanzas, there are twenty-seven references to "we" or "our." Never risking the individuality of "I," the speaker links himself arm in arm with his graduating brothers. Its conquering metaphors are oddly woven with metaphors of hesitation and doubt; the speaker is bound with his peers in boyish anxiety as well as manly determination. In spite of their very different occasions, genres, and tones, a similar stance found in his "Fable for Feasters": "I," the speaker, know nothing; you, the audience, are omniscient. This abject humility appears again with a vengeance in this graduation ode. The "I" shrinks to nothing, and the "you" expands to overtake the "I" in another kind of "we." The "we" that winks mischievously in the final lines of "Fable for Feasters" is a devious escape from the problems of authority and power. Here, though, in a public recitation of a graduation ode, the burdensome expectations of genre and audience require a monologic "we." Speaking as the collective voice of his class, the speaker sings of duty, gratitude, and great deeds through the plural pronoun:

But if this century is to be more great
Than those before, her sons must make her so,
And we are of her sons, and we must go
With eager hearts to help mold well her fate

In his iterations of "we," the speaker projects an ethos recognizable to members of his social class: deference to institutions and authority, regard for honor and fame, and the belief that men consciously shape their own destinies and heroically change the course of history. The political undercurrent here is the liberal belief in progress: "And let thy motto be, proud and serene, / Still as the years pass by, the word 'Progress!'" (Considering Eliot's later conservative politics, there is a neat irony of his extolling the virtues of liberal Victorian progress, punctuated with an earnest exclamation point.) This idealist strain, derivative of the nineteenth-century bourgeoisie, was manifested on the practical level in the elite structures of secondary education such as Smith Academy and Milton Academy. These two institutions, both Eliot's alma maters, were created to shepherd upper-middle-class scions into Harvard and Yale, thus replicating the class system. While the "deeds" to which the sons of the school are summoned are unspecified, there is one particular deed to which the speaker exhorts his graduating brothers: spreading the name of the school so that "Thy honor and thy fame shall but increase." In this context, "fame" refers to patrician accomplishment at an acceptable university or military academy. As a "duty," then, the replication of the class system looms even more largely than heroic deeds to which the twentieth century calls the graduating students.

Beneath the bombast and drabness of the poem, it reads, poignantly, like the voice of an adolescent trying to be a man. Flailing to assume the assured tones of maturity and wisdom, such a voice will have nothing wise to say—only a repetition of tested tropes. So the boy relies on an elevated diction and an elegiac tone to achieve his desired effects, and he turns, either out of habit or for want of a more inventive scheme, to a traditional rhetorical form, the Aristotelian four-part arrangement.[70]

Eliot recollected this performance almost fifty years later: "I was informed afterwards, by one of my teachers, that the poem itself was excellent, as such poems go, but that my delivery was very bad indeed."[71] That his peers were likely snoozing in their chairs at its recitation makes no difference to our analysis of this poem as a certain kind of success, "as such poems go," in his teacher's knowing phrase. It is the performance of a compliant schoolboy, a poem that soberly accomplishes its valedictory functions of praising and farewelling. More importantly, the poem has shown that its author has willingly adopted the manners and ideology of his class, gender, and education. Considering the poem's occasion, the real audience has determined its imagined audience: a combination of his peers and their relatives, the teachers and administrators of the school who are assembled for the graduation ceremony. But the poem conforms to the desires and expectations of the adults, not the peers—expectations that, however much they overlap with the obedient sons, have been determined by the Tradition, the literary conventions of an epideictic ode, and the social expectations of a graduation ceremony. Because the publicity of the occasion grants the young writer no room for jockeying, the audience and its ideology, voiced through the speaker, overtake the poem. That the speaker is unable to detach his own identity from that of his audience is a different iteration of his first rhetorical problem. Not only does the speaker know nothing while the audience knows everything; here the speaker has no identity at all but for the audience that gives voice through him.

"Song" ("When we came home across the hill")
Published in Harvard Advocate, *May 24, 1907*

After his graduation ode is proclaimed from the stage, Eliot spends one year at Milton Academy, a preparatory boarding school outside of Boston, and then another year, his first, at Harvard. This two-year hiatus from the publication of poetry ends with the appearance of Eliot's "Song" ("When we came home across the hill") in the *Harvard Advocate*. Four days after it appears, Eliot's first undergraduate poem is damned with faint praise by K. G. T. Webster in the *Crimson*. Far away from the fastnesses of his St. Louis home and the praise of his mother and teachers, Eliot hears this complaint from an instructor assisting in a comparative literature course: "Mr. Eliot's 'Song' is pretty and suggestive in its vague way. In general, *Advocate* poets—as well as others—should consider that sense hurts no poem."[72] Webster, an obscure scholar now immortal as Eliot's first public critic, has diagnosed the trouble: Eliot is an imitator rather than a disciple, hazarding a voice without much footing in sense.

Of the scant poems we have from Eliot's youth, this surviving poem is the first to attempt a description of loss or failure—a major preoccupation of the mature poet. The theme of loss is perhaps the reason its author has copied the clipped, tightly structured quatrains of *In Memoriam*: iambic tetrameter with an interlinked rhyme scheme of *abbc addc*, a variation on the closed Tennysonian form of *abba cddc*. The poem contrasts an idyllic setting—the bloom of spring—to the "faded" foliage of the beloved's wreath.[73] As Eliot's first critic has noted, the understatement here is so pronounced as to amount to a lack of statement: the poet observes the failure of the ideal, the reason for which is unnamed, nor is a specific emotion conveyed or identified.

The message of the poem is underdeveloped, and its speaker and audience are illegible. No sooner is the "we" uttered in the first line than it starts to fade like the beloved's wreath. In a biographical reading of the poem—conflating the young author with the speaker—it would appear that the author is unable to address himself to the problem underlying his experience. As a result, the "we" splits into indistinct identities: an "I" who never names himself, unable to summon a specific speaking identity, and a second person (the beloved), also never named. Preoccupied with describing the natural world, the speaker seems to have forgotten the beloved who has failed him. He refers to her only obliquely, by way of reference to "your wreath." By speaking past the beloved rather than addressing her, the poet indirectly accuses her of failure by noting that her wreath is faded, while the rest of nature maintains its freshness. Hamstrung by the propriety of his class—a capitulation to his audience's values—the courtier makes the accusation only elliptically.

Mayer, who follows such a biographical reading, believes the reason for this obliquity is that the speaker is, in reality, disappointed not in the beloved but in his own experience.[74] Thus, the attempt at the traditional "I-thou" arrangement, posited in the first line, is abandoned as insufficient. As a result, the audience is left out in the cold, with no explanation of who is speaking or why: the ghostly "I" is unable to plumb his own experience and speaks out of the side of his mouth to an indistinctly imagined "you."

While such a biographical experience may have directed the outlines of the poem, it is equally plausible to imagine that the young author, witnessing or reading about others' failed loves, adopts the tropes of the literary lament and dummies up a speaker and beloved. The result is a publishable poem, an artifact that wanly enacts a specific kind of experience through literary conventions. That the artifice of poetic lament has a relationship to real human loss is not entirely understood by the young author, and so the manipulations of those properties feel like the moving about of chess pieces rather than a compelling account of failure.

"Song" ("If space and time, as sages say")
Published in Harvard Advocate, *June 3, 1907*

In the immediate wake of his publicly criticized "Song" ("When we came home"), with its problems of ethos and pathos, Eliot publishes a revision of his two-year old poem "A Lyric," a conventional poem that is more successful in its handling of ethos and pathos. In this slightly revised version, the Jonsonian manner is kept, and the theme is the same, though the first stanza is improved both formally and thematically. Here the poet counters what the (now decapitalized) "sages" say about time and space not existing. "But let us live while yet we may," the poet argues, not because time does not exist—as the earlier version had it—but because "time is time, and runs away, / Though sages disagree."[75] In both the first and revised versions, the learned sages have claimed, counterintuitively, that time and space do not exist. But in the revised version, the speaker rejects the sages' version of reality.

The crux of the revision rests on the different logical relation of the same premise to the same conclusion: a switch made evident in the poet's substitution of "But" for "So." In the first version, the lovers' present enjoyment comes as an acceptance ("So") of the sages' hypothesis about time. In the revised poem, the lovers' present enjoyment comes in spite ("But") of what sages say about time. Poetically, the contradiction of a premise is more dramatic than the respectful following of a premise. Although Eliot is far from achieving his own voice as a poet, here his skepticism is evident. The poet refuses to escape into a metaphysical abstraction, insisting instead on the obvious, the real: "For time is time and runs away." Mayer sees in these subtle revisions "a sobering of adolescent romanticism by common sense."[76] That these revisions are accomplished squarely within the gather-ye-rosebuds tradition does not make them the less interesting.

Mayer helps to identify an audience concern when he notes that flowers "given" in the original poem are now "sent"—a more remote gesture. The poetic "butterfly," meanwhile, is reduced to the prosaic "fly." For Mayer, these and other revisions mark Eliot's growing aloofness: a "cultivation of detachment as a basic attitude, a way of regulating one's relations with the world and of safeguarding the self."[77] And, as Mayer indicates, that new aloofness is concomitant with Eliot's new milieu: the warmth and security of home in St. Louis has been exchanged for the ironic detachment of Harvard undergraduates and Bostonian culture.

Illuminating as Mayer's biographical suggestion is, the poem bears out this audience shift with even more specificity than he describes. The relation between "I" and "thee" does not change in the revised version, though "Love" as a sentimental title for the addressee is erased. What does change in terms of audience is that the wisdom figures who were merely topoi in the first poem are now present as a source of contention, their counter-authority transforming them into the anti-audience of the poem. In the revised poem, not only is their hypothesis about time rejected—or, more accurately, deemed irrelevant—the sages are themselves not the source of authority that they were in the earlier poem. In the first version, they are "Sages," whose authority on the topic of time is accepted and followed. In the second version, the demoted "sages" are shown to be at variance with the speaker. By splitting the speaker's attention among a beloved who is exhorted, an anti-audience who is resisted, and an authorial audience who overhears, the rhetorical situation of the poem becomes more complex. This nuance materializes as a result of the author's light resistance against an imagined authority. The author of the first poem was a sixteen-year-old who was living a sheltered life at home. The author of the revision is an eighteen-year-old freshman at Harvard, in his second year of living away from home. He is just starting to realize that authority might be gainsaid; that the narrow purview of familial, religious, and regional influences might be abandoned; and that a self might be created in the process.

"Before Morning"
Published in Harvard Advocate, *Nov. 13, 1908*

A year and a half earlier, in mid-1907, Eliot's "Song" ("When we came home across the hill") had been slapped for its vagueness, and his revised "Song" ("If space and time as sages say") was found by the *Crimson* to be sung merely "agreeably."[78] Now, after a considerable lapse of time, Eliot tries out yet another style in "Before Morning," with Edward FitzGerald's *Rubáiyát of Omar Khayyam* its closest model.[79] It is an extension of the manner Eliot approached in "Song" ("When we came home"), only the voice is even more disembodied here. No one is addressed in this poem, and no speaker announces himself: only a description of images is laid out.

> This morning's flowers and flowers of yesterday
> Their fragrance drifts across the room at dawn,
> Fragrance of bloom and fragrance of decay[80]

Considering his most recent poem, in which the roles of speaker and addressee are narrowly explicit, this experiment shows the author stripping himself of a prepackaged setup to see what results: What happens when a disembodied voice speaks to no one in particular? The outcome, alas, is another dull experiment, but it shows that Eliot never sits still.

As there is neither an addressee nor an explicitly evoked audience, the speaker is understood as the implied observer of the described scene, with the authorial audience shuffled off behind the speaker/observer. While placing the authorial audience over the speaker's shoulder is a commonplace of lyric poetry, the trouble is that no compelling reason for having the audience look on has been concocted. Of all the juvenilia, this audience is the most vaguely construed.

Mayer notes of this poem and its predecessor that a psychic distance appears in the upperclassman's writing, an "emerging fastidiousness" with regard to his relationship to self and experience.[81] Mayer's analysis can be extrapolated to apply to that self's relationship to his audiences. The young Eliot is still in reactive, rather than creative, mode, and he effaces the self by having no identifiable speaker: "By remaining unnamed as 'I' in the expression of its experience," Mayer explains, "the self becomes an uncertain source of experience."[82] Translated into the terms of this study, the speaker downplays his authority by disappearing. Although such a claim is not true as a general statement—the absence of "I" can universalize a perspective and grant it objective authority—the disappearance of Eliot's "I" here betrays a growing uncertainty. This distancing is a function of his emergent defensiveness with regard to an ironic audience of Harvard undergraduates, as we have already seen with his revisions to "A Lyric." As yet unable or unwilling to mobilize irony as a bulwark against an unsympathetic audience, the poet protects himself by relegating that audience to an uncertain limbo and by decoupling the "I" from experience. In his later notebook drafts, Eliot will experiment by fighting irony with irony, but here there is no dialogic exchange between speaker and audience shaping the meaning of this poem. A bare succession of images, learned from FitzGerald, is the most congenial form of poetry that the young author can imitate at this point.

Like "Song" ("When we came home"), "Before Morning" is another attempt at understatement whose point is so muted as to be nonexistent. What Eliot will learn from this unsuccessful experiment is that he must first *say* something for its point to be muted. He is also learning that the public stage of poetry brings with it a barrage of criticism—a withering sarcasm that surely confirmed the author's already tense fear of an audience's judgment. A month after the publication of "Before Morning," the *Harvard Lampoon* names "T. S. E." as the object of its parody, replacing Eliot's decadent flowers with the banalities of home milk delivery: "Bottle on bottle waiting for the day, / Clean bottles, milk bottles, bottles of dawn."[83]

"Circe's Palace"
Published in Harvard Advocate, *Nov. 25, 1908*

Perhaps Eliot has learned his lesson—that muteness itself is pointless until he has found a theme to be muted. With this next poem, Eliot looks beyond formal problems to address a real issue: the problem of sex. It is a theme that is more provocative than the smell of decaying flowers, as in his wanly rendered "Song" that only hints at adolescent romance. The next three poems—the last of his juvenilia—will attempt to deal with this reality, though they will do so with limited success.

"Circe's Palace" is the first appearance in Eliot's work of a dangerous woman who causes men pain, though this provocation, such as it is, alludes to Homer's *Odyssey*, a source that would have been acceptable to his audience. In this reading, the classical provenance helps Eliot to address a subject that would be touchy to conservative readers, and the most convenient model through which to refract this theme is a gauzy, fin-de-siècle decadence drawn from Swinburne. In Mayer's reading, the classical source is a topos that enables the speaker to hide from himself what he means: "As a neurotic vision of destructive woman and emasculating sexuality, 'Circe's Palace' is a remarkable revelation. Eliot the fastidious, sexually naive adolescent could not have published the poem aware of its implications (Bloomsbury found him to be unusually naive), yet the poem seems to have caught what Eliot knew instinctively."[84]

The ways in which the poem departs from its Homeric source bespeak an adolescent terrified and repulsed by sex and women. Eliot's Circe is nowhere present in the poem, only her cruel handiwork: Odysseus's men turned into animals. By implication, Circe is only dangerous, rather than dangerous and seductive, as in Homer. Also, Homer's Circe, once subdued by Odysseus, is ultimately his lover and a friend to his men, whom she restores to an improved human state. But Eliot's men have no such luck. The young poet is interested only in the emasculating nature of the goddess.

The pronoun "we" appears at the end of each stanza, both times changing the rhetoric of the poem. Both appearances of "we" interrupt the stanza and tell the audience something unexpected. The first stanza describes Circe's fountain, the suffering men, and the flowers that grow on them. It ends with an assertion, introduced without explanation: "We shall not come here again." Likewise, the second stanza describes listless animals inhabiting the garden. And again, the introduction of the second-person plural reveals something surprising about these animals: "And they look at us with the eyes / Of men whom we knew long ago." What this maneuver reveals is that Eliot has his doubts about straight description and the work that it can do. He resolves the problem of vagueness (theme taking over as description) by directly involving both the speaker and the addressee—an implied "you" packaged inside of "we." The identity of that "you" is ambiguous because it could be Odysseus's partners who are imagined or an unidentified silent listener. Whatever the effect, the rhetoric of this "we" indicates that Odysseus is talking either to the addressee of the poem or to his comrades, or possibly both—the hearer of the poem being turned into a comrade. In other words, the floating, voiceless description of the first stanza turns suddenly to implicate the speaker and listener and to draw them closer to danger; and the floating description of the animals in the second stanza turns abruptly into a relationship between the speaker-listener ("we") and their former friends. Eliot will attempt a similar maneuver in a number of subsequent poems, each time to different effect, until he perfects it in "Prufrock" and "Portrait of a Lady."

"Song" ("The moonflower opens to the moth")
Published in Harvard Advocate, *Jan. 26, 1909*

In hymn-meter, or ballad, form, the speaker addresses a virginal beloved, bearer of white flowers, who turns out to be inadequate: "Have you no brighter tropic flowers / With scarlet lips, for me?"[85] Here there is no emotion, only the desire for emotion. The speaker is passive, expecting the woman to bring passion to the relationship.

Like the passive speaker and the passive addressee, the audience is the traditional lyric audience who silently overhears. In the first stanza, a simple listing of white details is given in anecdotal form: a flower opens, a mist crawls, a bird flies. In the second stanza, an addressee is specified: she is "Love," twice addressed as "you." Unlike his revision to "Lyric" in which the endearment "Love" is expunged, here Eliot can risk such a title, because the beloved is revealed as far from ideal in this poem. Thus, the problem of sentimentality is avoided, and the smirking of Harvard undergraduates is forestalled.

The beloved turns out retrospectively to be the addressee of both stanzas: passively listening in the first, actively addressed in the second. She is addressed with a rhetorical question, her inadequacy taken for granted. The lyric form grants no space in which she might respond or object to her characterization. But the accusation seems to be overplayed: the speaker "wants *brighter* flowers, *tropic* flowers, filled with *scarlet* life from her," Mayer argues. "But his unconscious may reveal itself in the pallor imagery that subtly suggests that the deficiencies may be within himself, the source."[86] Mayer argues that the extremities of womanhood suggested by this poem and its predecessor ("Circe's Palace") seem less derived from cultural stereotypes—the Western tropes of woman as either virgin or whore—than from Eliot's "personal neuroses."[87]

However problematic his conclusions about women, the poet is here struggling to address his experience more forthrightly, directly accusing the beloved of insufficiency, unlike the indirect accusation in his first undergraduate poem, "Song" ("When we came home across the hill"). It is still a juvenile worldview and an unconscious that accidentally reveals its naiveté, as Mayer suggests. The poem is hardly an improvement formally. But the decision to assign the problem to a distinctly imagined identity reveals an artist who is trying to tackle the hard truths of reality, insofar as he grasps them, while grappling with crude tools of indirect expression. The rhetoric clarifies as a result: the speaker and addressee occupy the traditional lyric positions of "I-thou."

This poem and the following one, "On a Portrait" are written a few weeks after Eliot's discovery of Symons's *The Symbolist Movement in Literature* but before Eliot had access to the complete works of Laforgue ordered from France. Because of the dating, some scholars have tried to ferret out in these two poems some particle of French influence—Laforgue via Symons—avant la lettre. But Eliot's gestation period after encountering Symons was long—at least six months—and the change, when it comes, is much more striking than anything seen so far.

"On a Portrait"
Published in Harvard Advocate, *Jan. 26, 1909*

The danger of women is intensified here in Eliot's first sonnet, but so is feminine complexity and ambiguity. The portrait that the speaker observes is traditionally identified as Édouard Manet's 1866 *Woman with a Parrot*.[88] An impenetrable cipher, described as a "pensive lamia," the mythical monster only fascinates him from a distance: "Her dark eyes keep their secrets hid from us, / Beyond the circle of our thought she stands." Although figured as a possible threat, she is safely held outside of the ambit of the speaker's thought. Both "immaterial" as well as impenetrable, she can only be observed, rather than engaged.

Frances Dickey has argued that Eliot's poem presents two different subjectivities of the woman: "Either the woman is absorbed in some thought for which the painting offers no object, or else she is mentally, psychologically absent."[89] These subjectivities, both ambiguously present in the poem, map two competing views of artistic creation. The former view—the woman's absorption in an object unspecified by the painting or poem—is, Dickey argues, "the classic Cartesian conception of self that privileges inwardness and, following romanticism, the expression of inwardness through artistic creativity." The latter view—the psychological absence of the woman—"constitutes the subject out of flat surfaces whose hallmark characteristic is reflection or imitation."[90] To translate Dickey's painterly and philosophical terms into rhetorical terms, the poem foregrounds problems of voice and audience. Is voice claimed as subjectively authentic, or is voice claimed through imitation of others? Is it an inner (individual) voice, or a copied (community) voice? Is the object of the woman's gaze unknowable? Or is that mystery the point for the audience? For what reason does Manet or Eliot withhold from his audience an object of knowledge?

The poem ends with the viewpoint of the unknowable parrot. This shift from speaker to parrot complicates our understanding of the speaker, since the parrot, described as "patient" and "curious," seconds—or parrots—the observations of the speaker. The bird offers no judgment, but the speaker attempts to achieve more authority by invoking another mysterious observer—one as unknowable as the female being observed and described. The clinical viewpoint of the parrot mirrors the speaker's inability to make a human connection with her. Wanting to engage her but unable to conceive of how, the speaker shifts his viewpoint to that of a parrot, whose thoughts about the woman (if it has any) are likewise undescribed. The turn to the parrot is not exactly comic, but it does deflate any pretensions to authority the speaker holds. For Mayer, the poem represents an advance on the juvenilia, since it is the first poem "to dramatize an experience from within consciousness."[91] From a rhetorical perspective, this shift to the viewpoint of the parrot reveals the young poet's unease with the self-revelatory mode: the inner experience of a poet on the verge of coming to voice is bested in the final couplet by the quirky detachment of a bird prized for its ability to repeat the voices of others.

As with other conservative or defensive moves in the juvenilia, this shift to the parrot's viewpoint is of a piece with the poet's still-wary view of his audience. The object form "us" appears twice in the poem, but its identity is unclear: Does the "us" mark a plural speaker, speaker and audience, speaker and addressee, or speaker and unnamed character? Whatever its identity, it is disturbed by the first appearance in Eliot's juvenilia of the strangely elusive construction "one": "as if one should meet / a pensive lamia." As slippery as the identity of the lamia, this evasive "one" appears yet again in the next line: "An immaterial fancy of one's own." Since the audience and speaker are conceived as in league with each other ("us"), and outside of the circle of the woman ("her"), it is unclear what effect the author seeks with this construction. "You" in these contexts would not work, since no singular second person is specified (the woman being too distant to be addressed). And "we"—the natural choice for a poem whose speaker/audience has been conceived as "us"—would also be awkward in this hypothetical context. In "Prufrock," this "one" will be used to better effect, but though this earlier poem's lyricism hints at that later Prufrockian sound, the use of "one" here is a dodge for avoiding the "I" and its troublesome identity issues.

Dickey likewise views this evasion of the "I" as fundamental to the rhetoric of the poem, which she reads as broaching the problems of interiority and identity:

> The parrot's "eye" thus punningly merges with the poet's *I*. What would a parrot's *I* be? The romantic lyric *I*—expressing the unique inwardness of the poet—implies a conception of self that parroting would seem to cancel. That the pronoun *I* never appears in Eliot's poem except by implication in this pun indicates a disappearance of the speaker that exceeds the woman's evanescence. If the romantic self is predicated on expression of original thoughts and feeling, what kind of self can a poet have if he only repeats and imitates?[92]

Still an imitator rather than a disciple, Eliot will take many months to study the complete works of Laforgue, during which period he will make himself into an expert disciple of Laforgue and Symons—after which he will quickly move on to imitate yet other masters. Although this poem has not yet broken out of the boundaries delimited by the juvenilia, it already shows him querying the artistic limits and possibilities of imitation.

"Ballade of the Fox Dinner"
Recited May 15, 1909; printed privately in 1949 in William R. Castle's Fifty Years, *commemorating the anniversary of the Fox Club*

This slight, comic piece was written for a celebratory dinner at the Fox Club, perhaps an induction of new members.[93] Poking fun at club mates by name, it salutes the rituals of undergraduate inebriation and concludes with a mock-formal "Envoi." Its references to individuals must have amused its intended audience of drunken college students. But in such targeted comedy, the sentiments do not survive the circumstances, and the prankish banter and inside jokes are tedious to the non-elect. Even though the Eliot who writes this poem is concurrently immersed in Laforgue, the French author's sarcastic contempt—vigorously exploited by Eliot a few months later—here does not obtrude. This area of Eliot's creative self is cordoned off from public view, revealing just how tied to audience and occasion Eliot is: the boisterous celebration and fellowship take precedence over any experimentation Eliot may be conjuring in the back of his mind.

However, there is a shockingly new element in this poem, one that has not been noted before.[94] It is the appearance of the modern in the guise of slang, popular culture, contemporary events, and a rollicking, drunken good time. In a bit of foreshadowing, the poem that marks the close of Eliot's juvenile output also marks the beginning of his sustained engagement with popular culture.

It comes as no surprise—indeed, it is something of a relief—to hear that the young scion of a proper family has engaged with his college friends in drinking, gambling, defenestration, amorous adventures, and rowdy carousing. However, in a poetic context thus far distinguished by its staid decorum, what is surprising is that the author would use the medium of poetry to depict high-spirited debauchery and would deploy such slang and references to popular culture as "cocktail," "ginger ale," "booze," "summersaulting," and "demon Rum."[95] The *OED* categorizes "cocktail" as slang for a mixed alcoholic drink, dating its earliest appearance to early nineteenth-century America. Similarly, "booze," as a colloquialism for alcohol or spirits, was a common slang term.[96] Although variations on ginger beer as an alcoholic drink are centuries old, "ginger ale" as a compound (sometimes appearing with a hyphen) does not emerge until very late in the nineteenth century, the new expression marking the increasing popularity of the nonalcoholic drink at the turn of the century. And while the noun "somersault" is quite old, it had only recently been turned into a verb by the late nineteenth century. And, of course, the expression "demon Rum" was not only slang but a politically potent expression in the clamorous temperance battles of the turn of the century. The speaker's mandate to "temporize with demon Rum!" even plays impishly on the word "temperance."[97]

All these expressions found in the poem are less au courant than contemporaneous; slang was both more regional and slow moving in the preelectronic age. Slang usage can project trendiness, a concern (or neurosis) of the modern age, and it does so by signaling membership in a community, whether by region, ethnicity, class, or trade. What is more important than the modishness of Eliot's terms is their rough tenor, especially "booze" and "demon Rum," two terms that signal a sympathy with working-class grit and populist mudslinging. There is something transgressive in the poet's use of these terms, their louche drive elbowing aside somber literary conventions.

In addition to the thrum of the popular, there is an oblique reference in the poem to another current event, one that carries in it both the promise and threat of modernity. Appraising his happy-go-lucky friends, the speaker describes them as "A host of loyal graduates / Oblivious of bonds and stocks." Some of those loyal graduates would have needed a stiff drink to quell the anxiety that had been unleashed by the great Wall Street panic of 1907, which ruined many of their families' fortunes and jeopardized their own educations and futures.[98] The previous decade had seen huge market gains, reflecting a general surge in global prosperity, but also making millionaires out of speculators. It was not the first panic Wall Street had experienced, but it was the largest such crisis, lasting for two months and occurring amid a long economic contraction. The market finally recovered its confidence later in 1908, though it did not surpass pre-1907 heights until well into 1909.[99]

In spite of the vigorous, or even threatening, nature of such references to the popular and contemporaneous, they have no effect on the form or tone of the poem. The disorderly scene is surveyed, as it were, from within the prim confines of tetrameter quatrains. The contrast between such formal devices and the popular references heightens the irony Eliot intends and is a consequence of the tradition in which Eliot is writing. William Castle, the editor of the volume in which the poem was first published, acknowledges as much, insisting that Eliot's poem is "typical of these dinner verses."[100] So the poem must be heard not only as its occasion and audience require but as part of a poetic tradition of *vers de societé*: "brief lyrical verse in a genial, sportive mood and sophisticated in both subject and treatment. . . . Its characteristics are polish, *savoir faire*, grace, and ease."[101] As a category, it straddles both light verse and occasional verse. Within this tradition—whose undergraduate *vers* is perhaps more *d'ivrogne* than *de societé*—Eliot's poem manages both the sportive and the sophisticated, the popular and the literary. It is only within such a tradition that the joke of its mock-heroic invocation for example, can be understood: "Muse of the rye and ginger ale, / Muse of the Cocktail and the Bar."

As Grover Smith grumbles, the poem is a "trifling" piece.[102] The account of a good time is not, poetically speaking, a good time for its later readers. But the opportunity that the occasion has provided for Eliot is not trifling at all. It has given him an opportunity to approach his audience problem from a new angle. Even though the content of "Ballade" is unmistakably different from that of the rest of his juvenilia, the primary difference is that for the first time in his poetic career, Eliot imagines an audience that includes him as speaker, an audience that does not judge him by strict moral standards but celebrates him as an individual in the community. The poem extols the kind of easy commerce among "I," "you," and "we" that was seen only one other time, in his first poem, the Jonsonian "A Lyric." The ultimate value of that "we," however, is just as conventional as the Jonsonian "I-thou," which Eliot had adopted wholesale from the carpe diem tradition rather than turned to his own purposes. For in the collegiate contexts of hale fellow well met, the young Eliot has been bred to weigh exactly the values and bonds of the Harvard "we"; the raucous sons of the haute-bourgeoisie who are briefly "Oblivious of bonds and stocks" will soon sober up to their duties. In an unpredictable economic world far removed from the repartee of club dinners, they will capitalize on their Harvard relationships to advance their legal and business enterprises. Future business deals mark the foundation of their present friendships—which makes the "we" a rather hollow one.

It is unclear how consciously Eliot built this critique into his light-hearted toast, but it is unmistakably there. The speaker imagines that "twenty years" after the present dinner, the "faithful" friends will have parlayed their college hobbies into jobs: one Nick will direct some kind of gambling venture, another McNeil will have turned his amorous exploits into a more profitable "partnership with Venus," a certain Short will be known for "advertising booze," and one Talbot will be selling clothes.[103] The language of capitalism in the poem is as plentiful as the language of popular culture; the mix of the two is the cocktail of modernity. And the anxiety engendered by modernity—its alienation and discontinuity, its upheavals and exuberance—will become synonymous in the popular mind, less than twenty years later, with the poetry of T. S. Eliot.

Here is the paradox of the young author's "we," the final attempt of his juvenilia to forge an identity and find a place in community. While biographical reports and contemporaneous accounts paint a picture of a detached, overly formal undergraduate, Eliot was still a social figure, with a penchant for ribald humor. And unlike the pallid seriousness of much of his juvenilia, this poem reads like the performance of a high-spirited Falstaff enjoying himself and his friendships. For Eliot to ring the changes on such genial bonds in verse would cost him nothing. But the poem does forestall, in its inebriated haze, the vexed questions of personal identity and serious relationships to which neither his poetry nor his experience could offer any answer.

Forging a speaking identity and constructing an audience to whom he wishes to speak will be the tasks of the notebook. This poem, slight as it is, takes a new direction down that road. Abandoning for one evening the staid Tradition that has haunted his poetry so far, Eliot discovers that not all audiences for poetry are alike. And here, in May 1909, while Eliot is devouring Laforgue and preparing to write a new kind of poetry, we should consider that it is perhaps the boozy humor and crotch-scratching bluster of clubhouse doggerel—as much as the urbanity of Laforgue—that help to free Eliot from his restrictive notions of voice and audience.

This chapter has considered the ways in which literary indebtedness and good breeding set the parameters of Eliot's earliest rhetorical choices. We have considered only his juvenile poems and stories, but comparable parallels could be drawn with the young Eliot's essays. In one article published in *Harvard Advocate* a few weeks after his Fox Dinner performance, Eliot explores the "gentlemanly dignity" of New England sailors, of whom he counts himself a proud descendant. Eliot's "Gentlemen and Seamen" might as well have as its subtitle "Indebted and Well-Bred," for the author charts his own indebtedness to these early seafarers and praises their industry and manners, which they cultivated in a savage new world conspicuously lacking in both. Though lowly farmers, they maintained a "plebeian aristocracy" and saw no suffering or scarcity as an affront to their "pride or social position."[104] He concludes by exhorting his readers—the beneficiaries of men who had fewer occupations to choose from—to acknowledge their debt: "If . . . we have preserved the spirit of our old plebeian aristocracy, we should give them the grace of recognition."[105] Gracious indebtedness and aristocratic propriety go hand in hand with the young Eliot; this ideology works itself out not only in his rhetorical choices but in the very themes he addresses in his poems, stories, and essays.

Contrasting the early poems to the stories, one conclusion to be drawn is that narrative does not ignite Eliot's imagination as much as poetry does. The formulas of the adventure stories that he copies become repetitive, and so he drops the genre after a few tries. Poetry, on the contrary, allows him a broader reach. For the trying on and casting aside of various voices reveal more than just a fickle lack of identity on the part of an exploring adolescent. Unlike the predictable formulas of his stories, the various masks of his juvenile poetry disclose an Eliot who is by temperament a restless intellect, a poet in motion whose ear for the rhythms and sounds of language will eventually take him far beyond the domesticated savagery of his adventure stories.

A compelling voice is missing from the juvenilia, as is a coherent audience. Herbert Howarth has observed of the limitations of the juvenilia and the poet's audience anxiety: "Eliot willingly forgoes any largeness, any expansiveness, which might seem to claim public attention." The logical result of this anxiety, Howarth writes, is that Eliot instead "aims at unity and coherence, and is content to write a poem of very small compass if within the small compass he can produce the result."[106] One advantage of such narrow focus and compliant decorum is that these restrictions have enabled the young author to set his modest poetic inspirations on view: all of his extant juvenilia appeared in school periodicals or were recited in public.

Bracketing the singular exception of "Ballade of the Fox Dinner," the juvenilia's limitations of care, propriety, and circumspection—related to Eliot's fear of a disapproving audience—will soon be transcended in the purchase of a notebook: a private place where large poems and reckless gestures might be ventured. For this boundary to be crossed, the young poet needs more than ambition and a secluded workshop. He needs a model not only for a new voice in which to speak but for new audiences that will receive and respond to what he says.

CHAPTER TWO

The Notebook, Begun

The Clash of Laforgue and Baudelaire in the Poems of November 1909

> The taste of an adolescent writer is intense, but narrow: it is determined by personal needs. The kind of poetry that I needed, to teach me the use of my own voice, did not exist in English at all; it was only to be found in French.
>
> —T. S. Eliot, "Yeats"

The notebook does not begin with the notebook.[1] The place where Eliot begins to learn the use of his own voice is a poem that does not appear in the notebook, a sonnet entitled "Nocturne." Shockingly different from the innocuous confections he had been composing only months earlier, its blistering irony reveals the direct influence of Jules Laforgue. So why would Eliot's first poem in this new style be missing from a notebook that was given over, as Eliot explains the matter, to "working out the implications of Laforgue"?[2]

One explanation is that this breezily contemptuous poem, once composed, must have surprised its reticent author. The ramifications of that chasm—between the disdainful voice that had just erupted and the deferential voices he had been accustomed to using—warranted a notebook. For "Nocturne" charted a wholly new direction. And considering the conservative audiences for whom the adolescent Eliot had been writing, it was a potentially dangerous direction. Eliot's use of the notebook as a private place for experimentation represents a break from his former method of composing on whatever sheaves lay to hand and then publishing shortly thereafter. The sturdy, leather-bound notebook was a physical manifestation of a psychological reality: the double acknowledgment that such experiments needed to continue and that they needed to be hidden from view.

The medium-sized notebook—about 20.5 × 17 cm.—was purchased in Gloucester, probably in the summer of 1910, and intended as a workshop for Eliot's poems. A remarkable record of the transformation of Eliot's style, the notebook is a lively, bumpy account of a momentous shift, his adoption and transformation of the rhetorical moves and manners of the French Symbolists, American popular culture, ragtime, and slang—a process by which he became T. S. Eliot.

The Old Story: Eliot Finds His Voice in Laforgue

> [A] feeling of profound kinship, or rather of a peculiar personal intimacy, with another, probably dead author . . . may overcome us suddenly, on first or after long acquaintance; it is certainly a crisis; and when a young writer is seized with his first passion of this sort he may be changed, metamorphosed almost, *within a few weeks even*, from a bundle of second-hand sentiments into a person.
>
> —T. S. Eliot, "Reflections on Contemporary Poetry [IV]"

The event that sparks this change in Eliot's style is a thunderbolt in the form of a little book: Arthur Symons's *The Symbolist Movement in Literature*.[3] By chance, Eliot had picked up a copy in the library of the Harvard Union, where the *Advocate* had its offices, in December 1908. One chapter in Symons's book is devoted to the poetry of Jules Laforgue—a witty ironist with a mercurial style ranging from colloquial to scornful. Laforgue's sarcasm and informality are attributes that would seem ill suited to entice a proper scion such as Eliot. But such was the appeal to the younger poet that he sent to France for the complete works of Laforgue, which he signed upon receiving "Thomas Eliot 1909."[4]

While immersing himself in the strange world of Laforgue, Eliot writes no poetry for almost a year, with the exception of the romp "Ballade of the Fox Dinner." And then, in November 1909, a flurry of activity: six poems in total, three of which are formally successful poems that strongly mark Laforgue's influence. Eliot published the three Laforguean poems: "Nocturne," "Humouresque," and later, "Conversation Galante."[5] It is these three poems of which critics speak when they say that Eliot "found his voice" by imitating Laforgue.

That critics have long agreed on this narrative is understandable given that the three Laforguean poems were the only November 1909 poems in the public domain until the publication of the notebook in 1996. The source of this critical narrative is traceable as far back as 1917, the year Eliot's first volume of poetry appeared. Predictably, it was Ezra Pound who placed critics on the scent of Laforgue, in the early days when Pound and Eliot were log-rolling each other's works.[6] Other commentators soon caught on, and the mention of Laforgue as primary influence on Eliot became compulsory.[7] This narrative perdures in the critical and journalistic reviews of *Inventions of the March Hare,* where all of Eliot's early poems are finally on view, and in more recent scholarly accounts, where a neat summation of the old story is found: "The primary importance of Laforgue to Eliot was the sudden discovery of his own poetic voice."[8]

Considering the half-century sweep of Eliot's career, it would not be inaccurate to say that the poet suddenly discovered his voice upon reading Laforgue. Not inaccurate, that is to say, as long as the expressionist assumptions of "discovery" are not taken too literally, for a writer's voice is created rather than found. And if we wish to explore the nuts and bolts of that distinctive voice, then it is not the sudden transformation (magical, accidental, instantaneous) but the few weeks of struggle (trial and error, intentional, inventional) that provide the ground where rhetorical analysis can proceed: what raw materials are available for adoption, what is at stake in the various moves tried or rejected, and how conflicts are resolved. That Eliot specifies "a few weeks" as sufficient for a writer's metamorphosis suggests that his autobiographical hint describes not the arc of the notebook as a whole—the protracted investigations of Laforgue, Baudelaire, ragtime, slang, and American popular culture—but its beginnings, those few weeks of November 1909 in the immediate wake of his collision with Laforgue. This was the month in which the character of his writing changed radically, enabling him to articulate passions and sentiments that his previous poems had not risked. On the psychological level, Eliot's adoption of the French Symbolist was a kind of maturation, leaving behind the adolescent's "bundle of second-hand sentiments" and becoming finally "a person."

The three published poems originally written in November 1909 enact a thoroughly confident, Laforguean manner. This manner has been labeled "Eliotic," an understanding that is not so much inexact as it is curiously provincial. To contemporaneous and later commentators, the voice of these three poems sounded like Eliot's own because nothing resembling a Laforguean manner had existed in English-language poetry before. At the time of the poems' appearance, Eliot's startling act of ventriloquism appeared to be genuinely original in English, but it would have appeared derivative to any reader conversant with French Symbolism. Another reason that Eliot's first attempt at a Laforguean voice is mistakenly heard as the mature, Eliotic voice is that Eliot's first published volume of poetry will refine elements of his initial, wholesale adoption of Laforgue.

These three published poems, then, were strangely new to English speakers, though derivative from a continental perspective. As published poems, they formed the basis of how the transformation of Eliot's voice had been understood by critics. Now that the unpublished poems of the notebook allow greater access to Eliot's experimentation with French masters, adding the three other poems written in November 1909 results in a more complicated story than the sudden discovery of a voice through the influence of Laforgue.

The New Story: A Voice Divided, an Audience at Odds

"I doubt whether in any real poem only one voice is audible."

—T. S. Eliot, "The Three Voices of Poetry"

While Laforgue was a strong influence on Eliot's November 1909 poems, he was not the only, nor the first, influence.[9] That credit falls to Baudelaire. In his correspondence with Eliot in the 1940s, Edward Greene reports that Eliot told him that Baudelaire struck him first and with great impact.[10] Greene places Eliot's first encounter with Baudelaire as early as 1907 or 1908, a claim strengthened by the list of Eliot's coursework at Harvard, where he was enrolled during the 1907–1908 academic year in a "French 2a" course in French prose and poetry, a course that included nineteenth-century authors.[11]

Although often more voluble about Laforgue's impact, Eliot never denied Baudelaire's influence in his notebook poems. In his recollections of this stage of his development, Eliot sometimes mentions only Laforgue, but just as often his memory gives Laforgue the upper hand while acceding a supporting role to Baudelaire: "I had an outburst during my junior and senior years. I became much more prolific, under the influence first of Baudelaire and then of Jules Laforgue."[12] And elsewhere, Eliot confirms this double, if uneven influence: in a letter to René Taupin, Eliot describes his first poems as "almost pure Laforgue, with a little Baudelaire."[13]

If we restore Baudelaire's rightful if subsidiary place in the story of Eliot's coming to voice, then cracks in the Laforguean narrative begin to appear. In these first six apprentice poems, Eliot does not achieve a unified voice, as is often claimed. On the contrary, the voice of the November 1909 poems is a deeply divided one. As we will see in a fuller analysis of the three published poems, the corrosive irony of Laforgue at once produces a distinctive, if secondhand voice for Eliot's contempt. However, because that voice is so overpowered by Laforgue, Eliot struggles to redirect its purposes in the other three poems of the November 1909 grouping: "First Caprice in North Cambridge," "Second Caprice in North Cambridge," and "Opera." These latter poems—sequestered in the notebook and never published by Eliot—are serioso pastiches of Baudelaire with undigested remnants of Laforgue. Not only is the voice divided, the audiences of these latter poems are at war with one another. The audience that expects snide mockery cannot coexist with an audience of Baudelairean seriousness.

Restoring Baudelaire

Although we have Eliot's word that Baudelaire is a secondary influence on these first poems, and although the absence of Baudelaire in critical discussions of those poems is attributable to their seclusion in archives, the critic is still obligated to identify the evidence in the poems themselves. Here a seemingly formidable problem presents itself. Ricks's voluminous annotations of these poems identify no linguistic hints of Baudelaire until the December 1910 poem "Fourth Caprice in Montparnasse." If the eagle eye of Ricks finds no Baudelairean residue in any of the November 1909 poems, then it would seem that such influence is virtually untraceable.

Ricks's method of identifying sources relies on exact or close verbal correspondence between a word or phrase in Eliot and the original source. Such precise verbal echoes are not the only ways by which influence can be divined, however. Writers not only adopt the concrete phrasing and specific images of other writers; more generally, they adopt their moods, their rhetorical maneuvers, and their manner of seeing the world. Metaphorically speaking, we could say that while Eliot's volume of Laforgue, open on his desk, is avidly plundered for themes and technique, his volume of Baudelaire, up on the shelf, is more hazily recalled. The Baudelaire whom Eliot conjures in these November 1909 poems is the poet of industrial cityscapes, of the ugly and the grotesque, and of heightened, self-conscious suffering. That Baudelaire cannot in fairness be reduced to such poète maudit commonplaces is irrelevant, for we are not interested in finding our preferred Baudelaire, or even the nineteenth-century Baudelaire, but the Baudelaire of Eliot circa 1909. One of Eliot's recollections of Baudelaire's impact on his own work emphasizes this aspect of urban horror:

> I think that from Baudelaire I learned first, a precedent for the poetical possibilities, never developed by any poet writing in my own language, of the more sordid aspects of the modern metropolis, of the possibility of fusion

> between the sordidly realistic and the phantasmagoric, the possibility of the juxtaposition of the matter-of-fact and the fantastic. From him, as from Laforgue, I learned that the sort of material I had, the sort of experience an adolescent had had, in an industrial city in America, could be the material for poetry; and that the source of new poetry might be found in what had been regarded hitherto as the impossible, the sterile, the intractably unpoetic.[14]

It is this distilled version of Baudelaire—suffering, boredom, despair, all against a recurrent backdrop of drably urban environments—that is most evident in the three unpublished poems of November 1909.

The Use of Laforgue and the Use of Baudelaire

> There are two kinds of poet who can ordinarily be of use to other poets. There are those who suggest, to one or another of their successors, something which they have not done themselves, or who provoke a different way of doing the same thing: these are not likely to be the greatest, but smaller, imperfect poets with whom later poets discover an affinity. And there are the great poets from whom we can learn negative rules: no poet can teach another to write well, but some great poets can teach others some of the things to avoid.
>
> —T. S. Eliot, "Milton II"

For Eliot in November 1909, the useful, imperfect poet is Laforgue, and the less useful, greater poet is Baudelaire.[15]

The lesser poet is useful to Eliot in ways both technical and thematic. Even though Eliot's later views of Laforgue will be more critical, at this crucial stage what the apprentice needs is a Laforgue of masks and irony, of scorn for sentimentality, and of jaunty colloquialisms, a tone and a pose that is—in Edmund Wilson's nice phrase—"poignant-ironic, grandiose-slangy, scurrilous-naïve."[16] With this rhetorical map at his disposal, the young poet's style undergoes a brusque transformation. Laforgue's influence throughout the notebook is especially evident in the immediate expansion of timbre and scope for the voice. In the first three Laforguean poems of November 1909, Eliot strives for a broader tonal palette, achieved with nuanced turns as well as sudden shifts. Note, for example, the opening of "Nocturne," where the voice swoops into an arch timbre with the terse *frenchisme*: "Romeo, *grand sérieux*." These fleeting drolleries will become characteristic of the later Eliot. As with the opening line of "Nocturne," such tonal dives are often found at the beginnings of poems or sections:

> Madame Sosostris, famous clairvoyante
>
> —*The Waste Land*
>
> Ils ont vu les Pays-Bas, ils rentrent à Terre Haute
>
> —"Lune de Miel"
>
> And Life, a little bald and gray
>
> —"Spleen"[17]

Another example, this one in a title, "The Love Song of J. Alfred Prufrock," relies for its effect on a tonal mismatch that sets up one expectation and then quickly dips into a lower register. Eliot not only creates these swift, tonal descents; his ear is attuned to them in his own reading. His epigraph to "Portrait of a Lady" cites Marlowe: "Thou hast committed—" "Fornication."[18] Laforgue's fingerprint can be found not only in these tonal dives, but in the expressions of disgust and irritation that were wholly alien to Eliot's juvenilia. In "Humouresque," the marionette's brittle disdain—"Why don't you people get some class"—is poles apart from the drooping flowers of Eliot's erstwhile Victorian manner.

While Laforgue taught Eliot to explore the boring and attack the conventional, it was Baudelaire, the greater if less immediately useful poet, who demonstrated for Eliot how to inspect the ugly and the sordid. Thus, both French poets enable in the young American an expanded intellectual range and a more honest appraisal of the modern condition. Eliot's adoption of these French moves sharpens his vision; they enable him to see what he had not seen before.

Another consequence of the turn to Baudelaire is that the hold of strict form starts to loosen. It is not evident why Baudelaire should be associated with this change rather than Laforgue, because both French poets use regular and irregular forms in their poetry. Whatever the case, Eliot's bifurcated allegiances in these six poems are reflected in their forms: three poems that strictly model Laforgue and three that more loosely model Baudelaire. Thus, "Humouresque" adopts Laforgue's taut quatrains, and the other two Laforguean poems are written in tightly controlled forms: a sonnet and rhymed sestets. But while Baudelaire represents a world that Eliot wants to enter, *how* Baudelaire writes is of less import to him. Thus, turning away from Laforgue, the forms relax as Eliot addresses himself to the themes of Baudelaire: "First Caprice" starts out with a quatrain, as if Eliot had intended this form to sustain the poem, but this regularity is jettisoned when the poem takes directions the author cannot restrain. The other two Baudelairean poems see Eliot fascinated with his new, barely controllable voices, and he tries them out without regard for line length, rhyme, steady rhythms, or formal boundaries.

The Rhetoric of Voice and Audience in the November 1909 Poems

In the previous chapter, the voices of Eliot's juvenilia were revealed to be the derivative voices of his literary models and his audiences the oppressive presence of conservative authority. With the November 1909 poems—in spite of the radical changes in timbre, scope, and theme—the voice and audience still bear traces of earlier poses. Eliot is still without a unique voice, though now instead of imitating the staid voices of the Romantic tradition, he is overwhelmingly indebted to Laforgue and is struggling to harness Baudelaire to his own ends.

As with the audiences of the juvenilia, the authoritarian impulse of the audience of the November 1909 poems still causes the poet considerable anxiety, though that audience is no longer the feared-if-familiar Tradition, but a feared-because-unfamiliar audience. At this stage of Eliot's development, the audience of the November 1909 poems can be described as a distant, potentially hostile public whose cosmopolitan values the young Eliot can only barely glimpse. Those cosmopolitan values include scorn, sarcasm, refinement, and an echt highbrow sensibility that somehow engages the informal and colloquial. Vaguely French and unsettlingly erratic—for it is both sarcastic and serious—this urbane public appears on the horizon of Eliot's understanding to threaten the complacency in which he has so far been writing: more judgmental than high-minded relatives in St. Louis, more jaded than the dégagé irony of Harvard peers, and more serious than the artistic and intellectual sphere of Boston in 1909. Four years earlier, the Boston of 1905 must have seemed sophisticated indeed to the protected, recently arrived schoolboy from the Midwest. Now through the lens of Laforgue and Baudelaire, the frumpy, Puritan Boston of 1909 can be surveyed with French disdain.

This wariness-cum-daring reflects his conflicted attitude to his new audience and can be tracked, among other ways, by considering Eliot's retrenchment in his use of slang. In spite of his family's antipathy to informal modes of speech, the boy was addicted to slang. In one story written when Eliot was ten, the narrator relates the climactic good fortune of a hero: "The Govornor [*sic*] gave him a medal and said he was hot stuff."[19] The high-spirited narration reveals the ten-year-old's delight not only in slang but in its effect: a High Official at a formal awards ceremony and a zinger that deflates pretension.

In the previous chapter, I noted Eliot's turn to popular culture via slang and colloquial diction in "Ballade of the Fox Dinner" (May 1909). In that anomalous poem, Eliot exuberantly toasts his drunken clubmates—a most convivial audience. The warmth of his audience and the impermanence of the occasion allow Eliot to let loose a flurry of slang, bawdy remarks, and references to popular culture, current events, and capitalist ideology. But for the more seriously conceived, literary audience of the later "Humouresque" (November 1909), colloquialisms are not indiscriminately deployed. Slang appears only within quotation marks or is otherwise ascribed to the belligerent marionette: "who-the-devil-are-you," "snappiest fashion," "I swear," "Why don't you people get some class," and "Your damned thin moonlight."[20] Thus, Eliot's first use of slang expressions for a literary audience has a cordon sanitaire around it: a character other than the speaker lets them fly. Eliot cannot conceive of such speech in the mouth of a speaker whose persona mirrors his own. Likewise, even though the tone of the poems of November 1909 will swing wildly between sarcasm and seriousness, the speakers' diction avoids the direct expression of slang, preferring safer sources: the pot of common idioms and a Latinate vocabulary associated in the Anglo-Saxon mind with elevated poetry and formal discourse.

Another way of measuring the advances and retrenchments that have occurred in November 1909 is to observe how the use of personal pronouns has shifted since the juvenilia. In spite of radical advances in theme and manner, the same rhetorical problems of the juvenilia loom over the November 1909 poems: the deferential speaker, the conservative audience. The tensions of authority and identity can be felt in those personal pronouns; the young poet of November 1909 still has difficulty contriving a "we." Fortunately, the audience of the November 1909 poems is no longer the oppressive authority of the juvenilia—the "you" who overpowers or the "we" who overtakes the "I." Nevertheless, these new inventions betray different, if more complicated, rhetorical problems; they do not yet evoke the compellingly rendered audiences of later poems. The discussions of the individual poems below will track where these pronouns reveal distinctive aporia, but in sum, the speaker of these poems is groping in the dark for an audience, a "you" to whom his "I" never quite connects.

Aside from the identities of speaker and audience traceable in personal pronouns, another aspect of the rhetorical is what might be called the angle of expression. As the young poet tries to translate across the ocean the conflicting ideas and bizarre manners of the French Symbolists for an English-speaking audience, the problem of Laforgue versus Baudelaire comes down to the problem of indirect expression versus direct expression. For the moment, the young poet conceives of these two modes as being contrasting manners of expression as well as containing opposed worldviews. Thus, the two manners are at war, which is why the November 1909 poems are so clumsy. The oblique, Laforguean manner suits the young poet for expressions of scorn, as irony is the default mode for such attacks, while the direct, Baudelairean mode suits his expressions of suffering. What the young apprentice will learn in this first month of experimentation is that he cannot have both. At least, not yet.

The Poems
Poems of Nov. 1909 (Eliot at Harvard University, aged twenty-one)

THE THREE LAFORGUEAN SUCCESSES	
"Nocturne"	published Nov. 1909
"Humouresque"	drafted Nov. 1909; published Jan. 1910
"Conversation Galante"	drafted Nov. 1909; published Sept. 1916

THE THREE BAUDELAIREAN FAILURES	
"First Caprice in North Cambridge"	drafted Nov. 1909
"Second Caprice in North Cambridge"	drafted Nov. 1909
"Opera"	drafted Nov. 1909

"Nocturne"
Published Nov. 12, 1909, Harvard Advocate

One of Eliot's first poems to register Laforgue's influence, "Nocturne" brims with sardonic energy. Gone are the wispy longings, predictable flowers, and orotund speech. In their place is a riveting irony and a polemical viewpoint:

> Romeo, *grand sérieux,* to importune
> Guitar and hat in hand, beside the gate
> With Juliet, in the usual debate
> Of love, beneath a bored but courteous moon;[21]

In sonnet form, Eliot reworks the tragic love of Romeo and Juliet as a satirical tale. In this urbane vision, the love scene is so clichéd that even the moon is "bored but courteous," grudgingly fulfilling its duties as scene setter. Regretting the triteness of the episode, the speaker assumes the role of stage manager, interjecting some drama by having Juliet stabbed. The speaker is fascinated by the theatricality that results: "Blood looks effective on the moonlit ground." The speaker's delight in the macabre turns to contempt when he considers the inability of "female readers" to interpret his gruesome intervention properly. Misconstruing the death scene, such women project their own fantasies of a *Liebestod*: the lovers' "perfect climax."

Compared to the torpid manner of the juvenilia, the sarcasm of "Nocturne" fairly leaps off the page. Eliot has found an edgy voice and a relevant theme: the artificiality of romantic expectations and the suffocating inconsequence of courtship rituals. The voice rings with the clarity of sarcasm—an ironic manner that the speaker celebrates as "my best mode oblique." Such a new, indirect manner, spoken by a newly forceful identity, must temporarily subdue the formerly dominant audience: the only pronouns to appear here are "I" and "my"; there is no "you" or "we." Implicitly addressing an authorial audience for such satire, Eliot also explicitly targets an anti-audience: those "female readers" whose sentimentality has been shaped by nineteenth-century gender roles and culture. This first poem of Eliot's new style has as its locus of attention a (female) audience's misinterpretation and the speaker's caustic reaction to that incomprehension. The psychological pressure of the young Eliot's assault on upper-class rectitude leaves its imprint in the pivotal maneuver of the poem: condemnation. To cross into new territory, the adventurous yet defensive author must preemptively denounce his former audiences, whose conservatism, gender, or ignorance prevent their following him.

"Humouresque"
Drafted Nov. 1909; published as "Humouresque (After J. Laforgue)" Jan. 12, 1910, Harvard Advocate

Entitled simply "Humouresque" in the notebook, this poem is equipped with a parenthetical subtitle for its appearance in print: "(After J. Laforgue)." That initial "J." has a suspicious resemblance to Prufrock's first initial, and both are a pose. By adding to the published version the clarification that the poem is an homage, Eliot is doing more than citing a stylistic debt. He is protecting himself from an audience on whom he cannot yet depend. The declaration that the poem has been written "after" the style of a little-known French author forestalls criticism of its bizarre manner by signaling its intentional foreignness. It is not "Eliot" who has written this poem, the diffident author implies with his subtitle, rather "Eliot doing Laforgue." The late-added subtitle reveals a gap between the speculative work of the notebook and the various real publics to whom Eliot will present some of these poems.

"Humouresque" broaches the same problem as "Nocturne": how to speak when there is no audience to comprehend the author's meaning. As nonexistent audiences are the thematic concern of both poems, it is only natural for the stage to be marshaled again as the controlling metaphor. Instead of the speaker as stage manager and Shakespeare reviser, as in "Nocturne," here the stage is a puppet theater, since the stakes in puppetry are lower than in Elizabethan drama, however bowdlerized.

The poem begins by directly invoking Laforgue: "One of my marionettes is dead," a near translation of Laforgue's line, "Encore un de mes pierrots mort." Eliot's marionette is presented as "Half-bullying, half-imploring." That is, as an outsider with no audience, he must be both aggressive and defensive, tyrannical and pleading. Contemptuous of "fashion"—doing or saying what others do or say—the marionette's bullying reflects the young poet's frustration at having to cater to an uncomprehending audience. With no productive function other than bitter "Haranguing," the marionette is consigned to "Limbo."

Belonging nowhere and having no audience, the marionette dismisses frivolous people whom he derisively commands to "get some class"—an instance of the increasing use Eliot will make of popular expressions and colloquialisms.[22] But Eliot is not simply plugging in colloquialisms or platitudes as a way of imitating a technique of Laforgue; rather, the colloquialisms he uses are of a piece with his rhetorical conception of the poem. The marionette's bitter denunciation is thematically related to the anxieties of audience, behavior, and reaction that are the burden of the poem. To demand that someone "get some class" raises the question of social class. The nature of such an insult trades on the anxieties of acting inappropriately in the eyes of a judging audience, of revealing oneself as a rube for violating social customs. Likewise, the slang term "snappy" functions in the same way, here used in the marionette's call: "The snappiest fashion, just this spring's / The newest cry on earth, I swear." Dating from the late nineteenth century, the slang term "snappy" denotes "smart, clever, esp. of language" as well as "neat, elegant," while another usage means "irritable, irascible."[23] The use of slang in the elegant world of serious poetry is itself an irascible gesture learned from Laforgue. And the very term "snappy"—denoting both elegance and irascibility—points up the speaker's contradiction in his irritable rejection of society and his striving for a sophisticated, French-inspired manner.

Thus, the bullying side of the divided marionette. Its opposite, the pleading aspect of the marionette, is the ventriloquizing voice of the speaker himself, who is fond of this "bizarre" mask but distances himself from its toxicity by affecting bafflement: "I rather liked" such a marionette, he says bemusedly. As Howarth has described, this "low-pitched" phrase is resonant of undergraduate speech, though it does not stoop to the roughness of the marionette's slang.[24] As with the subtitle that deflects the hostility of the poet onto a foreign model, the split into a tyrannical mode (deflected onto the puppet) and a pleading mode allows the speaker to play the diplomat on behalf of his more troublesome nature. As with the strongly asserted identity of the speaker of "Nocturne," the speaker of "Humouresque" and his marionette-mouthpiece freely refer to themselves with "I" and "my." And as with the despised "female readers" in "Nocturne," the "you people" of "Humouresque" are opposed as the enemy.[25]

The speaker acknowledges that even though its logic has started from the wrong premises—thus making its argument null and void to the fashion set—the marionette, were it not stuck in Limbo but in "some star" instead, would have "A life!" Two months later in the published version, the hypothetically fulfilled "life!" is revised to the even more grandiloquent "a hero!" thus magnifying the irony of the protagonist's artistic pretensions. But such hypotheses of the hero's life are futile, and ultimately the wobbly bridge linking the marionette's contempt and the speaker's fond toleration cannot be maintained. The speaker must put off his own mask: "where would it belong?" he wonders. The final gesture of the poem is a similarly coded posture that positions the elegant speaker in the good graces of the audience by disguising his fundamental sympathy with the rancorous marionette: "what masque bizarre!" The rhetoric of the poem is a curious mixture of affirmation and denial, a poem whose formal success depends wholly on its debt to Laforgue, but whose deeper rhetorical confusion reflects the conflicted identity of the speaker and the elusive identity of an audience whom he presumes cannot hear him.

Eliot's inability to get a handle on his audience is related to the ambivalence with which he deploys slang. His exploration of the realm of popular culture is here hobbled by his thinking of literary audiences as solemn and censorious. The example of Laforgue is slowly chipping away at this presumption, but it will take some time for it to collapse entirely. In "Ballade of the Fox Dinner," Eliot effusively resorted to slang without any ambivalence. But in that poem, it is not the speaker's ethos nor the celebratory content that enables Eliot to let his guard down. It is the audience: his drunken clubmates, who are of no help in this later context, for they in no way resemble the kind of literary audience with whom Eliot desires to communicate on an extended basis.

It was the formal success—the ventriloquized novelty of Laforgue—that led Eliot at once to publish both "Nocturne" and "Humouresque" in periodicals. But a few years later when Eliot and Pound are scraping together Eliot's few poems to make up his first published volume, the rhetorical confusion and barely disguised hostility render these previously published poems unfit for inclusion. Eliot's later artistic advances lead him to conclude that of his first six poems written in November 1909, only one—"Conversation Galante"—is worth preserving.

"Conversation Galante"
Drafted Nov. 1909; published Sept. 1916, Poetry

As the only November 1909 poem to be preserved in his collected writing, it is worth noting the curious fact that it is the poem's draft date (1909), not its publication date (1916), that Eliot commemorates in all of his packaged, repackaged, and re-repackaged collections, from the first *Collected Poems, 1909–1935*, to *Complete Poems and Plays, 1909–1950*, to *Collected Poems, 1909–1962*, which turned out to be not quite so complete until several complete volumes later. Had Eliot followed standard usage, his various *Collected Poems* and *Complete Poems and Plays* would have carried the inaugural date 1917 to indicate the publication of *Prufrock and Other Observations*, or possibly 1915 at the earliest, to mark the initial appearance of "The Love Song of J. Alfred Prufrock," his first continuously collected poem to see print. Readers of Eliot's collected works may be genuinely puzzled to pick up a volume that announces its poems as dating from 1909, only to turn to the table of contents to see the first volume listed—shortened to the single word *Prufrock*—and its publication date of 1917. A reasonably curious reader might ask: to what, then, does 1909 refer? Aside from reminding himself of that momentous November (while neglecting to apprise readers that the poem to which that date refers was not published until 1916), Eliot is indulging in something of a boast with the date 1909: he would have us know that he was doing quality work at age twenty-one, never mind when it was published. Of the three November 1909 poems that were published, this creation is the most formally successful. For this achievement, Eliot will award the poem pride of place, writing it out on the first leaf of the notebook, an acknowledgment that will be sustained throughout his life in his continuous republications of it along with its labeled date of 1909.

Laforgue's sensibility as a whole spoke powerfully to the impressionable Eliot during the several months of gestation that preceded his November 1909 outpouring. But even before Eliot had received the complete works of Laforgue from Paris, Eliot had before him Laforgue's "Autre complainte de Lord Pierrot," courtesy of Arthur Symons. It was a terrific piece of luck that Symons chose to quote this poem in full. Voiced through the persona of a stock commedia dell'arte character—the naive and ridiculous Pierrot—Laforgue's poem records the increasingly absurd exchanges between a woman's gasps of love and a man's mocking non sequiturs. Beginning in the unlikely banality of geometry and ending in death, Laforgue's poem manages both to disguise and to reveal, in Symons's description, "suffering and despair, and resignation to what is, after all, the inevitable."[26] With such a poem as a provocative model, Eliot's first attempts seem less like studious imitations of Laforgue and more like discharges of pent-up pressure.

As with most of Eliot's Laforguean titles, the original, canceled title of the poem, "Short Romance," plays on a dual meaning embedded in a musical reference.[27] A "short romance" refers to a brief musical composition in a Romantic vein, and more ironically, to an amorous relationship cut short by some unexpected development. The poem presents a scene of two actors: lovers strolling in the moonlight. In a series of increasingly convoluted metaphors, the speaker mocks the cliché of the moon as a symbol of love. Rather than succor lovers, the moon ominously "lights poor travelers to their distress." The speaker seems more interested in trying out metaphors than in paying attention to the woman. Consequently, his observations bore her: they "digress," do not follow the pattern she supposes or wishes.

The poet continues in this derisive vein, mocking yet another Romantic topos, the piano nocturne as a symbol of "night and moonshine." The weight of the mockery is laid not upon the inadequacy of the symbol itself (the piano nocturne), but on the way in which its frivolous hearers pretend to perceive its delicate emotional shadings. The speaker protests that the nocturne is neither listened to nor enjoyed, but "seize[d]," violently appropriated to give substance to what has no substance: the vacuousness of the listeners. The female interlocutor is even more suspicious: "Does this refer to me?"

In the third stanza, the feminine—as "eternal enemy of the absolute"—derails the speaker's search for metaphysical truth with her frivolous charms.

She has not experienced true passion and is therefore all the more clever at manipulating "vagrant moods" to her advantage. Her "indifferent" cunning would undercut the artist's attempt to construct a poetics—one that will always seem "mad" to outsiders in its opposition to sentimentality. But Eliot's audience anxiety will not allow him to identify simply with the speaker, will not allow him to spout unhindered such an artistic credo. As with the final words of "Humouresque" ("what masque bizarre!"), which distance the speaker from the hostile marionette, so the final line of "Conversation Galante" is given to the woman in order to bracket the hostility of the speaker. Having been mocked by the man, her own rejoinder brings up sharply his dour polemics: "are we then so serious?"

As the battle between the speaker and the woman escalates, the personal pronoun of "our" breaks apart. The first appearance of "our" is a stagey version of "I" that reluctantly includes the woman: "I observe: '*our* sentimental friend the moon!'" But by the end of the poem, the meaning of "our" has shifted dramatically: "With your air indifferent and imperious / At a stroke *our* made poetics to confute—." Here the "our" refers to "I and fellow artists," excluding "you," the woman. It is the woman, however, who is allowed a "we" in the final line: "are we then so serious?" While that "we" is more stylistic than grammatical, it still suggests that the woman can imagine an "I-thou" relationship unavailable to the speaker.

The three Laforguean poems are formally successful, but they are just as derivative as the juvenilia. Eagerly modeling Laforgue yet defensively reigning in the dismissive gesture, Eliot manages just barely to restrict a destructive impulse. Although this level of self-consciousness—dismissing the dismissal—makes the poems acceptable for publication, the young poet is boxed in by such limitations. That is why the more interesting struggle of November 1909 takes place in the unpublished poems, where the mutually destructive clash of Laforgue and Baudelaire brings the young poet to an impasse.

"First Caprice in North Cambridge"
Drafted Nov. 1909

Although written in the same month as Eliot's first Laforguean creations, "First Caprice in North Cambridge" and its companion, "Second Caprice in North Cambridge," both strain against the limits of their French models, attempting unsuccessfully to redirect the Laforguean voice, broaden the theme, and grope toward a more nuanced sense of audience via the example of Baudelaire. By describing these poems as artistic failures, I do not mean to imply that Eliot rejected them. If he had perceived them only as embarrassments, he would not have carefully copied them into his notebook. As the following discussion makes clear, I suggest that Eliot's withholding them from publication is a later acknowledgment of their weaknesses. But their suggestiveness still provided him with artistic directions to pursue and rhetorical problems to be mastered.

Laforgue's irony turns out to have advantages and disadvantages for the young poet. As we saw in "Nocturne," the ironic pose is an effective vehicle for Eliot's scorn for fatuous social custom, but such sarcasm also undermines any attempts at emotional candor. "First Caprice in North Cambridge" records Eliot's discovery of the problem of corrosive irony. Set in the slum district just north of the Harvard campus, the poem begins with a direct treatment of the sordid. Modeling the cityscapes of urban decay, which he has learned from Baudelaire, the speaker reports without commentary such images as "dirty windows" and "Trampled mud and grass."[28] There are no personal pronouns in this poem, as if such a serious inspection of squalor is the job of an impersonal camera rather than a personal voice.[29] The images seem to be building to something decisive, but that movement is broken off with a dismissive conclusion, the intrusion of a personal voice: "Oh, these minor considerations! . . ." Fearing that he has drifted into the sentimental, the speaker reaches too quickly for its ironic antidote. After such a crippling turn—the seriousness of Baudelaire nullified by the sarcasm of Laforgue—the poem can only be abandoned as an unfixable failure.

In her chapter on the *Inventions* poems, Helen Vendler also points to these interruptions, the "throwaway undoings of an anteriorly-voiced serious emotion."[30] Like most critics, however, she attributes the cause of this problem to persona or voice rather than to audience: "Again and again, the early poems, after some tentative venturings into lyric seriousness, close by turning on themselves in self-mockery."[31] Mayer also ignores the role of audience in these poems, articulating the problem as one of artistic intention: "The title 'caprice' calls attention especially to these acts of detachment, which, as sudden shifts in attitude, insulate the observer [i.e., the speaker of the poem] from being implicated in what it sees; at the same time, the overtone of willfulness that 'caprice' carries subtly criticizes his shifty escapes from responsibility."[32] The phrase "shifty escapes from responsibility" implies that Eliot, at this initial, experimental stage, is entirely in control of his materials. But rather than consciously ironizing his escapes from responsibility, I argue that Eliot is ham-handedly feeling his way in the opposite direction: toward an engagement with human suffering. The problem of the moment is that he does not have the technical tools to manage it, and he instead worries about seeming too sentimental, a fear that trumps his empathy.

In contrast to the confused manner of "First Caprice," observe the more artistically coherent "Nocturne," in which the beginnings of a smoothly Eliotic manner can be seen: the confident and unified voice, its sureness of tone, its urbanity and anti-Romanticism. The problem is that the audience of this poem, while rendered more coherently than the audience of "First Caprice," holds assumptions that turn out to be just as constricted as those of the "female readers" it deplores: the expectation that the earnest and the sentimental will be hooted off the stage. It is this belligerent audience—courted and won in "Nocturne"—that is now feared in "First Caprice" and that provokes the speaker to dismiss preemptively his own imagined ridiculousness.

"Second Caprice in North Cambridge"
Drafted Nov. 1909

This companion poem, announced by title as a continuation of "First Caprice," maintains a focus on the sordid while attempting to redirect the abrasive irony of its predecessor. Human misery is the ostensible subject of the first poem, but its nearness to sentimentality had alarmed the defensive poet and destroyed the planned movement of the poem. Thus, the problem that the now-wiser poet takes up in the second poem is not human suffering itself but the rhetorical presentation of human suffering.

Although physically close to Harvard, the poor section of North Cambridge exists far from the principles studied in philosophy courses, and far from the "aesthetic laws" that govern high art.[33] Having learned his lesson in "First Caprice," in which he is unexpectedly ambushed by a hostile audience, the speaker now clearly specifies which audience he is addressing in this second poem: Harvard philosophers, whose "you" is linked to the speaker's "I" in "*our* definitions" of metaphysics and aesthetics. As in a university lecture, such logicians and philosophers are led by their speaker to acknowledge an aesthetic paradox: the images that, though seedy, should nonetheless stimulate "pity" in them.

In the previous poem, "First Caprice," detritus stands metonymically for human misery, the fragmentary nature of broken bits attesting to the uneasily approached problem of suffering. However, as a result of the uncertainty in which Eliot is composing, the difference between a delicate approach to suffering and earnest claptrap is not a distinction to be tolerated: all such sentiments have already been dismissed by his own pen as "minor considerations." And so the author must shore up in the second poem the rhetorical transaction he has destabilized in the first. The solution, then, of "Second Caprice" is to have the speaker fussily direct the mechanics of pity. Insisting didactically on its own effects, the poem begins:

> This charm of vacant lots!
> The helpless fields that lie
> Sinister, sterile and blind—
> Entreat the eye and rack the mind,
> Demand your pity.

This didacticism is not an advance over the first poem; it is instead a sign of insecurity on the poet's part as to whether his newfound tools are working. The rhetorical sleight of hand stipulates the work of pity and includes an unconvincing shift to the second person. The "you" whose pity is "demand[ed]" is not a hostile audience, but neither is it to be trusted to reach its own conclusions. Reminding himself that, like his audience, he is also a Harvard philosopher, the speaker attempts to soften the coercive force of the imperative "you" by shifting to the second-person plural: "Let *us* pause." The uncertain relationship of the speaker and his philosopher-peers is revealed not only by the impatient explosion that leaps out of the texture of the poem (discussed below) but by the speaker's distrust of a skeptical though not hostile audience whom he gauges would be unlikely to reach the prescribed aesthetic conclusions.

That the speaker is concerned with the problem of pathos—how to control his audience's sympathies—is evident in the first noun of the poem: "charm." The demonstrative pronoun—"This charm"—points to a specific attitude that is shared (or so the speaker presses) with the reader. *This* charm is nervously asserted even before the first, uncharming image is allowed to enter the scene: "vacant lots!" The strained exclamation point likewise attempts to compel the reader. Unlike the impartial descriptors that begin "First Caprice" ("dirty," "broken," "frail," "Trampled"), with their negative, if morally neutral connotations, the adjectives of "Second Caprice" are explicitly moralizing: "helpless," "Sinister," "sterile." The switch from neutrality in the first poem to moralizing in the second is a function of the speaker's wariness. The images of sordidness cannot be relied upon to do the work he intends, because he has not yet invented an audience adequate to his purposes.

The "charm" and "repose" supposedly evoked by industrial cityscapes are the speaker's attempt to turn by rhetorical force such images to his own ends. But the speaker's intention is undone by his bumbling into the cliché "rack the mind," followed by the slightly modified but still hackneyed "rack the brain."[34] Irritated that he has twice stumbled into the same platitude, he testily exclaims: "(What: again?)." As with the final line of "First Caprice," this sneer is Laforguean in origin, though here its brittle irony is sealed off from the rest of the poem. It is both parenthetically enclosed and buried in the middle of a stanza, whose lecture-hall tone continues uninterrupted, as if the contemptuous aside had never intruded. That the author of the poem foregrounds the speaker's stumbling reveals how conscious he is of the problem. The rhetorical clamps that keep this poem from flying apart are less awkwardly managed than in "First Caprice," but the tonal crash from analytical lecturer to petulant self-critic is abrupt and misjudged. Eliot's solution for defusing irony in "Second Caprice" is a cheap one, but it shows that he is working to solve the artistic question raised by "First Caprice." The serious and the ironic are at war with each other in both poems, and neither can seem to shape itself into a coherent whole.[35]

"Opera"
Drafted Nov. 1909

While "First Caprice" and "Second Caprice" have failed on the formal and rhetorical levels, the failure of "Opera" is ideological rather than formal. Here is yet another poem with a stage as its primary setting and whose argument signals the poet's struggle to invent an audience. By evoking the monumentality of Wagner's stage- and music-craft, Eliot takes aim at *Tristan und Isolde* as the pinnacle of Romantic self-expression. Whether the young artist believes his own critique is what is at stake in this poem.

In its engagements with the story of *Tristan* and its description of the particular orchestral effects that undergird those plot points, the poem must have been written in response to a performance of the full opera, rather than to orchestral excerpts shorn of narrative context. The adjectives describing the orchestral instruments are no fanciful projections. They are instead apt descriptions of the narrative use to which Wagner puts those instruments: the horns are "fatalistic," because they warn, in act 2, of the approach of King

Marke and his hunting party.[36] The violins are "passionate," since they are used for soaring melodies at moments of high drama and lovemaking. And the bass clarinet prefigures an "ominous" end, in its doleful accompaniment of Marke's monologue preceding Tristan's wounding. That Eliot here evokes the specific colorations of Wagner's music drama points to the author's affective engagement with *Tristan* and undercuts a reading of the poem as merely a polemic against the conventions and hyperemotionalism of nineteenth-century music.

In spite of the generic title "Opera," the poem takes as its starting point the specifics of *Tristan*. The title of the poem, then, refers not to the genre of which *Tristan* is an exemplar; rather, the title refers ironically to the non-operatic nature of the poet's own non-tragedy. As with the infamous act 2 reversal of *Tristan*, in which the glorious love duet is interrupted by startling dissonances, this poem stages its own reversal.

The speaker's descriptions of the overwrought music are self-consciously overwrought. Disdaining romantic love "torturing itself / To emotion for all there is in it," the speaker rejects such self-immolating love as unnatural: "Writhing" and "contorted." He dismisses the opera's unforgivable hyperbole with his own hyperbole: "Flinging itself at the last / Limits of self-expression." The speaker finally disallows the possibility of authentic tragedy: "We have the tragic? oh no!" Alas for us moderns, "Life departs with a feeble smile" and not with Isolde's orgasmic transfiguration. The banality of the speaker's experience in the face of such extravagant artifice leads him to believe that such intense experiences cannot apply to him. Such a brutal conclusion makes him feel irrelevant and isolated—a lonely prophet with no audience. The plural pronoun of "We have the tragic?" does not posit a sympathetic I-thou bond; rather, this "we" is stylistic, a rhetorical question whose answer is negative. The irony of the poem rests in how Wagner's mystical power over his audiences is resented as manipulative, while the speaker of the poem has no audience at all. And so he abandons the "we," reverting to the lonely "I": "I feel like the ghost of youth."

While the appearance of "we"—so vexed in the juvenilia—is stylistic here, it is still a parry in the direction of the audience. The implied audience of the poem is imagined as hostile toward Romanticism and as holding some sympathy for the isolated prophet-artist. Most significantly, it is the one poem of the November 1909 grouping whose audience most closely resembles the mature Eliot's audiences. Why then did this poem remain unpublished, since it does not exhibit the same destructive confusion of "First Caprice" and "Second Caprice"? The poem's inability to match its rhetoric to its argument points to the likelihood that this was not necessarily the argument Eliot wanted, or was able, to pursue. For unlike the speaker of "Opera," Eliot had an ambivalent relationship to Wagner, both impressed and skeptical. The poem, however, tracks only the skepticism, because a burgeoning artist with a "mad," anti-Romantic poetics could not be seen supporting the arch-Romantic Wagner.

Part of the historical context is the downgrading of Wagner's reputation at the turn of the century. Nietzsche had dismissed Wagner as a decadent in the 1880s, but the composer was still a hero to Mallarmé and other Symbolists. By the early teens, Wagner had been debunked by serious aesthetes as passé. In 1909, for example, the same year of Eliot's poem about *Tristan*, Proust had begun drafting *À la recherche du temps perdu*, adopting the same reverence for the composer as had the Symbolists. Just two years later, however, Proust was revising drafts and deleting references to Wagnerian aesthetics, except for those moments where he wished to suggest an antiquated atmosphere or old-fashioned ideas.[37] In spite of such snobbery among the elites, Wagner's music remained popular in opera theaters and concert halls. This double-edged, even contradictory, admiration-cum-resistance to Wagner's power forms the background for Eliot's own clash between his personal feelings and his artistic intentions.[38]

Contrast, for example, the poem's sarcastic dismissal of Wagner's emotional power to its probable origin in Eliot's own life. Igor Stravinsky, writing a brief memoir of Eliot a few months after the poet's death, recalls a lengthy conversation he and Eliot had upon their first meeting, during which they talked principally about Wagner: "Eliot's Wagner nostalgia was apparent and I think that *Tristan* must have been one of the most passionate experiences of his life."[39] Such an understanding of Eliot's youthful response to Wagner need not depend entirely on Stravinsky's recollection.[40] For, ten years after the notebook poem "Opera," *The Waste Land* would cite *Tristan* and the Ring cycle as passionate foils to bleak scenes of failed intimacy, giving a more accurate account of what Stravinsky calls "Eliot's Wagner nostalgia."

Another reason to attend to the poet's ambivalent relationship to Wagner has recently appeared with the opening of the Hale archive at Princeton. In a letter to Emily Hale of January 20, 1931, Eliot reminds her that they had seen *Tristan* together; subsequent letters describe his pain at hearing the opera, so strong are its associations with his doomed, protracted love for her. It seems that this performance of *Tristan* was what sealed his realization that he was in love with Hale.[41] However, it is not likely that the performance he saw with Hale was the one that inspired this poem. The height of the Eliot-Hale relationship occurred when he was in graduate school at Harvard, 1911–1914. His first performance of *Tristan* was likely an April 1907 production of the Metropolitan Opera on tour at Boston Theatre or a similar touring production in April 1908.[42]

At this early stage of his artistic development, Eliot's wariness of his audience provokes him not merely to cap the emotional volcano when its heat becomes too intense but to douse it entirely. A fellow flâneur, the speaker strenuously resists being identified with the hyperventilating "female readers" of lovers' death scenes, and so he stakes a polemical claim for the benefit of his newly courted, more worldly audience. The problem with such a pose—staged with wary regard of his still-misunderstood, still-feared audience—is that it comes at the cost of honesty. For the moment, the author trusts his newly found convictions more than his feelings. As he writes in an undated notebook poem, begging the listener's pardon, "I shall convince these romantic irritations / By my classical convictions."[43] Eliot would later remark that the greatest danger facing religious poets is writing what they would like to feel rather than what they actually felt.[44] In "Opera," the young warrior of anti-Romanticism writes a poem about how he wishes he had felt about Wagner.

The November 1909 poems show the young poet in a liberating free fall that is both giddy with promise and fraught with danger. The "I" and the "thou" of the juvenilia—never secure to begin with—are here subjected to interrogation, with uncertain results. As for the "I," the cobbled-together identity of his juvenilia has been blown apart, with nothing stable taking its place. Or, in Eliot's phrase, the "bundle of second-hand sentiments" has not yet become "a person." The desultory exertions of his juvenilia, in which one serious voice is imitated after another, have been abandoned in favor of the operatic extremes of loathing and suffering wholly alien to the formal reserve of his familial and cultural environments. As for the "you," the rigid provincialism of his former audiences has been rejected in favor of some other, faintly glimpsed and partially feared cosmopolitanism associated with the audiences of French poetry.

The six poems of November 1909 record not the finding of a voice or audience but a jettisoning of former voices and audiences. Within the resulting vacuum, the poet engages in an intense struggle whereby the different properties of Laforgue and Baudelaire, grating upon first meeting, achieve their first, unhappy resolution by allowing the Laforguean element to predominate, leaving the Baudelairean undeveloped. The most obvious sign of this imbalance is the publication of the Laforguean poems and the withholding of the Baudelairean ones.

In spite of the technical failures of "First Caprice" and "Second Caprice," it is affecting to watch Eliot struggle to integrate the larger concern of human suffering into his poetic range. It is not surprising that such first experiments fail, nor that the attempted solutions only raise more difficulties. What is remarkable is that a twenty-one-year-old, in the same productive month in which he has written three successful poems, has already reached the limits of what his short but fruitful apprenticeship with Laforgue has taught him. In the three Laforguean poems, Eliot employs a confident, sardonic voice and locates a narrow audience to applaud his hostile irony. For the shy, compliant boy of the juvenilia, those three poems represent the crossing of a definitive boundary, never to be uncrossed. In the Baudelairean poems, he takes risks that are even more breathtaking: essaying a voice that is divided and unmanageable, addressing himself to an audience that he neither understands nor fully trusts, and daring to broach—however clumsily—the vital theme of human suffering.

In the face of multiple technical failures, Eliot's consistent return to the problem of human suffering is the sign that his first solution—the triumph of Laforgue over Baudelaire—is not an adequate one. As a consequence, the more interesting story of the November 1909 poems is not Eliot's finding of a new voice but his sobering discovery that one of his primary concerns cannot be welded so easily into his new style. Much later, in his Clark lectures, Eliot will posit a more nuanced view of Laforguean irony: he will recognize that it too is an expression of suffering, that Laforgue's irony is never cynical because it is directed against a divided self that seeks wholeness.[45] But these are retrospective accounts of a matured writer. For now, the young Eliot hardly recognizes his own suffering in his scathing eruptions; he knows only the liberation of voicing them, their oblique expressions hiding even from their author what oppresses him. For suffering to be manageable in the climacteric of November 1909, the young author must project it outward. The suffering attaches itself not to fully realized characters but to sordid fragments and detritus, the partial expression itself a fragmentary approach to suffering, the adolescent slowly edging his way into maturity.

The unhappy solution of allowing the Laforguean voice to dominate while the Baudelairean one is consigned to the notebook is closely related to the technical problem of how suffering can be addressed artistically. Both problems remain unresolved at the end of November 1909. In the third chapter, I will track a second, more felicitous resolution of the Laforgue-Baudelaire nexus, in which suffering can finally be addressed head on and the two chafing, irresolvable elements are transformed into a compound that is, finally, uniquely Eliotic.

Clearing the Throat

The Poems of Early 1910

> Take the adolescent poet when he begins to write. He does not begin with a scientific spirit or much knowledge of his subject. His impulse is ejaculatory and imitative. He desires to extrude from himself some pressing and restless feelings in which he has become interested, and the shape they assume is decided by one or two admirations. These feelings, brought into the world tumultuously, respond to some facts in life or they do not. The first shock the poet has is when he discovers that something new to him and to him unique is valueless because it has already been better said by someone else.
>
> —T. S. Eliot, "Modern Tendencies in Poetry"

After the unresolved problems of November 1909—an indistinct audience, a divided voice, a thematic uncertainty—Eliot's pen falls silent for a month.[1] Perhaps it is the December break and holiday travel that distract him from the concerns of the notebook. But the very irresolution of those issues suggests another reason for why the artist in search of an audience would need an intermission before taking the stage again. Whatever the cause, January 1910 sees Eliot at his desk again, and the first poem that comes after this break is entitled "Convictions (Curtain Raiser)"—a poem whose thematic burden is the finding of an adequate audience.

Before considering what this poem signifies in the chronology of Eliot's development, a brief review of the major signposts of his poetic maturation is in order. We have seen how Eliot's first audiences are the typical ones of a nineteenth-century schoolboy: the authoritative judges and teacherly guides who monitor adherence to class and gender norms. To these audiences, the young Eliot responds with self-abasing decorum, even his impish "Fable for Feasters" lampooning its own servility toward the audience. Thus, Eliot's first rhetorical problem is the struggle to separate his identity from that of his audience: the Tradition represented by his Unitarian forebears, his reserved family, and his haut-bourgeois contexts in school and beyond. After Eliot encounters the robust example of Laforgue, he adopts that voice wholesale while making failed attempts to weld Baudelairean concerns to that manner. In this Laforguean mode, the young poet is content for a short time to be derivative, though he is less content to allow the captivating, if unusable, example of Baudelaire to fall to the side. The young Eliot soon begins to realize that this bifurcated identity, while thrilling and liberating, is just as secondhand as his juvenile identities. He has had his "first shock," discovering to his dismay "that something new to [the young poet] and to him unique is valueless because it has already been better said by someone else."[2]

This voice divided between Laforgue and Baudelaire can therefore provide no permanent rhetorical solution, not least because the poems of November 1909 grope unsuccessfully toward a theory of "we": the poet is unable to envision a distinct "I," a specific "you," or a relationship that binds them together. Yet, in the midst of such problems, striking gains are made. Notably, the grip of the juvenilia's speaker and audience has loosened: the sarcasm of Laforgue and the languor of Baudelaire have dispelled the good-boy ethos and the high-minded Tradition in which his juvenilia had been trapped. Nevertheless, old habits die hard, as traces of juvenile attitudes can still be heard in the speaker's deference to the imperiousness of his audience. All of these unresolved tensions become too great for the young author to explore psychologically or artistically, and what follows this impasse is a few weeks of silence.

Which short period of gestation brings us up to January 1910 and the tellingly entitled "Convictions (Curtain Raiser)." This poem so neatly addresses the above-named problems that the poem is later deliberately placed near the beginning of the notebook, *before* the November 1909 poems, as if it were a solution, an artistic manifesto arrived at and announced. "Convictions (Curtain Raiser)" reveals an author now writing with conviction to an audience seen more clearly as his curtain of rhetorical uncertainty is raised out of the way. Grouped together on a stage, the marionettes of this poem embody the tensions of an artist gesturing toward his audience, the puppets' staged mannerisms putting the author himself at a step removed from the ethos-pathos quandary. This objective distance gives him greater control over the rhetorical effects he seeks to achieve. And the assorted marionettes of "Convictions"—unlike the "dead," bullying puppet of "Humouresque" of November 1909—provide for Eliot a solution to his second rhetorical problem: how to imagine a new audience now that the prim authorities of his juvenilia have been banished from the theater. The aim of this chapter is to explain how this came about—how Eliot clears his throat, in both senses of that expression: how he clarifies his own voice and how he signals for attention to a new kind of audience.

Voice Lessons

As discussed in the previous chapter, the crises of November 1909 are easy to recognize, since their effects on the poems are so drastic. The advances—among them, an increased tonal range and a sharpened intellectuality—are as conspicuous as the problems: Laforgue's sarcasm is limiting, and Baudelaire's seriousness remains unexploited. By contrast with these marked changes, the crises of this next phase, January–June 1910, are harder to track because they are more diffuse and their trajectories are worked out haphazardly. The key breakthrough of early 1910 is the way Eliot solves the most glaring problem of the November 1909 climacteric. In a magical, original solution, the two previously warring elements of seriousness and sarcasm modulate, finally, into a coherent voice. The rhetorical advance that allows Baudelairean gravity to coexist with Laforguean irony is a three-in-one tool that enables Eliot to shift from one voice to another: a combination of shortened lines, tight rhymes, and snappy rhythms to mark an irony that is jaunty rather than destructive. This jazzy, tonal shift not only solves a major trouble of Eliot's notebook poetry, it is also one of the gestures that marks his mature poetry. Identifying the provenance of the technique, then, is no small matter, as it is not yet another source in the endless hunt for Eliot's allusions but a building block of his distinctive style.

Determining where Eliot learns this technique is not simple, as there are at least two sources, and perhaps even a confusion of the two sources in Eliot's mind. One source is popular culture, specifically ragtime. The other possible source is Laforgue himself or, rather, an element of Laforgue that Eliot had not been able to harness in his first month of experimentation.

Let us turn first to the possibility of ragtime. By the late nineteenth century, this African American art form had migrated from the domestic sphere to the minstrel show, dance halls, and vaudeville. Its musical form relies on standard marches as well as two-step or slow drag dance forms. Its sound is characterized by strongly syncopated melody and regular bass lines. On a piano, its chordal gestures are derived from rhythms originally idiomatic to the banjo, which the piano had come to replace as the typical ragtime instrument.[3] By the time of Eliot's birth, the cultural overtones of ragtime had become strongly racialized and sexualized, not only because of its African American origins but as a result of Tin Pan Alley's co-optations of its musical and verbal rhetoric. In what were called "coon songs" at the turn of the century, the (often white) composers of mass-marketed ragtime traded on notions of African American culture that caricatured dialect, slang, grammatical errors, and sexual proclivities.[4]

The melody in ragtime was not the only element that was syncopated or "ragged." The lyrics, too, had to accommodate the demands of ragtime melodies, which translated to rough-edged grammar (smashed rhymes and deliberate solecisms) and irregular language (the colloquial and the informal). As the critic Philip Furia has argued, ragtime "licensed the vernacular as a lyrical idiom and forced the lyricist to construct a lyric out of short, juxtaposed phrases marked by internal rhymes and jagged syntactical breaks"—exactly the kind of phrasing and rhyming that Eliot tries out in this phase of his notebook.[5] To give one famous example from Eliot's youth, the composer George M. Cohan's hit from 1904 truncates lines and speeds up words to produce a jagged rhyming effect:

> Give my regards to Broadway,
> Remember me to Herald Square,
> Tell all the gang at
> Forty-Second Street, that
> I will soon be there.

In addition to the "ragged" snippets that reveal the upbeat rhymes of "at" and "that," Furia notes, "with the ragtime device of matching short and long vowels to the eighth-note quarter-note pattern, Cohan's handling of colloquial formulas and place names seems effortless."[6]

Twenty years ago, a serious discussion of ragtime in a critical work on T. S. Eliot would have seemed inapposite. For much of the past century, Eliot's reputation as a high-art snob contemptuous of popular culture was part of the critical *acquis* agreed upon by both Eliot's detractors and defenders. This long-reigning orthodoxy has been handily demolished by David Chinitz's groundbreaking book, *T. S. Eliot and the Cultural Divide*, which finally presents a nuanced view of Eliot's productive and ambivalent engagement with popular culture. In an early chapter of his book, Chinitz excavates the history of ragtime and popular music as it relates to Eliot's formative influences, especially his childhood in St. Louis—the city that was the "acknowledged birthplace of ragtime during the first decade of his life."[7]

Chinitz's contribution to our understanding of Eliot's early poetry supplements the standard account of Eliot's coming to voice by imitating Laforgue.

It is not just Laforgue, Chinitz argues, but the metrical rhythms of American popular music that undergird Eliot's first efforts:

> What the apprentice poems of *Inventions of the March Hare* now enable us to see is that the acknowledged influence of Laforgue was complemented by the nearly suppressed yet indispensable influence of American jazz. It was the *convergence* of these elements—or their chemical interaction in the presence of the poet's mental catalyst—that produced the masterpieces of the *Prufrock* period. Laforgue showed Eliot how to adapt his voice to the popular material around him, and jazz gave Eliot a way to bring Laforgue into contemporary English.[8]

For Chinitz, the decisive evidence in the notebook dates not from early 1910 but from a year later, February 1911, and may be seen in the untitled poem beginning "The smoke that gathers blue and sinks." In that poem's unmistakable duplication of ragtime rhetoric, Chinitz finds a depiction of "proto-jazz performance and dance," in which the speaker "quotes an actual [ragtime] lyric, includes appropriate slang ('action,' 'the stuff'), and strikingly replicates the angular rhythms and sudden, unpredictable rhymes of popular ragtime lyrics of the period."[9] In surveying other references to popular music in the notebook, Chinitz concludes, "Eliot's patented cadences—his characteristic rhythms, the ways he uses rhyme, the tonal contours of his lines—were discovered in the sounds of popular music circa 1911."[10] Chinitz is careful to place the date at "circa 1911," when the poems of the notebook bubble over with references to popular song. We should note, however, that the earliest poem Chinitz cites as evidence for his thesis is "Suite Clownesque" from October 1910.[11] We will consider the implications for Eliot's rhetoric when those poems are discussed in later chapters. For now, the interest of Chinitz's thesis lies in what it can illuminate about Eliot's transition from the awkward contradictions of November 1909 to the Eliotic manner of early 1910, with its smoother voice and clearer audience.

In his study of the artists of Tin Pan Alley, Furia describes what he calls the "mosaic" art of the lyricist. Since a lyricist must often fit words to an already-existing melody, Furia bids us notice "not only the witty image and cleverly fragmented rhyme but how well the lyricist works within musical constraints (or subverts them), how deftly he matches the composer's phrasing with verbal fits (or shrewd misfits)."[12] Ira Gershwin—himself a master of that very art—dates this procedure back to the Elizabethan age, when the fitting of new lyrics to existing music was done "by satirists and parodists who, discarding the words of folk song and ballad, penned—quilled, if you like—new lyrics to the traditional tunes—lyrics which politicized, thumbed the nose, eulogized, or went in for out-and-out bawdry."[13] Gershwin expressly notes the devilish business of translation when it is added to the already thorny problem of fitting words to already-composed notes. The issue of translation takes us slightly off our path of tracing the historical origins of Eliot's technique. But the detour is a comic one: Gershwin reminds us that while W. S. Gilbert was famous mainly for writing lyrics that would be later set by Arthur Sullivan, Gilbert was also good (perhaps too good) at the reverse procedure: creating lyrics for already-composed melodies. Gilbert's English translations of opera libretti were noted, Gershwin explains, for their "tricky lyrics and recitatives loaded with puns." Even Gilbert's farcical translations of titles cued the listener less to the content of the opera and more to the wit of the translator. One would never guess the melodramatic seriousness of Meyerbeer's *Robert le diable* from Gilbert's heading: *Robert the Devil; or The Nun, the Dun, and the Son of a Gun.*[14]

To return to our historical survey, since the sixteenth century this "mosaic" procedure has marked a shift in tone: from folk song to satire, from earnest ballad to bawdry. The jamming of words into awkward line lengths and the breaking of grammatical sense to land on a rhyme became associated, historically, with the parodic instinct. According to Gershwin, the mischievous spirit of the lyricist has presided over fragmented lines and oddball rhymes long before ragtime picked up the procedure.

And, I might add, long before Laforgue was read by Eliot. At the very least, one could speculate that reading and imitating Laforgue enabled Eliot to hear ragtime not just as background music but as fodder for poetic creation. To concur with what Chinitz says of a later poem, the "point is not that Eliot extracted" his aesthetic from ragtime, but "that there is a fundamental convergence between Eliot's poem and the principal popular music of its era, particularly in the areas of structure, rhythm and allusion."[15]

Although it is essential to acknowledge Chinitz's work in popular culture, it is still not clear that Eliot's *earliest* unique voice and trademark rhetorical gestures—achieved in January and February 1910—can be attributed to popular sources. For if, as Chinitz suggests, the origins of Eliot's poetry are to be found in American popular culture, then for the purposes of this chapter some critical labor remains to be done. Namely, within Eliot's early experimentations with this three-in-one tool, Laforgue's own use of these techniques—the suddenly shortened line, the emphatic inner rhyme, and the jagged rhythms—

would have to be excluded as an influence from ragtime lyricists' use of those same methods for similar rhetorical ends.

So rather than ragtime, perhaps the source is as near to Eliot as Symons's description of Laforgue: "he will say to us, with a familiarity of manner, as of one talking languidly, in a low voice, the lips always teased into a slightly bitter smile; and he will pass suddenly into the slightly ironical lilt of"—here Symons cites the tight dimeter couplets of Laforgue—

Hôtel garni
De l'infini,

Sphinx et Joconde
Des défunts mondes[16]

As with a grinning sphinx or the mysterious Joconde, a jocund smirk underlies these crisp lines and assertive rhymes: an elusive tone that marries snappy rhythm to a languid, "ironical lilt." And so the crucial technical advance that Eliot mastered in January–February 1910 might be indebted only to Laforgue and Symons rather than to ragtime. Whether this technique is indebted to French poets rather than American music has already been assessed by an older Eliot, who weighed in on the matter in the last years of his life. In an interview with Donald Hall, Eliot claims, "My early *vers libre*, of course, was started under the endeavor to practice the same form as Laforgue. This meant merely rhyming lines of irregular length, with the rhymes coming in irregular places."[17] This recollection, offered fifty years after he had drafted the poems in question, cannot entirely suffice. However, since Eliot's memory so clearly recalls the technique he learned, it does lend some weight to the theory that his adoption was more consciously indebted to Laforgue than to ragtime.

Chinitz's claims about popular culture gain their traction in the 1911 poems, and my hunting in early 1910 for the first manifestations of what became evident a year later does not diminish Chinitz's general claim about the role of popular culture in Eliot's work. Rather, I wish to place Chinitz's ideas in the matrix of Eliot's early growth. My claim, then, is not that Laforgue and popular culture were roughly equivalent terms whose interaction produced the early Eliot, as Chinitz has it. Rather, when the early poems are read as a chronological map of his emerging concerns, the initial appearances and quick development of what would become a trademark rhetorical gesture—the jagged rhythm, tight rhyme and suddenly shortened line—can be seen as the means whereby the Laforgue-Baudelaire conflict of the previous months is mediated. Whether the source of that gesture is ragtime or Laforgue is probably not detectable, given the similarities of those sources and their nearly simultaneous uses in Eliot's early poetry.

In any case, in the first months of 1910, Eliot's perfection of this gesture is neither an end in itself nor another source to be exploited. It is a means for solving the more pressing problem of making the Laforguean and Baudelairean identities cohere in one voice. In November 1909, we had a mess of conflicting voices, with shifts that were spectacularly mismanaged:

> And a crowd of tattered sparrows
> Delve in the gutter with sordid patience.
>
> Oh, these minor considerations! . . .[18]

Only three months later, in February 1910, Eliot has accomplished an elision of voices, a shift in tone that is managed adroitly:

> "You let [Life] flow from you, you let it flow
> "And youth is cruel, and has no remorse
> "And smiles at situations which it does not see"—
> I smile, of course
> And go on drinking tea.[19]

Written in a loose pentameter, the woman's barrage ends with the words "remorse"/"see," which are answered by the speaker's "of course" / "tea," though not in the same pentameter. Left with little room to jockey in this salon warfare, the speaker's purse-lipped response shifts to dimeter and trimeter: two lines that enact a camp sensibility and a silent reserve (he smiles but does not speak). Masterfully done, it is the poetic equivalent of a slight shift of the eyebrows. As I will show, those eyebrows are arched at the authorial audience, not the woman.

As often occurs in the notebook, this successful maneuver has been preceded by a less successful attempt. In "Convictions (Curtain Raiser)," written in the previous month, the poem's approximate tetrameter suddenly gives way to a crude shortening of the line, drawing exaggerated attention to the chiming of "alone"/"monotone":

> Two, in a garden scene
> Go picking tissue paper roses;
> Hero and heroine, alone,

The monotone
Of promises and compliments[20]

Here is that same shift to dimeter and trimeter lines and the same emphatic rhyming, but there is not yet a corresponding shift in tone, no smirk underlining the scene. Appearing as they do in the middle of that satirical passage, the shortened lines and emphatic rhyme do not change the direction of the satire: no thematic purpose is served by the shift. It is as if Eliot needs to try the technique out here in "Convictions" before he can manage the tone a month later in "Portrait of a Lady."[21] He is giving himself voice lessons, cautiously expanding his technique, and then seeing what tonal ranges can be reached once the technique has been tried out. As might be expected from a youth who has picked up a new trick, he trumpets his accomplishment by using it everywhere in the next few poems, the shortened lines pealing off their rhymes.

From "First Debate between the Body and Soul" (Jan. 1910):

The street pianos through the trees
Whine and wheeze.

and:

Imaginations
Masturbations[22]

From "Portrait of a Lady" II (Feb. 1910):

(The need for self-expression
Will pardon this digression).[23]

From "Easter: Sensations of April" I (Apr. 1910):

With the smell of heat
From the asphalt street.

and:

Withered and dry
Long laid by[24]

From "Easter: Sensations of April" II (May 1910):

Daffodils
Long yellow sunlight fills

and:

> Smelling of earth and rain.
> And again[25]

From "Silence" (June 1910):

> That were so broad and deep
> So immediate and steep,

and:

> Are suddenly still.
> You may say what you will,

and:

> At such peace I am terrified.
> There is nothing else beside.[26]

Whether Laforgue, Symons, ragtime, or clubhouse doggerel are the operative principles in January 1910, what matters is what Eliot has learned: not how to blend voices but how to shift between them without grinding the clutch. Not all of the multiple excerpts cited above signal a shift in tone, but they show Eliot moving into and out of shortened lines in order to gauge the effect he might create. Given the control he exerts over these line lengths and rhymes, it is understandable that he would be so opposed, in a later essay, to describing these effects as *vers libre*, for there is nothing free about them.[27]

There are many lessons, techniques, expansions, and refinements that go into making up the authorial persona we recognize as T. S. Eliot. But it is this particular lesson learned in early 1910 that makes his poems lose their apprentice roughness and start to sound Eliotic. This lesson will enable, for example, the portentousness of Prufrock's "overwhelming question" to transition effortlessly into the jazzy syncopation of "Oh do not ask 'what is it?' / Let us go and make our visit."

Given the difficulty of determining the source of this trademark technique, one problem related to voice remains: If we are unwilling to concede the role of popular music in Eliot's adoption of that particular technique, believing instead that this tool has been inherited strictly from Laforgue, then how can it be said that it is not derivative in Eliot's hands? In other words, if Eliot is still imitating Laforgue—as he was in the derivative poems of November 1909—then what makes these poems of early 1910 distinctive rather than better imitations of Laforgue? The long answer to that question is worked out in the readings of the individual poems below. The short answer is that this technique expertly addresses those rhetorical features that had previously been unevenly handled—voice, theme, and audience. The three-in-one technique—shortened lines, tight rhymes, and snappy rhythms—modulates the voice, enables him to address a chosen theme directly, and signals to a specific audience. The poet now controls the device; its source no longer dominates him. As Eliot would later theorize the matter, he has changed from an immature poet who imitates to a mature poet who steals.[28]

Awaiting an Audience

In describing his poetic development, Eliot acknowledges the crucial link between voice and audience with which he struggled. He had been shocked to discover the derivative nature of his own work. As a result, he realized that he had to change the rhetorical conception of his audience: "He discovers that his poem must have a meaning apart from its meaning to him."[29] He must clear his throat and speak again, this time to an audience that will have different expectations than did the adolescent's audiences.

As I have already noted, the finding of an adequate audience is the very theme of "Convictions (Curtain Raiser)," which opens with a description of enthusiastic marionettes:

> They see the outlines of their stage
> Conceived upon a scale immense
> And even in this later age
> Await an audience open-mouthed
> At climax and suspense.[30]

With naive zeal, the marionettes imagine their reach to be considerable. And their artless belief in the power of art to impress is met by an equally credulous audience. For, the speaker wryly notes, even in this skeptical era, the marionettes "Await an audience open-mouthed / At climax and suspense." These ingenuous vaudeville-goers are the anti-audience of the poem, to be contrasted with the authorial audience. Using a favorite rhetorical maneuver—definition by contrast—the speaker implicitly commends his authorial audience for not being as gullible as the anti-audience. They, the authorial audience, are not impressed by the vulgar workings of vaudeville effect seeking. The problem, as will be discussed in greater detail below, is that the authorial audience is indistinct, for the speaker cannot imagine any positive quality for those readers.

The various marionettes of "Convictions" have been posed on a stage in stock situations to solve Eliot's second rhetorical problem: how to imagine an audience whose composition is different from the conservative audiences of his juvenilia. The contours of that solution can be divined in the speaker's attitude to the anti-audience, those gape-mouthed hordes. Getting the backstage view from the speaker, the authorial audience in the wings is flattered to be contrasted with the credulous rabble out in the auditorium. Eliot has taken this maneuver of defining an audience against its opposite from "Nocturne," in which the anti-audience—those sentimental "female readers"—contrasts with the authorial audience: sophisticated readers who expect the sentimental and the earnest to be hooted off the stage. We have seen how the authorial audience in "Nocturne" is just as narrow as the sentimental readers it presumes to deplore, for the sarcasm it expects is hardly more enlightened than the sentimentality against which it reacts. But with "Convictions," there is an advance over this construction of the audience by contrast. Because its marionette poses are so various (three stock situations are depicted), the authorial audience who observes is a more finely rendered group, one whose wit is trusted not to sour into sarcastic dismissal. In short, while the authorial audience of "Nocturne" is expected to *submit* to the effects that the speaker has marshaled in support of his anti-Romantic polemic (sarcastic denigration of the sentimental), the authorial audience of "Convictions" is invited to *observe* the effects of various poses on an anti-audience.

Needless to say, the speaker of "Convictions" has not lost his anti-Romantic convictions. His distaste for sentimentality cuts short with an irritated aside the woman's romantic exhalations: "(With more that I shall not repeat)." But this gesture, which was haughtily deployed in the earlier poem, is here placed as one among various gestures that are now coolly surveyed. Eliot has changed in this poem from an artist who hesitatingly attempts rhetorical effects to an artist who observes himself attempting rhetorical effects. Eliot critics often describe this maneuver, somewhat unhelpfully, as a heightened self-consciousness, as if it were a private, psychological trait of the speaker rather than an identifiable rhetorical strategy of the author. Critics have long identified the provenance of that strategy as Laforgue, and in examining the notebook poems, we can see exactly where this speaker observing himself first occurs, in what order Eliot is absorbing Laforguean mannerisms, and how each new absorption often represents a solution to a recently discovered problem.

There is a faint difference between the targeting of sentimentality in the November 1909 poems and the observation of such in "Convictions" of January 1910. This subtlety is perhaps the reason an older Eliot, dating the poems in a hurry before sending them off to John Quinn, at first assigned to "Convictions" the date "Nov. 1909." This first guess was then changed to "Jan. 1910" once Eliot recalled his reasons for promoting this later poem to the beginning of the notebook.

Compared to the rhetorical mayhem of the November 1909 poems, "Convictions" is a promising start in defining an audience, and the rest of the poems of January–June 1910 attempt to fulfill that promise. The result is several stanzas of a masterpiece, "Portrait of a Lady," as well as two other poems—"First Debate between the Body and Soul" and "Spleen"—whose theme, content, and manner forecast future triumphs. It is another momentous period of quick learning, in which the author's own broadening purview becomes coextensive with the adventurous expectations of his newly imagined audience.

The Poems

Poems spanning Jan.–June 1910 (Eliot, aged twenty-one years, at Harvard University)

"Convictions (Curtain Raiser)"	drafted Jan. 1910
"First Debate between the Body and Soul"	drafted Jan. 1910
"Spleen"	published Jan. 26, 1910
"Portrait of a Lady" II	drafted Feb. 1910
"Easter: Sensations of April" I	drafted Apr. 1910
"Easter: Sensations of April" II	drafted May 1910
"Silence"	drafted June 1910
"Ode" [Harvard Class]	published June 24, 1910

"Convictions (Curtain Raiser)" *Drafted Jan. 1910*

Although it was not written first, Eliot's placement of this poem near the beginning of the notebook, and his parenthetical title "(Curtain Raiser)" point to a certain thematic emphasis that Eliot wishes to apply to the notebook as a whole. The idea of staging, and in particular, the staging of emotion and the control of an audience's reaction, take priority in how Eliot belatedly reads an organizing theme into his early collection of poems. This poem's "meta" nature encourages the earlier, emotionally raw poems of November 1909 to be seen as poses tried out for effect rather than as serious positions once held. The placing of "Convictions" before the November 1909 inventions asks us to read those earlier poems not as clumsy stages in the growth of a poet's technique (as we read them in the previous chapter) but as provisional, deliberately rendered observations. Read in the later order that "Convictions" proposes, the unfixable disasters of November 1909 are now reframed. Rather than products of an incoherent collision of two powerful voices that attempt to coerce the judgment of the audience, those earlier poems are now set—like the three stock situations presented in "Convictions"—as yet more marionette gestures the audience is invited to observe. Whether such an attempt at reframing is convincing is another matter entirely. But seven years later, when Eliot decides upon a title for his first published volume, *Prufrock and Other Observations,* he will tip his hand regarding the nature of observing and its implicit analog, acting, as keys for understanding his early poems.[31]

The title "Convictions"—with its associations of judgment, penalty, feeling right—raises a number of questions. Of what is the poet convinced? What does he judge? And how is the authorial audience complicit in the poem's judgment or conviction? Mayer provides one answer: "By applying to his marionette's voices a term ["convictions"] that both Harvard and his family reserved for seriously held moral principles, Eliot undermines the assumed seriousness of received convictions, and signals his new allegiance to the world of art."[32]

The rhetorical configuration of the poem likewise raises a number of questions. Why, for example, have characters from earlier poems been transformed into marionettes, instead of being recycled as characters? What do marionettes do for Eliot that fictional characters cannot do? Why are the three scenes reduced to tableaus rather than given room to breathe as minidramas? Why, in other words, are the poses of the marionettes frozen rather than fluid? And what advance does the double audience (the gullible horde in the auditorium vs. the backstage intimates) represent for Eliot's developing rhetorical sense?

Eliot's turn to marionettes has been explained variously. My interest here is not in their historical provenance nor, primarily, in their psychological necessity but with their rhetorical effect in the poems.[33] The scenes, lovers, women, and philosophers of "Convictions" have all been recycled from previous poems. What is new is that the characters have been transformed into marionettes, and that the relationship of those marionettes to the audience has been reconfigured in two ways: physically, the stage metaphor is made explicit, and rhetorically, the distance between the speaker and his subject matter is widened. In "Convictions," the "monotone" of a lovers' exchange refers back to the humdrum conversation between Romeo and Juliet in "Nocturne."[34] The stock patterns of love duets are satirized in both poems, but there are three significant differences in the presentation of the later poem, differences that reveal a poet thinking hard about his relationship to his audience. First, whereas the lovers in "Nocturne" enact a mini-drama (Juliet is stabbed; Romeo is relieved), the lovers of "Convictions" are reduced to a simple tableau without dramatic action, the better to focus attention on the theatricality of their relation to the audience. Second, whereas in "Nocturne" the stage director's cues provoke differing reactions from the anti-audience and the authorial audience, in "Convictions," the focus of attention is the stage manager's gesturing itself, not the object toward which he is gesturing. And third, whereas in "Nocturne" conventions are staged in order to be mocked, in "Convictions" the staging of convention becomes the subject matter of the poem. Although mockery is implicit in such a setup, the difference between satirizing and the staging of satire allows the author more breathing space: he can point to the implicit relation between him and his audiences—both the anti-audience and the authorial audience. The real subject of the poem, then, becomes the relationship of speaker and audience.

In the third stanza, an argument among "Paladins" who exchange cant about eudaemonia points back to the speaker and audience of "Second Caprice"—the Harvard philosophers and aestheticians whose sympathies the speaker had attempted to coerce. In "Convictions," one of the philosopher-marionettes claims loudly, "strive for social happiness / And contact with your fellow-men." This ideal of human community is voiced by a puppet because the speaker cannot concur with it. At present, the speaker sees himself as a lonely prophet, with no community or audience. But rather than stage himself as a coercive speaker-philosopher as he does in the awkward "Second Caprice in North Cambridge," he can objectify that relationship on a stage, with the ridiculous sight of philosopher-marionettes arguing among themselves.

In the fourth stanza, an aristocratic lady confesses to romantic unfulfillment, with the speaker—who is bored or embarrassed by her predictable longing—sardonically abbreviating her confession, "(With more that I shall not repeat.)" Here appears a version of the speaker of "Nocturne" but in a softened, more lightly ironic pose. Here also is another version of the Laforguean lady, first seen as a group ("female readers") in "Nocturne" and as an individual in "Conversation Galante."

In terms of the rhetoric of the poem as a whole, the repackaging of previously used scenarios is striking. The same characters from earlier poems appear, but now all of them appear as marionettes in a vaudeville show, facing a live audience. The most telling difference is the change from "Second Caprice," whose situation is a speaker-philosopher addressing an audience of fellow philosophers, to "Convictions," whose situation is an artist observing and commenting on the codified gestures of marionettes and their predictable effects. The audience of "Second Caprice"—fellow philosophers earnestly addressed and emotionally coerced by the speaker—are here reduced to ridiculous marionette philosophers. With such an objectifying move, the marionettes in their various poses can now be dissected like insects. The speaker ironically notes that the marionettes conceive their stage "upon a scale immense." Like the puppet-actors, the anti-audience is similarly ridiculous: "open-mouthed" at the spectacle. As with the "female readers" of "Nocturne," the audience to whom the marionettes play is not the authorial audience of the poem but another anti-audience, as no self-respecting readers of Laforgue would consider themselves gullible to the conventions of puppetry. The most important character is the speaker: a version of the artist who stands above it all, pulling the strings.

It may seem but a small step from "Humouresque"—in which a speaker observes a bullying marionette—to "Convictions," in which a speaker observes an array of marionettes. The difference, however, is more significant than adding more characters to the stage. The distinction lies in the relationship of the speaker to his observed phenomena. In the earlier "Humouresque," the speaker is involved in, and barely able to extricate himself from, the brutal sarcasm of his "dead" marionette that has sprung to life. By contrast, two months later in "Convictions," the speaker is the playfully ironic stage manager, wholly detached from the enthusiastic, deluded marionettes who enact their roles for an equally deluded public. This is the "conviction" Eliot has achieved as an artist: the cool scrutiny of rhetorical machinations. Such poise is noticeably absent in the outbursts of November 1909, as especially seen in "Second Caprice," which didactically attempts to coerce the emotions of its audience. Another poem of November 1909, "Humouresque," likewise reveals a lack of poise, speaking not with the world-weary irony of the mature voice but with the high-handed snottiness of an adolescent. Thus, with "Convictions," the rhetorical advance over "Humouresque" may seem small in terms of technique, but it is significant in terms of attitude. It allows the brutal dismissiveness of the marionette in "Humouresque"—which is really a partial mask for the speaker—to melt into a more jocular irony in "Convictions." Such a shift marks more than just the technical advance of an artist but the expansion of a mind. The increasing rhetorical sophistication is of a piece with a maturation in judgment.

Since most of Eliot's letters to his parents were destroyed, there is little biographical data from this time in his life to illuminate the personal maturation that parallels his poetic maturation. But the cool detachment that Eliot achieves in this January–June time frame does coincide with his increasing detachment from his parents. Eliot would have traveled home to St. Louis for the Christmas break in December 1909, where, flushed with the exhilaration of writing a French-inspired poetry, he requested permission to spend a year in France. It would have required a detached will to survive the frantic worries of his beloved mother, who wrote him at Harvard, in April 1910, a few months after his holiday visit: "I cannot bear to think of your being alone in Paris, the very words give me a chill."[35]

As often happens in the notebook, Eliot's initial solutions to rhetorical problems do not quite work, requiring further refinement. "Convictions" is Eliot's first attempt at poetry as observing rhetorical maneuvers, and it succeeds only in mapping out the solution to the problem, rather than actually solving it. Its failure becomes evident once the map ends: the tableaus have been staged, the expectations of the anti-audience have been separated from the expectations of the authorial audience, and then . . . what? Having drawn an authorial audience up into his metanarrative, the speaker finds he has nothing to say. The detached rhetorical maneuver that the poet has achieved has deprived him of his best subject matter: those inane targets of the earlier poems. And so the poem ends on a breezy, vague note: "My marionettes (or so they say) / Have these keen moments every day." Eliot has not yet discovered what he wants to say to this audience, because the burden of this poem is the discovery of the ways in which he relates to that audience.

Mayer also notes an equivocal element in the rhetoric of the poem: "Eliot is ambivalent about these fluent puppets, distrusting their eagerness to speak, yet delighting in the stage business."[36] The puppets' facility with stock conventions is not the problem; it is the authorial audience that causes the speaker's ambivalence. The anti-audience, in its gape-mouthed appreciation, already knows how to react. But having jeered at their naive reaction, the speaker does not know how to stage-manage the presumably wiser reaction of his authorial audience. Aside from observing the gap with him, what further reaction does the speaker expect from them? What message does he have to communicate to them? He does not know.

Another clue in identifying the rhetorical difficulty of the poem can be found in the pronouns. There is a palpable ambiguity in the speaker's parenthetical "they": "My marionettes (or so they say)." The plural pronoun could possibly refer to the marionettes: what they say of themselves. However, it is more likely that, as an idiomatic expression (the anonymous whispers of what "they say"), the phrase suggests an audience who watches and judges—the very problem of potential audience hostility that the speaker is seeking to defuse. Thus, the phrase is more than just rhythmic filler to extend the line and provide a rhyme. As we saw in the previous chapter, Eliot is not plugging in colloquialisms as a way of imitating Laforgue; those platitudes are congruent with his rhetorical conception of the poem.

In spite of the important technical advance that the poem represents, the flubbed ending keeps Eliot from publishing it. After all the elaborate stage direction that pulls various marionettes on stage, reveals the hollowness of their poses, and distinguishes the authorial audience from the gape-mouthed hordes, ultimately the speaker has no sense of a larger purpose for his backstage observations of this spectacle. Its inconclusive conclusion corresponds to its ambiguous position: promoted to the beginning of the notebook, second only to "Conversation Galante," yet never published. Because the poem presents such a novel breakthrough—observing rather than acting—it is initially proudly set out of chronological order near the beginning of the notebook, as a way of marking how the subsequent poems are to be understood. The poem is never published, though, because it marshals an array of characters to make a statement and in the end cannot do so. The elaborate machinery of the poem grinds to a halt, and another poem is taken up.

"First Debate between the Body and Soul"
Drafted Jan. 1910

Scribbled on loose leaf, the multiple crossings-out of this poem show Eliot frittering away at adjectives, fussily aiming at local precision while sentences that defy grammatical sense are left dangling. That the poem is never written out in fair copy on the pages of the notebook reveals something about its unresolved nature as well as Eliot's drafting procedures. The evidence of this manuscript suggests that at the beginning of his apprenticeship, Eliot initially used loose leaves for sketches and rough ideas. Then, once the shape of the poem had become apparent to him, he would transfer the poem in fair copy to the notebook for further editing and discard the loose leaves. As the notebook progresses, this ordered division of labor breaks down, and the secured leaves of the notebook are used not only for fair copies but for sketching as well. This slow evolution reflects Eliot's wary temperament—Virginia Woolf will describe Eliot as "infinitely scrupulous, tautologous, & cautious."[37] At first the notebook serves as a museum for finished, or nearly finished, poems, with the messy process of drafting hidden in discarded loose leaves. Then, once Eliot becomes more comfortable, he uses the notebook as a true drafting tool, where he feels no compulsion to clean up, content to allow deleted mistakes and alternative readings to linger. The loose leaves of "First Debate between the Body and Soul" have survived because they were deliberately laid into the later pages of the notebook, their fragmented ideas interesting enough to keep Eliot from scrapping the poem entirely but not unified enough to warrant a fair copy.

The body and soul to which the title refers are traditional opposites, long serving as tropes of the material and the spiritual, the terrestrial and the transcendent, the sinful and the sacred. Whatever Eliot intends with this contrast, a "debate" engages these polarities, acknowledging their unresolved nature. The pressure of the poem testifies to a personal, intense experience of suffering. Its raw themes—sexuality, fear, the clash of imagination and experience—are ones for which the young author cannot feign detachment. For this reason, his preferred (and recently discovered) mode of observation does not avail him here. The word "Debate" in the title is later given the modifier "First": at some point in the poem's evolution, Eliot realized that the debate would need to continue elsewhere. Of the poems written in early 1910, "First Debate" is the most confused. Some clarity regarding the poem's aims can be had by looking forward a year to "Bacchus and Ariadne: Second Debate between Body and Soul" and to "Rhapsody on a Windy Night." But if we are patient with the poem's confusion rather than jump ahead to its later resolutions, we can get a better sense of how Eliot is expanding his approach to voice and audience in this time frame.

With increasing confidence, Eliot wades further into the territory of the ugly, the prohibited, the unspoken. Remarkably, he does so without glancing over his shoulder at a judging audience. The most obvious sign of this progress is that Eliot here refers openly to masturbation, without a fussy windup or recourse to scatological humor. In a post-confessional age, a reference to masturbation seems unremarkable, but to understand it as transgressive for the young poet, we have to recover the moralistic context of his upbringing. A sense of that context can be gleaned from a letter that Henry Ware Eliot Sr.—T. S. Eliot's father—wrote to his brother on the topic of sex education, a letter that—although recently published—has already been overquoted: "I do not approve of public instruction in Sexual relations. When I teach my children to avoid the Devil I don't begin by giving them a letter of introduction to him and his crowd. I hope that a cure for Syphilis will never be discovered. It is God's punishment for nastiness."[38] The severity of the father's judgment will be passed on to his son, who will sustain a similar disgust about sexual matters for much of his life. So even though Eliot's open reference to masturbation in the poem is transgressive (a letter of introduction to the Devil, surely), by likening it to defecation, the son's attitude mirrors the stern moralizing of the father. The Tradition cannot be wholly repudiated.

Exactly one year earlier, the poet had written a furtive poem about sexual longing. To his innocent beloved, he had wanly requested more passion: "Have you no brighter tropic flowers / With scarlet lips, for me?"[39] Such demure posturing is now cast aside as inadequate to his poetic needs. Having broached the taboo of masturbation, there is, perhaps, a slight holding back, an instinctive caution in the face of new danger. Eliot opts not for crude slang but for the clinical term that fortuitously rhymes with other Latinate suffixes: defecations, sensations. This neutrality confers an aura of serious inquiry, as does the equation of masturbation to other bodily functions. The ambiguous grammar of the word that precedes it also adds resonance to this sexual term: "Imaginations"/"Masturbations." The seemingly plural "Imaginations" is missing a crucial apostrophe, which sets these concepts in apposition.[40] The implicit possessive raises the somatic taboo to an acceptably figurative level: mental masturbation is a common metaphor. But Eliot no longer seems concerned with what is acceptable to his old audiences, who have been abandoned in this phase of his writing. His playing with the figurative level of imagination(')s masturbations has less to do with hiding from the judgment of a hostile audience and more to do with framing his sexual conflicts in relation to his other struggles.

As vexed as the trials of sexuality are, the more troublesome conflict outlined by the poem is the incommensurability of imagination and experience. On the one hand is the pure idea, to which the philosopher is "devoted" but that is rejected because it is unattainable and empty. On the other hand is brute reality, which oppresses: "The cosmic smudge of an enormous thumb / Posting bills / On the soul." With their sexually depraved connotations ("turpitude," "leering"), the sensations of the world cannot be redeemed by the imagination.

Given the incommensurability of experience and imagination, and given that this first debate between them yields no dialectical movement, the posited solution is a forced one, a violent yoking of the intellectual with the terrestrial in the image of a "supersubtle peasant." The author immediately apologizes for the ridiculousness of a figure with neither grounding in reality nor precedent in literature. A monstrous birth, it is buried in parentheses: "(Conception most unpleasant)."[41] Having conceived the image however, the speaker entertains its possibilities, figuring this "supersubtle peasant" as a kind of god from whom he might beg aid: "Assist me to the pure idea." This rustic-philosophy-as-deliverance would enable the speaker to be detached from the intractable problems of imagination and experience, enabling him to see nature "without love or fear." Yet this resolution is unsustainable: the poem reaches for a detachment that is wholly beyond the means of its rhetoric. And so the proposed resolution falls apart: eventually, "life evaporates into a smile." Here Eliot's smile revisits an earlier image, derived from Laforgue and Symons: one already found at the conclusion of "Opera" and that will reappear in "Portrait." His several variations on this image of a futile smile reveal how powerfully it speaks to the poet's experience. The ambivalence of the image pulls in different directions: for the well-bred young man, the smile is the polite nonresponse that maintains elaborate pretenses. But for the Laforguean ironist who "smiles with an exasperating tolerance," the smile is a kind of "frivolity" that is an escape from "the world as it appears to the sober majority."[42] The smile maintains the social façade at the same time that it critiques the "sober majority" who impose it. Eliot's later verse retains this connotation of smile as meaning a false veil behind which one hides: "People change, and smile: but the agony abides."[43]

Perhaps because the struggles are too intense, and because this poem is his first to address several of these struggles at once, the poem does not achieve a satisfactory form of expression. Eliot's mind was a dialectical one, often reveling in apparent opposites, but "First Debate" is not truly dialectical.[44] Stuck in the polarities of imagination and experience, the debate finds no common ground on which to tread. As a consequence, it moves toward a cheap resolution that is recognized as such. The poem is no debate, rather a staging of a deeply divided self, whose presentation is not adequately turned toward an audience. The poet's foggy sense of audience is a consequence of talking to himself, working through his own suffering in his head.

The poem is as divided as the realms of imagination and experience that are pitted against one another. When the poem attempts to clarify the speaker and audience, its rhetoric betrays confusions typical of this phase of his apprenticeship: an unclear, though sympathetically plural "our" is repeated in the refrain, whereas the speaker turns to "one" and "me" elsewhere. More significantly, at the very weakest point of the poem—its yoking of opposites in a "supersubtle peasant"—the rhetoric becomes rashly acrobatic. As described above, once the image is presented, it is immediately regretted in parenthetical disgust. Even more strangely, after this sniff the abortive image is repeated, this time with an added detail:

Absolute! complete idealist
A supersubtle peasant
(Conception most unpleasant)
A supersubtle peasant in a shabby square

That scenic detail of the "shabby square" is mannered, as if the author hopes that by repeating a facile idea and adding grimy atmospherics, a kind of Baudelairean credibility might be lent to the scene.

It is in this phase of his writing, though not in this particular poem, that Eliot does manage to integrate a Baudelairean mode into his poetry. Looking back on this integration, Eliot will describe it in terms quoted in the previous chapter: "I think that from Baudelaire I learned first, a precedent for the poetical possibilities, never developed by any poet writing in my own language, of the more sordid aspects of the modern metropolis, of the possibility of fusion between the sordidly realistic and the phantasmagoric, the possibility of the juxtaposition of the matter-of-fact and the fantastic."[45] Such fruitful juxtapositions will eventually determine the shape of such poems as "Rhapsody on a Windy Night," and they are what "First Debate" tries ineffectively to do.

Another forced element of the poem's rhetoric is the unprepared shift that first presents the rustic philosopher in the third person but then addresses him in the second: "A supersubtle peasant in a shabby square / Assist me." To make this address work, the author would have had to revise the rhetoric, to apostrophize the peasant, rather than describe him: "O supersubtle peasant / Assist me." But while such a revision might have solved the rhetorical confusion, it would have been tantamount to concocting something like a prayer, and neither is acceptable.

It is no wonder this poem never made it past a sketch: the author has painted himself into a corner. The poem is not observational enough for a writer whose subsequent successes rely on a detached pose, a speaking self that can survey its own divisions. Although it is a failed experiment, the poem does show Eliot moving further into the Baudelairean mode. One sign of improvement here is that the failures of the poem are due to overreaching rather than to a panicked interruption by Laforguean sarcasm. With increasing courage, the young poet is working through his own suffering.[46]

"Spleen"
Published Jan. 26, 1910, Harvard Advocate

With its three short stanzas, "Spleen" bites off more than it can chew. It first presents a parade of women, reduced via synecdoche to their hats. Their feminine composure and "conscious graces" at their Sunday rituals provoke an aside, the sudden self-consciousness of an awkwardly named "you"—a strange, new leap in the direction of a sympathetic audience.[47] This inward turn of self-consciousness, whose "you" seems to coincide with a lyric "I," is a detour from the parrotings of social custom. Without transition, another digression leads us (or "you") from tea in an interior setting to an alley full of cats. Then enters a scrupulously dressed character by the name of Life. He is "a little bald and gray," and his fussy manners keep ultimate questions at arm's length. In the speaker's gently ironic parentheses, he waits "(Somewhat impatient of delay) / On the doorstep of the Absolute."

It is all too much for such a short poem. But we know where it is headed: an awkward, punctilious dandy; a "you" in league with an "I"; self-satisfied women at tea; the suffocating artificiality of social rituals; languid digressions; unmarked transitions between patrician settings and dingy alleys; the motifs of avoidance and paralysis; and an atmosphere of suffering lightened by irony. Immediately recognizable as a precursor to "The Love Song of J. Alfred Prufrock," "Spleen" is so close to the themes, gestures, and manner of that more famous poem that Eliot does not allow its later republication or collection.[48]

"Spleen" appears in the same month as "Convictions," a poem that marks Eliot's change from an artist who had been attempting rhetorical effects to an artist who observes his speakers attempting rhetorical effects. Whereas "Convictions" discovers the pose of observation but cannot direct that technique to any artistic purpose, "Spleen" exploits the two consequences of its observational stance: awkwardness and inaction. Awkwardness is the first consequence of the self-conscious pose, because self-observation reveals the gap between one's inner world and the phoniness of social convention. The other consequence of self-observation is indecisiveness, a fatal failure of action. "Spleen" links both awkwardness and inaction: heightened self-consciousness brings with it the knowledge that one's inner world does not conform to the customs used—apparently without difficulty—by everyone else. The realization that social conventions are arbitrary might be liberating for someone who is coming of age. For someone such as Eliot who is still crushingly indebted to that culture, with no means of escape, the knowledge causes paralysis.

With his observational pose, Eliot's increased distance enables him to watch these two consequences (awkwardness and inaction) play out artistically without succumbing to personal despair. His increased sense of rhetorical distance is another advance that allows him to weld Laforgue and Baudelaire together without glaring contradictions. Many commentators have noted that "Spleen" is indebted to both French authors, and this study notes, by way of addition, how hard won that union is. The title is a reworking of Baudelaire, though the word "spleen" was a common one for Laforgue and for French Romantic poets. The poem's observation of the domestic and the urban also seems indebted to Baudelaire, especially in its tone of detached seriousness—the very pose that Eliot first attempted but could not sustain in "First Caprice in North Cambridge." As Mayer has noted, "Spleen" is also a tribute to Laforgue's series of Dimanche poems, in which "life is depleted through the mechanical routines by which it is lived."[49] But since Eliot's Laforgue is so closely tied to Symons's Laforgue, Symons himself is as much a source for the poem as the two French poets. These lines of Symons could well have planted the seeds of "Spleen" in Eliot's mind: Laforgue "thinks intensely about life," Symons claims, "seeing what is automatic, pathetically ludicrous in it, almost as one might who has had no part in the comedy."[50] Symons's critical explanation—"life [as] automatic, pathetically ludicrous"—has been rendered in artistic form in "Spleen," without much transformation. Symons's language is even copied by Eliot: Laforgue, Symons claims, "composes love-poems hat in hand," while Eliot's figure of Life waits "hat and gloves in hand."[51]

There is no "I" or "we" in the poem, but a clumsy turn to the second person appears out of nowhere: "Your mental self-possession" is said to be disturbed. The implied "you" here signifies a leap of sympathy on the part of the speaker, but the slight effort at coercion is graceless. It is not so domineering as the browbeating that "Second Caprice" gives its readers, though it is not so suave as Prufrock's invitation to "you and I." What is exceptional about this appearance of the second person is that it is the first time in Eliot's serious poetry that the imagined audience, directly addressed, is almost trusted to agree with the lyric speaker's point of view. What is missing from its rhetoric is the voice of a lyric "I" that wholly lays claim to the identity of a balding, dithering misfit.

In spite of such problems, the serious content expressed in a light tone is the surest sign that Eliot has succeeded at balancing Laforgue and Baudelaire. Eliot manages this lightness by playing up the contrast between the claims of the Absolute and the inadequacies of the character, named Life, who appears in the last stanza.[52] This late-introduced character waits "(Somewhat impatient of delay)." The coy parentheses delay the grammatical resolution, and the wry "Somewhat" douses the energy of "impatient." The contradictions of the poem's content slowly bring a smirk into the final stanza, even though, as I will show, Eliot has muddled his attempt at the three-in-one tool. Eliot's ideas mature simultaneously as he masters the rhetoric needed to express them.

W. H. Bizley has puzzled through the rhetoric of "Spleen" in terms similar to those of my own analysis here. The problem with the poem, according to Bizley, is that Eliot "got the idea before he got the technique."[53] In its phrasing, Bizley's claim seems to be the inverse of my argument, which claims that Eliot tries out various techniques before the rhetoric is assured. My own understanding of rhetoric belies Bizley's binary of technique/idea, and so I think that Bizley and I are in agreement about the problem with the poem, though we describe it differently. Summarizing the poem, Bizley finds that it has a compelling idea driving it: "One's 'mental self-possession,' which sounds dignified and strong, cannot stave off the incessant interruption, the awakening brought about by domestic trivia and their 'unwarranted digression.'" For Bizley, though, the technique is what is lacking to pull it all together: "to see a joke, and to tell a joke, are two different things," Bizley remarks. "I think we must admit that Eliot's stiff verse with its cumbersome rhymes sounds rather more like the 'dull conspiracy' itself than any rallying wit."[54]

A careful look at the rhetoric of the poem reveals that it is exactly in this place—where Bizley notes the presence of the idea but the absence of the technique—that Eliot has attempted rather wanly the three-in-one technique:

"Your mental self-possession / By this unwarranted digression." The lines are short and the rhyme is tight, but there are several problems with this couplet. The diction is too Latinate and not colloquial enough to serve as a contrast to the women's world of hats and teas. As a consequence, the double rhyme of "possession" and "digression" occupies a literary rather than ragtime register. Also, instead of syncopated rhythms, sober iambs are served up. Finally, the length of the couplet is not markedly shorter than the lines that precede it. Eliot's initial attempts to use this tool are circumspect, because his uninhibited deployment of contrasting voices in November 1909 had yielded only incoherence. Here in January 1910, Eliot's pendulum has swung back to the side of restraint.

The problem, then, is not that Eliot has the idea but not the technique, as Bizley claims. The problem is that the technique *is* the idea, and Eliot has neither. Eliot has not yet managed the technique—the tell-tale tonal shift—that will allow him to tell the joke: a technique that is inextricable from the idea of ethos (a lightly ironic speaker), the idea of logos (the world surveyed with both anxiety and detachment), and the idea of pathos (an urbane audience that gets the joke without extraneous gesturing). Fortunately, the next poem Eliot writes finally masters the technique he has been attempting.

"Portrait of a Lady" II
Drafted Feb. 1910; published with parts I and III (both drafted later), Sept. 1915, Others

The draft version of this familiar poem is bound to surprise its readers, especially lines 16–21:

> Oh, spare these reminiscences!
> How you prolong the pose!
> These emotional concupiscences
> Tinctured attar of rose
>   (The need for self-expression
>   Will pardon this digression).[55]

The outright accusation, apologetic parentheses, and unmeasured tone of this passage are not promising. They are exactly the kinds of extraneous gesturing of which the young author is struggling to rid himself. Once these six lines are cleanly excised—a cough that clears his throat—the resulting poem speaks in the assured voice of a major talent. He has no mentor to guide his efforts; he has been experimenting in this new style for only three months; he has a mere nine apprentice poems behind him. And yet Eliot has managed to pen an extended section of an enduring masterpiece. When this section is published five years later, the draft version will require only minor editing when it is sewn together with its other two sections. For readers of the drafts, what is remarkable is how the assured tone exists side by side with the intemperate gesturing. It is the judgment of Eliot's later editing that determines the poem as much as the creating mind that first imagines its shape.[56]

In the deleted outburst quoted above, the lines of battle are too obviously mapped out for a *guerre de salon* that is conducted subterraneously. By declaring his "need for self-expression," the speaker compromises the detached pose that the rest of the poem sustains. This detachment is thematized a few lines later:

Another bank defaulter has confessed:—
I keep my countenance—
I remain self-possessed.
Except when a street piano

The loss of self-control described in these lines is obliquely reported rather than dramatized, whereas the lady's gushing is quoted directly. The speaker's reference to his own self-control comes immediately after a bank defaulter's confession. The speaker, by contrast, has *not* confessed; he remains reserved and remote. Here, the speaker's ethos mirrors the scrupulousness of the poet's own personality.

In this poem, the Laforguean lady—seen one month earlier in "Convictions"—escapes from her two-dimensional caricature. This more convincing portrait is likely a result of Eliot's drawing not only from his emotional experiences but from social experiences as illuminated by Laforgue. Conrad Aiken has argued that the woman is based on a fixture of the Cambridge social scene: "our dear deplorable friend, Miss X, the *precieuse ridicule* to end all preciosity, serving tea so exquisitely among her bric-a-brac."[57]

Both the speaker of the poem and the lady use the pronouns "I" and "you," but to different effect. The woman's recourse to such pronouns and possessives is calculating, her repeated "I-thous" attempting to forge a relationship from which the speaker backs away: "'But what have *I*, but what have *I*, *my* friend / 'To give *you*, what can *you* receive from *me*?'"[58] By contrast to the lady's barrage of first- and second-person pronouns, the speaker relies on narration to describe himself and to address the audience. The one exception is the speaker's unrestrained exclamation, aimed (silently) at the women and later deleted: "How you prolong the pose!" Once deleted, the speaker's other references to "you" will be to the audience: "You will see me any morning in the park." Seen against the vexed references to "you" throughout the juvenilia and his own coercive attempts to wrestle "you" into shape in the November 1909 poems, the assurance of this "you" cannot be overstated. The speaker's questions are likewise aimed at this intimate "you": "How can I make a cowardly amends / For what she has said to me?" And: "Are these ideas right or wrong?" This "you" is an audience that sympathizes with, rather than judges, the speaker's difficulties.

This chapter has tracked Eliot's increasing rhetorical sophistication, which in this phase of development has included his setting aside crude signaling in favor of understatement. He is feeling his way toward a theory he will later label "the objective correlative," which is something more than mere understatement but the conviction that, given a reliable audience, one's images are doing their intended work.[59] Relying on poetic objects rather than directing emotional traffic requires an observational strategy in place of a persuasional strategy. "Convictions" marks Eliot's crucial discovery of the observational pose as an antidote to the aggressive posturing of the November 1909 poems, all of which had clumsily sought to direct the sympathies of their audiences. "Portrait of a Lady" II continues the observational pose, its premise—set in the first nine lines—the examination of a lady's plot to ensnare the speaker's sympathies. The poem is an observation of the attempted, if unsuccessful, manipulations of someone other than the speaker. It is as if Eliot were looking backward at his previous speakers and inviting his audience to do the same: here is what sly, if ineffective, rhetorical machinations look like.

In response to the lady's accusation ("youth is cruel"), the speaker responds not with reported speech but with narration: "I smile, of course / And go on drinking tea." The speaker's response is not encased in quotation marks because these lines are addressed not to the woman but to the authorial audience of the poem. His response includes the loaded phrase "of course," which is notable not only for its conversational tone but its target: it is the first moment in the poem in which the narrator is winking at the audience. *Of course*, this is how guerilla warfare is conducted in the parlors of the well connected. This nudge signals to the readers that by observing the lady, they are in league with the speaker. This fundamental change in the speaker's relationship with his audience is an extension of the path desired in "Convictions" and attempted in "Spleen." Such a shift—from distrusted, manipulated audience to audience as confidant—is what enables the rhetorical shape of "Prufrock" and other great poems to germinate in Eliot's mind. He no longer fears the hostile judgment of his audience; rather, he can count on their sympathy, stage-managing their emotional responses with subtle maneuvers rather than overt attempts at regulation.

The rhetorical organization of this poem is more complicated than an audience overhearing a conversation between onstage actors. Instead, the audience is addressed by the speaker who is himself observing another character. The identity of the speaker is an artful welding of two separate aspects of the speakers of the apprentice poems. In "Portrait of a Lady" II, the speaker is both a stage manager (as in "Nocturne" and "Convictions") as well as a character (as in the other November 1909 poems). In a few months' time, Eliot will pen another section of the poem, whose opening lines will place the woman's too-obvious ploys in contrast with the speaker's more agile rhetorical power:

> Among the fog and smoke of a December afternoon
> You have the scene arrange itself—as it will seem to do—
> With an "I designed this afternoon for you"[60]

This later section will frame the poem as a battle of dueling stage managers. But while the lady's coercive tactics are explicit in the section composed first (part II), the stage-managing metaphor becomes explicit only later (part I). Here in part II, the rhetorical emphasis is on the speaker as stage manager *and* actor. This double role enables him to participate in two relationships. The first relationship is what criticism on the published poem has so far examined. Concentrating on voice and persona, most analyses understand the poem as a study of the vexed relationship between the speaker and the lady, drawing different conclusions as to how culpable either character is. For example, citing various critics on either side of the critical binary, Cyrena Pondrom has nicely summarized this problem and planted her flag in the middle: "Some critics have associated Eliot's sympathy with the woman, and others, often dogmatically, with the man. . . . In fact, Eliot, chameleon-like, refuses to ally the poet's views with either figure in 'Portrait' but instead offers a critique of the gender roles that each acts to the fullest, and suggests a bleak assessment of the possibility of genuine and compassionate human love."[61] Perhaps the chameleon-like nature Pondrom sees—and the critical battle to decide which character Eliot favors—are indicators of the poem's rhetorical objective, which is less to target a lady than to woo an audience by means of targeting a lady. Seen in its chronological place in the notebook and examining the hard-won rhetorical dynamic Eliot has finally achieved, another portrait emerges. After three months of trial and error, Eliot has drafted a poem that enacts the almost-solidified relationship between a persona who speaks in modulated tones and an audience who is trusted to hear and sympathize. That relationship is "almost" solidified because the outburst of lines 16–21 is the one moment in the poem in which the speaker's old audience anxieties resurface. Even read with these lines in place however, the poem stages with finesse the anxieties of a recognizably Eliotic speaker who confides in an audience. In this view, the bleakness Pondrom and others observe in the relationship between the speaker and lady is mitigated by the intimacy of the relationship that has been built between the author and his audience.

"Easter: Sensations of April" I and II
Drafted Apr.–May 1910

Whereas "First Debate between the Body and Soul" proposes the contrived oxymoron "a supersubtle peasant" to resolve momentarily the claims of the intellectual and the sensual, in "Easter: Sensations of April," Eliot summons a more believable image of the actual poor, in this case, a "little negro girl" who "repeats her little formulae of God."[62] Observing the girl's geranium brought home from Sunday school, the speaker notes that it has become desiccated. The whole of this remembrance is confined now to "the sweepings of memory." The poem is not about the contemplation of immediate or recent experience but about the haunting memory of experience.

As with the rejected passage from "Portrait of a Lady," the most telling part of "Easter: Sensations of April" is its one deleted line: "She is very sure of God." It is, as Ricks reports, a manifest borrowing from Symons's chapter on Villiers de L'Isle-Adam. The "last word of Villiers," Symons reports, "is faith"—"faith against the evidence of the senses, against the negations of materialistic science, against the monstrous paradox of progress, against his own pessimism in the face of these formidable enemies. He affirms; he 'believes in soul, is very sure of God'; requires no witness to the spiritual world of which he is always the inhabitant."[63] In Symons's analysis, Villiers pits faith against the liberal values of the nineteenth century, especially its materialist and political notions of progress. More importantly for the absorbing mind of Eliot, Villiers pits faith against the senses. In Eliot's poem about sensations, he comes up to the lip of Villiers's theology and then backs away, as if dogmatic notions—whether large, like Villiers's peculiar brand of Catholicism, or small like the girl's "little formulae"—were somehow incommensurate with the sensations of spring. It is not the task of this study to root out the theological and spiritual concerns of Eliot the proto-convert; such biographical trajectories are difficult to pinpoint, especially in such dicey contexts as poems, which are artistic representations rather than autobiography or history. But considering its source—its dogmatism, its direct signaling of the problem of faith—this deleted line provides a window into Eliot's rhetorical concerns.

Because of the unstable nature of the draft, it is unclear whether the line "She is very sure of God" was meant to be the final line. Also unclear is whether the unsatisfactory line ruined the movement of the poem or whether Eliot stopped the poem with that line, only to delete it later. Whatever the case, reconsidering the line, Eliot is not so sure. Something about its very certainty—the speaker's certainty about the girl's certainty—must have made him queasy.

The colon of the title "Easter: Sensations of April" separates rather than brings together dogma and sensation: another debate between soul and body, the abstract doctrine of Christ's resurrection and the compelling earthiness of geraniums, heat, perfume. "Easter: Sensations of April" is in an unresolved draft form, rather than a neat fair copy. And as he attempted in his failed "First Debate"—another unresolved draft—here Eliot reaches for some experience beyond his own that will resolve his contradictions: the experience of a "little negro girl" who "repeats her little formulae of God." The repetitions of "little" in reference to the girl and to her prayers suggest an attitude of baffled if gentle incomprehension on the part of the speaker. Although this attitude can be read as condescension—race, class, and gender are all operative categories in this white, haut-bourgeois male's rendering—it is Eliot's nostalgia for the elemental that determines the shape of the poem and that seeks for resolution to the body/soul, intellect/sense divide. As discussed in the first chapter, Robert Crawford has noted the contrary vectors of this nostalgia: on the one hand, a genuine fascination with alterity, and on the other hand, a source of comedy or dismissal. However, in this poem, the tone is not one of comedy, nor even a detached curiosity, but a poignant longing to resolve personal contradictions. It is this sense of lostness, the speaker's unnamed solitude and pain, that keeps Eliot's forays into the mind of the poor from being read merely as condescending slumming or exploitative curiosity—even though, paradoxically, Eliot's constructions of the other are often problematic. Here, the deletion of the line "She is very sure of God" is a capitulation to the unknowability of his subject. Whereas Villiers's published writings enable an observer to make claims about Villiers's theological certainty, Eliot realizes, belatedly, that one cannot make such assumptions of a young girl. As his studies in epistemology deepen, Eliot will explore poetically and critically what can be known, or claimed, about another and about the self. The deletion is delicately polite, an acknowledgment that binaries cannot always be sustained, that others may have their doubts too.

The first part of this poem has no number written at the top; it is only the Roman numeral II on the second poem, laid in as a loose leaf, that later connects the first poem to the second. Like the geraniums of its companion poem, the daffodils of the second part again call up sensations and memories. This time the poignancy of memory is trumped by irritation—it is a muted Laforguean rejoinder to the Baudelairean concerns of the first section. The irritation is reported rather than dramatized.

At the beginning of this chapter, I claimed that the trajectories of this phase of his writing (January–June 1910) are more difficult to track than those of November 1909. One reason for this complexity is that the problems Eliot addresses in these months are increasingly personal. While the November 1909 poems see Eliot attempting to solve various rhetorical problems, here in the new year vexed problems—of sexuality, of mind and body, of human suffering and isolation—are not merely poetic matters to be resolved with the appropriate technique. Here, in his second poem pitting the body against the soul, Eliot is not even sure of what the problem is. He is still struggling to make sense of the scope of the problem, which is why the conclusions are so forced, or deleted, and why the unfinished poems are abandoned rather than worked over for new directions.

It should be noted that the resolutions in "Portrait of a Lady" of February 1910 are coterminous with a new direction in Eliot's experimenting: his debate poems. As he looks to explore problems of personal moment, Eliot must first figure out how to modulate his voice to smooth out contradictions, allowing various modalities to exist within the same poem. And Eliot has to construct an audience who will not judge him but sympathetically hear him. The rhetorical problems that "Portrait of a Lady" finally resolves in February 1910—a modulated voice, a sympathetic audience—enable the messy, unresolved debates between body and soul to unfold.

"Silence"
Drafted June 1910

Alongside the various trajectories pursued in this chapter, there is another pattern that links the January–June 1910 poems: the expansion of the body/soul debate into different territory. This expansion is not a full resolution or even a partial one, for the debate poems continue for another year. But with "Silence," surprising new terms are added to the conflict: peace, stillness, and silence. A troubling experience—whether remembered or invented—is described in his poem "Silence." Lyndall Gordon has connected this poem to an earlier one, Eliot's January "First Debate between the Body and Soul"; that earlier poem "calls on the Absolute to rescue the soul from the 'mud of physical sense.' He was rewarded, not immediately, but six months later, by the Silence in the Boston street."[64] Like Gordon, Ronald Schuchard understands the poem as straightforward biography: he confidently declares the poem a record of "an ecstatic visionary experience."[65] The experience of "Silence" is not named as baldly as "God," for the speaker has neither theological nor philosophical "formulae," little or big, to encompass the experience. What is most significant about the poem is what it does not say. There is a striking absence of the very formula one might have expected Eliot to use in such contexts: the Absolute. That Eliot avoids this philosophical construct for naming his experience is an indication that the experience rendered in the poem exists outside of the boundaries set by the intellectual games of his philosophy courses and outside of his irony about them.

The outward forms of life are symbolized by the "garrulous waves" of passers-by who quarrel about the "thousand incidents" of their busy lives.[66] In the middle of this "sea of experience," which is figured as "broad and deep / So immediate and steep," the poet imagines it all falling away to reveal some inner calm. The portent of this peace terrifies the poet, its undeniable reality leading him to the conclusion "There is nothing else beside."

Regarding spaces and silences, Ricks draws attention to a revealing passage from Pascal's *Pensées* Eliot has marked in a book that had quoted it: "Le silence éternel de ces espaces infinis m'effraye." Eliot refers to this phrase again in his *The Use of Poetry and the Use of Criticism*, where he challenges I. A. Richards's "inconceivable immensity of the universe": "It was not, we remember, the 'immense spaces' themselves, but their *eternal silence* that terrified Pascal. With a definite religious background this is intelligible."[67] It is not that the spaces exist, Eliot recalls, but that they exist and say nothing.

Such a distinction sends us back to "Silence," in which stillness, silence, and peace are not used interchangeably: "peace" is the experience that terrifies the poet. But "Silence," which headlines the poem, announces its mute refusal, or inability, to describe the import of that tremendous experience.

This realization about his experience-beyond-sense-experience is of great moment for the speaker, but what it portends is neither articulated nor understood. As a consequence, it cannot be described as a conversion poem, as it conveys no content. But the terrifying peace is a felt experience rather than an abstract value or rational truth. In its evocation of stillness, terror, absence, and presence, the poem peers into the abyss of existential experience. Such an experience, in the course of human events, does not necessarily lead to any particular theology. In another artist, it might be described as a psychological maturing, a recognition of the void at the root of the human condition. And such a secular import may be what the twenty-one-year-old author intended.

While this may be the young poet's intention, an older Eliot will also claim, famously, "We had the experience but missed the meaning."[68] And Eliot's post-conversion poetry will take similar, equivocal if freighted experiences as his starting point. Gordon gives "Silence" particular weight in her account of Eliot's spiritual development. She argues that Eliot had an actual experience

> which, [Eliot] said, many have once or twice in their lives and are unable to put into words. "You may call it communion with the Divine or you may call it temporary crystallization of the mind," he said on another occasion. . . . For some, such a moment is part of an orthodox religious life, for others—like Emerson—it is terminal, sufficient in itself, and gratefully received. For Eliot, though, the memory was to remain as a tantalising reminder of an experience beyond his grasp.[69]

Gordon contends that Eliot was at first not conscious of the religious implications of the silence, only that it was opposed to the world of ordinary sense experience: "The revelation in the spring of 1910, at the age of twenty-one, had no immediate repercussions but remained the defining experience of his life."[70] Whether this unpublished poem can be made to bear such determined biographical weight, there are a number of factors that support Gordon's conclusion: first, as I have said, "Silence" eschews familiar philosophical concepts in describing the experience. Second, the poem comes directly on the heels of "Easter: Sensations of April," which hesitantly evokes "God." Third, Eliot's post-conversion poetry will follow the pattern set by "Silence," contrasting the "twittering world" with states of simplicity and surrender, still points and hidden realities.[71]

That "Silence" is so tight lipped about its meaning is a consequence of the contexts Eliot had at his disposal—familial, religious, cultural, and philosophical—none of which were adequate to the description or interpretation of such an experience. Reflecting on the religion of his childhood, an older Eliot grumbled, "In the Puritan morality that I remember, it was tacitly assumed that if one was thrifty, enterprising, intelligent, practical, and prudent in not violating social conventions, one ought to have a happy and 'successful' life. Failure was due to some weakness or perversity peculiar to the individual; but the decent man need have no nightmares."[72] Peter Ackroyd has described Eliot's childhood religion of Unitarianism as "Puritanism drained of its theology."[73] In this description, we see an older Eliot's contempt for it: the narrowness of its cheerful, duty-bound ethos and its blindness to darker realities. Eliot's rejection of such vacuous pieties had been evident since well before his conversion in 1927. However, it was not until the publication of *Inventions of the March Hare* in 1996 that we have been able to track how the young poet was striving for a feeling and language of God that went beyond the civic obligation and moral rectitude that were the standard conceptual markers of the Boston Brahmin class. Starting in 1910, these poems reveal how Eliot began to feel his way toward an articulation of the numinous that went beyond the clichés of his lukewarm Unitarianism. It is yet another trajectory begun in this phase of his writing, and again, its forward momentum depends upon the satisfactory rhetorical resolutions achieved by February 1910. The young, careful author needs to invent a sympathetic audience before he can explore such forbidding territory.

That sympathetic audience is put to a crucial test in "Silence," for it is not only a numinous presence that troubles the speaker but an auditing presence that threatens the speaker's confidence, a doubting "You" who suddenly appears in the antepenultimate line:

> You may say what you will,
> At such peace I am terrified.
> There is nothing else beside.

A skeptic who "may" controvert such an experience, this "You" is at least partly a projection of the restrictions of class, culture, and education that hamper a frank description of the numinous. Here also, Eliot's Harvard context presses in close: the agnostic, intellectual milieu that scorned fundamentalist naiveté proffers a formidable "you" indeed. Despite these skeptical contexts, the "you" of "Silence" is no enemy. By addressing this audience directly—a "you" he has begun to trust since "Portrait"—Eliot asserts more imaginative control over his authorial audience. He insists to his audience's face on the primacy of his own experience over social expectations. Unlike the previous "yous" of the juvenilia and of the early sections of the notebook, this "you" is not a feared cynic who must be defensively preempted but a skeptic whose incomprehension is both politely acknowledged ("You may say what you will") as well as gently challenged. It is a "you" that exists on the halfway mark between the domineering audiences of his juvenilia and the nearly trusted confidant to whom "Prufrock" is addressed. As we have seen many times in the notebook, an improvement in rhetorical style coincides with a maturation in judgment.

"Ode" ("For the hour that is left us fair Harvard, with thee") *Published in Harvard Class Day program of events, June 24, 1910, and simultaneously in* Harvard Advocate, Boston Evening Transcript, *and* Boston Evening Herald

Wrestling inwardly with the terrors of experience, the troubling propulsions of sexuality, and the vertiginous divide between body and soul, the young author wisely sequesters such problems and capitulates to the needs of his public audience on graduation day. Composed in the same month as the unpublished "Silence," the sentimentality of this class ode is jarring. The poem gallops along in anapests, heedless of the ideas that its author clearly does not believe:

> For the hour that is left us Fair Harvard, with thee,
>   Ere we face the importunate years,
> In thy shadow we wait, while thy presence dispels
>   Our vain hesitations and fears.[74]

The institution of Fair Harvard, whatever its glories, can hardly mollify the "hesitations and fears" that his private poems have been exploring. Unlike his Smith Academy graduation ode, however, which grinds on for fourteen stanzas, this farewell is mercifully short. It is a thoroughly traditional poem in the style of late Victoriana, even its use of "thee" and "thine" signaling nineteenth-century formality rather than sixteenth-century intimacy. Churning on anapestic rhythms and ballad form, the poem avoids any ideas other than nostalgia and gratitude. All the signs point to the fact that this public poem is a command performance—the last one, thankfully—of the good-boy ethos that was the hallmark of Eliot's juvenilia.

With the composition of his graduation "Ode" in June, Eliot is only eight months into his apprenticeship. In spite of immense gains in intellectual range, voice, and audience, he predictably reverts to a safer style for this moment of public commemoration. We finally hear the last gasp of the juvenilia in his Harvard "Ode": the stagey "we," the anapestic thumping, the avoidance of challenging subject matter. As with the soon to be deleted burp in "Portrait of a Lady" II, such problems are no longer crippling issues in need of resolution but the residue of old habits that can be swept away. Eliot's poetry now moves forward with increasing confidence, tackling the most vexed problems of his intellect, deploying a modulated voice that shifts fluently among modes, and addressing a trusted audience that follows his own widening compass.

He has become T. S. Eliot.

CHAPTER FOUR

Raising the Voice

The Sequence Poems of Fall 1910

> The imperative intimacy [with another author] arouses for the first time a real, an unshakeable confidence.
>
> —T. S. Eliot, "Reflections on Contemporary Poetry [IV]"

He has become T. S. Eliot. And, of course, he is still in the process of becoming T. S. Eliot.[1]

It would be imprudent to draw exact inferences between Eliot's public graduation and his poetic maturation. Nevertheless, the public reception of a diploma does coincide with the private assertion of authority, the professional identity of a master's degree with the vocational identity of poet. The problem with these simultaneously maturing identities is that rather than being complementary, they are in conflict. They present Eliot with a choice. And by choosing to go to France rather than graduate school, he opts for his vocational identity as a poet.

Leaving Boston behind is a subtext of Eliot's 1910 poems, which Lyndall Gordon describes as "mostly rejections of family and Boston life."[2] That Eliot conceived of his Paris year as an escape rather than as a basis for scholarly study helps to contextualize such rejections as preparations for something new, a sifting through and clearing out of old allegiances in a manner that is different from the social critiques leveled in his November 1909 poems. His momentous decision to chart his own course, even as it deviated from his parents' expectations, must have taken its toll: in May 1910, one month before graduation, Eliot contracted scarlet fever, and his mother hurried to Boston to be with him.

Eliot spoke of his possession by Laforgue as giving him an "unshakeable confidence."[3] This description is worth attending to, for we should not underestimate the strength of character required to buck the pressures of such a proud inheritance, especially since Eliot was tied by bonds of filial piety to his family. The emotional coloration of the phrase "unshakeable confidence" refers not only to the authority Laforgue has given him to write but to the courage to claim a personal and vocational identity in the face of resistance. Although his later assessment of Laforgue's poetry will become critical, throughout Eliot's life his emotional debt to Laforgue remains one of gratitude. Critics who describe Laforgue's influence on Eliot as primarily stylistic—one of many masks tried on and adapted—do not give adequate weight to the strains that attend Eliot's maturing, both as a young man and as a writer. The poetic authority he has claimed, largely through his appropriation of Laforgue and Baudelaire, has more at stake than a play with voices or technical range. Its broader consequences license a steely will and a poet's identity that will eventually lead him far away from his narrow compass. At this point in his life, Eliot does not see himself as a trailblazer or iconoclast. He is a young man whose ambition for writing poetry has been quickened and who recognizes that the tensions between this determination and his family's expectations have become unignorable. While the poems of his leather-bound notebook are unpublished and unseen, their consequences are no longer private.

However disguised, some trace of the pain that this quarrel must have caused his mother can be detected in her letter of protest. Her objections of maternal solicitude can be heard clearly enough: "I cannot bear to think of your being alone in Paris, the very words give me a chill. English speaking countries seem so different from foreign. I do not admire the French nation, and have less confidence in individuals of that race than in English." Another worry—that her son's stand is a kind of rejection—is more muted. Of all the arguments Eliot presented to his parents, one of them must have been that a year in France would allow him to ferret out the "particular genius" of its people and culture. Conscious of her own lack of education, Charlotte Eliot responds with wounded pride, throwing her son's words back at him in disapproving scare quotes, "I suppose I am not enough of a scholar to know what is termed the 'particular genius' of any people."[4] Eliot's request to spend a year abroad causes a small rift in the normally affectionate exchange between mother and son. Perhaps she has intuited that a year in France is more than just a yes to poetry and a no to philosophy, because for the first time in his life, her son declines the part of obedient boy capitulating to his parents' expectations or concerns.[5]

Breathing Deeply

One breathes deeply when one is relieved or when one wants to recite a long passage with authority. Now that Eliot has claimed an authoritative, multivalent voice, the next task is to deploy the voice in longer passages and more complex ideas. The hallmark of the poems written in the fall of 1910 is the sequence: poems whose ideas are lengthened via sectional variations. Of the fourteen poems Eliot composes in this period, all are parts of a sequence or a larger whole.[6] Like a singer whose control of breath permits long-limbed lines or an orator pacing elaborate phrases, Eliot begins to extend his thought, inventing in deeper breaths, with more variations on an idea.

Two poems from the previous year seem to point to an affinity with the sequence form: "First Caprice in North Cambridge" and "Second Caprice in North Cambridge." As discussed in chapter 2, these inventions are not sequence poems in the same sense that he now uses the form. Insofar as "Second Caprice" tries awkwardly to fix the rhetorical problems discovered in "First Caprice," the second poem is less a variation than a mulligan. By contrast, the sequence poems of late 1910 are planned as distinct variations on a theme. His only other attempt at the sequence form so far has been the tremulous, unfinished poems of "Easter: Sensations of April."

The sequence poem is the form of all of Eliot's most significant mature poetry. "The Love Song of J. Alfred Prufrock" is the only exception to this rule—though even that long monologue is structured in distinctive sections, some of them set off with asterisks. With his lyric sensibility, Eliot discovers at this stage of development that the sequence allows him to maintain his lyric stance. He can invent in longer periods without having to turn to epic, discursive, narrative, or dramatic modes.

"Neat, Complete": The Whole (Rather Than the Part)

One concept that brings together the upper-class elders of the "Mandarins" sequence, the debutantes and suitors of "Goldfish," and the vaudevillians of "Suite Clownesque" is the idea of completeness. As Ricks notes, Eliot's use of "complete" is Shakespearian, meaning perfect or accomplished. The word "complete" appears in each of these three sequences, and variations of it abound: "fixed," "assuring certainties," "eternal truths," "Infinite," "real," "absolute," "self-embodied," "Concentred."[7] Against this system of completeness pushes a hazy congeries of ideas: "shifting," "uncertain," "hesitate," "accident," "fears," "shadow," "Inconsequent." The two lists presented here do not function as synonyms and antonyms so much as two realms that exist in tension with each other. Some words, such as "interrogate" and "fate," seem to straddle both.

In "Mandarins," "Goldfish," and "Suite Clownesque," there is an element of nostalgia for those who appear to have achieved completeness. Completeness and certainty—contending with partiality and uncertainty—are either ideals that are longed for or illusions that are mocked. For Eliot the young philosopher-artist, both philosophy and aesthetics make nominal, unconvincing appearances in these three sequences. Philosophy and art both purport to identify completeness, but Eliot the comedian-skeptic sees through such claims and explores that gap in these poems.

Notably, all characters gesturing at completeness are associated with roles. In "Mandarins," the role is aristocracy—those who look without seeing, a superior obliviousness. In "Goldfish," the role is the theater of courtship—lover and beloved. And in "Suite Clownesque," the roles are the personages of vaudeville—comedian, singer, actor, dancer.

"Scattered Thoughts": The Part (Rather Than the Whole)

The unpublished sequence poems discussed above—"Mandarins," "Goldfish," "Suite Clownesque"—track one path Eliot takes, and these explorations of the "Neat, complete" are written before his departure for Paris. An opposing track Eliot pursues in this period involves a theme he had sounded in his first experiments of 1909: the partial and fragmentary. At this point in the notebook's chronology, these explorations of the fragmentary are themselves fragments: the Hamlet section of "Prufrock" and "Preludes" I and II. Later fitted into longer sequences, these verses offer such material as detritus, debris, scattered images and thoughts. Fragmentation, both as theme and technique, is on display in these not yet complete (though eventually published) poems, whereas the contrasting topos of completeness is worked out in the completed (though never published) sequence poems. All of these images of the fragmentary have been reclaimed from his "Caprice" poems of a year earlier and are now set in a broader context.

The images of partiality, debris, and fragmentation that appear in these poems are authentic if incoherent. They are objects rather than human characters. Not until "Prufrock" will Eliot manage to address the theme of completeness while simultaneously casting his eye on the fragmentary—all done through the medium of a human character's consciousness, rather than a camera's eye. But that feat is still on the horizon. Here in the fall of 1910, such problems remain unresolved and account for why only those poems that explore the fragmentary (the Hamlet section of "Prufrock," "Preludes" I and II) are published, while those sequences that attempt to understand the whole ("Mandarins," "Suite Clownesque," "Goldfish") are never published.[8] It is because the fragmentary is more convincing, while the complete is incomprehensible, for Eliot can find no metaphysical or epistemological ground from which the whole can be surveyed. With some ambivalence, Eliot positions himself with diffident fragments, distancing himself from abstract certitudes: "Between the theoretic seas / And your assuring certainties / I have my fears."[9]

Vox Populi

How does he dispel those fears? By launching himself "for some Hesperides / Of street pianos and small beers!"[10] It is popular culture—the genial occupations of drinking, strolling, street pianos, vaudeville shows—that explodes, rather than resolves, the philosophical questions described above. The doorway to popular culture cracked open by the slang and popular references of "Ballade of the Fox Dinner" (1909) and "Humouresque" (1909) is flung open wide in this period. Conrad Aiken describes his Harvard days with Eliot as "perhaps the most creative period of American slang," inventions in which Eliot "took enormous pleasure."[11] It is strange that slang—exuberantly deployed in "Ballade of the Fox Dinner" and more carefully cordoned off in "Humouresque"—should start up again during this phase, because the immediately preceding experiments had seen Eliot toying with boundaries of informality but stopping short of slang's coarseness. Perhaps the renewed interest is due to the effects of finally commanding a coherent voice with varied textures and timbres. As a result of this consolidation, Eliot can push the boundaries of the voice even further with the vigor of contemporary slang.

While these sequence poems of late 1910 do not represent Eliot's first turn to the popular, they do mark his unabashed exploration of the territory for serious artistic ends. The more explicit turn to the popular might be explained by Eliot's recognition of philosophy as a cul-de-sac. We have seen how his decision to go to France is a rejection (a temporary one, it turns out) of philosophy. Popular culture presents another avenue to explore—a different destination rather than a resolution. If these speculations explain why the popular is licensed in this period, then a related question remains: Why is the popular ultimately suppressed? For the poems that explore the partial are the ones that are published; the three sequences that explore completeness and that mobilize popular discourse are left in the privacy of the notebook. One reason for not publishing the "complete" sequences is that they are not as artistically convincing as the "fragmentary" poems. Another reason for burying these poems is that Eliot may fear that the presence of popular culture risks trivializing the philosophical problems explored there. Eliot's increasing dexterity with serious literary voices has validated his literary ambitions, and so the role of the popular as an explicit source is not yet to be trusted for this genteel son of Tradition.

Later in his life, Eliot will embrace the role of "popular entertainer," but only after he has succeeded as an avant-garde poet. We would have had a radically different view of Eliot—who for much of the twentieth century was known as the high priest of high art—if these early sequences had been published.[12] Some of his earliest poems that he did choose to publish engage with popular culture: Eliot's first readers sensed the rhythms of ragtime in several poems, heard the contemporary slang of "Humouresque," and noted the speaker of "Portrait of a Lady" reading "the comics and the sporting page."[13] But it is not until ten years later, in drafts of *The Waste Land*, that Eliot deploys the popular for more deliberate effect, and even that poem's uses of popular culture are themselves muted. In Eliot's and Pound's editorial interventions, *The Waste Land* is given the same treatment as these early poems: much of the rough, the vulgar, the popular, and the American are edited out, while the literary, the serious, and the European are played up. In the notebook poems we have evidence of this process, the first instance of how Eliot starts with some subterranean inspiration for a poem, some "acute personal reminiscence"[14] or a lively, rough wellspring that is ultimately edited out once the poem nears completion or publication. Eliot's penchant for universalizing has always existed in productive tension with the roots of his experience.

An Audience in Suspense

In the poems of fall 1910, the stock situations of vaudeville are used yet again but to different effect than in "Convictions (Curtain Raiser)" of earlier in the year. "Suite Clownesque" (Oct. 1910) provides a useful measuring stick for gauging the progress of how Eliot imagines his audiences. In the first section of the poem, whose setting is a vaudeville stage, the people in the auditorium (the audience in the poem) are described as a group "Who still continue in suspense // Who are so many entities / Inside a ring of lights!"[15] Unlike the undifferentiated horde of "Convictions," this later audience of "so many entities" is played to without disdain by the author. It is a neutral audience in the poem, something halfway between an anti-audience whose ideology the author rejects and an authorial audience whose expectations define an ideal audience. This invention of a neutral audience is an important advance in his mastery of rhetoric during this time frame. By bridging the gap between hostile, unmovable audiences who misunderstand his work and ideal audiences who meet the author's expectations at every turn, Eliot has imagined an audience that does not hold his expectations but that is yet persuadable, one that can be moved from the neutral to the authorial position. This audience "in suspense" is suspended between the two incompatible constructions of audience between which Eliot has been flipping. By positing this middle way, the author has achieved not exactly a eureka moment but a small addition to his rhetorical arsenal. This neutral audience is less important than his discovery of a friendly authorial audience, but it allows him to mediate between two poles that had, as of yet, seen none of each other and whose bare hostility had all the markings of an amateur writer.

The following audience typology is gradually coming into focus in Eliot's work:

Audience in the poem: These audiences are always described, evoked, or addressed by the speaker. Up to this point in Eliot's development, the audience in the poem has been either hostile (the sentimental "female readers" of "Nocturne," the female addressee of "Conversation Galante") or skeptical (the "You" from "Silence"). These hostile or skeptical "anti-audiences" had always been differentiated from the kinds of ideal audiences Eliot imagines. But "Suite Clownesque" adds another kind of audience in the poem to Eliot's rhetorical bag of tricks: a neutral and even friendly audience evoked or addressed by the speaker.

Audience of the poem: These are the audiences conceived by the author, the readers whom the poem imagines and constructs. Up to this point, I have named them "authorial audiences," which is something close to what Wayne Booth might call an implied reader.[16] I will continue to call them "authorial audiences," but Eliot's growing rhetorical skill calls for a more nuanced vocabulary in describing their variety. These authorial audiences can range on a continuum from hostile to skeptical, to neutral, to friendly. Months earlier, in a single poem, "Nocturne," Eliot made a stark contrast between a hostile audience in the poem (the "female readers" with their sentimental expectations) and the hostile audience of the poem (the authorial audience who sarcastically dismisses those female readers). This hostile audience of the poem is in tune with the author's own caustic attitudes. But, as discussed in chapter 2, the poem's divisive contrasts, while freeing Eliot from suffocating gentility, soon reveal limitations. Since that early poem, we have seen Eliot slowly broaden his notions of audience. In "Silence," for example, the skeptical audience in the poem ("You") is suspicious of—though not hostile to—transcendent intimations, while the audience of the poem is more accepting, the readership to whom the poem is addressed.

The second person serves as a barometer of Eliot's conception of audience, and this "you" often straddles the audience in the poem and the audience of the poem. Up to this point, the clearest example of a friendly audience of the poem has been found in "Portrait of a Lady" II (Feb. 1910): "You will see me any morning in the park."[17] And in the fall of 1910, we get several more versions of a "you" who is not hostile. How a "you" in a published poem is understood is a complicated matter. When readers come across a "you" in a private note addressed to them by a friend, the "you" is equivalent to the reading self, presuming no complicating factors intervene. But a "you" in a published poem (or the draft of an eventually published poem) is another matter. The clearest "you" is one specified by the text as a particular character, such as in the Browning monologues whose addressees are fully realized, fictional creations to whom their speakers respond and whom they manipulate or are manipulated by. This "you" is a character, whom the authorial reader observes while the speaker addresses him or her. However, when a reader comes across a "you" in a poem that is not specified in this way—especially a "you" that is implicitly singular—there are a range of readerly responses. On one end of the continuum, the reader perceives the "you" as an artificial construct, some persona projected by the poem distinct from the breathing, living reader. On the other end of the continuum, the reader responds to the "you" as to an address, imagining the reading self as coterminous in some way (if not equivalent) with the "you" projected by the text. The "you" blends the neutral audience in the poem with the friendly audience of the poem, finally bridging the gap that Eliot has been working to close since "Nocturne."

The Poems

Poems spanning Aug.–Oct. 1910 (Eliot turns twenty-two years old, just before his move to Paris)

Hamlet section of "Prufrock"	drafted before Oct. 1910
"Mandarins" 1–4	drafted Aug. 1910
"Goldfish (Essence of Summer Magazines)" I–IV	drafted Sept. 1910
"Preludes" I and II	drafted Oct. 1910
"Suite Clownesque" I–IV	drafted Oct. 1910

Hamlet Section of "The Love Song of J. Alfred Prufrock" Drafted sometime before Eliot's departure for Paris in Oct. 1910

Besides the Hamlet passage, other unidentified fragments of "Prufrock" were possibly drafted before Eliot sailed for France. Eliot describes the composition of its earliest parts in a letter to John Pope:

> The poem of Prufrock was conceived some time in 1910. I think that when I went to Paris in the autumn of that year I had already written several fragments which were ultimately embodied in the poem, but I cannot at this distance remember which. I think that the passage beginning "I am not Prince Hamlet," a passage showing the influence of Laforgue, was one of these fragments which I took with me [to Paris], but the poem was not completed until the summer of 1911.[18]

Eliot's conjecture about the Hamlet stanza's date of composition is buttressed by correspondence between Pound and Harriet Monroe around the time of the poem's publication. The Pound-Monroe correspondence not only helps us to date one of the earliest fragments of the "Prufrock," it also illuminates the precarious, in-between status of those lines. By focusing our attention on the weakest point of a poem that has long been universally admired, we can peek inside its temporal construction to see how Eliot is slowly ratcheting up his skill level.

In their negotiations, Pound defends the poem against Monroe's uneasiness, with the Hamlet passage and the closing stanzas the focus of contention:

> Now as to Eliot: "Mr. Prufrock" does not "go off at the end." It is a portrait of failure, or of a character which fails, and it would be false art to make it end on a note of triumph. I dislike the paragraph about Hamlet, but it is an early and cherished bit and T. E. won't give it up, and as it is the only portion of the poem that most readers will like at first reading, I don't see that it will do much harm.
>
> For the rest: a portrait satire on futility can't end by turning that quintessence of futility, Mr. P. into a reformed character breathing out fire and ozone.[19]

Without Monroe's side of the correspondence, it is difficult to reconstruct exactly what her objections were. That she disliked the futility expressed in the conclusion is probable enough. And Pound's scare quotes—that the poem seems to "go off at the end"—read as a direct reference to her letter. Another view of Monroe's objections is proffered by John Gould Fletcher, who describes the maneuverings between the antagonists. Writing to Amy Lowell on December 22, 1914, Fletcher recounts that Monroe "had written EP saying that ['Prufrock'] was too much like 'Henry James carried to the Nth degree' and had received the usual insulting note in reply. She got frightened and intends probably to print it."[20] Whatever Monroe's reservations about Hamlet or Henry James, it is not likely that she wished the poem to "end on a note of triumph," in Pound's fulminating phrase.

Fletcher provides another illuminating account of the poem before it saw print. Although he shared some of Monroe's objections, he had encouraged her to publish the poem.[21] Writing to Amy Lowell, Fletcher recounts, "[Monroe] also showed me another thing ['Prufrock'] by Pound's latest discovery, T. S. Eliot, which was very, very Huefferish, and trailed off badly towards the conclusion. . . . I told her that I thought it fairly good."[22] It is revealing that the poem's earliest readers—Monroe, Pound, and Fletcher—either complain about the poem's conclusion or remark on the awkwardness of the Hamlet passage. Even Eliot recalls that section as derivative. Later criticism, however, tends to hear the Hamlet section as coherent with the rest of the poem and the final lines as its musical, apt conclusion. Once we reexamine the composition history of the poem and observe the stopgap solutions with which Eliot ventures to pull the uneven sections together, we will come closer to recapturing this provisional feel of the poem's formal structure.

Although this passage begins with a negation ("No! I am not Hamlet"), the exclamation sets the speaker not so much in opposition to Hamlet—Prufrock is a member of the royal court—as in ambivalent relationship to the kind of audience he seeks. On the one hand, he is part of the onstage crowd, willing to "swell a progress." Yet as a "Fool," he claims a role that is uniquely distant from both the mandarin court and the rabble. The Shakespearean fool speaks most directly to the authorial audience's sense of what needs to be said to a deluded protagonist. It is a serendipitous discovery, this fool figure. It clarifies Eliot's concept of audience and gives him a role that is both self-consciously acted and directly communicative.

If "Spleen," published in January 1910, is the first, clumsy draft of "Prufrock," then the Hamlet section, written some months later, functions as a stepping-stone to the finished poem. As suggested in the previous chapter, the rhetoric of "Spleen" fails in the inability of its lyric "I" to lay claim to the identity of a balding, dithering misfit. By drafting a section that begins with negation ("No!") and that continues by defining a "ridiculous" character, Eliot is sketching the contours of Prufrock's rhetorical situation: how he imagines himself relating to—and partly rejecting—his audience's expectations. If the Hamlet section is weak, as its first readers were inclined to think, it is not because it is derivative of Laforgue. As Pound intimated, that "early and cherished bit"—so essential for Eliot's conception of the poem—is redundant in the finished work. The stanza of Prufrock-as-not-Hamlet names too directly what the rest of the poem dramatizes indirectly.

"Mandarins" 1–4
Drafted Aug. 1910

As a whole, the "Mandarins" sequence explores the ideology of superiority that infuses Boston Brahmin culture. The term "mandarin" evokes a pompous officialdom that is obscure or out of reach, and "mandarinism" connotes Byron's "type of cultivated indifference."[23] The mandarins of this sequence seem to be a variation on Eliot's marionettes. And so, as with stock situations of the marionette stage—mooning lovers, wilting females, and inane philosophers—here Eliot turns his attention to objectifying his social milieu on another stage.[24]

Part I concerns an "indifferent" mandarin who does not condescend to the temptations of popularity. Dispassionate and vacant, he serves only "his own intrepid dignity."[25] The misalignment of that phrase—dignity cannot be intrepid, though actions, persons, and intentions may be—points to Eliot's inability to decide whether this particular mandarin is to be scorned or praised, an indecision that fractures the poem. The speaker calls him "A hero!" but given the title of the sequence and the character's stiff pomposity, the appellation sits uneasily.

The published version of "Humouresque" also designates an ambiguous figure "A hero!"—the repeated exclamation mark linking the two characters. This figure of the saluted hero, ambivalently acclaimed, recurs in Eliot's early work because it galvanizes his ideas about identity and audience. The heroes of both "Humouresque" and "Mandarins" 1 are exalted above a crowd. Their heroism consists in an integrity that is "Indifferent to all these baits / Of popular benignity." The Hamlet passage of Prufrock likewise sets itself in ambivalent, exclamatory relationship to a hero: "No! I am not Hamlet"—(the title of "Prince" added later). As with the "mad poetics" of the previous year's "Conversation Galante," in "Mandarins" Eliot continues to theorize an aesthetic of the difficult, setting his teeth against some future, uncomprehending public. Such a benighted audience serves Eliot's imagination in much the same way that, a year earlier, the tradition of Boston Puritanism had served him: as a negative commonplace with which to contrast his target audience. This is *not* my audience, the young Eliot insists—but such an anti-audience implies no positively constructed authorial audience.

Eliot's critique of the anti-audience in "Mandarins" 1 is not simply a repetition of the gestures of "Conversation Galante," in which a female companion is rejected for trying to confute his "mad poetics." In terms of audience construction, the advance of "Mandarins" is that Eliot here clarifies an insight for himself and for his dimly grasped audience that by rejecting the genteel tradition of his forbears, he is not thereby seeking popular fame. Such an ambition would be vulgar, and there are some elements of his upbringing to which Eliot still clings. Thus, it is too easy to conclude that the poems of 1910 are merely rejections of family and tradition. Rather, they are a sifting of allegiances, some of which are rejected, while others are turned to his own purposes.

The final line of "Mandarins" 1 calls attention to the theatricality of the mandarin's stance: "The rest is merely shifting scenes." The mandarin's statuesque isolation from his audience is staged after all: "merely" the trickery of official costume and heroic pose. As with so many of the notebook poems, Eliot gains traction by observing the ineffective posturing of others. The ambiguity of the poem resides in Eliot's skewering the mandarin pose at the same time that he paradoxically adapts a mandarin aloofness to deflect charges of fame seeking. He is a "hero!" who is simultaneously undercut—the exclamation point an ambiguous cross between a smirk and a cry. This irresolution accounts for why the poem reads like an unsettled hybrid of Laforgue—who mercilessly flays Romantic notions of heroism—and Eliot's later *Coriolan* poems, which sympathetically explore the contradictions of political power and heroic ambition as they play out before a capricious populace.

The second poem in the sequence, a satire of overrefinement, is less ambiguous. It hits its target more squarely because Eliot's own artistic identity is not twined with the object of critique: two snobbish ladies, another mandarin type. The first stanza refers to the nonverbal etiquette by which the speaker cues his ability to interpret the scene. First, the ladies' seniority is remarked in the delicate social register "of uncertain age"—with a knowing wink to the common expression. Their age is not spoken, and neither is vulgar gossip. By reminding us archly of what is not said—"(No persiflage!)"—

the speaker points to a context in which lightly contemptuous badinage might be expected from cultivated peers.

Himself a master of these ideological nuances—what is known but not said—the speaker guesses that "By attitude / It would seem that they approve / The abstract sunset (rich, not crude)." The speaker's careful "It would seem" mirrors that cautious, mandarin judgment the ladies apply to the sunset: they applaud the natural phenomenon as if it were a painting. Sunsets, in such an ideology, have a tendency to Romantic lushness, an excessiveness the ladies would by their class and education be expected to deplore. Although it has gained their approval for being so "abstract," the sunset still is dangerously "rich," though not so overstated as to be "crude"—the qualified refinements of their aesthetic judgment. Nor is oversaturated realism to be found in this drawing room; the ladies' gowns are as abstract as the sunset. Their dresses, with "outlines delicate and hard," intertwine in "patterns [that] move / From the shoulder to the floor." In this two-dimensional cubism, the body part of shoulder is nailed to the floor.

In the section's final lines, the rhetoric and the grammar converge in an abstract effect: "You have the other raise / A thin translucent porcelain, / Murmurs a word of praise." The unprepared turn to an addressee ("You") pulls in the reader, who had previously been listening to the lyric voice but is now suddenly implicated in staging the undramatic drama of the parlor. Like the dresses zigzagging to the floor, the second-person grammar of "You have" bends in cubist fashion to the third person without signaling the shift. The confusion between "You have" and the implied "[she] Murmurs" is a throwback to the distinctive opening line of "Mandarins" 1: "Stands there, complete"—a completeness that is implied rather than given. This grammatical uncertainty serves the evocative rhetoric of the poem.

As with the first two sections of "Mandarins," part 3 stages the regarding gaze of an audience. The object of study is a fat, self-regarding mandarin. Rather than looking out toward the world, he inspects "the corner of his nose." This mandarin is in turn regarded by the ornamental cranes on a screen who—in contrast to his sober, intellectual laziness—are very non-mandarin: "pert, alert," and "frivolous." The obese mandarin takes no notice of the cranes noticing him or of the authorial audience noticing both him and the cranes. Like the mandarin of part 1, he is an "indifferent idealist" who envelops the universe in the smallness of his "fist." By contrasting the cranes' impertinence with the mandarin's indifference, Eliot seems to be testing moral attitudes toward the world as well as critiquing the condescension such moral views can imply: it is hard to gauge whether the cranes' "frivolous" nature is better than the mandarin's "World in fist."

The section ends with deflating exclamations that steer clear of judgment: "And what of all that one has missed! / And how life goes on different planes!" This mandarin has "missed" much because his narrow world encompasses only those bits of scenery in which he stages his repose. For the authorial audience, this mini–theater piece "goes on different planes": the cranes exist on a literal, two-dimensional "plane" (the screen). But the thinness of this "obese" mandarin's life is also observed on another plane, by the speaker and the authorial audience. Hence all of the angles of regarding, observing, and judging to be found in "Mandarins": the meta-observation that "life goes on different planes" implies that one can "miss" otherwise essential elements in the type of moral distillation in which the mandarins indulge. Compared to the condescension of his milieu, the speaker's own moral attitude is admirably refined, nearly avoiding the superior condemnation of others' superiority. The lightness of the rhetorical conception is partly indebted to that breathing space afforded by the sequence form.

The final line points to a type of observation that the young poet wants to make but that he has not yet mastered: "And how life goes on different planes!" Such a line teases us with the later poet's genius at the same time that it reveals the hollowness of this particular sequence. The later poet will become a master at exposing the different planes of existence in which we live: the tortured longings, the existential fears that are covered up by social habits and routines. But in this sequence the buried life is not exposed. Its pressures do not leak out from under a façade. As a consequence, the blithe exclamation point that ends the line strives too much for effect. Its happy clatter does not contrast with a serious underside.

In part 4, the speaker turns to his audience, offhandedly confessing that he has something else to say: "Still one more thought for pen and ink!" The nonchalance is calculated—as is that affectedly casual exclamation point—for he needs to pitch his concluding poem some notches below irony and above earnestness. The thesis of the final poem of the sequence is "How very few there are, I think / Who see their outlines on the screen." Even with that cautious mandarinism of "I think," the speaker can still remark the distressing lack of self-awareness of his fellow mandarins. They move, regardless and thoughtless, through the conventions of their social class. So the speaker shrugs, adopting the very indifference of the class he critiques. He avers that it is, after all, a good thing that these ladies and gentlemen, garbed in their ornamented gowns and smoking jackets, go for strolls amid cherry trees, their talk neither serious nor trivial. In spite of his critical distance, the speaker ends up backhandedly approving of the quintessential mandarinism of the Boston Brahmin class. The speaker's final jab manages to register one notch higher on the irony scale: "How life goes well in pink and green!"

The best balance he can strike in this moral equation is reflected in his description of the decorous reserve of the conversation: "nor intellectual nor mean," "graceful, not too gay"—which precisely names the constricted etiquette of Brahmin culture. While it shuns vulgarities and frivolity, it also avoids meaningful inquiry. The poet holds this culture up for critique, but neither can he quite escape from it. As a result, the shrug he offers in response is not entirely convincing, though it avoids high-handed moralizing in the face of realities he clearly cannot accept. Another rhetorical advance is disguised as a parenthetical aside: "I find it good / (Even if misunderstood)." Here are the seeds of a different rhetorical attitude: the idea that an audience that misunderstands is not necessarily hostile.

In this fourth poem of the sequence, there are many corrections in both pen and pencil that have been made at different times. Such vigorous emendations point to a use of the notebook for revision that is previously unseen. Messily written poems and unfinished jottings have predated "Mandarins" 4, but they appear on loose leaves laid in, not on the bound pages of the notebook. On the verge of leaving for Paris, Eliot is either quicker to place poems in the notebook before they are polished, or he has come to care less about their finality, at last content to use the notebook as a place for rethinking rather than just recording. The change in intention—from the carefully inscribed fair copies to the scrawled jumble of revision—signals another breath of relief, a giving-up of control. He allows himself to appear on the page as a writer in process.

"Goldfish (Essence of Summer Magazines)" I–IV
Drafted Sept. 1910

In the late nineteenth century, the goldfish occupied a peculiar place in the class structure of America. They were colorful, tiny fish that could be owned, cared for, and even bred for profit by the poorest of the poor, and the elaborate aquaria in which goldfish could be displayed struck a fad among the wealthiest. The goldfish connected Americans to its exotic origins in China, provided an object for an increasing domestic interest in natural history, and offered a dreamy observer a respite from practical affairs. In his 1883 book *The Goldfish and Its Systematic Culture with a View to Profit*, Hugo Mulertt describes the reasons why goldfish, for the past forty years (1843–1883), have been "tenderly cared for" by so many Americans

> merely because they are beautiful, and besides being in a sense pets, upon which to lavish much solicitude and attention, served the purpose of an animated ornament, than which is it difficult to find a more beautiful and desirable substitute. The very fact of their being denizens of a different element than that in which the most familiar domestic animals and pets live, served to surround them with a halo of fascination that prompted their admirers to expend upon them any amount of time and pains to keep them in a flourishing condition, and ever ready to be displayed before the chosen guest in the household.[26]

For Mulertt, the beauty and uselessness of goldfish—and their inhabiting a different element than mere humans and dogs—made them prized. They were "a kind of superior being."[27] As the author explains it, goldfish were easily bred but easily killed, and in need of protection from predators, as almost any other fish in the same environment would kill them. Goldfish lived in an enclosed, protected culture whose primary purpose was leisure. Describing the Chinese origins of goldfish and the exalted class to which they most belonged, the author writes, "The mandarin, in person, may sometimes be seen in the markets buying fish for his aquaria, which, indeed, are often made of carved ivory, and inlaid with gold."[28]

Goldfish were, in short, the animal kingdom's version of mandarins. And if their Chinese origin were not enough to connect Eliot's goldfish to the mandarins of his previous sequence, then Mulertt's description of the mandarin's difference from—and stilted engagement with—popular culture is sufficient to qualify Mulertt's book as a possible source for Eliot's ideas: the mandarin is "sometimes" spied "in person" in the vulgar marketplace buying a goldfish. Symbolically, goldfish represented the mandarin class, as the decorative fish were favored by them and whose fragile, behind-the-glass beauty mirrored mandarin aloofness. Yet their mass-market availability made them transcend class boundaries, since even "the deserving widow or invalid" could have a go at raising them.[29]

Which brings us back to Eliot's title: "Goldfish (Essence of Summer Magazines)." Ricks admits to some unease with the title, describing it as "enigmatic." Even without the source of Mulertt's how-to text, Ricks still manages to catch Eliot's conjunction: "There is a suggestion of the wealthy leisure class," Ricks speculates, "floating among 'summer magazines' where their essence is catered to."[30] As with the stagings and regardings that attend the "Mandarins" sequence, here goldfish in a bowl—the wealthy leisure class—are set as part of the scenery, ornamental objects of an audience's gaze. The title's awkward parentheses conjoin in a stilted way the mandarin goldfish with the commercial marketplace of popular magazines.

In part I, the hackneyed tunes of "Merry Widow" and "Chocolate Soldier" are interminable, recalling the tedious rounds of summer engagements: "So many nights and afternoons— / August, with all its faults!"[31] The ultimate meaning of such tedium is nowhere to be found. "What answer?" the speaker asks of the thrumming waltz as it "assaults / The tired Sphinx of the physical." The answer, like the Sphinx, is inscrutable.

The final stanza returns to the waltzes that "Float and fall"—an image that recalls the leisured, ornamental goldfish of the title, here turned more sharply to evoke a waltz's weaving and bobbing: "Like the cigarettes / Of our marionettes." The reappearance of marionettes not only links the poem to Eliot's (and Laforgue's) other poems that lampoon mindless social ritual but to the other mandarins, clowns, and vaudevillians that populate the sequence poems of 1910. The bizarre spectacle of smoking marionettes—combining sophistication and playfulness—is encoded as not the speaker's own but "*our* marionettes." Likewise, the answer asked of the Sphinx is one that "We" are unable to make out. The "Goldfish" sequence, in its welter of first- and second-person pronouns, will propose variations on the speaker-audience relationship. By contrast, the previous sequence has only the single appearance of "You"—deployed in cubist, rather than rhetorical, fashion. But here in "Goldfish," the second-person plural is casually dropped in—there is no staged shift to "you," as in "Mandarins." This appearance of "We," rather than calling attention to its construction of audience, quietly confirms what has been implicit since the beginning of the poem: the assumption that the audience is in close agreement with the speaker.

The final line dismisses the superficiality of the whole scene as "Inconsequent, intolerable." The first word is nicely judged: the assured "Inconsequent," rather than the predictable "inconsequential." The scene is not just tedious but unendurable—to the speaker as well as the audience. The balanced if compromised shrug that had concluded the earlier "Mandarins" sequence is no longer acceptable, and Eliot's new sequence signals an intention to query more aggressively the problem of the individual caught in meaningless social ritual.

The second poem of this sequence rehearses a different attitude. Rather than disgust, a clamorous jollity is the keynote of the poem. Hailing his addressees directly as "Ladies," the poet calls to them on a moonlit night as they organize an outing, armed with "sandwiches and ginger beer." The title of this section—"Embarquement pour Cythère"—refers to the destination that this group of high-living dandies seeks out in a small touring boat. That a Greek island famous for its status as the crossroads of the Mediterranean is their destination is as nonsensical as the idea that the touring party would need to return eventually. Their cigarettes are lit, as in an Edward Lear sketch, "at the evening star," the image collapsing the grand canopy of stars with their smaller world of glowing butt ends. Since the frivolous revelers have no need to return from their voyage, the poet asks, "why should we not proceed . . . // To porcelain land, what avatar[.]" Eliot's use of "avatar"—as the incarnation of a deity, a soul, or an idea—here bears the weight of both religion and philosophy. The incarnation of this porcelain land manifests its "law" as "blue-delft-romance." This scene is dismissed with the final line: "Philosophy through a paper straw!"—the disgust coded as flippancy.

The third poem rejects both disgust and flippancy as inadequate responses to the "intolerable," trying instead to force a way through the thickets of trivial custom to something more meaningful. But the poem's solution is a slippery, ambiguous "ideal." The first stanza evokes lazy, semiformal summer afternoons on a portico overlooking the sea—like the Eliots' own summer home in Gloucester, whose spacious wrap-around porch commanded a view of the harbor.[32] Amid the usual clutter of "cakes and tea," the speaker makes "guesses at eternal truths / Sounding the depths with a silver spoon," the speaker here ironically juxtaposing fastidious upper-class customs—the bric-a-brac of a tea set—to the Absolute.

In the second stanza, a "you" is addressed whose identity is hard to pin down: perhaps merely an imagined addressee, perhaps the reader, or perhaps some version of the speaker's interior self who observes his external self engaged in social duties. Amid such aristocratic ease, the speaker wonders if "you" might "hesitate" to question "How much is simple accident / How much one knows" and other questions of meaning or fate. Such preoccupations, when asked in such a way and in such a setting, seem more like breezy conversation topics—what in other contexts might be called dorm-room philosophy—rather than the beginning of a rigorous inquiry. The answer to such clichéd inquiries is itself a cliché, which the speaker seems to choose among any number of possible answers, a signal that his offering is merely provisional. He offers it: "Play to your conscience, through the maze / Of means and ways." The ambiguity of the imperative mode builds on the ambiguity of the phrasal verb: "to play to" means to act in such a way as to gain favor or approval. Implicit in this expression is the awareness of an audience: "to play to a gallery" or "to play to certain prejudices." What is genuine is put aside, while a role is donned to generate some desired effect on an audience. This sense of "play to" then deeply contradicts the notion of what a conscience is. One's own conscience can be obeyed, disobeyed, or even appeased, but "you" won't fool your conscience merely by "playing to" it. The rhetoric of address—the imperative mode of "Play to your conscience"—is implicated in this moral muddiness. Here Eliot's authorial audience is played to, bringing them in on the joke/problem. As with so many of Eliot's mature poems, the audience of this poem is challenged, flattered, accused, and implicated.

The result of appearing to be conscientious (as opposed to *being* conscientious) is that you / the speaker can "weave the crown of your ideal / Bays / And Rose." Here the speaker, in a Laforguean move, indicts his own self-consciousness, whose heroic "ideal" is the bays of the victor-poet's wreath. Regrettably, such laurels have been gotten by conniving and self-congratulation, all under the appearance of philosophical rigor and authenticity. Concerned that his indictments of upper-class culture are too easy, the speaker has turned on himself and on the "you" who is coterminous with himself.

In the final poem, part IV, the speaker is presented with the same problem as in the conclusion of his "Mandarins" sequence: some kind of resolution to the problems explored in the first three poems is called for or at least a decent parry in that direction. As we saw in "Mandarins" 4, that poem's unsatisfactory resolution was a compromised shrug, the poet refusing to strike a blow against the constricted etiquette of Brahmin culture. Here in "Goldfish" IV, the poet casts about for a more convincing conclusion and turns—at first unconvincingly—to the figure of an oracle, an external authority that distances the speaker from any answer that is given, and then—surprisingly—to popular culture.

The date of the sequence is given as September 1910, a time of year when the Eliot family routinely left their summer home in Gloucester to return to St. Louis. The poem opens with a listing of the "débris" of fall: postcards, shoes, letters, all of them reminders of the summer that is now past. While the speaker sifts the contents of a bureau drawer, the poem registers a more existential cleaning out. A copy of a barcarolle is found in the drawer, evoking the waves of the sea, which are "Bearing what consequence to you / And me." This matter turns out to be less consequential than imagined: "Some minor problems of the soul."

The "you" of the poem seems remotely related to the "you" of the previous poem; namely, some version of the speaker's self. Yet the "you" and "I" cannot be coterminous, because the "you" of part IV is the expert skipper of a craft sailing across the seas of stanza 2 and carrying the "I" of the poem. The skipper's specialized vocabulary is not only "nautical" but "complete." Nautical language is sufficient for the problems associated with the world of seamanship. So the "me" of the poem (the speaker) is content to give up and be guided, and to "contemplate / The aged sybil" he sees in "your eyes." Anthony Cuda has pointed out that Eliot will revisit this crucial sense of abandonment in the concluding verses of *The Waste Land*, with the same nautical imagery and rhetorical "you" skippering the boat.[33] As with the uneasy answers afforded by *The Waste Land*'s oracular epigraph and closing, the sybil of this early poem offers scant comfort: "These problems seem importunate / But after all do not exist." His anxiousness thus deflated, the speaker nonetheless retains his "fears," which exist somewhere between the "theoretic" seas that could swallow him up and the "assuring certainties" of a materialist skipper—a "you" whose oracle waves away such problems. Rejecting both Scylla and Charybdis, the speaker sets sail for "some Hesperides / Of street pianos and small beers!" This final image engages both the metaphysical properties of an idealist solution—the Hesperides as an Isle of the Blest where such problems would be solved—and the anti-metaphysical properties of a materialist universe where such problems are of no consequence: small beer.

As his "Goldfish" sequence nears its end, Eliot is reaching for a more convincing conclusion than the evasive shrug that ended "Mandarins." Tellingly, the rhetorical conception of "Goldfish" IV is as complex as it is confused. The "you" of the poem is no passive addressee but an active agent who makes oracular pronouncements for the speaker's benefit, whose hand is "expert with sail and oar"—to use the language of *The Waste Land*. Such an identity clearly cannot be the equivalent of the authorial audience, yet this "you" is no anti-audience either, because the author makes no attempt to distinguish the ideology of this "you" from the ideology of the authorial audience. The "you" of this oracle then is awkwardly mixed up with the audience's identity—

as if the author wished his audience might solve these problems for him rather than vice versa.

Added to these problems is a vexing identity issue, abetted by the textual issue of a missing quotation mark. In the second stanza, the speaker of the poem—self-identified as "I"—leaves off where the quoted "Barcarolle" begins. But it is unclear where this new voice ends, as no close quotes punctuate the voice. Other speaking identities intrude, apparently, inside this quoted voice. Marionettes, risen from the grave (another kind of oracle) bear their news in the plural voice: "'We beg to call to your attention / 'Some minor problems of the soul.'" This "We" is clearly not the combined "you" and "I" from elsewhere in the poem.

By the third stanza, the ship of identity has been righted. In this stanza, the "you"—whose "assuring certaintics" repel the speaker—resembles the authoritative audiences of earlier poems, notably the threatening, auditing presence of "Silence": "You may say what you will." Like the closing gesture of "Silence," which validates the speaker's own experience in the face of an uncomprehending auditor, so this poem also rejects, lightly, the convictions of this "you" by sailing off to his pop-culture Hesperides.

As before, when he tries to invent new rhetorical vistas, Eliot's reach has exceeded his grasp, a failure that he recognizes. Not only does Eliot decline to publish this sequence, he has also deleted in pencil the entirety of poems III and IV. He will not even let them stand in their inadequate state as models to be later corrected or plundered.

"Preludes" I and II
Drafted Oct. 1910; published with parts III and IV (drafted later), in Blast, *July 1915*

Considering the failure of "Goldfish" to conclude with an adequate and comprehensible rhetoric, these two "Preludes" represent a signal triumph. Turning from the impossible task of "completeness" and instead taking up the more tractable path of fragmentation, the rhetoric of these two poems is adequate to the task—Eliot here retooling a Baudelairean style that he had botched in the "Caprice" poems of the previous year.

The musical title is indebted to Chopin's *Preludes*, to which Eliot refers in "Portrait of a Lady" I. Chopin's peculiar use of the term may serve to explain the evocative nature of Eliot's poems. Before the nineteenth century, the term "prelude" was largely used to designate a short piece, often improvisatory, to precede a hymn or other longer piece. Chopin was the first to use the term as a generic cover for his sharply etched character pieces that are unburdened by the programmatic, literary connotations other Romantic composers gave such character pieces. Nor do Chopin's preludes serve as an introduction to some other work.[34] It is in this Chopinesque sense—a haunting characterization detached from narrative specificity and an independent piece that introduces nothing else—that Eliot uses the term "prelude."

"Prelude in Dorchester (Houses)" is later published as the first of the "Preludes" with the Roman numeral I in place of the descriptive subtitle. In reclaiming the rhetoric of Baudelaire, in which urban grit is calmly observed, the opening poem must resolve the lingering problems of "First Caprice" and "Second Caprice"—those notable failures in which Laforguean sarcasm undercuts seriousness, and a distrusting speaker overcompensates by directing the emotional traffic for his audience. "Preludes" I begins similarly to "First Caprice": an eye roves dispassionately over an urban setting of poverty and filth. "First Caprice" is in many respects the model for the later, more successful poem: both begin with serious observations of decaying urban fragments, and both end with a surprise exclamatory line.

In "Preludes" I, the speaker is absorbed into the anonymity the urban setting affords him, the drab routines of the poor contrasting with the overrefinement of Eliot's other poems. Recording the phenomena of rain, trash, dinner smells, and domestic details ("broken blinds and chimney pots"), the speaker is completely detached, neither ironic nor judgmental, with no conclusions or explanations to offer.[35] The lack of moral judgment combined with a steady attention to detail have the effect of focusing the reader's attention on the images—"burnt-out ends of smoky days," "grimy scraps." Not only does the speaker of the poem abstain from emotional response, he declines to direct the emotional response of his audience. This holding back is an important advance from the previous year, as the author now relies on his audience to see and feel as his speaker sees and feels. Of course, subtle rhetoric is still rhetoric: by turning his premises into assumptions—that is, by making the explicit implicit—Eliot has effectively maneuvered his audience into position with a minimum of pressure. This is the genius of "Preludes," and it is of a piece with his increasing mastery of rhetoric in the notebook.

The final line—that moment where poets are most tempted to make transcending gestures—is awarded extra weight as the only separated line in a poem whose preceding twelve lines constitute one stanza. The final, separated line ends in an exclamation point in this otherwise muted poem. The setting apart and exclamatory punctuation seem to signal a shift in emphasis or change in direction, some transcendent leap or explanatory gesture. But such formal signals of difference are belied by the content of the line, which says nothing new: "And then the lighting up of lamps!" Placed near the beginning of the line, the word "then" promises consequence but delivers only chronology. That exclamation point is a sly little jest. Given the cool seriousness of the poem, it is a gesture that seasons rather than mars the tone. Compare the line's delicate balance of tone, its subtle undercurrent of irony, to the distorting sarcasm of the final line—also separated and exclamatory—of "First Caprice": "Oh, these minor considerations! . . ." Where the earlier poem is torn between its warring audiences' expectations, the later poem is master of its tone and shaper of its audience.

In spite of this finesse, Eliot, ever careful, deletes the exclamation point after the poem's first publication in 1915, and typographical inconsistencies in subsequent editions make it unclear as to whether the final line should stand alone. The ripple of irony, so balanced and carefully managed in the notebook, is obscured in the published versions. With the final line of "Preludes" I—with or without the exclamation point—all three problems evident in "First Caprice" and "Second Caprice" are definitively solved. First, the voice is a coherent and unified entity that shifts imperceptibly between a pensive torpor and a muted irony; and second, the speaker trusts his audience to be compelled by the impartial recording of urban fragments. The first problem had been solved by February 1910 ("Portrait of a Lady" II), but not in tandem with the second one.

The third problem—finding a rhetoric adequate to address human suffering—is also solved. For the first of the "Preludes" refers not only to urban fragments but to detritus that curls around "your feet." This presence of the second person is deftly evoked by transferring it to a possessive adjective. At the same time, a fragment of the human body is snuck into the scenery. An advance of "Preludes" over the "Caprice" poems is the connection of urban waste to the human body and therefore to the human person. In "First Caprice," by contrast, humans are kept out of sight for fear of sentimentality: its street piano must somehow be operated by a person, and the offstage wailing of "children's voices" must imply their bodily counterparts, but the corporeal makes no appearance in those earlier poems.[36]

The second poem in the "Preludes" series, subtitled "Prelude in Roxbury," is later published with Roman numeral II in place of the subtitle. It is another urban scene of drabness and routine, this one set in the morning. In this second poem, the phenomenon of fragmenting the human body is continued. Grover Smith notes the "depersonalizing character" of "Preludes," with their disembodied hands and feet unconnected to a personality.[37] Such a depersonalizing effect is the consequence of a cubist rendering of human fragments—a cubism first seen in "Mandarins" 2. But Eliot's depersonalizing is not dehumanizing, rather the opposite. For with such fragmentation, Eliot's Puritan temperament is put on hold, and instead of rendering judgment on moral beings, he can observe fragments in a detached way. The disembodied hands and feet of "Preludes" are the human equivalent of the broken glass and disintegrating bricks of the "Caprice" sequence of the previous year. In this manner—fragmentation extended from urban detritus to the human body—Eliot's preferred topic of human suffering is smuggled in through the back door. He cannot yet gaze into the eyes of poverty or despair, but he can examine its hands and feet. The problem of finding an adequate rhetoric to address human suffering is the third and only problem left over from "Second Caprice." As a consequence of such maturation, the rhetoric of "Preludes" is serious but not sentimental; it is compassionately engaged and dispassionately observational. The coarse protections of irony, sarcasm, and flippancy, previously used to guard against hostile audiences, are unnecessary here, and Eliot deploys restrained irony to subtler ends, as he does in the concluding line of "Preludes" I.

The first two poems of "Preludes" are not just variations; they are developments as well. They move forward by taking different angles. The variation of "Preludes" II is that the rhetoric moves beyond the objective observation of "Preludes" I, which simply records the facts of detritus. In the second poem, the recording eye slips into a worldview that is recognizably the speaker's, a judgment that comments on the street imagery, where early commuters wait at coffee stands: "With all other masquerades / That time resumes." With this evocation of time, the routine of getting coffee before work is implicated as one of those "masquerades" that pulls the world from its dreary sleep time into an even more dreary real time. Such reflections cause the speaker to think of the trudging of time and the bleak facelessness of crowds condemned to weary routine.

The voice of "Preludes" I and II presents the serious subject matter of Baudelaire tempered by the rhythmic accentuation of Laforgue/ragtime; namely, Eliot's late-mastered tool of the line brought up short with an emphatic rhyme:

And now a gusty shower wraps
The grimy scraps

—"Preludes" I

From the sawdust trampled street
With its muddy feet

—"Preludes" II

With such effects, the tone of the poem is muted—restrained rather than deadened—ragtime undulating through the languor of Baudelaire. With the Laforguean/ragtime element modulating rather than swamping the prevailing tone, "Preludes" finally succeeds where the "Caprice" poems had failed. Targeting a sympathetic Baudelairean audience, "Preludes" successfully reclaims this observational mode from the domineering contempt of his Laforguean audiences of the previous year.

"Suite Clownesque" I–IV
Drafted Oct. 1910

The turn to popular culture at the end of "Goldfish" IV purports to resolve questions of meaning and identity, but its conclusion—blithely sailing off for the land of mass entertainment—is a rather surprising one. The waltzes, sandwiches, cigarettes, photographs, and boat rides of that sequence had signaled ambivalent vectors of frivolity, tedium, glamour, and escape. And so the deus ex machina of the poem's conclusion rings false, popular culture providing an escape from problems rather than a solution. As a consequence, Eliot's ambivalent relationship to popular culture becomes the next issue to be sorted out. The upper-class contexts of "Mandarins" and "Goldfish" now move off to the wings, and in "Suite Clownesque" the venue is vaudeville, that rich ground of turn-of-the-century popular culture.

B. F. Keith was an iron-fisted entrepreneur credited with institutionalizing the vaudeville form, and Boston was the center of the Keith empire. As an undergraduate at Harvard, Eliot is more likely to have seen vaudeville in Boston than in St. Louis as a boy. Some of the productions he would have seen were Keith productions, as no other mass-produced variety programs could gain a foothold in Boston or its environs.[38] Keith's vaudeville was famous for the novelty of its continuous performance: entertainment seekers could enter the theater at any time from late morning through late evening, staying to watch repetitions or until the act they saw upon entering retook the stage. For his own poem, Eliot has subverted this continuous form, instead packaging his sequence of four poems like other vaudeville programs that "build" toward a climax, some star turn or effective crowd-pleaser reserved for the penultimate act.

Of the various forms of popular culture in 1910, vaudeville was most finely attuned to its audience's pleasure. A live form, vaudeville took the temperature of its audience's approval in measurements of laughter, catcalls, rapt attention, and applause. Unlike the medium of film later in the century, for which the delay between production and audience approval required intervening censors, vaudeville never established a censor system because its managers kept their fingers on the pulse of its audience's approval. As managers reminded their underlings, anyone could be fired immediately if their act strayed into blue territory. Vaudeville had been codified out of a desire to market the haphazard organization and shady reputation of burlesque and variety to a middle-class, family-oriented audience.[39] B. F. Keith himself boasted of the "purity" of his vaudeville productions.[40] Like the French term *vaudeville* itself, which was commandeered by American entrepreneurs looking to overlay their mass productions with a sheen of high culture, the title of Eliot's poem trades on the ambivalence between rowdy entertainment and an awkwardly Frenchified pretension: "Suite Clownesque."

According to Albert F. McLean Jr., the content of vaudeville—though the skits were not thematically connected and were often contradictory—was the Myth of Success: "the American Dream of opportunity, prosperity, and happiness."[41] In deference to the Protestant moralism of the late nineteenth century, the base materialism of this impulse had to be disguised, McLean argues. The working- and middle-class audiences of vaudeville pined for material success, and yet they knew from experience in the factory or office that such success was hard to come by. Some indirection was therefore necessary: the translation of "happiness" into sex appeal, for example, fed into—indeed, created—the mass cult of glamour, upon which the mystique of vaudeville stars thrived.

Eliot chooses four stock skits for each section of his sequence: the comedian, the ingénue, the dandy, and the dramatic playlet—this fourth act interrupted by a surprise reappearance of the comedian. Comic acts were rarely the "star turn" of a vaudeville program, the comedian being only one of countless stock figures. That Eliot chose the comedian to be the bookend figure of his sequence matters, as the sharpness of the "new humor" was more in tune with his purposes than the sentimentality or spectacle of other vaudeville acts. Jettisoning the broad, humane humor of the late nineteenth century, the comic acts and quick-patter jokes of vaudeville exploded the myths of urban life and made its humiliations, rootlessness, and instability the object of its sharp scrutiny. While vaudeville as a whole was built on the Myth of Success, the new humor poked holes in that myth's empty promises. Vaudeville humor was a weapon of critique.[42]

So when Eliot introduces his comedian in section I, it is curious to note that this comedian says nothing funny. Eliot is not interested in the content of his act; instead, he is fascinated by the control the comedian wields over his audience. Many of Eliot's earlier poems had observed the ineffective rhetorical posturing of others. By contrast, this comedian is a master rhetor: playing to his audience, the comedian leans across the proscenium the better to invoke intimacy with them. In spite of the comedian's skill, the speaker of the poem sees through the charade: "It's all philosophy and art."[43] Like Eliot the philosophy student / emerging artist, the comedian has claims on both ways of looking at the world, the philosophical and the artistic. The physical details of the comedian correspond to these two modes of art and philosophy: one is his "broad dogmatic vest," which describes the artistic front he presents to an audience. The second detail is the comedian's nose, descriptive of his philosophical attitude: upturned, his "sceptic" nose "interrogates" both the stars and the audience. These two details—broad vest and upturned nose—track the comedian's dual relationship with the audience in the poem. On the one hand, the vest-wearing comedian is a master of the performance art that enables him to be completely in command of an audience. He "gets away with it" by employing such perfectly timed comic gestures as spreading his toes apart to underscore a point. On the other hand, he is a master of skeptical philosophy. His upturned nose implies a haughty dismissal of the very audience he is charming as well as a corrosive disbelief in the metaphysical quandaries of the stars. Yet in this first section, the speaker dismisses the comedian—and that part of the author who would play this role—as having his entire being "Concentred in his vest and nose." It is *all*—which is to say *only*—philosophy and art. Eliot's skepticism targets what is false but does not yet lead him to an alternative.

In part II, a skit involves ingénues who narrate with ragtime sauciness their story of playing hooky. The fingerprints of ragtime are all over this poem, from the coyly sexualized content, to the girls' extroverted call-and-response with the audience, to the crammed rhymes of "one in the *centre* / (Who would *venture* to be a *dissenter*)." It is such an exuberant tour de force that the young author blurs the line between writing a poem *about* vaudeville and writing lyrics *for* vaudeville.

On seeing soldiers from their streetcar, the girls jump out to catch up with them. Their tale stops just short of bawdy revelation though, the girls apparently "perplexed" at what is supposed to happen subsequently. In this winking aside, the girls invite the theatergoing audience in the poem as well as the audience of the poem to "construe" their question as an implicit admission of licentiousness. The girls want money and a good time, and they have just found willing soldiers to entertain them. Both audiences, of course, know exactly where the girls and the soldiers will "go to next." Although the pseudo-naive girls are the ones telling the story, the author wordlessly signals to the audience (or its adult membership) the crucial, sexually charged information that supplies the punch line of the joke.

This maneuver of the unreliable narrator is one of the ways the poem conveys its double meanings. Another part of the poem's rhetorical organization is indebted to the coy game of revelation and innuendo that vaudeville played with its middle-class audiences. Eliot is not merely reporting the subject matter of a skit he has seen, he is translating the rhetorical parries and thrusts of vaudeville into lyric poetry—a very different medium. In a verbal construct, Eliot cannot passively rely on a visual system: meanings must somehow be signaled through discourse. Whereas on the stage of Keith's vaudeville palaces, the semiotics of skirts would communicate silently, Eliot has to set up the terms of the purity code in the first three lines. There the audience learns that the girls' skirts are "down to the ancle." At the same time that this detail signals family entertainment, we learn that there are seven of these girls, all "under age"—contradictory signs that position this skit on the extreme edge of the purity code. Similarly, on a vaudeville stage, the visual of a shaken finger could be a straightforward bid for attention. Or it might signal a negation, a warning that a line must not be crossed. Eliot manages both contradictory meanings—come hither, but don't be naughty—with recourse to the jagged rhymes of ragtime: "Just while they *linger* shaking a *finger*." A sign of how tightly it has been conceived, the poem is filled with such in-and-out gestures, from the inversion of the girls' refrain ("Hello people! / People, hello!"), to their jumping on and off the streetcar, to their ambiguous motives: skipping school (signaling deviance) to "peek" around town (signaling the clean motives of tourism).

Sections II and III of "Suite Clownesque" are both "glamour" poems, trading on notions of sexual power and happiness, yet the third section does more to expose the hollowness of this pose.[44] The speaker of the third section is another type, the urban dandy in which Laforgue meets vaudeville. The dandy's meticulousness of dress and his studied pose reflect his consciousness of the audiences that watch him. Audiences multiply like mirrors in this poem, where everyone looks at everyone else. The speaker is followed around by adoring "girls" who constitute one audience in the poem. Another audience in the poem who watches the speaker is "everyone" on the beach. A third audience in the poem is a "you" whom the speaker anxiously addresses over and over. Then, of course, there is the audience of the poem who watches all this watching. In spite of the speaker's anxiety to please and be admired, he himself is paradoxically "Just out of reach"—the stage his prison of isolation and the only system that validates his identity.

Like the comedian of part I for whom questions of identity and meaning are merely the speculations of philosophy and art, the dandy is concerned only about his effect on his audiences. Blithely shaking "cocktails on a hearse," he too is untroubled by larger meanings signaled by the cosmos or by death. The only activities that engage his attention are the summer occupations of the leisure class: the beach by day or Broadway by night. In spite of all the extroverted camaraderie, the intimacy of friendship or romance is absent. Whereas the traditional lover would target a singular beloved to seduce, the entertainer on the stage clamors to attract the attention of a larger audience. Strutting in his "quintessential flannel suit," he describes himself as "First born child of the absolute." A more extroverted cousin of Prufrock, this speaker surveys his domain and asserts hopefully, "I guess there's nothing the matter with us!" This assertion is immediately undermined, however, when he seeks approval from the "you" of the poem: "Do you think that I'm all right?" He claims to be "Neat, complete," but his question betrays an incompleteness, a desire for approval and intimacy. That a charismatic womanizer would momentarily drop his mask to ask such a question is a foreshadowing of Prufrock, the ditherer who sets aside his rationalizations to admit, "And in short, I was afraid."[45] The dandy's desire for approval is not quite so poignant as Prufrock's admission of vulnerability. Given the similarity in their situations, it is worth noting the similarity of their rhetoric: in "Suite Clownesque" III and later in "Prufrock," the speakers' fears are addressed not to the respective girls or women but to the "you" in the poem, some trusted companion who holds the place of the authorial audience.

In the last section of the poem, the vaudeville program seems to be nearing its predictable conclusion: the hero gets the girl, while "village girls" dance with "smiling boys" who sport the signature rattan canes of the vaudeville circuit. The audience, having seen the preceding crowd-pleaser, is exiting during this last act—a mild if expected insult to performers—choosing not to sit through its "discovered masquerades." Amid the bustle of this denouement—on stage and off—the comedian from the first act interrupts, his unexpected entrance through the colonnades falling like "a shadow dense, immense." The comedian "explodes" in sinister laughter. The speaker, in turn, repeats his own dismissal of the comedian as being "Concentred into vest and nose"—trivially preoccupied by mere philosophy and art. Yet the speaker repeats his ambiguous description of the comedian, this time parenthetically, as "(The most expressive, real of men)." The order of adjectives here seems to suggest that the speaker, as a type of the philosopher-comedian author, finds this dominating figure expressive and therefore the most "real."

Although the speaker cannot share in the self-confidence of this figure who seems to have it all figured out—how to please an audience and how not to be bothered by philosophical quandaries—he cannot ultimately condemn the comedian's shallowness. In spite of his craven playing to an audience and his hypocritical disdain of them (a duplicity with which he "gets away"), he ultimately *exists*: his expression may be crude and even morally questionable, but at least he is real. Eliot ultimately has his speaker qualify his dismissal of the comedian's dismissal, reaching a point of balance beyond which it would be difficult to go: a wary and suspicious maintenance of irreconcilable tendencies.

The four-poem sequence is both a celebration of vaudeville's exuberance and communal spirit and a critique of its crass materialism and hollow happiness. By the end of the poem, the magic of vaudeville falls apart, and the glitter is revealed as stage paste. The ground from which Eliot launches such a critique is unclear. The only thing that is clear is that Something Else intervenes. Some "shadow" falls.

In the months leading up to his departure for Paris, Eliot conducts an imaginative review of the meaning-making systems of his culture that he is soon to leave behind: the aristocratic ease and superiority of Boston Brahminism in "Mandarins," the rituals of courtship and leisure in "Goldfish," the materialism and success myths of popular culture in "Suite Clownesque." And he finds all of these systems wanting. Even so, as Helen Vendler has argued, he proves by his recurrent use of these discourses that he cannot do without them.[46]

Vendler and Chinitz seem to occupy contradictory positions on the subject of Eliot's engagement with popular culture. Surveying the superficial happiness evoked and critiqued in "Suite Clownesque," Vendler has argued that Eliot has judged popular culture inadequate as an answer to pressing questions of meaning and identity. Because of its sparseness of content, Vendler concludes that the effects of popular culture on the poet's voice are negligible: "[Eliot] has judged the jazzy but semiotically empty discourse of the smart set as a language suitable only for 'shaking cocktails on a hearse,' usable as a decorative accent but not as a substantial matrix."[47] However, Eliot's temporary abandonment of popular culture after "Suite Clownesque" is a consequence of several problems. It is not just that popular culture is unable to provide adequate answers to questions of meaning and identity, as Vendler argues. Eliot's turn from popular culture also involves his inability to square its claims with his serious literary ambitions. He is still the genteel son of Tradition.

As Chinitz has shown, Eliot's forays into popular culture, beginning with ragtime rhythms, leave their mark on the poems even when he turns away from the content of popular culture. The exuberance of popular culture has sunk its roots too deeply into his consciousness for him to repudiate its influence. However, Chinitz's emphasis on the subterranean effect of ragtime on Eliot's cadences, while convincing, does not explain Eliot's decision to keep these "complete" poems in the privacy of the notebook and elides the fact that they are artistically inferior to the "fragmentary" poems. Chinitz's valuable exploration of popular culture in the notebook poems explains how the "complete" poems got onto the notebook page—not why they never made it to press.

Unlike "Mandarins," "Goldfish," and "Suite Clownesque," the two poems of his unfinished "Preludes" do not constitute a critique of a system. Eliot has too little familiarity with the poor to critique the economic and social structures that entrap them. Unrestrained by the facticity of poverty, he is able imaginatively to empathize with the poor, and in doing so he casts off the problems of the capricious sarcasm that had hobbled his earlier attempts at empathy. In "Preludes," he forges a rhetoric of interiority that paradoxically requires an empathetic audience. This interiority-cum-audience-empathy stands in relief against the social and cultural systems in which the upper-class Eliot is caught. The other sequence poems of 1910—"Mandarins," "Goldfish," and "Suite Clownesque"—record respectively his dissatisfaction with the systems of Brahminism, courtship, and popular culture. These poems are marked by an intellectual and emotional thinness because their author has neither the wherewithal to critique those systems from a coherent philosophical viewpoint nor the courage to fully articulate his sense of entrapment within them. These are the problems he now sets out to solve.

Trembling with Pathos

The Paris Poems of Late 1910 and Early 1911

> [Charles-Louis Philippe] has an intense pity for the humble and oppressed, a pity still more akin to that of Dickens' Russian disciple Dostoievski; and a pathos which as in Dickens and Dostoievski both, trembles on the edge of the maudlin. . . . The pathetic, even when wholly sincere, is a dangerous speciality; and that which, to the author, is the most pathetic, is not always so to the reader.
>
> —T. S. Eliot, preface to *Bubu of Montparnasse*

Getting his parents to fund a year in France involved some subterfuge on Eliot's part.[1] Announcing an intention to study French literature, Eliot presented the prospect of a year abroad as necessary for understanding the "particular genius" of the French people. This surprising announcement, which entailed turning his back on philosophy, did not please his mother, who wrote to him after the initial kerfuffle: "I have rather hoped you would not specialize later on French literature."[2] Although she had encouraged her son's literary abilities as a hobby, Charlotte Eliot did not approve of her son becoming a journalist or critic and was even less keen on poetry as a profession, a resistance that would only increase in subsequent years. She enlisted her son-in-law, an English instructor, to weigh in on the matter: "Sheff wrote early in the fall," Charlotte related to her son, "that he thought before the end of the collegiate year your ideas would crystallize and you would know better the best direction for your literary activity."[3] Charlotte Eliot hoped that the "best direction" would mean a sideline rather than a profession. Her ambivalence ran deep, however: in this same letter, she also expressed hopes that her son's literary work would receive the recognition that she had sought for her own work.

In hindsight, the poet's year abroad and his increasing interest in literature appear to be natural developments. For as an intelligent, well-read student, Eliot would have been expected to pursue graduate study.[4] A year abroad as preparation for "specializ[ing] later on French literature" might have been predicted for someone of Eliot's class and education. By so lobbying his parents, Eliot was playing to the only sympathies he could hope to stir in them, though in itself this tactic is no evidence of subterfuge. Perhaps the most generous interpretation is that Eliot hoped that becoming a French professor would inspire his own poetry on the side.

Eliot's own recollections, however, tell a different story. The intention to prepare for graduate work in French literature appears only in correspondence with his mother; that intention appears nowhere in Eliot's contemporary letters from France or in his later descriptions of that year. Instead, the evidence collectively points to an intention to write poetry: "Mais ce n'est pas un accident qui m'avait conduit à Paris. Depuis plusieurs années, la France représentait surtout, à mes yeux, la *poésie*."[5] It was not an accident, Eliot stresses, that led him to Paris. Since he had come under the scandalous influence of Laforgue and Baudelaire, France had represented *poetry*—the italicized, exciting kind of poetry he had been absorbing, not the academic study of Old Masters.

Even more telling was the plan Eliot conceived for himself once he arrived in France in 1910. In a later interview, Donald Hall asked Eliot whether he had ever considered writing Symbolist poetry in French. Eliot's illuminating response: "I only did that during the romantic year I spent in Paris after Harvard. I had at that time the idea of giving up English and trying to settle down and scrape along in Paris and gradually write French."[6] In December 1910, a few weeks into his French experiment, he idly wonders, writing in his notebook, about the prospects of such ad hoc work versus the dull stability of academia: "The world is full of journalists, / And full of universities."[7] Both careers seem unworkable, and the lines are deleted. What is retrospectively labeled as "Eliot's Paris year" was thought of, at least for a while, as a more permanent arrangement. Given Eliot's sense of discretion, it is unlikely that he discussed the plan to remain in France with his parents. Even though his escape turned out to be only temporary, what mattered for the poetry was that Eliot had escaped at all: he was liberated from his familial contexts, social environments, and professional expectations. In spite of what his parents apparently believed, Eliot went to France intentionally to become a poet, not a professor of French literature—the latter an invention he has long forgotten by the 1959 interview with Donald Hall. In 1910, the fiction of preparing for an academic career in French literature provided the cover he needed. For Eliot's rebellion to be funded, it had to be disguised as a combination of professional exigency and Grand Tour.

After his arrival in France, Eliot eagerly adopted a new identity. His dress changed to match the cultivated urbanity he observed there, and his handwriting evolved over the course of a few months from the careful, rounded hand of his Harvard days to a spiky, tighter script. Adrift from familiar contexts, Eliot kept up with the external forms of behavior. He worked on his language skills and attended philosophy lectures. He wrote chatty, observational letters back to relatives in the States.

Nevertheless, this blithe persona disguised a different reality. His experiences of escape, exploration, and freedom were overshadowed by the difficulties of being alone in a foreign country. "When I was living [in Paris] years ago," Eliot recounted to a friend, "I had only the genuine stimulus of the place, and not the artificial stimulus of the people, as I knew no-one whatever, in the literary and artistic world, as a companion—knew them rather as spectacles, listened to, at rare occasions, but never spoken to."[8] Given the warm friendships he developed with Jean Verdenal and Alain-Fournier in Paris, this recollection may exaggerate the extent of his solitude, but it does reflect the genuine alienation that is found in the Paris poems.

And so the scheme to remain in France was abandoned as untenable; within the year Eliot resumed his quondam plans for graduate study in philosophy back at Harvard. One reason for beating a retreat was that there was no one in Paris to feed his literary ambitions. Even with such friends as Alain-Fournier, who was well connected in the literary establishment, and Jean Verdenal, who was possessed of opinions musical and literary, none of his acquaintances seemed poised to show Eliot, via example and instruction, practical ways to achieve a career in poetry or journalism. Unlike London of 1914, where Eliot arrived on a fellowship, there was no Ezra Pound in Paris of 1910–1911.

Aside from an absence of mentors and promoters in Paris, there was another major hurdle to Eliot's absorption into French culture. As soon as he set foot in France, Eliot experienced the steep learning curve of mastering a second language. What little information we have about Eliot's emotional state in Paris refers explicitly to this struggle: "It is hard to talk to the little ones," Eliot wrote to his young niece, "because they don't talk French very well yet, and I don't either."[9] In a letter to his cousin, Eliot described his first few weeks in Paris as the period of his greatest difficulties with the language. For someone as articulate as Eliot, the loss of linguistic facility must have been a humiliating experience. That loss of language is part of a complex of experiences that could anachronistically be called culture shock.[10] When persons find themselves immersed in a second culture, even when they have been prepared for it with language study, they are bound to encounter on an hourly basis situations of misunderstanding, helplessness, and disorientations both cultural and linguistic. The cumulative effect of these problems can provoke a range of emotional responses, particularly anger, hopelessness, and despair.

Eliot's alienation and despair brought him to the brink of sexual panic. Reflecting back on his problems in Paris, Eliot writes to his friend Conrad Aiken, "I have been going through one of those nervous sexual attacks which I suffer from when alone in a city. Why I had almost none last fall I don't know—this is the worst since Paris. I never have them in the country." It is poignant to hear Eliot specify that he had *almost* no nervous sexual episodes: it is both exact and evasive. He testily concludes the matter, "I should be better off, I sometimes think, if I had disposed of my virginity and shyness several years ago."[11]

Eliot's helplessness, alienation, and sexual anxieties as a foreigner enabled him to explore situations of vulnerability and extreme pathos in his own poetry. For such anxiety and alienation to be used as literary fodder in his own notebook, he required only some kind of literary model. Under the guidance of his French tutor, Alain-Fournier, Eliot had read Charles-Louis Philippe's *Bubu de Montparnasse*, a novel about a prostitute and the underworld of Paris. Prostitutes show up in Eliot's Paris poems: "Rhapsody on a Windy Night," "Ballade pour la grosse Lulu," and "Preludes" III, the draft version of which begins with phrases from Philippe's novel: "Son âme de petite putain" (her little whore's soul).[12] Trembling with pathos, Eliot walked the streets of Paris encountering prostitutes, but his propriety restrained him: "One walks about the street with one's desires, and one's refinement rises up like a wall whenever opportunity approaches."[13] And one's personal pronouns become vague, so as to distance oneself from the terror of sexual abandonment.

Stripped of the comforting if restricting routines of his social class and collegiate schedule, Eliot was left to face his alienation head on. A year of unignorable alienation—as opposed to the harder-to-name alienation felt in Boston—enabled him to analyze his condition more forthrightly. As a result, his emotions take rhetorical and imagistic form in the notebook poems. A number of those poems deal with a torpid character locked inside his head. In these poems—"Entretien dans un parc," "Bacchus and Ariadne," "The smoke that gathers"—the speaker projects himself into external reality only by force of will. Other Paris poems thematize notions of apathy and indifference. Eliot's mind lingers over a line from Webster's *The White Devil*: "I have caught an everlasting cold"—an evocation of chronic, low-grade misery.[14] Lost for months in an alien culture, the young Eliot battered against the walls of his solipsism and the lassitude that crept in its wake. In the ten-line "Interlude in London," the word "indifferent" and its synonyms—"apathetic," "Careless"—choke the poem.[15] Embroiled with his apathy is fear: the dueling emotions of alienation. "The Triumph of Bullshit" records his fear of being misunderstood, and "Entretien dans un parc" explores his dread of "the fire of ridicule."[16]

Among the Fog and Smoke

One of the images to which Eliot repeatedly turns in the Paris poems is fog or smoke. Such images appear throughout the notebook, but they take on particular intensity in the poems of 1911. Whether generated by nature, factories, or cigars—fog and smoke make air visible, calling attention to a normally transparent medium. In Eliot's work, the appearance of smoke allows his speakers to observe what is otherwise unseen. Smoke thus represents the mysterious, or what a later poem, clogged with perfume and steam, describes as "the unconscious, the ineffable, the absolute."[17] Hung with grime, humidity, or burnt particulates, haze does more than lend gothic atmospherics to the urban settings of the poems. More significantly, fog represents the intersection of matter and spirit for Eliot. Permeated with smoke, many of the 1911 poems build toward "Rhapsody on a Windy Night," which is the most evocative expression of the matter/mind, body/soul problem, or what another 1911 poem describes as "the relation of life to matter."[18]

The only other term that occurs in the notebook with as much frequency as smoke is the word "indifferent" and its synonyms. Curving languorously or hanging thickly, the slow movement of smoke is an apt metaphor for lethargy and indifference. Eliot explicitly connects smoke with indifference: one Paris poem has "apathetic, with cigars / Careless," and in another poem a man twists "a hopeless cigarette."[19] With a similar turn to the indifferent, the speaker of "Portrait of a Lady" escapes from the salon into the narcotized companionship of a "tobacco trance."[20] And Prufrock disgustedly compares his futility to the detritus of cigarette smoking: "the butt ends of my days and ways."[21]

Slow and dissolving, smoke is not only the poetic repository of Eliot's indifference and helplessness, it is the abstraction of time made visible. The ubiquity of the metaphor in Eliot's work raises it to a conceit: all of those evenings, dusks, mornings, and afternoons . . . wafting, curling, and clinging.

Where there is smoke, there is time: "And indeed there will be time / For the yellow smoke that slides along the street."[22]

Eliot identifies the source of this recurring fog as the factory smoke that blew across the Mississippi in St. Louis.[23] Images of fog and smoke stretch back into Eliot's juvenilia, where incense of "altar-smoke" is paired with "sanctuaries of the soul"—sacrificial smoke by which the profane is translated, via burning, into the plane of the sacred.[24] By the time he begins the notebook, Eliot's smoke has been scrubbed of such associations with the sacred, though not of its connection to the metaphysical. Smoke or fog usually appears at the beginning of a poem, where an abstraction of time (often the evening) is made sensate by particulates smelled or seen in the air. In chronological order:

> This morning's flowers and flowers of yesterday
> Their fragrance drifts across the room at dawn
>
> —"Before Morning" (1908)[25]

> The yellow evening flung against the panes
> Of dirty windows
>
> —"First Caprice in North Cambridge" (1909)[26]

> The winter evening settles down
> With smell of steaks . . .
> The burnt-out ends of smoky days.
>
> —"Preludes" I (1910)[27]

> The morning comes to consciousness
> Of faint stale smells of beer
>
> —"Preludes" II (1910)[28]

> Among the fog and smoke of a December afternoon
>
> —"Portrait of a Lady" I (1910)[29]

> —Let us take the air, in a tobacco trance
>
> —"Portrait of a Lady" I (1910)[30]

> Across the room the shifting smoke
>
> —"Interlude: in a Bar" (1911)[31]

> The smoke that gathers blue and sinks
> The torpid smoke of rich cigars
>
> —"The smoke that gathers" (1911)[32]

And cigarette smoke of corridors
And cocktail smells in bars

—"Rhapsody on a Windy Night" (1911)[33]

When the evening is spread out against the sky

—"The Love Song of J. Alfred Prufrock" (1910–1911)[34]

The yellow fog that rubs its back upon the window panes
The yellow smoke that rubs its muzzle on the window panes
. . . .
Let fall upon its back the soot that falls from chimneys;

—"The Love Song of J. Alfred Prufrock" (1910–1911)[35]

Well! and what if she should die some afternoon,
Afternoon grey and smoky, evening yellow and rose;
Should die, and leave me sitting pen in hand
With the smoke coming down across the house-tops

—"Portrait of a Lady" III (1911)[36]

Shall I say, I have gone at dusk through narrow streets
  And seen the smoke which rises from the pipes

—"Prufrock's Pervigilium" (1912)[37]

Smoke has seeped so thoroughly into Eliot's thinking that neighboring images pick up the smell: the walls of a bar are said to "fling back the scattered streams / Of life."[38] In "Prufrock's Pervigilium," boys "drifted helplessly together," their bodies blending together with the smoke from their cigarettes.[39] And the opening image of lovers in "Bacchus and Ariadne" makes no sense until the suspension of smoke is detected behind it: "I saw their lives curl upward like a wave / And break. And after all it had not broken—."[40]

The metaphor of smoke functions in three distinct ways, often overlapping: (1) As particulate hung in air, smoke represents the relation of mind to matter, the invisible made visible, the mysterious given form. (2) As atmospherics, the lethargy of fog and its lack of direction signify the emotions of indifference, confusion, and uncertainty. (3) As abstraction, the slow-moving, dissolvent nature of smoke represents time.

Audience, Voice, and Message Problems, Resolved

Surfacing during his Paris year, the poet's extreme emotions and anxieties were rich material for exploration. However, the artistic problem in presenting such material, as Eliot later described Philippe's work, is that such presentation "trembles on the edge of the maudlin." In this phase of his development, the problem he struggles with is not maintaining control of his materials or his rhetoric. With the exception of "The Triumph of Bullshit," he has already learned that lesson by early 1910, when he managed to shift seamlessly between voices, without letting any one voice dominate. Now that he has developed a flexible voice and targeted a mostly sympathetic audience, the problems he works out in Paris are related to logos and pathos: finding an adequate imagery and form to express his alienation and striking a stance that will elicit sympathy from his audience without crossing over into the maudlin. The critique Eliot later makes of Philippe is exactly the tension with which he struggles in the Paris poems: "The pathetic, even when wholly sincere, is a dangerous speciality; and that which, to the author, is the most pathetic, is not always so to the reader."[41]

His experience in Paris is one of stark alienation; his literary model is Philippe's brand of pathos. The result is a series of poems of exceptional power and pity: "Rhapsody on a Windy Night," "Preludes" (III), "The Love Song of J. Alfred Prufrock," and "Portrait of a Lady" (I). Many of his earliest poems had attempted to make oblique reports on human suffering, resulting in depersonalized body parts juxtaposed to images of brokenness. By contrast, in his Paris poems, fully realized characters find elaborate forms and compelling images for the expression of alienation, ennui, and fear.

Even with the major successes of the Paris period, Eliot still manages to write some weak poems, which his good editorial sense kept him from publishing. The weaker Paris poems are of a different sort than the groping uncertainties of the earliest notebook verses. In general, they reach inadequately rather than fumble awkwardly. A number of these Paris poems read as forced attempts to wring philosophical meaning from vexed encounters ("Fourth Caprice in Montparnasse," "Bacchus and Ariadne," "Entretien dans un parc"). At the other extreme, some read as unconvincing attempts to shrug at the absence of meaning ("Inside the gloom," "He said: this universe").

The suspicion and fear of authorial audiences with which he has been struggling throughout the notebook reach a climacteric with one of his first Paris poems, "The Triumph of Bullshit" (November 1910), where he curses at an uncomprehending audience. The first few Paris poems reveal a brief fumble amid the poet's disorientations on arrival. Shortly, his audience problems—problems of trust and rhetorical organization—are given firmer resolutions in the late Paris poems. The author's fear of ridicule and of being misunderstood does not disappear from his poetry; rather, this fear is put to productive artistic use. He no longer defensively protects himself from hostile or uncomprehending audiences. Instead, he explicitly announces his fear, turning to a sympathetic audience to share in it. For the most part, the authorial audience is no longer the source of his fear: he can finally trust his audience to follow him sympathetically. Even when the fear of an audience does surface—"Oh do not ask 'what is it?'"—it is deftly handled, woven into the fabric of the poem's rhetoric rather than tearing it apart.

Among the many measures of this advance, which will be detailed in discussions of each poem below, one instance might be summarized here. The various sections of "Portrait of a Lady" provide instructive contrasts because the three sections of the poem, written at different times, explore roughly the same dilemma and maintain the same characters. As we saw in chapter 3, the first-drafted section of "Portrait" (later published as section II) contained some intemperate gesturing that is later deleted. Four lines explode at the lady's pretentiousness and are aimed at her directly, the audience in the poem: "Oh, spare these reminiscences! / How you prolong the pose!" And two lines parenthetically apologize to the audience of the poem for this outburst: "(The need for self-expression / Will pardon this digression)."[42] Both the invention and the deletion of these lines reveal an author uneasy about the expectations of his audiences. By contrast, the section drafted nine months later in Paris requires no restraining. A few lines from this draft are later cut for publication but only because the lines are repetitive or awkward, not because of audience problems. Eliot has finally grasped the character of his audience. "Portrait" (I), as well as "Rhapsody on a Windy Night," "Preludes" III, and "Prufrock," are all more sure-footed than anything he has written previously.

After the disorientations of his first months in Paris, his confidence in addressing a poetic audience is matched by a personal confidence. Nearing the end of his momentous year abroad, Eliot writes to his former professor of fine arts: "My opinions on art, as well as other subjects, have modified radically."[43] He is a changed man. Even as the Parisian sophisticate brags to his former professor about his maturation, he realizes that he has yet to undergo the crucible of reentry into America, where he fears that his literary dreams will be suffocated. In the summer of 1911, preparing for the long trip back across the ocean, he finishes "Prufrock," whose speaker imagines waking from a watery dream and drowning in the stifling confines of the Boston establishment and the airless halls of academic philosophy.

The Poems
Poems spanning Nov. 1910 to July 1911 (Eliot in Paris, aged twenty-two years)

"The Triumph of Bullshit"	drafted Nov. 1910
"Portrait of a Lady" I	drafted Nov. 1910
"Fourth Caprice in Montparnasse"	drafted Dec. 1910
"Entretien dans un parc"	drafted Feb. 1911
"Interlude: in a Bar"	drafted Feb. 1911
"Bacchus and Ariadne"	drafted Feb. 1911
"The smoke that gathers blue and sinks"	drafted Feb. 1911
"Inside the gloom"	drafted late 1910 / early1911
"The Little Passion: From 'An Agony in the Garret'"	drafted Feb. 1911–July 1911
"He said: this universe is very clever"	drafted Mar. 1911
"Rhapsody on a Windy Night"	drafted Mar. 1911
"Interlude in London"	drafted Apr. 1911
"Ballade pour la grosse Lulu"	drafted July 1911
"Preludes" III	drafted July 1911
["The Love Song of J. Alfred Prufrock"	dated July–Aug. 1911—discussed in chapter 7]

"The Triumph of Bullshit"
Drafted November 1910[44]

The thematic concern of this tart little poem is the gap between an artist's "good intentions" and an audience's incomprehension.[45] Eliot's juvenilia, as we have seen, had been acutely conscious of his audience's conservative expectations; since the beginning of the notebook, Eliot has been wary of the even greater danger of hostile audiences. When those audiences in the notebook are pegged as female, the wariness increases. This distrust now comes roaring out in "The Triumph of Bullshit," where "Ladies" serve as a convenient target for the speaker's rage. The self-parody in the poem does not deflect attention from its target of sentimental women, nor do the scatological elements push this poem into the territory of good-humored bawdy. Unlike the contempt hurled at social convention in earlier poems, the anger here is disproportionate as well as unfocused. The only other poem Eliot writes in the same month as "The Triumph of Bullshit" is section I of "Portrait of a Lady"—yet another lady who misunderstands.

Poems do not necessarily spring from the biographical experiences of the artist. These imagined "Ladies" are literary, not biographical, and they reflect the audience problems Eliot has been negotiating since his juvenilia. But the surprising anger of the poem bespeaks a source in the poet's life. As for the target, those Ladies bear a suspicious resemblance to his mother's society connections. (Charlotte Eliot was an active member of several women's groups, including the St. Louis Woman's Club and the Wednesday Club, which had an artistic and intellectual character.) As for the anger itself, perhaps it has something to do with Eliot's transition to France and the anxiety that attends such momentous changes: feeling vulnerable and lost, Eliot lashes out in anger at imagined critics. In this November of Eliot's jangling nerves and culture shock, "The Triumph of Bullshit" lays bare the extreme form of the problem he has been grappling with in the notebook: How does one communicate when an audience's expectations guarantee incomprehension? That Eliot, in the extremities of emotional turmoil, reaches for this theme again is another indication of how central this problem is to his development as an artist.

The speaker of the poem is an artist, a floundering writer of "versicles." Uncomprehending and hostile "Ladies" constitute the audience in the poem—an audience that points backward to the "female readers" contemptuously dismissed in "Nocturne" and forward to the vacuous debutantes of Prufrock's circle. The Ladies themselves are dismissive of the speaker-poet's failures: "Awkward insipid and horridly gauche." Each stanza is a variation on the theme of the speaker's poetry as overrefined, derivative, and ineffective. The Ladies' mocking, nursery-rhyme dactyls are all interrupted with the speaker's refrain, abruptly shifting to pounding iambs and spondees: "For Christ's sake stick it up your ass." For his part, the speaker courts the very criticisms he affects to reject: to those critics who would charge him with obscure vocabulary, the speaker responds with such diction as "galamatias" and "cabotin." As for the admonition that he is "frequently crass," the speaker exuberantly proves the charge with his scatological refrain.

The Ladies' inventory of the speaker's defects is crowned by their critique of his intentions, such as his ineffectual staging of emotion. The penultimate line of each stanza builds to the criticism that strikes closest to the speaker's heart: "Attempts at emotions that turn out *isiculous*" (second stanza) and "Quite innocent—'he only wants to make shiver us'" (third stanza). Both accusations turn on the concept of emotional coldness. In the second stanza, the speaker has attempted to communicate a warm emotion, but the effect leaves its female readers as frozen as the word it describes: "isiculous" deriving from an obsolete spelling of "icicle."[46] In the third stanza, the Ladies' accusation sums up the poet's ineffectiveness. Compared to a child with a "box of new toys," the speaker is charged by his hostile readers with seeking mere effect through novelty. The hostile audience in the poem judges that the speaker "only wants to make shiver us"; the speaker's attempts to move his audience are as clumsily ineffective as the ungainly metathesis of that phrase.

The final stanza switches rhythmic and tonal gears, slowing to an iambic pace. In its stagily archaic diction ("thyself," "shalt pass"), it seems to be moving toward a moderated conclusion, wherein the poet would humbly invite his critics to consider his sincerity in spite of his failures. Capitulating to his critics, the speaker admits that his own theory, lying in fragments on the ground, cannot be said to have accomplished its aims. Only its "good intentions" can be said to exist, not their successful realization. But the speaker drops this pose to get the last word in. Rammed up the anuses of his critics, his verse fails as poetry but triumphs as bullshit.

The despised ladies who are the audience in the poem contrast with the audience of the poem: serious male artists who share the speaker's disdain for sentimentality and who sympathize with the vexed problems of artistic communication. With its insistent scatology, the poem harks back to the homosocial air of Harvard undergraduates and the sympathetic audience of "Ballade of the Fox Dinner." However, unlike the parodic "Envoi" that concludes that light-hearted poem, here Eliot chooses FitzGerald—hardly a greater contrast could be found—to bring this jittery poem to conclusion. The effect of swerving into FitzGerald's Romanticism is tonal incongruity rather than parody. The poet is looking to contrast the bitterness of the poem in order to gain momentum for the final refrain.

The poem's ire, while seeming irrationally aimed at an undeserving target, is in effect a crystallization of the very problems of audience anxiety that Eliot has been struggling with for more than a year in the notebook and that his later Paris poems will finally resolve. With its boorish and repetitive content, its instinct for polemic rather than observation, the poem represents an uncharacteristic step backward for an artist who had been demonstrating increasing mastery on many fronts. Whatever provoked this poem, the poet is in danger of letting his finely tuned irony revert to an adolescent crudeness. Within the notebook's trajectory of advances, "The Triumph of Bullshit" is an instance of how Eliot's path also involved cul-de-sacs and detours.

After the frantic gesticulations of "The Triumph of Bullshit," Eliot regains his countenance and remains self-possessed—mostly.

"Portrait of a Lady" I
Drafted November 1910; published with part II (drafted earlier) and part III (drafted later), September 1915, Others

The same month of Eliot's jarring dislocation to Paris sees him composing two poems in radically different styles: the crude scatology of "The Triumph of Bullshit" and the fine-brush reserve of "Portrait of a Lady." Aside from sharing chronological and physical space in the notebook, there would appear to be little connection between the two poems.[47] But both poems target women who have entrapped the speaker; both audiences in the poem are unsympathetic forces "upon whom [his] attentions have waited." Here in "Portrait" I, Eliot resumes his tactic of observation in order to dilute the lady's power. Unlike the earlier section of "Portrait," with its (eventually) deleted stanza of accusation and apology, the tone of this section is assured throughout, with no intemperate gesturing. A few lines are later edited out, but these moments are repetitive or unnecessary rather than disruptive.

Eliot returns to his analytical portrait of this Boston society matron who preys on the sympathies of a well-mannered young man. The stage-managing metaphor, implicit in the section drafted earlier, now becomes explicit, as both speaker and lady attempt to gain the upper hand: the lady by "design[ing]" an afternoon for him, the speaker by distancing himself from her.[48] That distance is signaled in the distinction between her directly quoted speech and his own reported interior narrative (her direct speech versus his indirect speech). Like the stage-managed scene of Juliet's feigned death—whose consequences are disastrous—traps and stratagems are the dominant metaphors of this section. The notebook version is more explicit about traps and disasters: "disturbing things" are deliberately left unspoken, whereas the revised version leaves the strategy more obscure: "all the things to be said, or left unsaid."

The proximate cause of their meeting is an intimate tea following a concert at which a Polish pianist—the latest subject of upper-class frisson—has explored the delicate terrain of his countryman, Chopin. Yet the specificity of the occasion is undercut with the speaker's "let us say"—as if the scene is always set this way, no matter what the occasion. In the section of "Portrait" drafted earlier, Eliot had finally perfected his "we"—intimately addressing an almost-trusted audience. Now the speaker effortlessly distinguishes the "we" and "us" within one line: "We have been, let us say, to hear the latest Pole." "We" here refers to the lady and the speaker, while "us" encloses the speaker and the authorial audience. Even though this "us" signals a generic "one" as much as the authorial audience, the transition is so smooth that the rhetorical organization of the poem is finally assured.

Just as the "We" and "us" of the line refer to different audiences, so the "you" of the poem shifts identity. The "You" who has the scene "arrange itself" is the lady, whom the speaker mentally addresses in his head, while the "us" of "Let us take the air" is presumably a male companion with whom he escapes the lady's grasp. This companion is the same authorial "you" of "You will see me any morning in the park" of the previously drafted section. Mayer describes the rhetorical work accomplished by this shifting pronoun: "Although this 'you' is consistent with Eliot's use throughout the early poetry of the second person in the sense of 'one' as a device to escape responsibility, here it is also part of the rhetoric of the sophisticate, whereby the young man mentally addresses himself to a kind of knowing auditor who will recognize his cleverness, approve his gambits, and solve his uncertainties (Are his ideas right or wrong? Should he have the right to smile?)."[49]

The *success* of the speaker's tactics depends upon the audience's recognizing the *failure* of the lady's tactics. Her first strategy is the engineering of the scene; her second strategy is calling attention to what is already apparent—that she has "designed" the afternoon for him. Her third volley is a defensive move: she wants to prove that she is intelligent and sensitive, yet she does not want to be upstaged by intellectual talk, since her preferred plane is the emotional, where she can dominate. And so she breezily notes that the refinement of Chopin's music is such that it should be played "only among friends / Some two or three." Her casually unspecific number specifies the speaker and herself, and she thus avoids the faux pas of brazenly declaring off limits a normally acceptable topic of conversation: postconcert discussion in which attendees voice their opinions of the performance. The speaker precisely describes the erotic undertone and power plays of social chatter: "the conversation slips / Among velleities and carefully caught regrets."

With these preliminary moves out of the way, the game to win the speaker's sympathy begins in earnest, with the off-stage trumpets ("remote cornets") signaling the commencement of hostilities. Launching a provocative accusation, the lady digresses into a compliment and ends with an expression of gratitude, all run together to prevent interruption:

"You do not know how much they mean to me, my friends
And how, how rare and strange it is, to find
In a life composed so much, so much of ways and ends
(Indeed I am not social—you knew it? ah, I knew you were not blind!
How keen you are!)
—To find a friend who has those qualities
So rare and strange and so unvalued too
Who has, and gives
Those qualities upon which friendship lives
How much it means that I say this to you!
Without these friendships—life, what *cauchemar*!"[50]

Reverberating somewhere between insult and invitation, her ploy first charges the speaker with the offense of undervaluing intimacy. Reversing course, she then implies that the speaker does value intimacy, having those very "rare and strange" qualities in which friendship thrives. Finally, an expression of her own vulnerability forestalls any defensiveness on the part of the speaker: "How much it means that I say this to you!" The apotheosis of her maneuvering is the pretentious exclamation, "life, what *cauchemar!*" whose gaffe exposes her straining for effect. As Ricks has pointed out, she should either say "what a nightmare!" or "*quel cauchemar!*"—not a mixture of the two.[51] Yet in spite of her domineering tactics, her ploys do not have the desired effect. Together, the speaker and the authorial audience observe her failed tactics.

In my earlier discussion of the first-drafted section of this poem, I had described the rhetoric of that section as a space the speaker carves out between a character whom he observes and a sympathetic audience whom he addresses. The resumption of this poem presents an ethical problem, insofar as its rhetoric lays the groundwork for its ethics. By adding another scene, the author raises the stakes of its ethics: Why return? To scoff yet again at the benighted woman? The intimacy forged between the speaker and authorial audience becomes increasingly compromised by the speaker's embarrassment at his own moral and social obligations. His squeamishness is a sign that ridicule is an ethically impoverished response. Yet the speaker has trouble moving beyond seeing this lady as a ridiculous figure. As a consequence, the portrait of her trembles on the edge of the maudlin; as a character of sympathy, she hovers somewhere between bathos and pathos.

This uncertainty is reflected in critical discussions of the poem. Given the apparent pretentiousness of the lady, Grover Smith's critical defense of her serves as a typical case. Smith's reading leans in her favor too much, imagining that her "buried life" is poignantly presented rather than pathetically mocked: "Her appeal, moreover, to her 'buried life, and Paris in the spring' conveys to [the speaker] an unmanageable fact, that she is no mere instrument of monotonous music but a wasted human heart. Matthew Arnold's poem 'The Buried Life' contributes to her phrase the sense of the incalculable, unconscious vital principle, the essential humanity beneath all appearance. But equally there is a sense of a lost past, a vanished joy."[52] The allusion to Arnold, rendered by Smith as granting pathos to the lady, can reverberate in other directions: as yet another pretentious allusion or as the lady's claim to a rich interiority that the speaker doubts. Thus, it is impossible to determine the author's sympathies here. How the audience's attitude is subsequently shaped has less to do with the rhetoric of "Portrait"—that is to say, with the power that the poem has to shape an audience's attitude—than in the ethical assumptions that readers already bring to the poem. An author cannot control such assumptions, which makes talk of an authorial audience always ideal rather than real. That Eliot allows these various attitudes full play is a sign of how far he has come in his development. Only a few months earlier, in the February 1910 section of "Portrait," he was still apt to gesture frantically, attempting to coerce the authorial audience's reaction. The speaker's angry mockery of the lady is later deleted—"Oh, spare these reminiscences!" But that such lines were still tentatively proffered in the earlier section shows Eliot's ill-advised attempts at control.

In this November 1910 section, the speaker's self-ridicule is more obvious: "Inside my brain a droll tom-tom begins." This self-ridicule offers a solution to the problem of why the author returns to expand the poem. It is a more ethically clear solution than the dubious effects of ridicule-cum-sympathy directed at the lady, but neither self-ridicule nor self-awareness fully solves the problem, hence the critical disagreement as to who comes off worse, the lady or the speaker. Critics cannot agree on where the sympathies of the poem lie; indeed, the speaker himself seems not to know ("Are these ideas right or wrong?"). Such disagreement is a sign that the authorial audience has become wrapped up in the complex—and, in its draft form, confused—rhetorical schema designed by the author. These insoluble ethical and rhetorical problems lead the author to revert to the same deus ex machina attempted in the earlier section of "Portrait": at the climax of his embarrassment and impatience, the speaker escapes, without transition, from the confined salon to the imagined camaraderie of an intimately addressed other. In the earlier section, the speaker had escaped in this manner:

> —I take my hat. How can I make a cowardly amends
> For what she has said to me?
>
> You will see me any morning in the park
>
> —"Portrait of a Lady" II[53]

In the November 1910 section, the speaker escapes again:

> Inside my brain a droll tom-tom begins
> Hammering a prelude of its own
> Capricious monotone . . .
> That is at least one definite "false note."
> —Let us take the air, in a tobacco trance
>
> —"Portrait of a Lady" I

As we will see in chapter 8, when Eliot returns a third and final time to these scenes, it will be to draft a more satisfying resolution—narrative, ethical, and rhetorical—than these two sections deliver.

Rooting for the lady, rather than examining the social structure in which both characters are caught, Smith accuses the young man of "injudiciously protract[ing] his acquaintance with the lady until he cannot go free without embarrassment and cruelty." Stepping further into the traps of the poem, Smith projects onto the speaker a motive of being afforded "a certain intellectual amusement" by the lady's ridiculousness, which keeps him returning.[54] At the risk of projecting a motive as arbitrary as Smith's, I would suggest that Eliot's returning in imagination to these scenes mirrors the problem of visitation etiquette. In the poet's quasi-aristocratic class, one did not casually drop a society matron simply because she was pretentious. (The resumption of the poem also prompts a new epigraph, a complaint of recurrent pain, inescapable if mild: "I have caught an everlasting cold.") The culture of such social rounds involved the silent endurance of the members of one's class, hence the liberation Eliot felt when Laforgue gave him a language for directing pent-up rage at its restrictions. The author of this poem is just as stuck in the rounds of visitation as the speakers of his poems are stuck inside their heads. The poetry, for Eliot, involved observing and articulating this conundrum rather than escaping it. Those fleeting moments of imagined escape are never real but wildly fantastical in the Paris poems, as if abandoning the universe of Cambridge would be closer to a fairy tale than to a viable strategy: ragged claws, butterflies, mermaids, and chattering apes populate the overworld that is Not-Cambridge. The underworld that is Not-Cambridge is the world of poverty, brokenness, and prostitutes—a world that is more sympathetic to Eliot but just as unreachably other as the world of mermaids.

Vendler comments on the paradox at the heart of Eliot's critique-cum-acquiescence in this discourse: "He has mimicked, satirically, the inherited repressive discourses of his class, but has been unable to dismiss them utterly—admitting, by his recurrent recourse to such straitened exchanges, their importance in his aesthetic and ethical formation."[55] So Eliot remains stuck: in his head, in his class, in his social rounds, even when he has critiqued them in his poetry. And even in Paris, where he had fled to escape them all.

"Fourth Caprice in Montparnasse"
Drafted Dec. 1910

It is unclear why Eliot begins another city poem under the rubric of "Caprice," with the obvious success of "Preludes" behind him and the adequacy of its rhetoric to the themes of urban detritus and human suffering. The "Caprice" sequence, by contrast, had been disjointed: the seriousness of Baudelaire derailed by the sarcasm of Laforgue. Perhaps Eliot sees the success of the first two "Preludes" as a way to rescue the "Caprice" poems. Though this poem is numbered "Fourth," the third poem is unaccounted for—either never written or discarded.

Eliot is writing on the Left Bank, near Montparnasse, where he would have gone walking, but his original title for the poem is "Fourth Caprice in North Cambridge." The American city is later crossed out and "Montparnasse" penciled above it, with no other change to the setting of the poem. As Mayer has noted, in Eliot's Paris poems, familiar landmarks like the Seine or the Eiffel Tower do not appear. Eliot's cities are interchangeable: "They are not poems of Paris but of the City of Matter," Mayer argues, "and their cityscapes are not important in themselves, as aspects of a distinctive city, but only in relation to a consciousness compelled to confront through their matter its destiny and vocation."[56]

The crux of the poem is a contrast: beggars who are indifferent and a speaker who is not. Both stances result in uncertain effect. Observing a rainy scene, the speaker compares soaked houses to mendicants begging for alms in the dreary weather. They are "without regrets / For unpaid debts."[57] More problematic for the speaker, the houses/mendicants are "Indifferent if derided." This short, three-word line yokes together the two conflicting emotions of Eliot's Paris year: apathy and fear of ridicule. A grammatical ambiguity uneasily tethers indifference to mockery: "if" here embracing *when*, *despite*, or *perhaps not*. The indifference of the mendicants is hard to pin down. Are they indifferent to the mockery of those who decline to help them? Or merely unapologetic for their neediness? Or are they indifferent to whether they succeed in getting alms? Whatever their stance, it presents a challenge to the speaker, who reverts twice to tight, ragtime rhymes in his attempt to articulate the ambiguity. As an artist, the speaker cannot imagine himself indifferent to the jeers of an audience. Yet somehow these beggars have achieved a spiritual indifference: oddly detached from their vocation, they remain "Hand in pocket, undecided" rather than begging with outstretched hands. This aporia—one among many "scattered thoughts" that have no apparent resolution—provokes the poem to an impasse. The only remaining maneuver is to move to the refrain and to pose an unanswerable question: "But why are we so hard to please?" That pronominal shift to "we" blurs the identities of speaker and audience. The question in which the "we" is set addresses itself both to the speaker's desire for meaning and the audience's expectation of coherence, neither of which is satisfied. However, the conspiratorial "we" does show that this artist knows who his audiences are: both the addressee—the audience in the poem—and the authorial audience outside of the poem.

This poem is successful in so far as its "scattered thoughts" gaze without judgment at the detritus and confusion of the world. But its final gesture repeats, less disastrously, the same error as "First Caprice"; its final complaint is only a milder variation on "Oh, these minor considerations!" To dubious effect, the gesture self-consciously points to the very discontent that his "Caprice" poems can neither resolve nor satisfactorily articulate, even though its audience is nicely rendered. As a result, he writes no more "Caprice" poems, leaving them all unpublished.

"Entretien dans un parc"
Drafted Feb. 1911

Aimless and prosy, the slackness of this poem's conception is not apposite to the intensity of its reported emotions. Nevertheless, it does strike a new note of intimacy, of a speaker on the verge of revealing himself to a reader. As an experiment in this direction, it moves Eliot toward "Prufrock" primarily because it allows him to articulate the painful restraints of courtship rituals as they affect a hyperconscious young man.

The poem exists in the same social world as "Portrait of a Lady," presenting a speaker who struggles to make his intentions known. A century after these poems have been written, it is difficult to recapture the cultural norms that guided social interaction, but Vendler is not exaggerating when she claims that the quasi-aristocratic milieu in which Eliot was raised was "almost inhumanly restrained in what it allowed by way of permissible conversation between the sexes."[58] This restraint would have included the impossible expectation that suitors could convey their intentions with the conversation limited to art or the weather. Such a charged if futile atmosphere is described by the speaker's "Struggling intention that becomes intense."[59] As poetry, it is a feeble line, but its author is attempting to ferret out the word "intense" as buried inside "intention." Unspoken intentions, especially for a suitor, are a matter of great personal intensity. The cultural pressures to leave those intentions unspoken only compound the anxiety of the speaker (and possibly the woman), exacerbating the ridiculousness of the situation.

The poem's dramatic action hinges on a wordless gesture. Shamed by his own irresolution, the speaker experiences a "sudden vision of incompetence." By way of reaction, he wills himself to "seize" the hand of his walking partner. This sharp gesture surprises both the speaker and the woman, who accepts it. The world does not fall apart; indeed, she even smiles at him: "as if, perhaps, surprised to see / So little her composure disarranged." There is a measure of self-awareness in his "perhaps." The speaker knows his own internal anxieties; yet, because of a lack of genuine connection, he suspects that he may only be projecting his anxieties onto the woman. Even though the point of courtship is to have one's advance accepted, his success brings the speaker no comfort. He grumbles inwardly, "All the scene's absurd!" Having screwed his courage to the sticking place, his own feelings still do not line up with traditional romantic expectations ("what we feel, or not"). Wherever such social conventions are subjected to scrutiny, the speaker experiences them as moments of embarrassment and ridicule. The theatrical metaphor slides in: the "scene" is ridiculous and exasperating, and somewhere out of sight an audience (not the authorial one) sits in judgment, stirring the "fire of ridicule." It is noteworthy that this outburst—the "absurd!" scene, stoked by the "fire of ridicule"—marks the last appearance in the notebook of such intemperate anger.

The transition from the interior fear of "the fire of ridicule" to the external "blind alley" follows the same course Eliot has set elsewhere. Once again, the futile anger at imagined audiences and the cul-de-sac of introspection are left behind by turning to seedy materiality: the detritus and graffiti of the alley. Hovering as a self-contained stanza, the couplet begins and ends with dashes, signaling the unnamable:

—Up a blind alley, stopped with broken walls
Papered with posters, chalked with childish scrawls!—

Lacking a subject or verb, the two lines come as a relief, a moment of meditation and observation before the hazards of his hypothetical conclusion. Yet the image of the blind alley is not an escape: it is a metaphor of the speaker's walled-off interiority, defaced with posters and handwriting, the evidence of now-absent others.

The final stanza fantasizes a way out of these difficulties: "if we could have given ourselves the slip / What explanations might have been escaped—." In this hypothesis, where their awkward selves have been evaded, no explanations would be required, no confusion remain over "ends unshaped." This fantasy is deflated by reality: "We are helpless." Nonetheless, the speaker is still intrigued by the woman's vague acceptance of his advance, however ambiguously interpreted and however threatening to his own composure. In the midst of trailing ellipses, he wonders: "Still . . . it was unaccountable . . . odd . . ." The speaker wonders whether, like industrious creatures, one might arrange such matters and control their outcome: "Could not one keep ahead, like ants or moles?"

This attempt to control the effects of self-abandonment leads to the remarkable final lines that posit a deity who might intervene to solve these intractable problems. But this unsettling possibility is immediately rejected and reabsorbed into the quiet irony of composed masks: "Someday, if God— / But, then, what opening out of dusty souls!" Here is found the first, tentative broaching of the term "God" in relationship to the speaker's self, though it is a rhetorical gambit rather than a record of a visionary moment. The content of such a hypothetical encounter cannot even be articulated; the Dickinsonian dash holds a world of uncertainty within its mute slimness: "Someday, if God—." The halting recommencement of the following line ("But, then, what") marks the speaker's uneasy recovery and his admitted unwillingness to consider what such an "opening" of souls might portend. He knows only that it would be a dirty business, like an airing of closets better kept shut.

"Interlude: in a Bar"
Drafted Feb. 1911

The scene is set in a squalid, smoke-filled bar, a setting that is both hazily unreal and sordidly realistic. As with other Paris poems, the opening image of smoke straddles the mind/body divide: the smoke in the room hovers around the figures "that pass / Pass through or clog the brain."[60] The life that the bar encloses is described in a series of paradoxes that also span the mind/body divide: "Visionary, and yet hard; / Immediate, and far." The speaker circles back to the word "hard," expanding it into a simile that prefigures the poverty and despair of the Thames daughters in *The Waste Land*: life is "scarred / Like dirty broken fingernails."

The title of this poem—as with "Preludes"—refers to a short musical composition, one that is placed between or before more important pieces. This short sketch avoids large conclusions and rests in ambiguous observation and depersonalized images. Human figures are "forms," and only the detached "finger nails" are given life in this poem, but it lacks the coherence of the other "Preludes" and is not published as a consequence.

"Bacchus and Ariadne: 2nd Debate between the Body and Soul"
Drafted Feb. 1911

The rhetorical problem here is identified in the phrase "tendencies unknown and questions never spoken."[61] How does one gesture toward mystery without sounding, on the one hand, obscure, and on the other, banal? The mysteries to which this poem addresses itself include human isolation (a "ring of silence" is contrasted with the violent "world of contact"). The other mystery—the road that leads out of isolation, directed by longing—is the path of human flourishing. The failure of the poem lies in the gap between the speaker's certainty that such a path exists and his inability to reveal it. The poem's gesture toward "tendencies unknown and questions never spoken" also suggests the legitimately hidden and mysterious overlap with cultural repression and self-deception. Nothing is ever simple in Eliot.

The springboard of the poem is a painting of the lovers Bacchus and Ariadne, perhaps a Titian painting of the same title, described as "exuberant" in Eliot's London Baedeker.[62] Imitating smoke—Eliot's preferred metaphor for the unknowable and for the body/soul intersection—the lovers "curl upward like a wave" that seems to break but ultimately does not. While the "drums of life" are sounding in the lovers' heads, by contrast the speaker is trapped in a "ring of silence." Whatever thoughts he manages are a result of willful exertion, like a train that appears in the middle of a desert.

Time makes its inevitable and destructive entrance, prepared for by the rough "world of contact" and the dissolving "winds beyond the world." Both images smack of gothic bathos, Eliot here clumsily moving the poem toward the solution he wishes to propose. The goal of human flourishing—and the path out of isolation—is distilled in the concluding image of a chrysalis. The pupa of a butterfly represents transformation, the body and soul evolving into some other state. The state that the speaker longs for is one that is frank, idealistic, yet not naive: this would be "triumph."

Amid some grammatical ambiguity, the final stanza links the pure idea/intellect to feeling/body: the butterfly, locked in its pupa cell, "meditates its wings"; that is, the insect imagines its way out of an earthbound state while being fed by the decaying earth. The poem ends with a hollow if resonant pattern of repetition and distillation, the epistemological ground of the poem asserted rather than shown: "I am sure it is like this / I am sure it is this / I am sure." By proposing such an idealistic solution, Eliot veers toward a philosophical dilettantism. Unlike the wishful thinking of this poem, Eliot's best works explore the impasse of his problems, observing his own fantasies of escape rather than proposing viable solutions.

"The smoke that gathers blue and sinks"
Drafted Feb. 1911

As with the parks and public venues that are recurrent backdrops for the Paris poems, the setting of this poem is a public bar where the speaker weighs his alienation from others by observing them at a distance. The atmosphere of the bar is inert and sleepily drunken, the air filled with the blue smoke of "rich cigars" and the pungent smells of liqueurs.[63] Humanity is depersonalized, appearing only as "overoiled" or drunk "machinery" rather than as individuals. The lethargic stanza peters out with ellipses.

The second stanza abruptly changes direction with "What, you want action?" The tone and pace contrast: a sexualized content, strong rhymes and short lines brimming with allusions to popular music. The first attraction hauled out on stage is "A lady of almost any age / But chiefly breast and rings" who sings a raucous popular song begging for love. This diversion is dismissed as "hardly strong enough." The second act sees a dancing "negro" reduced, like the woman, to body parts. In a visual pun, Eliot encloses this character's "(teeth and smile)" with two parenthetical lips. By distilling these two figures to body parts, Eliot points to the ideological charge of their performance: the woman is reduced to her overbearing sexuality (breasts) and her femininity (rings), while the male is reduced to his crowd-pleasing minstrelsy—the broad, toothy smile a common racist depiction of African Americans, especially performers. The poem attempts to hold together, without resolving them, the opposed states of lethargy and enthusiasm, meaning and meaninglessness.

"Inside the gloom"
Drafted late 1910/early1911

As with so many Paris poems that are infected by an atmospheric gloom, this poem queries "the relation of life to matter."[64] Its setting of a murky attic connects the poem to the garret of "The Little Passion," written around the same time. Both poems evoke the pension where Eliot lived on the upper floors, mulling over his isolation and searching for meaning.

Increasingly impatient with the aridity of philosophical speculation, Eliot harnesses the irony—as well as the astronomical content and stanzaic structure—of Laforgue's "Litanies des premiers quartiers de la lune." Eliot represents various philosophical positions as constellations: the stars take up "their stations" with attendant connotations of fixity and armed combat. The constellation positions are designated with their mythological or zoological names, such as Scorpion, Major Bear, Pegasus, Cassiopeia, though their squabbling and posturing make their proportions seem less mythic than cartoonish. Occupying points on an astronomical chart, their rigid positions are unconnected to other ideas and take no part in genuine dialogue. The inconsequential debate among the stars provokes the final constellation to suggest that all such metaphysical queries are caused merely by "indigestions." Even this dismissal is not as searing as the speaker's final word: "So they cried and chattered/As if it mattered."

Eliot's less successful Paris poems move between extremes of emotional states, trembling with the pathos of forced ecstasy (the unconvincing eureka that concludes "Bacchus and Ariadne"), untempered rage ("The Triumph of Bullshit"), or despair ("Inside the gloom"). Eliot manages to temper the nihilism of this latter poem with the knowing wink of his own exasperation. This poem is as much a critique of the meaninglessness of philosophy as of the author's own psychological pain: the tempest of philosophy is acknowledged as existing only in the narrow confines of the speaker's small room/mind. The constellations take up their positions not in the broad firmament but in the claustrophobic squalor of his "garret room."

"The Little Passion: From 'An Agony in the Garret'"
Loose leaf version drafted Feb. 1911–July 1911; notebook version 1914

The effect of the title is Laforguean: a pinprick to the overdrawn.[65] This "little" passion is not the Christian drama of salvation. Its agony is one of ennui and isolation rather than torture and murder, and its setting is not the garden of Gethsemane but a bar and a garret. In spite of such deflationary tactics, the poem is serious in intent and tone, Eliot having learned to adapt Laforgue for uses other than dismissive contempt. Rather than mock the pretensions of an overindulgent speaker, the circumscription of "little" and "garret" in the title highlights his alienation and disconnection.

In spite of the speaker's isolation in a garret, the drafts are unique among the Paris poems in that they describe a tenuous relationship the speaker has with a talkative bar patron. In the solitude of his attic room, the speaker recalls their numerous conversations and one comment in particular. The bar where they would meet is one of the "dark retreats" where the man postpones, or at least marks, his journey to the cross amid his night wanderings in the city.[66] The crucifixion to which the man moves is "inevitable" rather than chosen. In the concluding stanza, the speaker notices the man's "hopeless" cigarette and his ambiguous smile: "A washed-out, unperceived disgrace." The disgrace refers presumably to the existential nature of the man's suffering, as his cross is barred from grace, holds no promise of redemption. The "Little Passion" fizzles with despair instead of exploding into transformative miracle.[67]

In a remarkable letter to Emily Hale, Eliot sheds light on this difficult poem when he explains one of the most disturbing events of his life, which occurred in Paris in his pension, sometime before Christmas 1910. Eliot had been befriended by an older, gay Englishman, Matthew Prichard, a former assistant director of the Boston's Museum of Fine Arts and a friend of some of the same patrons whom Eliot had known in Boston. At this vulnerable point in his life, Eliot felt himself dominated by this man, whose views on aesthetics and philosophy he respected. His terror was provoked not by an attempted seduction but by what seemed to be an attempt to possess his soul. (Prichard appears in Eliot's poetry as Mr. Silvero in "Gerontion.") Eliot describes a few moments alone in his upper room when he felt hung over an abyss, in utter despair.[68] By presenting a moment of horror in a garret, along with remembered conversations of a powerful, if disgraced man, this poem seems to have its sources in this terrifying experience.

Three moments in these two drafts point toward "Prufrock." First, the crucified souls are "pinned, and bleed," a formulation that reaches forward to Prufrock's predicament. In the later poem, though, the static of the paschal mystery will be cleared away for the more apt metaphor of an insect display. Second, a telltale "our" points to empathy and shared suffering. Eliot's revision of a line shows him edging closer to suffering: "his soul is spread" is emended to "our soul[s] are spread." As Eliot struggles to clarify the rhetoric, he is asking himself, who is included in the circle of intimacy and talk of suffering?

Most significantly, Eliot tries out a new manner of expression that he will use to startling effect in "Prufrock." Having mastered the oblique modes, Eliot now toys for the first time with the possibilities of a direct, lyrical statement of pain. If this claim that Eliot has not yet tried direct statement seems surprising, consider all the indirect ways in which Eliot's notebook poems have so far addressed suffering. In November 1909, the personal claim "I feel like the ghost of youth" is refracted through simile.[69] Several months later, another seemingly direct confession—"At such peace I am terrified"—is qualified by reference to a skeptical "You" who possibly disagrees.[70] Likewise, in September 1910, the apparently direct "I have my fears" is undone fore and aft by an auditor's "assuring certainties" and the speaker's own dismissal of his problems as "small beers."[71]

More often, the speaker's direct statements have not been personal revelations of intense emotion but veils drawn over the emotion: "I keep my countenance— / I remain self-possessed."[72] Where intense emotion has appeared, the speaking "I" is nowhere in sight: "And what of all that one has missed!"[73] So far in the notebook, loneliness has never been directly attributed to the speaker's self: "A lonely cab horse steams and stamps."[74] And human misery has, until Paris, been transferred to the impersonal "one" and to disembodied fragments: "One thinks of all the hands / That are raising dingy shades."[75]

Now we finally hear a direct statement of pain. As with his first, circumspect uses of slang in "Humouresque" placed in the mouth of the marionette, Eliot carefully frames this statement. It comes in the form of reported speech from which the speaker distances himself. An unbalanced character holds ideas that, the speaker shrugs, are "seldom well digested." As with the court fool who has freedom to speak the truth, the clarity of this man's self-awareness stings the speaker like a reproach: "I feel / As if I'd been a long time dead." This direct statement of suffering will license Prufrock's rare, devastating moments of honesty: "And in short, I was afraid," and "I do not think that they will sing to me."[76] It is significant that direct statements of pain, spoken through the "I," appear in the notebook during the same period that petty explosions of irritation and outrage disappear. He can trust the former lines to do their work without fear that the latter emotion will interrupt to undercut its sincerity.

"He said: this universe is very clever"
Drafted Mar. 1911

Like an obsessive worrying at an insoluble problem, Eliot returns to a claustrophobic interior. The familiar Paris garret is here rendered as "an attic / Up six abysmal flights of broken stairs."[77] At the time of writing, Eliot was living at a six-story pension at 151 bis rue St.-Jacques, and he was also immersed in the lectures of Henri Bergson at the Collège de France.[78] Bergson gave wildly popular lectures, the hall thronged with auditors long before the lectures began. Extending into many disciplines and exerting a broad effect on the culture at large, Bergson's philosophy promised, according to one rapturous admirer, "intoxicating novelties" and liberation from their "prison of materialism."[79] In describing his own intellectual development, Eliot often recalled this impressive spectacle of *la ferveur bergsonienne*, even though his later repudiation of the philosopher led him to dismiss his time in Paris as "a temporary conversion to Bergsonism."[80]

The first stanza of the poem rehearses a view of scientific determinism in which the universe works out its own ironclad rules. The second stanza serves as a quasi-Bergsonian response in which the universe is a "geometric net" whose processes divulge the Absolute. This godlike figure is compared to a "syphilitic spider" that devours everything. Ricks puzzles over this strange image, offering the explanation that syphilis "deals death in love and sex, and so—in some species—does the female spider."[81] While this explanation ties together the discordant elements of sexually transmitted disease, the breeding habits of spiders, and the meaning of the universe, it skirts the appalling nature of this view: it seems no more attractive than the scientific determinism it repudiates. Perhaps Eliot's incipient resistance to Bergson is detectable in the off-putting simile. Eliot intimates that the multidisciplinary Bergson offers an irresistible philosophy, but in spinning out a systematic explanation its web ultimately "tangle[s]" and kills. Later, Eliot would describe Bergson's troubling promise of immortality as a kind of seduction.[82]

Eliot continues drafting, drawing below the second stanza a line that marks off these lively, public debates from the more private stanzas that follow. The third stanza relates uneasily to the first two because it does not describe a worldview but an event. Or more accurately, two events juxtaposed: the "dramatic" crucifixion of an outsized life contrasted with a timid life spent on "officechairs." Given that the first two stanzas contrast determinism with absolutism, it may seem that the third stanza adds a theologian's view to the scientist's and the philosopher's. However, it is more likely that the crucifixion of the poem is de-Christianized to contrast the banal incoherence of personal experience (stanzas 3 and 4) with the intolerable comprehensiveness of scientific and philosophical thought (stanzas 1 and 2). That the poem is not concerned with the theology of salvation but with the incommensurability of the mundane with the meaningful is evident in its decoupling of the crucifixion from theology. The outsized life is described not in terms of soteriology, materiality, or philosophy but as "dramatic," which is to say, theatrical. While the monumental life—whether criminal or divine—provokes the outraged response of public execution, the timid life is constricted to meaningless routine and the narrow ambit of a garret. It is not a momentous crucifixion in the public square but a little crucifixion in an attic.

Since the little passion, or meaningless crucifixion, provides no rejoinder to scientific determinism or Bergsonian philosophy, the poem begins to fall apart. The pentameter quatrains and tight rhyme scheme of the first three stanzas give way to a halting, irregular conclusion whose content mirrors its incoherent form. Life is like an article that, instead of being fully written, is pasted together from "old clippings."

In any number of notebook poems, Eliot has sketched ideas, trends, or conventions with which he struggles. In this poem the stakes are even higher, since the struggle itself is called into question. On the one hand, Eliot fears a material universe with no meaning. On the other hand, he fears being trapped, against his will, into accepting an external system of meaning: the scientist's universe is so "clever" that even the motions of atoms cannot escape its laws. Although guided by different laws, Bergson's universe likewise entraps everyone "inside her." That such systems of meaning are imposed or unavoidable is highlighted by the unchanging attribution "He said." Monotone and monolithic, this same "He" introduces all of the conflicting ideas; there is no distinguishing "another said" or "a third said." This absence of variation—along with the absence of an authorial position—suggests that Eliot does not intend merely to juxtapose competing systems of meaning, implicitly valuing one over another. Instead, he bridles at the notion that his free will and judging intellect are perhaps not the deciding factors in what the universe means, if the universe can be said to mean anything at all. In the face of scientific determinism and Bergson's Absolute, the problem of free will looms even larger. The detached skepticism of Eliot's earlier critiques of philosophy is here flecked with metaphysical panic.

Unable to occupy a meta-position from which competing systems of meaning might be chosen or avoided, the speaker resorts to the incoherent scraps of experience that surround him: "I am put together with a pot and scissors." The poem necessarily stumbles in articulating how a timid life contrasts with a crucified life. The final stanza, deliberately flat, has become Eliot's predictable way out of insoluble difficulties. The conclusion registers disaffection with mere intellect but neither compellingly inhabits the problem, as his best Paris poems do, nor attempts a positive solution, as his unsuccessful Paris poems do. "Rhapsody on a Windy Night" will transform these fears and aporias into strange imagery and compelling music, in a way that "He said: this universe" has not been able to manage.

"Rhapsody on a Windy Night"
Drafted Mar. 1911; published in Blast, *July 1915*

"The poem is indeed bizarre," remarks Piers Gray, in an admiring summation of how "Rhapsody on a Windy Night" works its eerie magic on the reader.[83] Compared to the audience that Eliot constructs in other notebook poems, "Rhapsody" represents a high-water mark in the trust required of its audience to follow strange byways. Here Eliot explores alienation not only as it is projected onto a bleak urban landscape but as it is plumbed from within a dissolving consciousness. The intimacy of the poem is thus more disturbing than that of other city poems, such as the "Caprice" sequence or "Preludes," with their more objective frames of reference. In describing the genesis of "Rhapsody," Eliot recalled its experimental character as having no formal model. After having consciously imitated Laforgue, Eliot claims, "there were things in the next phase which were freer, like 'Rhapsody on a Windy Night.' I don't know whether I had any sort of model or practice in mind when I did that. It just came that way."[84]

It would be an exaggeration to say that "Rhapsody on a Windy Night" has been ignored, but it is curious to note how many of Eliot's important critics have played the game of acknowledging it as a major poem while at the same time declining to explain how it works or what it means.[85] Those critics who do seem to have a grasp on the poem tend strongly toward the philosophical. For example, Piers Gray's reading is compelling and scholarly, steeped as it is in Bergsonian philosophy. However convincing his interpretation, I find that with Gray—as with many critics who read the poems through the lens of Eliot's philosophical preoccupations—the line is blurred between a source and an allusion. Many readings of "Rhapsody on a Windy Night" are better at explaining the ideas of Bergson than the ideas of the poem—which are admittedly harder to pinpoint. Indeed, the philosophical critics cannot agree on whether the poem swims wholeheartedly in a Bergsonian sea, or whether it critiques Bergson's philosophy.

And so, rather than offer another gloss on the poem's relationship to Bergson's philosophy, I wish to focus on the poem's self-presentation to a reader. In the poem's draft form, Eliot can be seen working hard—perhaps too hard—at making the logic of its imagery apparent to the reader. In the second stanza, a streetlamp urges in the imperative mode:

> "regard that woman
> "Who hesitates toward you on the *corner*
> "You see the *corner* of her dress
> "Is torn, and stained with sand
> "And the *corner* of her eye
> "Twists like a crooked pin."[86]

Two more corners appear in a subsequent stanza. Part of the weirdness of the published poem resides not only in the imagery but in the way those images flow from one to the next. Here in the draft, however, the five repetitions of "corner" are deemed too obvious, and they are later edited down to two. However locally botched, this linguistic effect—the repetition of the same word to refer to different things—is transformed in later stanzas into a truly imagistic logic, such as the "twisted things" that weave through the poem. Even more disconcerting is the imagery of mechanical response in the fourth stanza.

With little transition, we first get a cat's tongue that "Slips out" to eat decaying food, then a child's hand grabbing a toy, then vacant stares of alienated passers-by, and finally a crab automatically locking onto a stick that the speaker offers. The cat and the crab frame two images of human disinclination: the vacant child and the alienated passers-by. A small illumination that the draft version reveals is Eliot's care with pronouns. Originally, the cat "flattens himself" and sticks out "his tongue." Later, the masculine pronouns are switched to neuter, distancing the cat from any human affect. The crab, in no danger of being anthropomorphized, retains the masculine "him."

Much could be said about Eliot's meaning here: what the poem has to say about automatic responses, for example. Note instead the way in which Eliot draws the reader through these images, inducing a cumulative effect of unthinking automatism everywhere. A crab gripping a stick is not in itself a striking image. But as the climax of a series of images, the effect is unnerving, as it compares the animalistic response of the crab to the preceding images of human motivation. The humans depicted in the poem are isolated not just from others but from their own desires. As images of alienation, both the cat and the crab will come back in "Prufrock" to comment on human lack of motivation.[87]

In addition to the logic of imagery that guides the reader through the poem, another deliberate effect the author deploys is an ambiguous syntax. The agrammatical placement of phrases mirrors the logic of juxtaposed images by which the poem proceeds. In original form, the opening is grammatically unsettling, its phrasing without apparent syntactical subordination or relation:

Along the reaches of the street
Held in a lunar synthesis
And all the lunar incantations
Dissolve the floors of memory

Revised, the grammar of these lines is clarified, though not entirely. The word "Whispering" hovers uncomfortably between an adjective and present participle:

Along the reaches of the street
Held in a lunar synthesis,
Whispering lunar incantations
Dissolve the floors of memory

Other sentences in the poem retain their improvisatory meandering. The final stanza is ripe with such ambiguities:

> Here is your number on the door
> Memory!
> You have the key

Is memory simply named by the speaker, or is it apostrophized as the "You" of the following line? Or is the addressee—"You"—the one who invokes memory? It is disorienting, though not exactly confusing, as the poem hangs together through the force of its conception.[88] Other, more radical ambiguities of the draft are clarified, but even the published draft contains moments that are tantalizingly unclear. What does it mean that the moon smiles "into corners"? The general sense is clear enough: she looks into corners with a smile. But we generally smile *at* things, not *into* them, unless they are mirrors or cameras—both of which imply a receiving consciousness, which a corner is not. The overall effect is of oddity, of something slightly amiss.

Another logic that holds the poem together is the patterning of its sounds. Aside from the obvious poetic effects such as rhyme and alliteration, there are numerous repetitions of words in close contact: "a *lunar* synthesis / And all the *lunar* incantations"; "The midnight *shakes* my memory / As a madman *shakes*"; "A crowd of *twisted* things; / —A *twisted* branch"; "And a *crab* one afternoon in a pool / A *crab* green." Even more insistent are the threefold repetitions: "The street-lamp sputtered / The street-lamp muttered / The street-lamp said"; and "The lamps sputtered / The lamp muttered in the dark / A lamp hummed"; and "cross and cross across." While one repetition generally creates a localized sonic effect, two repetitions in such close quarters create an effect quite different from mere alliteration. Here, all of these repetitions evoke a mind singularly focused on external details as a hedge against its dissolving consciousness. Such quiet obsession is the linguistic equivalent of a madman shaking a dead geranium.

In spite of the poem's reliance on sonic repetition, the trademark Laforguean/ragtime line appears only twice in the draft. The first appearance—"Its divisions, / Definite precisions"—is later changed to an internal rhyme. Only one remains in the published version, after slight revisions: "That smells of dust and eau de Cologne, / She is alone." In spite of the tightness of rhyme (a sought-after effect throughout "Rhapsody"), it is likely that this ragtime effect is not exploited here because it calls attention to the abruptness of the shortened line. If this effect had been overused in "Rhapsody," it would have created syncopations and rhythmic shifts that would have drawn attention away from the liquid haze in which the poem moves.

Another key to the soundscape of the poem is its momentary lapse into French. Eliot has conflated lines of Laforgue: "La lune ne garde aucune rancune." The shift to French creates a music of internal rhymes, smoothed over with the creamy alliteration of its "l"s and "n"s. That the moon would harbor no grudges is a function of her having "lost her memory." Thus, on the level of idea, the line is linked to memory and pain. But the purpose of keeping it in French is not to remind us of its source—Laforgue was then largely unknown to English readers—but to exploit the alliteration and consonance of the line. Likewise, the internal rhyme "divisions and precisions" distills the aural music of Laforgue and forecasts the sounds of Prufrock's "visions and revisions."

There are other logics that hold the poem together, including its dialectical structure, its chronological framework, its contrasts of light and dark, and its variations on a theme. In downplaying the poem's purported ideas—its philosophical argument with Bergson and its dialectical structure—I do not mean to suggest that these elements hold no rhetorical purchase on a reader, only that those logics seem to depend at least in part on how much individual readers know of Bergson. By contrast, the logic (or illogic) of its grammar, imagery, and sound hold "Rhapsody" together in a manner that is neither philosophical nor architectonic. The structure of the poem—not its outline but its very bones, the way a reader is pulled from one line to the next—reveal an artist trembling with pathos, discarding heavy-handed imitations of Laforgue and strictness of form, and feeling his way into something strange and new. This unnamable oddness is what has stymied readers and critics, which is perhaps why philosophical critics have rushed in to fill the poem's silences, where others acknowledge its power but can only blink strangely at it.

"Rhapsody" is the culmination of the Paris poems. ("Prufrock," by contrast, is the culmination of the notebook as a whole.) With the exception of "Entretien dans un parc," which points toward "Prufrock," the other, shorter Paris poems have been building toward "Rhapsody" in the ways in which they aspire but fail to reach the luminous intensity and odd coherence of the long poem. "Rhapsody" finally succeeds because it suppresses Laforguean doubts and sarcasm, proceeding instead with an undiluted, serious tone. It follows its own logic of images and sounds rather attempting to wring philosophical meaning from vexed encounters, as in "Fourth Caprice," "Entretien," and "He said: this universe." Those poems are too logical and pat, their conclusions rooted in ideas rather than affect. "Rhapsody on a Windy Night," by contrast, is Eliot's most personal exploration of alienation, launched from an unstable space of inner consciousness rather than from the safe distance of a camera's eye or the superior critique of a philosopher.

"Interlude in London"
Drafted Apr. 1911

Freshly returned from an April visit to London, Eliot writes to his cousin Eleanor Hinkley about the glories of the Parisian spring, "It is such a revelation that I feel that I ought to make it known."[89] Eliot complains that London, by contrast, had been rather dreary: "At London, one pretended that it was spring, and tried to coax the spring, and talk of the beautiful weather; but one continued to hibernate amongst the bricks. And one looked through the windows, and the waiter brought in eggs and coffee, and the *Graphic* (which I conscientiously tried to read, to please them)."[90]

This playful discussion of London's bad weather is turned to different purposes in the poem, though a trace of the letter's intimacy persists in the verse. It is unclear whether the letter was written before the poem or vice versa, but the chronology matters less than that both make use of the same personal material in different contexts. In the letter, the archly impersonal "one" is deployed for humorous effect, whereas the opening lines of the poem engage a plural "We" who are locked up inside during a spring rain: "We hibernate among the bricks," lulled by the dreary rhythms of tea.[91] Another difference from the letter is that in the poem there is an absence of troublesome social obligation and the divided self it implies. The epistolary speaker had felt he "ought" to praise the Parisian spring, he had "pretended" that spring had come to London, and he had tried to please his hosts by feigning interest in their illustrated newspaper. Indeed, the rhetorical situation (letter-writing) is itself a social obligation. But since no one is obliged to write poems, the poetic speaker and his companion are free to be "Indifferent," "apathetic," and "Careless." Against such lethargy, spring can make little progress; it barely succeeds in breathing life into what is "mouldy" and "broken." Whereas the letter's speaker, writing in flowering Paris, had attempted to "coax" a past-tense London spring into being, the poem's speaker, hibernating in present-tense London, seems to unconsciously oppose it. There is a close correspondence between the poem's reluctant spring and the speaker's apathy, a situation Eliot will rework in *The Waste Land*.

Even though "Interlude" is ostensibly set in London, there are no recognizable London landmarks. As with the Paris poems, London is once again a city of matter rather than a geographically distinct place. "Interlude" is a slight poem, a less interesting version of the other Paris poems, with no advances to its credit. Yet, while the poem neither sets itself new challenges nor resolves old problems, it is worth noting that the opening "We" of the poem implicitly shares the speaker's circumstances with some larger portion of humanity. While this plural pronoun appears only in the first line, the rhetorical stance of the poem is maintained without modification throughout its ten lines. The intimacy of the letter, then, speaks to the situation of the poem. Perhaps Eliot's affectionate tone with a beloved cousin has merged with the sense of audience that he has been constructing throughout the notebook. Even in his less successful poems, there are quiet and unobtrusive signs that Eliot is increasingly comfortable with the rhetorical terrain that he has sketched out.

"Ballade pour la grosse Lulu"
Drafted July 1911

In July 1911, Eliot sets off from Paris for Munich and northern Italy, on his final tour of Europe before returning to the States.[92] Somewhere along the way, he must have come across a run of recent issues of the New York weekly the *Outlook*. The magazine itself is the main target of the poem's ridicule, and three people are satirized who appear in the July 1911 issues of the *Outlook*: Lyman Abbot was editor in chief, and contributions from Booker T. Washington and Theodore Roosevelt appear prominently in five of those July issues.[93]

The speaker is provoked to disgust with American culture as represented by the *Outlook*, a periodical that panders to readers' obsession with sports and sensational news: the clichéd mass-market Christianity on offer, business tycoons and their gospel-of-wealth rationalizations, university presidents and their talk of "Virtue," all of it mixed up with the hawking culture of capitalism.[94] More problematic is the speaker's distaste for the racial politics of the *Outlook*. By granting an interview to "Booker T." (dismissively abbreviated), the periodical lends seriousness to a life story roundly mocked by the speaker: its headline " 'Up from Possum Stew!' / Or 'How I set the nigger free!' " To all of these journalistic instincts—which the speaker perceives as pandering and trivial—he retorts, "But, My Lulu, 'Put on your rough red drawers / And come to the Whore House Ball!' " The whorehouse, it is implied, is at least honest about its desires and its business model. (Loretta Johnson has claimed that in oral tradition, Lulu variously appears as "black Lulu"; her sexual appetite thus converges with King Bolo's "big black bastard queen."[95]) While the title of the poem and its scatological critique are indebted to Villon's "Ballade de la grosse Margot," Eliot's refrain is also indebted to Villon's refrain: "Nous deffuyons onneur, il nous deffuit, / En ce bordeau ou tenons nostre etat" (we flee from honor, honor flees from us, / in this brothel where we ply our trade).[96]

As usual, the poem dramatizes the problem of audience: most of its figures speak cloyingly, patronizingly to their audiences. The *Outlook* itself panders to the lowest common denominator: Lyman Abbot "kindly" explains "to You" that God is in his heaven (all's right with such a world); Rockefeller explains his money as divinely granted, believably so for his audience, since he is "fresh and frank." It is no different from prostitution, the author implies.

It is easier to stomach this poem if we bracket the racism and see its exuberant scatology as lampooning the rationalist-religious ideology of the *Outlook* and, more generally, fatuous commercialism disguised as ethical practice. Adapting Villon's "aggressive disrespect," the poem derives its energy from vituperating these targets.[97] Unfortunately though, the poem's racism cannot be so neatly bracketed from its critique: the racism is interwoven with its cultural and economic critique, all of it launched from the fastnesses of Brahmin culture. This quasi-aristocratic culture of European descent valued lineage and decorum, even as it relied on mercantile success to help it flourish. Many notebook poems have skewered the city of Eliot's forebears, but whatever its limitations, Boston culture is ultimately preferable to the politicking and money-grubbing of New York culture, all of it tainted by unacceptably liberal racial views. It is cartoonish, dyspeptic, and not at all funny, this outsider's critique of New York. As a result, it is much less successful and nuanced than "Prufrock," which is an insider's critique of Boston.

"Preludes" III
Drafted July 1911; published with "Preludes" I, II, and IV, July 1915, Blast

The nine-month gap between the first two "Preludes" and the third results in a change in strategy, one that reflects the influence of his Paris year. The first two "Preludes," written shortly before his departure for France, had focused on a desolate and externalized landscape: "the sawdust trampled street / With its muddy feet."[98] As with the "Caprice" poems, those two "Preludes" had juxtaposed depersonalized fragments of the human body (hands, feet) to urban litter. There had appeared a surreptitious "you" fitted inside the possessive adjective in the first prelude: "withered leaves around *your* feet." But this reference to a personalized addressee is so unobtrusive it could almost be missed. More palpable in those first two "Preludes" is the impersonal construction of "one" and the misery of mass humanity: "One thinks of all the hands / That are raising dingy shades / In a thousand furnished rooms."[99]

By contrast, the insistence on the second person in "Preludes" III is overwhelming: "you" or "your" appear nine times in this sixteen-line poem. For Gray, this insistence reveals the influence of Bergson, the "harsh consciousness of consciousness contemplating itself."[100] The philosophical focus on "harsh consciousness" goes hand in glove with the rhetorical conception that hammers away at an explicitly named "you." In spite of this shift in focus between the second and third "Preludes," the coherence of the eventual four poems is a result of all of them rendering, in different ways, "the contemplation of selves . . . in deep loneliness," as Gray has argued.[101] Eliot is able to smooth over the difference between the first two poems and the third by moving from abstraction ("One thinks") and generality ("a thousand furnished rooms") to specificity: "Preludes" III sympathetically examines one instance of all those lives in dingy rooms with uncertain light.

Eliot has imitated—or perhaps "learned" is the better word—this sympathy for a suffering individual from Charles-Louis Philippe. The scene from Philippe's *Bubu de Montparnasse* on which Eliot draws is one of great pathos. In chapter 4 of the novel, Berthe, a prostitute, wakes next to her lover and pimp, Bubu, recalling that she must tell him that she has syphilis. In a room with gray curtains, dirty windowpanes, and filthy sheets, Berthe is depicted as physically and emotionally coterminous with her surroundings. Her hair is disheveled; her feet are dirty and yellow; her ideas lie in a heap inside her head ("ses idées étaient couchées en tas dans sa tête").[102]

The weight of what Berthe recalls ("Elle se rappela tout") in the novel—her obligation to her lover—becomes transformed in the poem into a higher "vision" of what all this misery means: "You had such a vision of the street / As the street hardly understands."[103] In the draft version of the poem, Eliot does not desexualize the content. The epigraph conflates phrases from *Bubu* to name her "little whore's soul" ("Son âme de petite putain"). By deleting this epigraph before publication, the prostitute simply becomes a lower-class woman, and Eliot again reveals the difference between his exploring, artistic self, and his cautious, public self.

The scene from *Bubu* that Eliot plunders has an odd rhetorical swerve: from the impersonal French construction of *on* to the intimate address of *tu*, where the reader is suddenly addressed: "On éprouve un sentiment de déchéance à cause des réveils d'autrefois où les idées étaient si claires qu'on eût dit que le sommeil les avait lavées. Quand tu auras dormi, mon frère, tu n'auras rien oublié."[104] Absorbing not only the images and ideas of this passage but its rhetorical stance as well, Eliot must have been struck by the intimate and vaguely sinister address to the reader: "mon frère."

How this insistent "you" functions rhetorically is different from the previous poem's passing evocations of the addressee. Mayer provides a fine account of the rhetorical force of the poem: "The burden of the woman's night is to achieve a kind of 'vision,' which affects both her and the observer, whose passive witness to her suffering is itself a form of revelation that alters his perspective. The observer, a forerunner of Tiresias, shares her anxiety-ridden experience through a sympathy that penetrates her soul."[105] The poem's most compelling effect is this contrast/conflation of the observing male speaker and the waking woman. That the woman is insistently invoked as "you" further implicates the reader in the suffering and the sympathy of the poem's vision. Both speaker and audience tremble with pathos for this woman, which is an explicit sympathy quite unlike the distant observer of mass humanity in the first two "Preludes."

Eliot's year in Paris, 1910–1911, decisively influenced his poetry just as Laforgue had changed his style and themes in November 1909. While his initial engagement with Laforgue and Baudelaire had manifested itself as a growth spurt, the year in Paris represents a broader and deeper maturation. After the initial fumble of "The Triumph of Bullshit" of November 1910, Eliot's Paris poems culminate in gratifying, if unexpected resolutions to his intractable audience problems. "Preludes" III solves the audience problem by blurring the speaker's observational stance with the female character and the audience, both of whom seem to be welded together in the poem's "you." "Rhapsody" solves the audience problem not by trying out a new maneuver to cajole or convince but by imagining that the problem never existed in the first place. With its strange logic and eerie effects, "Rhapsody" seems to have been composed by an author who has never doubted his audience's ability to follow his haunting and haunted reveries. Without the protection of social masks, the speaker of "Rhapsody" explores his alienation through the bleak landscape in which he walks and—the greater risk—through his own dissolving consciousness. "Prufrock," as we will see in chapter 7, likewise solves the audience problem not by moving predictably from mistrust to trust but by holding the two attitudes in ambivalent tension.

Just as "Convictions" of January 1910 had marked a significant shift—from attempting rhetorical strategies to observing those very attempts—so the Paris poems, taken as a whole, represent another sea change in his rhetorical and ethical formation. Whereas "Convictions" had revealed in one blow a speaker who has magically resolved one rhetorical problem by widening the distance between himself and his subject matter (by observing rather than arguing), the Paris poems do not reveal one easily identifiable shift. Rather, the Paris poems show an increasing mastery on rhetorical and ethical fronts: his speakers are personalizing their own alienation, claiming their suffering and inviting audiences to share in it. This shift is evident not in one poem but in the entire nine-month stretch, in both the successful and unsuccessful poems. This shift—an intensely personal speaker sharing his suffering with his readers—closes the gap that impersonal observation had opened up: a too-wary and too-impersonal distance from his audiences.

The best Paris poems—"Portrait" I, "Rhapsody," "Preludes" III, "Prufrock"—synthesize previously introduced themes of the notebook, resolve remaining rhetorical difficulties, and add a newly personalized tone, in keeping with the poems' deeper and more direct sympathy. The influence of Baudelaire, from whom Eliot had learned to stare unblinkingly at suffering (and thus obliquely to sympathize with it), has been softened by Philippe, from whom he has learned to sympathize more directly with suffering.[106] This shift toward greater trust and intimacy leads inevitably to Eliot's toying with the possibilities of candid, lyrical statement. His first, careful forays in this direction coincide with the disappearance of petty explosions of irritation and outrage. His speakers, heart in throat, take the risk of speaking directly to an audience.

The Short and Surprisingly Private Life of King Bolo

The Bawdy Poems and Their Audiences

> He had a tongue in his head, and it burred out "Good night, ladies. Good night, sweet ladies! Good night, good night!" It also sang, and it very often sang something ribald.
>
> —Jules Laforgue, "Hamlet"[1]

Intimations of Eliot's bawdy verses started to leak out during the author's lifetime.[2] Confidants of the poet teased the public about their existence, and Eliot himself joked with interviewers about a character named King Bolo. In the 1980s, biographies and a volume of letters offered the first idea of the scope of the obscene verse. Then, in 1996, *Inventions of the March Hare* was published. In an appendix judiciously labeled "Poems excised from the Notebook," the editor reproduced several pages' worth of obscene verse—including the Columbo and Bolo poems—that Eliot had torn out before selling the notebook to John Quinn. Reviewed in the popular press and dissected in scholarly journals, these poems became notorious for their scatological and pornographic content and more troublingly, for the violence, racism, misogyny, and homophobia of such lines as "The only doctor in his town / Was a bastard jew named Benny" and "'Up from Possum Stew!' / Or 'How I set the nigger free!'" and the jolly tinker whose "whanger" "ripped up my belly from my cunt to my navel."[3] Commentators have alternately shrugged at these poems, explained them, explained them away, or expressed astonishment or outrage at their content.[4] Most recently, with the 2015 publication of the magisterial *Poems of T. S. Eliot*, the scattered appearances of the Bolo sequence have been sewn together in a composite to which the editors have given the title "The Columbiad" and where all forty-nine stanzas are finally on view, awaiting the judgment of the future.

By way of entering this debate, I want to consider three questions that scholars have not yet thought to ask about these poems: (1) Did Eliot really try to publish his obscene verses in Wyndham Lewis's *Blast*? (2) Was the elderly Eliot still composing Bolo verses? (3) And if so, were they written in the same racist and misogynist vein as in his youth? Without sufficient proof and without looking carefully at the available evidence, scholars have assumed that the answer to all these questions is "yes." I would like to offer multiple reasons for responding with a qualified "no" on all three counts.[5]

Although these three questions seem to address narrow issues of historical fact, their answers open onto the contested spaces of what these poems mean and why they have provoked such disapproval. The first question, whether Eliot really intended to place bawdy lyrics in *Blast*, is not only one of historical accuracy; it is also one of audience and thus of understanding the poems' rhetoric. For whom did Eliot write these poems, where did he imagine they would appear as he was composing them, and what public and private venues did he, in point of fact, seek for their readership? The belief that Eliot tried to publish obscene poems in *Blast* has led some to think, erroneously, that Eliot took these verses more seriously than he actually did, that he had the poor taste to believe that their circulation outside his immediate circle of friends was appropriate, and that he was foolish enough not to realize that they would damage his reputation. Correcting the historical record on this matter, while a salutary task in its own right, has another consequence: it restores to Eliot his consciousness that these verses were extremely transgressive.

The second and third questions—how late was Eliot writing Bolo poems, and what is their content?—are likewise not just concerns about chronology or accurate paraphrase. Both questions touch on Eliot's bigotry in light of his later conversion: What are we to think of an elder statesman and Christian convert who wrote poems of spiritual humility for public consumption while supposedly scribbling away at racist and misogynist poems in private? The belief that Eliot continued to compose these obscene poems throughout his life has led some to claim, erroneously, that these verses should be viewed not as juvenilia but as an abiding interest of his middle and late periods.[6] As a result, they see the poems as reflecting an ongoing sexual dysfunction, a lifelong immaturity, and a committed misogyny, whereas the poems are more understandable, and less scandalous, as expressions of youthful sexual frustration and facilitators of juvenile masculine bonding.

Eliot's Alleged Intention to Publish His Blue Verse

That Eliot seriously intended to publish "The Triumph of Bullshit" and "Ballade pour la grosse Lulu" in *Blast* is a commonplace that no one has yet questioned.[7] Although this interpretation precedes Ricks's edition of *Inventions of the March Hare*, critical agreement regarding Eliot's intentions seemed to be cemented by a skewed reading of two quotations that appear in that volume. On the title page of the appendix, Ricks offers without commentary the following excerpts, passages that have been repeated in nearly every critical discussion of these verses:

> [Eliot] to Pound, 2 Feb. 1915:
>
> > I have corresponded with Lewis, but his puritanical principles seem to bar my way to Publicity. I fear that King Bolo and his Big Black Kween will never burst into print. I understand that Priapism, Narcissism etc. are not approved of, and even so innocent a rhyme as
> >
> > . . . pulled her stockings off
> > With a frightful cry of "Hauptbahnhof!!"
> >
> > is considered decadent.
>
> Wyndham Lewis to Pound, before July 1915:
>
> > Eliot has sent me Bullshit & the Ballad for Big Louise. They are excellent bits of scholarly ribaldry. I am longing to print them in *Blast*; but stick to my naif determination to have no "Words Ending in -Uck, -Unt and -Ugger." [8]

The reigning interpretation of this episode is that sometime in early 1915, Eliot sent "The Triumph of Bullshit" and "Ballade pour la grosse Lulu" to Lewis, hoping that he would publish them in *Blast*. Lewis considered the possibility (so the story goes) but ultimately demurred, explaining his decision both to Pound and to Eliot, with the latter humorously complaining about the rejection. In spite of the unanimity of this interpretation, however, this narrative seems hard to credit. I would like to construct a more probable scenario for the correspondence among Eliot, Pound, and Lewis—one that attends carefully to what these letters are saying and not saying, and one that takes into account a number of important contexts that have so far been ignored.

To understand one of those contexts, it will be helpful to look back five months to September 30, 1914. The war only a few weeks old, Eliot wrote to Conrad Aiken, offering a Bolo verse turned in the service of a patriotic war poem: British heroes sink a German warship, and all are drowned except for the German cabin boy, who "was sav'd alive / And bugger'd, in the sphincter." Ironically commenting on the prospects for the poem's publication, Eliot continues: "The poem was declined by several musical publishers on the ground that it paid too great a tribute to the charms of German youth to be acceptable to the English public. I acknowledg'd the force of the objection, but replied that it was only to be regarded as a punitive measure, and to show the readiness and devotion to duty of the British seaman."[9] This letter to Aiken shows that Eliot was, without question, joking about publishing these Bolo verses. Five months later, writing to Pound, Eliot would adopt this same pose of an unfairly rejected author. The repartee among Eliot, Lewis, and Pound was only the continuation of a motif that Eliot had sounded previously and would extend for some time: namely, pretending to lament that his Bolo sequence would never "burst into print."[10]

To return to the February 1915 exchange, why Pound was involved at all seems to be that Eliot and Lewis had not yet met one another.[11] Pound had probably encouraged Eliot to send some poems to Lewis for editorial consideration: Eliot's introductory gesture—"I have corresponded with Lewis"—elides but implies "as you told me to." Subsequently, "Rhapsody on a Windy Night" and "Preludes" were published by Lewis in *Blast* in July 1915. Whether Eliot sent obscene verses to Lewis in the same letter as "Rhapsody" and "Preludes" is of less consequence than why Eliot sent him such verses. Eliot often sent blue verse to literary friends and editors with no intention of their being broadcast further. That Eliot sent such poems to Lewis is, in itself, no proof that he wanted them published.

If we look closely at what the letters actually say, it turns out that Lewis nowhere attributes the idea of printing the poems to Eliot. Lewis writes, "Eliot has sent me Bullshit & the Ballad for Big Louise," which indicates Eliot's action, but not its intention. Further, Lewis writes, "I am longing to print them," which—read as ironic or not—ascribes the intention to publish to himself rather than to Eliot. Another often-missed cue in this correspondence is that Eliot does not bemoan the rejection of "Bullshit" or "Ballade" (the only poems of which Lewis acknowledged receipt).[12] Eliot instead refers to the wider corpus of obscene verse: "I fear that King Bolo and his Big Black Kween will never burst into print." While it strains credulity to imagine Eliot seeking publication for "Bullshit" or "Ballade," vulgar as they are, it is frankly impossible to imagine Bolo's pornography getting into print with Eliot's imprimatur. The clues to the tongue-in-cheek tone are unmistakable: Eliot accuses Lewis of holding "puritanical principles" (an absurd claim), he sulks histrionically over the imagined rejection, and "decadent" rhyming is given as a primary reason for the refusal. Likewise, when Lewis pretends to be torn between his ban on vulgarity and his "longing" to print the poems, he is not reporting an editorial dilemma but working up a comedic bit for Pound's amusement.

Whether Pound was joking is a different matter. In response to Lewis's feigned reluctance, Pound suggests, "I dare say Eliot will consent to leaving blanks for the offending words."[13] If Pound is in on the joke, then this riposte simply belabors it. But it is likely that Pound was not quite attuned to the prank; his irony was more heavy handed than his correspondents'. In any event, Eliot has nothing to do with the intention to publish: that Pound would "dare say" what Eliot would agree to demonstrates that Eliot was not included in this side conversation about making the offensive poems more palatable.

At the same time that Eliot and Lewis were joking for Pound's amusement, Pound himself was engaged in the serious business of getting as many of Eliot's poems into print as he could. Indefatigable and generous, Pound was in the midst of a long battle with Harriet Monroe to speed up her publication of "Prufrock" in *Poetry*. After trying unsuccessfully at the *Smart Set*, Pound was able to place "Portrait of a Lady" in Alfred Kreymborg's *Others*, and he directed Eliot to Lewis's *Blast*, where two poems were placed. Pound himself republished several of Eliot's poems in *Catholic Anthology*, later claiming that the whole purpose of publishing the volume in London was "in order to get 16 pages of Eliot printed in that damned city."[14] In the four years preceding his arrival in London, Eliot had published nothing. In 1915, by contrast, Eliot scored twelve publications or reprints, and Pound's intervention was directly responsible for all of them. And so, when Lewis and Eliot kidded to him about publishing "Bullshit," Pound smelled blood in the water.

What happened next in the correspondence between Pound and Lewis is telling. Pound sent Eliot's "Portrait of a Lady" to Lewis, ending with the warning: "If you want to use this Portrait you'll have to get his permission. =or I will have to."[15] In the midst of his tireless crusade to get Eliot published, why does Pound suddenly recall the niceties of permission? Did Eliot, appalled, get wind of Pound's suggestion that "Bullshit" be published with blanks? In response, perhaps Eliot made it clear to Pound that nothing was to be published without his permission. I am conjecturing about such a rebuke, of course, but it would explain Pound's uncharacteristic submissiveness.

The explanation that Eliot might have offered the poems as potentially anonymous contributions falters on the hazards of British obscenity laws. As brash as Pound was, he knew that something like blanks would be needed, and not even a newly arrived foreigner such as Eliot could have believed that the censors, especially vigilant during wartime, would overlook such obscenity. Government censors were on the lookout, and a variety of social purity organizations pressured government agencies to act. As Celia Marshik has explained, the consequences for writers included "visits and surveillance, public proclamations and warnings, and threatening letters as well as trials for obscene libel."[16]

As an editor, Lewis was keenly aware of the pressures of censorship. In June 1914, in a dustup regarding the first edition of *Blast*, Lewis's publisher, John Lane, had required that three lines from Pound's poem "Fratres Minores" be blacked out. Chastising Lewis for letting the poem make it so far into press, Lane reminded him of their earlier agreement: "that there would be no sexual disagreeableness or anything which could possibly be construed into libel in it."[17] The release of *Blast*, dated June 20, 1914, was delayed until July while two women at the Rebel Art Centre crossed out the lines by hand. For Pound as author and Lewis as editor, it was an irritating, humiliating episode. The offending poem by Pound—with its use of the word "testicles" and an oblique description of orgasm—had markedly less "sexual disagreeableness" in it than anything in Eliot's obscene verse. Several months later, the second edition of *Blast* was due to be published, again by Lane. With the memory of their mutual tussle with Lane fresh in his mind, Lewis expresses to Pound his "naif determination to have no 'Words Ending in -Uck, -Unt and -Ugger.' " With this context restored, it is not only obvious that Lewis is joking about Eliot's verse presenting him with an editorial dilemma, it seems that he is still licking his wounds.

A number of factors have contributed to our misunderstanding of the correspondence among Eliot, Lewis, and Pound. The misreadings of the letters themselves are part of the problem, and these forgotten contexts are another part: (1) Eliot's unmistakable joking about publishing Bolo, joking that both precedes and follows the 1915 episode; (2) the atmosphere of blustery friendship and literary ambition among the three men; and (3) the widely known realities of British censorship and Lewis's particular history with Lane. In the scenario I am sketching, it was Pound's ambition for Eliot and his bullying manner that came up against an in-joke between two men who were playing to Pound's audience and who were modeling the kind of virile one-upmanship that Pound encouraged. In the static that ensued, Pound missed the tone of the joke and barged ahead with his own plans for Eliot's future.

So far as we know, at no other time in his life did Eliot attempt to publish his obscene verse.[18] A scenario in which all three men were kidding—or at least Eliot and Lewis were—seems more likely than one in which Eliot momentarily took leave of his senses.

Eliot's Alleged Composition of Bolo Verses Late in Life

Only one critic has contested the scholarly consensus regarding how late Eliot was writing Bolo verses. Valerie Eliot was in a position to know the most about the composition history of the Bolo poems, but she published only two sentences about the matter, and her terse claim has been ignored by critics. Responding to a discussion in the *Times Literary Supplement*, the poet's widow contested the idea of Bolo's late composition: "It is not true, as William Baker asserts . . . , that T. S. Eliot was still writing his 'King Bolo' limericks 'in the late 1950s.' Almost all were written during his Harvard days and none later than 1916."[19]

That Eliot kept composing such racist and misogynist poems up to the day he died is another canard, abetted partly by misreadings of the archival evidence and partly by the tantalizing presence of the letters up to 1922 (published in 1988) combined with the long delay of the subsequent volumes (letters from 1923 to 1938 were published between 2011 and 2019). Many scholars have described the existence, dating, and content of what they imagine to be late Bolo stanzas without offering any credible evidence to back up their claims. For example, Bryan Cheyette confidently dates the last Bolo poem to 1964 and gives a blanket description to cover the fifty-year span: "These [Bolo verses] are a long cycle of bawdy, racist, and astonishingly vulgar doggerel which Eliot began writing for a few friends while a student at Harvard and was still writing a year before his death in 1965."[20] Cheyette's claim is influenced by the work of Gabrielle McIntire, and both Cheyette and McIntire have written illuminating chapters on Eliot's Bolo poems, which I will rely on below. However, for the moment, I want to focus on some of the factual claims they make about the poems' dating and content.

McIntire and Cheyette certainly have good reason to suspect that Eliot was composing installments of the Bolo epic later in life. Eliot himself seemed to confess the deed in a 1959 interview for the *Paris Review*. Donald Hall asks, "Do you write anything now in the vein of *Old Possum's Book of Practical Cats* or *King Bolo*?" Eliot's initial response seems to refer to both types: "Those things do come from time to time!" After mentioning some incomplete cat poems, he concludes the discussion with an arch reversion to "one": "Oh, yes, one wants to keep one's hand in, you know, in every type of poem, serious and frivolous and proper and improper. One doesn't want to lose one's skill."[21]

Note that this admission—if that is what it is—offers no proof of misogyny, racism, or anything offensive. Once we have examined more recent evidence and identified the important shift that Bolo undergoes in the late 1920s, we will be more likely to see this interchange as a complicitous wink to an interviewer looking to debunk Eliot's saintly authority.

McIntire claims that the Bolo poems "form part of an extensive cycle that Eliot continued to write throughout his life."[22] She offers as evidence for this claim numerous references to the Bolo sequence in Eliot's letters:

> In the John Davy Hayward Bequest at Cambridge University, for instance, Bolo emerges in a letter to Clive Bell in 1941, nearly fifteen years after an intense correspondence on the subject with Bonamy Dobrée reaches its peak in 1927—astonishingly, the year of Eliot's conversion—and roughly thirty years after Bolo's first incarnation. Furthermore, Conrad Aiken indicates in December 1964, less than a month before Eliot died on 4 January 1965, that Bolo was still a topic of interest. Writing to Eliot at the time, Aiken expresses regret that this year they would not have their usual exchange of Columbo and Bolo poems: "But o dear we shall miss our annual meeting in New York and the exchange of Bolos and lime rickeys at the River Club or Vanderbilt." . . . What perhaps is most astonishing about this body of work, then, is that Eliot continued to write and circulate the Columbo and Bolo verses through his whole life.[23]

For McIntire, what is presumably "astonishing" about this evidence is not merely that Eliot kept writing poems about Columbo and Bolo "through his whole life." Rather, what is troublesome is left unstated: that any appearance of Columbo or Bolo is necessarily racist, misogynistic, or otherwise offensive. Once this same evidence is probed in more detail, however, such assumptions begin to fall apart. The 1941 letter to Clive Bell in which, as McIntire indicates, "Bolo emerges," in point of fact contains no Bolo verses whatsoever. Eliot instead is thanking Bell for some bit of praise, then he remarks on his scheme to complete several long poems (*Four Quartets*), which prompts this single sentence: "I may even take in hand the long neglected task of putting in order the epical ballad on the life of Chris Columbo (the famous Portuguese navigator) and his friends King Bolo and his Big Black Queen."[24] As Eliot ages, the old joke about publishing Bolo becomes a different, if still obvious joke about giving the sequence a scholarly treatment.

That Bolo "emerges" in this letter to Bell is true enough; however, he does not emerge in his poetic guise—namely, as the hero of an epic trafficking in problematic tropes—but in his tamer, prosaic guise as the subject of a mock editor's scholarly project. The crucial error that critics make in discussing Bolo's longevity is failing to distinguish between the Bolo *poems* and the Bolo *prose*, the former occasionally alarming, the latter mostly tedious. A typical passage of Bolo prose, describing the "behaviour of the primitive inhabitants of Bolovia," notes that they are "a notoriously lazy race. They had two Gods, named respectively Wux and Wux. They observed that the carving of Idols out of ebony was hard work; therefore they carved only one Idol."[25] Such jokes about Bolovian theology or mock discussions of a scholarly edition are hardly "astonishing" at all.

In drawing attention to the differences in tone, form, and content between the Bolo poems and the Bolo prose, I intend to offer clarity rather than plead for a full exoneration. For the Bolo prose has its own ethical problems. Even in these seemingly banal passages I have quoted, Eliot reworks an American prejudice about African Americans as lazy, and he repeats an offensive epithet created years earlier: the "Big Black Queen." Each of these three words creates problems of racial othering and sexual fetishizing. Similarly, even though the Bolo prose is tamer than the poetry, lampooning tribal customs still betrays a condescension toward indigenous people. In spite of these qualms, I believe I can still press my point: I am not claiming that the Bolo prose is thoroughly innocent, only that the ethnic humor found therein pales in comparison to the starker prejudices of the Bolo poems. In the Bolo prose, the later Eliot has turned from a poetic corpus of colonialist expansion and sexual deviance toward a mock-sociological study of Bolo's tribal customs. It blurs a useful distinction to place the mild Bolo prose, whatever its problems, in the same moral category as the Bolo verses that spew racial slurs and revel in sexual violence. In addition to urging historical and factual accuracy in this discussion, and to identifying the generic conventions and rhetorical aims of the Bolo verse and prose, I am also suggesting that we maintain a delicate ethical balance between distancing ourselves from troublesome prejudices and resisting the facile superiority that comes from scolding a dead person.[26]

"Putting in Order the Epical Ballad": A Bolovian Chronology

At this stage of discovery, what can be safely claimed about the dating and content of the Bolo poems and prose? The first thing to note is that the character of Christopher Columbo—as the oversexed hero of an epic sea journey—is not Eliot's invention. Columbo first appears in a bawdy sea song that scholars variously date to 1876, after 1877, and 1893.[27] Eliot's use is therefore part of a long folk tradition of repetition and variation. Some of the Columbo stanzas that have been preserved in Eliot's notebook are nearly word-for-word transcriptions of preexisting stanzas, some are adaptations (or "dud" variations as Chinitz and Ricks describe them), and others are entirely his own inventions.[28] For the purposes of chronology, I do not distinguish below between verses Eliot has transcribed and verses he has composed; both types are attributed to his hand. However, because a point of contention is whether Eliot kept writing *new* Bolo verses late in life, I note the difference between the first time a Bolo stanza appears and its subsequent repetition in correspondence.

In their richly annotated edition of *The Poems of T. S. Eliot*, editors Christopher Ricks and Jim McCue are able to date many of the Bolo and Columbo poems. But several Bolos contain no clear evidence for precise dating. Nevertheless, there is sufficient evidence to place all the Bolo poems into distinct chronological periods. The Bolo poems that were excised from the *Inventions* notebook can be roughly dated to the late aughts and early teens. The Bolos that appear within the letters are clearly datable, because Eliot almost always dated his correspondence. That leaves roughly twenty Bolos with no chronological slot. These remaining Bolo poems, housed at Yale, were not published in *Inventions* because they were not clearly linked with the notebook. These twenty-some stanzas were from a smaller pocketbook, of which only six pages remain.[29] As I explain below, I date this pocketbook to the late teens.

Act 1, Bolo Begun: Poems 1906–1914

Certainly the vast majority, and probably all, of the Bolo poems were composed at Harvard. Having examined the correspondence of Eliot's Harvard friends, Robert Crawford concludes that the exchange of Bolo verses was part of their fellowship as undergraduates (1906–1910).[30] Aiken expands this time frame, claiming that "hilariously naughty *parerga*" on the subject of King Bolo served as a "sort of cynical counterpoint to the study of Sanskrit and the treatise on epistemology," extending the sharing of Bolo stanzas into Eliot's graduate student days in America (1911–1914).[31] Given the contemporaneity of the *Inventions* notebook (begun 1909), some of those verses exchanged among Harvard friends most likely include the Bolo stanzas that were written on its leaves. It is also likely that these same Bolo verses are the ones that Pound saw a few years later in London.[32] From the Pound-Lewis correspondence cited above, we know that "Bullshit," "Ballade," and other obscene poems predate 1915.

This American period (1906–1914) saw the zenith of Eliot's sexually violent and racially offensive Bolo stanzas. Sexual violence and racial slurs are likewise salient themes in other poems from this period such as "Fragments" and "Ballade pour la grosse Lulu." The verses excised from the notebook were probably not penned after 1914, by which time the notebook had lost allure as a place of invention. This arc of Bolo poems, begun at Harvard, ends with his departure from America in 1914.

Act 2, Bolo Collected: Poems 1915–1923

With Eliot's removal to London, a new stage in his life begins. Almost all the Bolos that are datable to this second period have been collected from his time in America and transcribed into a pocketbook rather than newly composed. As an artifact, the pocketbook probably dates to the late teens, even though its contents date from much earlier.[33] My guess is that this smaller pocketbook was purchased later than the *Inventions* notebook as a way of "putting the epical ballad in order," because these pages have generally neater handwriting and only Bolo poems appear on them, as opposed to the *Inventions* notebook, where Bolos are interspersed with the other poems.

Only two new Bolos appear during this period: a brief couplet in 1915 and two stanzas in 1923. As early as 1915 a shift in attitude is detectable: these Bolos are already starting to sound mock intellectual rather than shockingly ribald: "pulled her stockings off / With a frightful cry of 'Hauptbahnhof!!' "[34] Eliot has a new set of friends to entertain, more witty and learned than his drinking companions from Harvard. The shift from Harvard social clubs, with their regular dinners and occasions, to the London avant-garde, with its epistolary culture, is one possible reason Eliot started collecting Bolos more deliberately in this smaller pocketbook. Columbo, Bolo, and his queen make a crashing exit in a letter to Pound (Sept. 3, 1923) and then disappear for a few years.

Act 3, Bolo Transformed: Poems and Prose, 1927–1932

The next datable appearance of Bolo is 1927, when a new arc begins. In this arc, Bolo begins his shift from hero in a poetic sequence to a specimen in a prosaic study. The impetus for the revival is an extensive discussion of Bolovian customs that Eliot had initiated with Bonamy Dobrée. The first appearance in this vein is May 10, 1927, where, as we have already seen, Eliot introduces Dobrée to the Bolovians as a "notoriously lazy race."[35] In subsequent letters, he continues in this vein, explaining their cultural customs and liturgical rites. Along with the change from poetry to prose, a concomitant shift can be traced from the historical and sexual matters of the Bolo poems to the anthropological and theological matters of the Bolo prose. This shift in 1927—when Bolo becomes mostly an anthropological/theological joke—exactly corresponds with Eliot's conversion to Christianity. What is a sticking point for McIntire and others is an implied, distasteful hypocrisy: that Eliot, in their understanding, seems to be writing ethically suspect verse in the same year that he adopts a pose of spiritual humility. But now we can see that Eliot's conversion carries with it a deepened commitment to theological discourse and a new interest in the sociological organization of Christian society: the two discourses that Eliot then playfully satirizes in his Bolo prose.

The Bolovian banter with Dobrée continues through 1927, with a few more references in 1928 and 1932. This burst of activity coincides with the creation of the "London Bolovian Society," which Eliot proudly announces to his old college friend, Howard Morris.[36] Nevertheless, within this discussion very little new verse appears—just a pair of stray stanzas to Morris in late 1929 and two others to Theodore Spencer in 1932.[37]

Act 4, Bolo Mourned: 1940–1964

Aside from one recycled stanza that appears in 1934, Columbo/Bolo—whether dressed in verse or prose—seems to go underground again for a number of years. Columbo resurfaces in a letter to Hayward on August 29, 1940, but the stanza is recycled, having originally appeared in the *Inventions* notebook.[38] In a letter a few months later, also to Hayward, Eliot quotes a Bolovian description he had sent to Dobrée years earlier: "As King Bolo said to the Queen in presenting Columbo, 'he hunts with the Quorn and shoots over his own coverts.'"[39] Appearing after a long gap, these repetitions point to a lethargy surrounding the topic of Bolo. In the midst of this time frame, a third transformation materializes, legible in a letter to Hayward on November 25, 1940. No longer the sexual adventurer of the poems or the object of anthropological study in the prose, now Bolo is hailed wistfully as a former way of life, Bolovian custom providing the pseudo-ancient salutation: "Well, as the Bolovians used to say (and often I feel nostalgia for that blessed isle) 'Wux-ho!'"[40] The following year, the nostalgia endures, Eliot again signing off, "So meanwhile, as the Bolovians used to say (for their happy island has now disappeared): 'wux-ho!'"[41] Also in 1941, as we have already seen in Eliot's letter to

Clive Bell, he jokes about "putting in order the epical ballad"—the imagined scholarly treatment a sure sign that Bolo is a fixed, dead canon.[42]

From early 1932 until his death—a thirty-three-year drought—Eliot seems to have composed no new Bolo stanzas. A previously unrecorded Bolo poem does appear in a 1956 letter, but it is almost certainly recycled. Writing to his Harvard friend Nick Brooks after a bout of illness, Eliot begins, "I've been slow getting round my friends for their letters of condolence on my approaching demise," and he continues:

> So you see that I have some of the resilience of our epoch making heroine the Black Queen—
>
> That vast voluptuous vestal
> Who, as you may have forgotten—
> Was always Bright and Full of Beans
> As well (you may also have forgotten this)—
> As well as Blandly Bestial.[43]

Even though the first recorded instance of this stanza comes from a 1956 letter, Eliot is writing to a Digamma Club friend with whom he had shared Bolos at Harvard.[44] In the poem, Eliot twice reminds Brooks of what has been "forgotten." Thus, the internal and external evidence of the poem suggests that this verse is recycled, one with which his correspondent has long been familiar. Note, also, the queen's transformation: reshaped into a "vestal," if ironic, innocent, she indulges no longer in violent sex but in the "Blandly Bestial" pastime of flatulence.

As with this 1956 letter, occasional repetitions of previously composed Bolos appeared in the latter part of Eliot's life. The last appearance of such is from late 1963 or 1964. We have already heard Aiken's lament in 1964 that there would be no "exchange of Bolos" in the coming year because of Eliot's ill health. Like other tantalizing references, it seemed to suggest the existence of newly composed stanzas. But the last Bolo that Eliot sent to Aiken is the same one that he had first shared with his friend exactly fifty years earlier, in 1914:

> Now while Columbo + his men
> Were feasting at the Passover,
> King Bolo and his Big Black Queen
> Rolled in tea-kettle-arse-over.
> They all sat round the festive board

And dined—on fried hyaenas.
And the King said: "mine's a piece of tail
With a juicy bit of penis."[45]

Similar to the variations that occur in oral tradition, the small divergences of this 1964 stanza from its earlier versions are largely inconsequential. To neglect one of these variations, however, would be to miss a significant shift, though to overlook it would be easy, since it is a change of omission. In a 1927 variant of this stanza, Eliot had jokingly insisted to Dobrée that the stanza was corrupt and that it "should read": "Now the Jewboys of Columbo's Fleet / Were feasting at the Passover."[46] By 1964 though, the anti-Semitic sneer has been deleted or forgotten. Previously scornful of "Jewboys" and once maltreated by a "bastard jew" who had scorched his penis, the 1964 Columbo is now "feasting at the Passover" not only with Bolo and his queen but with all his men, joining with—and indistinguishable from—their brother Jews.[47]

David Chinitz was the first to discover that the Bolo stanza that has given the most offense—the one about the "bastard jew named Benny"—was not Eliot's invention at all but a stanza that appears in the Columbo folk ballad of popular tradition.[48] Chinitz notes that finding a source does not exonerate this ugliness in Eliot, but the earlier reference does allow Chinitz to express some relief "that this instance of vulgar Jew-baiting originated in the imagination of another."[49] Likewise, by pointing to the disappearance of "Jewboys" in the 1964 stanza, I am not exonerating Eliot, early or late, on the score of anti-Semitism, merely noting that this prejudice seemed to become less impulsive as he aged.

General Notes on Dating and Chronology

It is probable that Valerie Eliot was exactly right: no new Bolos were written after 1916. Only a small handful of newly recorded Bolos date from 1916–1932, and it is possible that their originals, predating 1916, have simply been lost. Even if those stanzas were newly composed, we can still trust Valerie Eliot's general sense of where Bolo belongs: Eliot was mostly finished composing Bolo verses by the time he left America. The few stanzas that appear after this time—such as those offered for Dobrée's instruction in the 1920s—are recycled rather than newly composed.[50] Those rare Bolo poems that are perhaps written later have lost their vicious bite: the earlier sexual violence and racial prejudice having largely given way to puerile jokes about farting, buggery, and genitalia.[51] The later Bolo prose is mostly a send-up of academic pedantry. Eliot continued with the Bolo prose somewhat beyond the verse, with a strong burst in the late 1920s, but he was mostly finished with that by 1930 as well. As many Eliot scholars have noted, the poet had a roving intelligence; he was always abandoning a style or concern once he had mastered it or used it up. So one reason Bolo resurfaces in the late 1920s is that Eliot can fit Bolo into a new form (prose explanation) and a new set of concerns (anthropology and theology). This production of Bolovian prose involves the repetition of old Bolo stanzas and, perhaps, the composition of a few new verses. In the early 1940s, he twice expressed nostalgia for Bolo as a figure of his youth, which shows where the whole business stood in his own mind.

It is understandable that McIntire and others, coming across Bolo references in the letters, would assume that Eliot was still churning out such verses when he was in his seventies. To be sure, scattered Bolo references, in hard-to-reach archives, held out just this intriguing possibility. However, with the bulk of the letters now becoming publicly available, a more complete search does not bear out that conclusion. Given the shift in the 1920s when Bolo became a different kind of joke and given Eliot's valedictory tone regarding Bolo in the 1940s, it is unlikely that a hidden cache of Bolo poems datable to the 1920s or later will ever surface. If a few more Bolos pop up in unexpected places, I doubt that they would mar the broad picture I am sketching here: that a middle-aged and then elderly Eliot did not set himself to the task of composing Bolo verses as a way of expanding the already existing sequence.[52]

The Bolo Poems versus *The Columbiad*

The first complete edition of *The Poems* (2015) will no doubt become the standard reference for discussing the Bolo sequence in the future, because the volume finally publishes the remaining stanzas from the Yale archive and the other Bolos from as yet unpublished correspondence. The newly published Bolos in turn are brought together with the previously published stanzas from *Inventions* (1996), fixing some minor errors in the process. The luxurious detail, scholarly apparatus, and new format of the Bolo poems augur both opportunity and risk for critics.

A potential hazard of the explanatory material is that the carefully dated sources may encourage the reader to mistake an appearance of a Bolo stanza for its date of composition, thus reinscribing the fallacy that Eliot spent his life composing the sequence. Another problem concerns the textual history: the editors have prudently declined to print every variant of the Bolo verses—

a practice that would have further consecrated these lightweight poems.[53] However, the absence of variants and their dates means that the new edition, while exhaustive in many respects, cannot guide a scholar in tracking conceptual and attitudinal shifts, nor can it help distinguish when Eliot wrote a new Bolo from when he repeated it.

It is worth recalling that even though Eliot collected a number of the Bolo stanzas in an early pocketbook, he did so for his own reasons, not as preparation for publication. Eliot himself never collected all the poems, nor did he direct anyone else to do so. *Poems* has spruced up and regularized the Bolos, and the danger here is that the new presentation confers a seriousness of purpose that the originals were not intended to convey. Likewise, the editors' imposition of a formal title, *The Columbiad*, and the format and numbering of stanzas confer literary authority: they are no longer improvised poems but a textually coherent mock epic. Yet another problem with *The Columbiad* is that the settings of the Bolos pinball around the globe, but the editors soft-pedal this chaos, imposing a quasi-narrative by beginning the sequence with Columbo's dealings with Spanish royalty and ending with his "Regain[ing] the Spanish shores"—the trajectory of the historical Christopher Columbus.[54] And finally, the editors frame the entire sequence with Eliot's mock-Elizabethan stage directions from the *Inventions* appendix—the "Enter" and "Exeunt" of the king and queen.

All of these editorial choices bestow a spurious wholeness on fragments whose narrative, geographical, and characterological unity was never intended by their author. The world of Bolo was an imaginarium from which Eliot drew for ad hoc purposes of entertaining close friends. Although it had distinct, if shifting, logical markers and recurring themes and names, the Bolo sequence was never a narrative with beginning and end. In their section entitled "Improper Rhymes" and their composite of the Bolo stanzas, Ricks and McCue have not made arbitrary or unwarranted decisions, but future commentators on the Bolo poems will need to distinguish what is editorially engineered from what is authorially intended.[55]

Where a critic or scholar wishes to discuss the Bolo poems as a sequence or the bawdy poems as a genre, *Poems* and *Inventions* offer conflicting visions of whether these poems constitute a separate corpus (where they are grouped as an appendix in *Inventions*) or an uncomfortable cross between regular poems and "improper rhymes" (where they are variously interspersed or grouped in *Poems*). Because *Inventions* has been available to scholars for much longer than has *Poems*, the scholarly dialogue so far has been more influenced by the *Inventions* scheme. By consigning the obscene verses to an appendix in *Inventions*, Ricks's edition separates them from the other poems alongside which they had been composed, allowing Eliot's later anxiety about these inventions to color our understanding of them.[56] I have tried to avoid replicating this problem by repositioning two of the excised poems back in their chronological order: both "Bullshit" and "Ballade" are precisely datable and so were discussed in chapter 5 along with the other Paris poems of 1910–1911. In this chapter however, I consider the Bolo poems and "Fragments" together for several reasons. First, their reception history since 1996 recommends their being grouped together in order to join the dialogue that has sprung up around them as a corpus. Relatedly, the rhetorical and ethical issues the bawdy verse raises are distinctive because of their transgressive content. Grouping them together enables me to address such issues in one place. Second, even though the Bolos were written over the span of seven years, their thematic cohesiveness lends itself to a generic rather than chronological consideration. Finally, considering their overall effect as bawdy verse allows me to address the question of why Eliot's rhetorical development—so strong and cumulative elsewhere in the notebook—seems to flag in this genre.

The Poems

["The Triumph of Bullshit"	drafted Nov. 1910—discussed in chapter 5]
["Ballade pour la grosse Lulu";	drafted July 1911—discussed in chapter 5]
"Fragments"	ca. 1910–1911
Columbo and Bolo verses	ca. 1910–1916

"Fragments"
Drafted ca. 1910–1911

As Chinitz has shown, Eliot's "Fragments" is deeply indebted to the traditional bawdy song known as "The Jolly Tinker" or "The Highland Tinker." Both the tradition's and Eliot's versions feature a "grotesquely over-endowed itinerant" (in Chinitz's sly description), whose enormous "whanger" (in the poem's not-very-sly description) provokes chaos among those who witness or suffer its depredations.[57] Given the strong correspondences between Eliot's poem and traditional versions, it seems clear that Eliot was not writing variations on a theme but copying out verses he had heard delivered elsewhere. Even so, Chinitz argues, Eliot's text is more than just a record of what the young poet has heard sung: "By affixing the title 'Fragments' and numbering the stanzas 1, 2, 13, 24, 25, 41, and 50—as if 'The Tinker' had been preserved, like Sappho, on tattered papyrus—Eliot ironically invests the song with a spurious antiquity. . . . Eliot's elevation of 'The Jolly Tinker' to the status of classical (or Modernist?) fragment mocks the pretensions if not of Art then at least of philology, with a playful and self-parodic gesture of which Eliot was certainly capable."[58] The humorous numbering to which Chinitz refers is not assigned at random. It has its own logic, with contiguous numbers suggesting a thematic correspondence and distant numbers suggesting a narrative gap. For example, 1 describes the tinker's "four and twenty inches hanging to his knee," while the immediately following verse, numbered 2, mathematically doubles the already ridiculous size: "his eight and forty inches hanging to his feet." (Although tumescence possibly causes the increase, note that his "inches" are still "hanging." Hyperbole is the more likely cause, the huge numbers signaling the poem's delight in implausibility.) Likewise, the mother and daughter are linked, respectively, by the adjacent 24 and 25. By contrast, the cook makes a dire future-tense prediction of the tinker in 41: "he's a gona fuck us all." The immediately following verse skips to 50 and the perfect tense: "he's a gone and fucked us all."[59] The shift from future to perfect tense is probably Eliot's invention, since it is related to the joke about the poem's antiquity. Those pedantically precise numbers signal the ravages of history and the painstaking attempt to preserve its remnants. The leap from 41 to 50—from prediction to accomplishment—denies us the prurient scenes, the mayhem of eight lost verses in which the prediction would have been accomplished. The poem's a gone and teased us all.

The poem does more than just cross the traditions of bawdy with the conventions of philology. As a map of Eliot's rhetorical development, "Fragments" stages an ambivalent relationship to two different audiences. The first audience is the private atmosphere of clubrooms at all-male Harvard, where Eliot first exchanged bawdy lyrics among friends. The second audience is ostensibly a scholarly audience, though here it can be read as a code for a Symbolist readership whose difficult expectations Eliot has been managing since November 1909: both Symbolists and scholars are cool, critical, and public audiences. By transforming this oral song into a written document of pseudo-philological interest, the author/curator of "Fragments" has created not a bridge between the two audiences (homosocial clubmates and Symbolist scholars) but a vantage point from which both audiences could be observed.

These two audiences—the hearties and the aesthetes—were not constructed by Eliot but inherited from his Harvard contexts. "Fragments" neatly encapsulates in its two audiences the anxieties surrounding the cult of masculinity that Kim Townsend has explored in his book *Manhood at Harvard*. For a variety of reasons—some of them having to do with the Civil War—by the end of the nineteenth century, the new word "masculinity" had entered the vocabulary, and men found themselves approaching every issue that affected them—personal, professional, and social—with a changed sense "of having to present themselves as manly," Townsend argues, "and a clear sense of how womanly they would be considered if they did not measure up."[60] Townsend shows how athletes and men of action became the new standards of masculinity, while scholars and artists—once figured as solitary geniuses and Romantic heroes—had to scramble to define their vocations as manly within this changed value system. In the student body at all-male Harvard, other categories of race, ideology, vocation, temperament, and social status broke in unexpected ways across this fault line of masculinity. So to explain how Eliot fit uneasily within these vexed categories, and how a defensive sense of masculinity suffuses them, we must first examine the categories as Townsend lays them out in his illuminating study.

One class of student at Harvard clearly does not apply to Eliot: these were the bright but poor scholarship students whom William James admiringly dubbed the "undisciplinables."[61] (From the usual, and less charitable perspective, they were loners, grinds, or eccentrics.) Serious students with academic ambitions, they were contemptuous of the celebrated "Harvard indifference." James's undisciplinables, however, were the outliers. Most students at Harvard were hearty joiners: debating, musical, theatrical, and literary societies, final clubs, and athletic teams were hubs of energetic social life. (Harvard indifference applied only to one's grades and the outcome of sporting events.) Within this wide majority, there were two types of "hearties." One was a fast set, whose identity depended upon money—especially old money—the conspicuous ways it was spent, and the careless manners associated with cosseted privilege. These students would reside on the Gold Coast: the expensive, private dormitories along Mount Auburn Street with luxurious amenities such as plumbing and electricity. Another group, whose members intermingled with but were not coterminous with the fast set, was the social elite. (A boorish aristocrat was not necessarily welcome in these circles.) As Townsend describes them, these men set a tone at Harvard. They mixed with Boston society, not only with Brahmins but with leaders in business and industry, cultivating connections to a broader social world for practical advantage.

For both the fast set and the social elite, their notion of masculinity was tied to being men of the world: hearties were men of action, whether in their athletic contests, debating tournaments, socializing, or angling for professional advantage. Their indifference to schoolwork was part of the masculine pose, with serious academic pursuit figured as feminine. The elective system, unique to Harvard at the time, abetted these masculinist attitudes. Instituted by its long-standing president Charles William Eliot, the elective system had abolished the prescribed, classical curriculum. President Eliot's intention was to encourage masculine independence: to compel a young man to choose his own occupation and those courses that would prepare him for it. A healthy social life and an indifference to schoolwork were the elements that unified different types of hearties: athletes, aristocrats, elites, social clubbers, and pre-businessmen.

Set against the hearties were the aesthetes. Since poetry and literature were in danger of slipping into effeminacy, it required vigilance to keep arts and letters on the masculine side of the binary. Van Wyck Brooks, a contemporary of Eliot's at Harvard, felt compelled to defend aesthetes from the charge of effeminacy in the *Advocate*: "I desire first of all to make plain that the word 'aesthetic' indicates not a flabby, purple and altogether repulsive state of mind, but the outlook on life of certain clear and sensitive persons who are quite honest and straightforward and by no means effeminate."[62] Wallace Stevens, like Van Brooks a student of Irving Babbitt, composed a journal entry while at Harvard entitled "Poetry and Manhood": "Those who say poetry is now the peculiar province of women say so because ideas about poetry are effeminate. Homer, Dante, Shakespeare, Milton, Keats, Browning, much of Tennyson—they are your man-poets."[63] At Harvard, literary figures such as Henry James and philosophers such as George Santayana were considered outsiders by virtue of their lack of manliness; any suggestion of homosexuality was frowned upon by Harvard men.[64]

As a hearty and an aesthete, Eliot fit into both categories and many of their subcategories, though he fit into none of them perfectly. The homosocial dynamics of his bawdy verse can be seen as an attempt to shore up the difference: to ratify his manliness as an aesthete and to enhance his credentials as a hearty. Like the members of the fast set, Eliot lived on the Gold Coast, and he had the pedigree of a family name. But he did not fit perfectly into this class: although he was well off, he was neither excessively rich nor from old money, nor was his preferred mode the boisterous pranks and high living of the fast set. As for the other category of hearty—the social elite—Eliot did mingle with Boston society in the parlors of Brahmins and the boxes of opera houses. As the son of a brick manufacturer, he sat comfortably within the ranks of the many students whose parents were part of the industrial class. However, he also found the artificiality of their social rituals maddening and suffocating, pointedly ridiculing them in his notebook poems. Standing aloof as a future academic or artist, he had little use for the networking ambitions of his peers who were looking for jobs in industry or the business world.

With his very poor grades in his first year, Eliot initially aligned himself with the hearties by consciously adopting their Harvard indifference. As a consequence, he was put on probation at the end of his first semester and given a talking to by his father. Nevertheless, the loafing persisted for several more semesters.[65] This casual attitude toward academic study stood in clear contrast with his record at Smith Academy and Milton Academy, where he had been a good student, a contrast that reveals how strongly he was pulled into the orbit of the hearties in his first years at Harvard and how the camaraderie of these circles filled a need for belonging in him.[66] He joined clubs such as the Southern Club and the Digamma Club (later renamed the Fox Club). Those private clubs provided not only social atmosphere and meals for students—Gold Coasters were unlikely to cook for themselves—but access to alcohol when Cambridge was still a dry town.[67] In Eliot's first year, he tried out unsuccessfully for the crew team, an attempt to add the identity of athlete to his bona fides as a hearty.[68] And heeding the advice of his clubmate Harold Peters, Eliot entered Eugen Sandow's course of exercise and strength training to increase his chest size.

But Eliot was also an aesthete. Beginning in his first year, he published a modest number of essays, reviews, and poems in the Harvard *Advocate*; by his third year, he was on its editorial board. As editor, he moderated a telling exchange in its pages between opposing viewpoints: "an ancient controversy—that between the sport and the grind." (Note that the terms of the point-counterpoint are *not* sport and aesthete.) Eliot identified with both sides: "No one need hope to settle the dispute. But if all prejudice and misunderstanding are cleared away, it is possible for each partisan, while retaining his own opinions, to see that there is much reason in the other man's contention."[69] While Eliot was never a remarkable student at Harvard, neither did he idle in introductory classes, as the elective system enabled his lazier peers to do. Although his course was somewhat eclectic and his grades average, he finished Harvard's three-year elective course with an AB and a further year for his MA. As Crawford has described, in all Eliot took twenty-five courses in languages, humanities, and government, a program that would later be considered something like a major in comparative literature.[70] Above all—and though it was not yet public knowledge—it was the seriousness with which Eliot experimented in his notebook that tagged him as an aesthete.

It was out of these warring allegiances and the anxiety about masculine identity that Eliot's bawdy verse was born. As Crawford has argued, the Columbo sequence is "an offensively crazy, overemphatic performance of maleness."[71] In "Fragments" and the Bolo poems, Eliot could give free play to all his anxious classifications of people—sexual athletes, overperformers, conquerors, businessmen-sailors, aristocracy, gay men and straight, voracious women, rapists, buggerers, and lovers—and free rein as well to all his anxious attitudes regarding social etiquette, professional ambition, sexual desire, and racial and cultural taboos.

The bawdy elements of the song reproduced in "Fragments" gesture to the flesh-and-blood comrades whose shared rituals of drinking and bonding included the risqué intimacy of bawdy songs, an intimacy reinforced all the more strongly because of the taboo content. Sung or shared among other males of the same social class, this form of bonding enacts a safe rebellion against the moral rectitude of their upbringing. These songs showed Eliot exactly what he was missing in his serious verse: a warmly receptive audience, wily and misogynist in its sexual banter, whose shared values and expectations included the (temporary and private) rejection of the genteel mores of its own class.[72] A clear line can be drawn from the performance of Eliot's "Ballade of the Fox Dinner" to the exchanges of the obscene verse. It is the same clubroom atmosphere; only the element of bawdy has been turned up a notch. Although it lacks the hard, critical edge and superior ironies of the Symbolist aesthetic—and lacks also its keen intelligence—the subversiveness of the bawdy tradition is one element that links it to an otherwise very different audience, the Laforguean readership that first captured Eliot's imagination.

The very oddness of "Fragments," in which bawdy is pushed through the sieve of philology, marks it as a dead end rather than a way forward. Its two different audiences—the one heartily welcoming, the other coolly dispassionate—are brought together in ironic counterpoint rather than substantive dialogue, which is why it is the only poem of its kind in the notebook.

Columbo and Bolo Verses
Drafted ca. 1910–1916

While the character of Christopher Columbo was adopted from oral tradition, the characters of King Bolo and his queen were apparently Eliot's creation, a sometime foil and sometime mirror to the oversexed European adventurer.[73] The preexisting variants of the story are almost entirely taken up with the sea voyage, beginning with Columbo's request for ships and ending with his men finally spying a "whore" on "the coast of Cub-y," whence they swim to shore and make frantic use of her services: "In fifteen minutes by the clock / She made nine hundred dollars."[74] In this traditional version of the ballad, the culminating scene is a sexual conquest underwritten by commercial exchange, an initiatory relationship that stands as shorthand for the future partnership between the Old and New Worlds. In the oral tradition, the Old World, sexually rapacious of territory, ends by getting the "clap," while the New World is a wealthy "whore": enriched if abused.[75]

Chinitz argues that Eliot's unique contribution to the Columbo tradition is the way his verses develop an antecedent folk song along the lines of Robert Burns's or Walter Scott's balladry.[76] Eliot's sequence does extend beyond the narrative borders of the traditional versions, since Eliot's is set both before the famous sea journey, where Columbo engages with Spanish royalty, and after his arrival in the New World, where he interacts with the newly met characters of Bolo and company. Eliot's extension of the tale even stretches to Columbo's triumphant return to Spain.[77]

On the level of technique, the poems are clearly doggerel, deliberately composed as such. Jonathan Gill points out how the use of the letter "k" for many /k/ sounds characterizes the "Kween" as a "simpleminded, illiterate heroine, who cannot spell but who knows obscenity when she sees it."[78] Likewise, Gill records, other calculated errors and unlettered rhymes such as "soda" and "loader" contrast with witticisms like the rhyming of "sink'd her" and "sphincter."[79] Such "paradoxical rhetoric of blackface minstrelsy," as Gill describes it, is one of many links between the bawdy verse and the serious verse, whose crammed rhymes and jazz effects are central to their technique and tone.[80]

On the level of history, the colonialist background and homosocial atmosphere of the Bolo sequence are aptly described by McIntire. The Bolo verses, she argues, "comically portray the history of early colonialism in the Americas as an orgy of uncontrollable desire and deviant sexuality."[81] The history of colonialism is one of violence, and the scene of the crime is here suppressed: the slave trade is nowhere mentioned in the Bolo sequence. When Columbo first arrives in the New World, Bolo's African tribe is already conveniently, if ahistorically, in place. In Eliot's history of colonialist expansion, the return of the repressed is found everywhere in the narrative, particularly in the centrality of sexual violence and racist tropes. The narrative both celebrates and critiques these violent tropes, the literary analogs of the violence of slavery. In her explanation of how the poem effects this ambiguous truce, McIntire points to such moments as the styling of "King Bolo's Big Black Bassturd Kween." Such a "potent moment of naming," McIntire argues, is disturbing "because of the element of racial hatred it speaks, while it also already troubles that racism by pointing to its own absurdity, turning the critical glance back upon itself to disclose more about the speaker than about the queen."[82]

Although the peculiar violence of these racist and misogynist tropes is new in Eliot's work, this obscene history of colonialism circles back to Eliot's earliest attitudes to "savage" cultures found in his adolescent stories written at Smith Academy.[83] In his juvenile story "The Man Who Was King," the narrator had lamented that the French had come and "educated the natives to wear clothes on Sunday and go to church, so that now they are quite civilized and uninteresting."[84] Even for the sixteen-year-old Eliot, civilization is ultimately less interesting than indigenous culture. A few years later—away at college and liberated from the constraints of his overly civilized adolescence—the young poet breaks all the taboos he had been trained to observe. Rather than civilizing the tribe of Bolo, Eliot's Columbo is himself a sexual libertine. His encounter with Bolo is not an agon of the civilized with the uncivilized but a meeting of equals. This equality of cultures is what is radical in Eliot's critique of the colonialist enterprise. By contrast, Jonathan Gill argues that Bolo and his queen are the "dangerously sexual savage[s]" to Columbo's "European decency, order, and civilization."[85] This is not the case: both Columbo and Bolo, representatives of their respective cultures, are raucous, lawless, and libidinous. Their first meeting imagines Columbo's sensing (literally smelling) the presence of Bolo's tribe before he encounters them:

> Columbo sniffed around the air
> And muttered "I smell whore"
> And ere they'd taken twenty steps
> Among the Cuban jungles

They found King Bolo & his queen
A-sitting on their bungholes.[86]

As might be expected when two different cultures meet, there are differences to work out, but they turn out to be superficial. After some initial "disrespect" and "quarrel[s]," Columbo and the queen quickly "terminated the affair / By fucking on the sofa."[87] Sex is the ultimate equalizer, as is the pregnancy that results from it. In a later stanza, the queen is pregnant with an "embryonic prince" whose paternity is unclear: "His prick is long his balls are strong / And his name is Boloumbo."[88] In the queen's progeny, Bolo and Columbo become indistinguishable.

More bountiful than sex is the amount of excrement to be found in the sequence: Columbo defecates on Queen Isabella's table, shits his breeches, and carries "forty tons of bullshit" as cargo.[89] King Bolo's culture exhibits the same preoccupations: his men "mounted in a banyan tree / And shat upon their sovereign."[90] McIntire notes that excrement is the "great, expendable form of currency and expression" in the Bolo sequence.[91] In McIntire's reading, the ubiquity of excrement is Eliot's comment on the "relation between colonialism and waste, pillage and bodily excess," a relation in which the raped and shat-upon body stands for the pillaged territory of colonial expansion.[92]

While McIntire helps us understand the historical background of the Bolo poems, Cheyette helps us understand the artistic trajectory: how Bolo morphs into Sweeney and is then abandoned. In his discussion of the Bolo poems, Cheyette concentrates on the issue of race, particularly the difference between how blackness functions in the Bolo sequence and how Jewishness is figured elsewhere in Eliot's work. In the Bolo sequence, the characters of Bolo and his queen embody racial, cultural, and sexual border crossing; likewise, in Eliot's poetry and prose, the figure of the Jew embodies "boundary-crossing disorder and uncertainty."[93] The odd difference that Cheyette notes is that Jewish boundary crossing is condemned, while black boundary crossing is celebrated: "Characterized by fluidity and boundary-crossing of all kinds, as well as outrageous forms of sexual and racial caricature, these [Bolo] poems use exactly the same motifs of sexual depravity, disease, and excremental sliminess which epitomize his Bleisteinian 'jew.' But whereas 'the jew' is discounted as the creator of cultural confusion and uncertainty, King Bolo's 'bullshit' is embraced by Eliot."[94] In Cheyette's reading, this black transgressiveness, which Eliot extends in *Sweeney Agonistes*, is ultimately unsustainable. Hence, *Sweeney Agonistes* remains unfinished. The disorder that Eliot abhors, Cheyette argues, leads him away from Bolo and Sweeney and toward classicism and conservatism as a way to police literary, religious, and cultural borders. Cheyette's own analysis of Bolo's fading away is at odds with his now-untenable claim that Eliot was "still writing [Bolos] a year before his death in 1965" and fits instead with my own claim that the Bolo poems were a preoccupation of his early period.[95]

What we are left with, finally, are the same ethical questions with which we started the chapter, and here McIntire offers a fine summary of the problem and fascination of these verses: "They play recklessly on prohibitions while offering a satirical poetics of desire and memory whose comic edge is always in danger of collapsing into the outright racism, homophobia, and misogyny that they ventriloquize, repeat, and critique."[96] By pushing the boundaries of decency and the limits of doggerel, do the poems make us laugh because they are "utterly inane," as in McIntire's estimation, or are they just not very funny for the same reason?[97] The fluttering moral register of the Bolo sequence is of a different quality than "Ballade pour la grosse Lulu," with its supercilious racism and flat-footed air. In the Bolo poems, the tropes of racism, misogyny, and homophobia are simultaneously harnessed and chewed up by raucous, transgressive energies. As a consequence, the author is ambivalently complicit in the moral quandaries the poems pose: he can seem, at times, to identify more with that transgressive energy than with the taboo content, though this ambivalent quality does not prevent hackles from being raised in individual readers.

Regarding the significance of these poems, Ricks has argued that if the Bolo poems are suppressed, then one misses the essential contribution that Corbière offers to Eliot's later poetry—the rough world of sailors and scatology that make later figures such as Sweeney intelligible. In Ricks's telling, Eliot's transition from "the Laforguean velleities of 1917 to the Corbièresque bluntness, such as 'Sweeney Erect,' of 1920" makes sense only with respect to the bawdy verse.[98] While this gap between "Prufrock" and the later quatrain poems may indeed have been bridged by the obscene verse, an even earlier transition can be observed by placing the bawdy verse back into the chronology of the notebook. Written on the same pages as "Portrait of a Lady" and "Suite Clownesque," the obscene verses reveal a different kind of gap: the stark difference between two audiences, namely, the easy camaraderie of the sharers of bawdy and the nervous skepticism of the earliest Laforguean audiences. This was the audience gap—also a confidence gap—that Eliot was seeking, if not to close entirely, then to bring together more nearly. Taking account of the convivial audience of the obscene verse helps to illuminate how Eliot moved from the clumsy mistrust of the first inventions to the distinctive trust-cum-hesitance of "Prufrock."

As with Eliot's serious verse in *Inventions*, the obscene verse is of a piece with his experimentation and increasing mastery. The bawdy verses, like his serious verses, are rhetorical constructs whose voice is aimed at a specific audience and pitched for certain effects. In the serious verse of *Inventions*, such as "Portrait of a Lady" and "Prufrock," Eliot's critique of social custom and his exploration of poverty and alienation required that he cross mental borders that were strongly policed by his class and education. And perhaps the most difficult boundary to cross for someone of Eliot's class and temperament was the erotic boundary. As Alex Zwerdling reminds us, the "cultural dispensation from which Eliot emerged demanded virtual silence on the subject of erotic life. . . . Sex in these poems [from *Inventions*] is never associated with pleasure or love: it is anxious, sordid, urgent, unwanted, unfulfilled, at best masturbatory, at worst a crucifixion in a garret."[99] Because the obscene verses adopt a tone of hysterical buffoonery rather than squalid fear, they do not breathe exactly this same atmosphere of anguished sexuality found in the serious poems. Nevertheless, the scabrous verse still pushes against the same sexual and erotic boundaries as other poems in *Inventions*.

Even though the obscene poems can be seen as part of the same project as the notebook as a whole, they were detours from his artistic development in a noteworthy sense. Often categorized as bawdy verse, they are also occasional poems. Although they were not written to commemorate a public event, they are still "occasional" in the sense that they were written for a specific communal setting: the social clubs of Harvard. We, their tardy and unwelcome readers, cannot recreate through the texts the living atmosphere of Eliot's exclusive, homosocial circle. That audience was wholly sympathetic because it would always be private and circumscribed. The poems speak to the already-known friends of the poet and to those, like Lewis, who were introduced by known friends. The bawdy verses do not seek to create a new readership, which is why they never seem to improve. Their fumbling, jerky quality can be partly attributed to the audience for whom they were performed: like a composer's études, they were concoctions thrown off to entertain, experiments in rhythm and rudeness, with no need to worry about an audience's potential rejection.

Once Eliot moved from Harvard to England, the class and profession of men with whom he shared such lyrics changed, but key identity markers remained the same: the maleness of the club, their youth and sexual anxiety, a view of women's sexuality as passive, and an aggressive sense of themselves as shapers of their respective worlds. Compared to his new London coterie, Eliot was inexperienced, both sexually and literarily, and so he leads the charge with his Bolo poems. (None of his correspondents seemed to have written them, only received them.) Eagerly sharing via letters what had been sung at social clubs, he overcompensates with the bravado of the insecure, hoping to recreate in a new environment some of the atmosphere of Harvard.

We are now in a position to understand how the historical analysis with which we opened the chapter is related to the rhetorical analysis of the poems—how, in other words, these three aspects of audience are interdependent: (1) why Eliot never sought a public venue for these poems, (2) why the thrill of writing them waned early, and (3) why their rhetoric is essentially private. The obscene verses—especially the Bolo sequence as it expanded in the late teens—project a circumscribed audience whose expectations were titillation and friendly bonding. These expectations were bound to disappear as Eliot's relationships changed and the cultural atmosphere altered: Bloomsbury bohemians would not be so easily shocked as Harvard undergraduates. With such a low bar of titillation, it is no surprise that the poems are dully repetitive and, for all their sexual and racial boundary crossing, artistically unadventurous. But perhaps this judgment is too severe. Even as a ten-year-old boy, in his *Fireside* compositions, Eliot revealed a good ear for bad verse. That Eliot used such woeful doggerel as a vehicle for such ethically bad material is a way of satirizing the badness of both. Eliot might have been playing in ways that are too bad to be judged as merely bad.[100]

For the apprentice author of *Inventions,* the audience of the Bolo poems was private and real—the specific nameable friends of the young Eliot—while the audience for the serious verse was imagined and aspirational. For a lonely artist who was struggling so mightily to wrestle a new audience into shape, the freedom and ease of writing for a warmly accepting audience must have been a psychological relief. The audience for the bawdy verse kept him moving in the artistic direction toward which he was already oriented.

The serious poems in the notebook, both the successes and the failures, were what made Eliot famous, because they called into being a peculiarly modern audience that had never existed before. By contrast, the obscene poems, because they were written for several dozen people, might seem to be interesting only because they were composed by a poet who famously became "T. S. Eliot." This seems to be the conclusion reached by many reviewers and scholars. Once placed back into the chronology of their making, however, the obscene poems reveal a liberated sense of audience, rather than the stepwise rhetorical mastery achieved elsewhere in the notebook.

Eliot would probably be exasperated to know that scholars were writing somber analyses of his bawdy poetry. One of his recurring jokes is that a pedant by the name of Prof. Dr. Krapp will take up the task of writing commentary on his Bolo poems.[101] Exasperated Eliot might be, but he could not be surprised at this state of affairs, since he deliberately chose to preserve the obscene verse. The influence of the obscene poems on his artistic project is perhaps the reason Eliot could never bring himself to destroy them, because they offered strangely occluded evidence of his expanding vision and his rhetorical aims. As a young man tossing off such bawdy poems, he probably had little thought of what might become of them after they had been shared with their intended correspondents. Even so, once Eliot's fame escalated, he could easily have gotten rid of the obscene poems still in his possession. He was not averse to burning sensitive material. Instead, he cut them out of the notebook and sent them to Ezra Pound, who valued the poems and who Eliot knew would preserve them. And sometime in the future, Prof. Dr. Krapp and his colleagues would set to work on them.

"Prufrock," Abandoned

How the Poem Was Written, How It Was Received, and How It Works

> I often feel that "J.A.P[rufrock]." is a swan song.
>
> —T. S. Eliot, to his brother Henry

On December 4, 1950, at a poetry reading at New York's Ninety-Second Street Y, T. S. Eliot abandoned "The Love Song of J. Alfred Prufrock," a poem he dismissed as "embarrassing." A recently discovered recording of the event is a revelation: it is the only known audible recording of the poet making impromptu remarks. For anyone used to the measured cadence of his recordings and broadcasts, or to the self-assured prose of his letters and essays, it comes as something of a shock to hear the same voice—its thin nasality, its unplaceable accent—wandering around in grammar that does not always line up, hemming and hawing through an introduction. It seems impertinent to transcribe here Eliot's uhs and ums, his hesitations and repetitions, but his speaking off the cuff clearly charmed the audience, who laughed sympathetically:

> An author—a poet rather tends to like best what he's written most recently. Uh, and uh, therefore, he reads it best. The early things are become rather remote, and also, you see from a later stage of, uh, of uh, exercise and training, you see all sorts of flaws, uh, in maturity, which are embarrassing. And it's difficult to read one's early poems with the same conviction. And therefore it's best to uh, to leave the things that you think you do best until the end. Umm. So I shall begin . . . taking, um, period by period. I know I shall disappoint some people, but, um . . . I *am* rather embarrassed with, uh, with "Prufrock." [*audience laughter*] Uh . . . nnn . . . now I, I feel it's uh . . . it's rather an, exposing an adolescent personality.[1]

Eliot was always leaving "Prufrock" behind him. As early as 1916, a year after he had first published the poem, Eliot wrote to his brother Henry, "I often feel that 'J.A.P.' is a swan song."[2] And as late as 1959, when asked by a journalist about "The Love *Life* of J. Alfred Prufrock," Eliot responded, "I'm afraid that J. Alfred Prufrock didn't have much a love life"—though Eliot's mischievousness is aimed less at his own poem than at the journalist's misremembering the title.[3]

The unfortunate journalist aside, it is easy to remember what "Prufrock" is about. The poem has long been a cultural commodity—a comforting joke about coffee spoons or timidity, a predictable reference for *New Yorker* cartoons, its author a recurrent answer in crossword puzzles. What is not widely remembered is that Eliot abandoned "Prufrock" before he had even finished it. With the full drafts of "Prufrock" now available, and with the flurry of interest in "Prufrock's Pervigilium" now becalmed, it is time to approach it anew, to see how the poem was written in stages, to discover what it meant to its first readers, and to imagine how such an approach might change the way we now understand this beloved, much-anthologized poem.

How It Got Written: The Drafts of "Prufrock"

The story of how "Prufrock" got on the page is a complicated one. Over a six-year period, there were short sections written and preserved, then long sections drafted, deletions and wrong turns, a lengthy fallow period, and finally, the limp toward publication at someone else's urging. Articulating the stages of the drafts allows us to see the reason for the long delay: a gaping hole in the middle of the poem, into which "Prufrock's Pervigilium" was later added, then whittled down. Eliot worried over this middle section for a number of years, coming up with various solutions and making last-minute changes before sending it off for publication. The published version of the poem still retains evidence of its most perilous gap at line 75: the transition from a bottom-dwelling crab to a Boston drawing room. It is a disorienting leap that begins with the inapposite conjunction "and"—slyly pretending that before and after are clauses of logical sequence or equal grammatical standing: "I should have been a pair of ragged claws / Scuttling across the floors of silent seas. // *And* the afternoon, the evening, sleeps so peacefully!"[4]

The successive drafts reveal Eliot circling this crux, first offering large-scale, then small-scale solutions:

1. 1910, Harvard: Hamlet passage and other short, unidentified sections
2. 1911, Paris and Munich: long draft with four pages left blank in the middle (manuscript at Berg Collection)[5]
3. 1912, Harvard: extended draft, with "Prufrock's Pervigilium" added on the reserved middle pages (manuscript at Berg)

4. 1913, Harvard: revised draft, with double spaces setting off distilled "Pervigilium" (typescript at University of Maryland)[6]
5. Oct. 1914, London: fair copy, with four asterisks, then deleted, then changed to a row of dots, setting off middle section (typescript with autograph corrections at *Poetry* archives, University of Chicago)
6. June 1915, Chicago: publication in *Poetry*

In the earliest extant version of the poem (#2 above), "Prufrock" is unfinished, with two large sections unconnected to each other. The first section is parenthetically subtitled "Prufrock among the Women" and runs from the familiar "Let us go" through the stanzas beginning "For I have known them." Following this section, two leaves (that is, four pages) are intentionally left blank for a projected middle section. This large gap is followed by the final stanzas of the poem, beginning "And the afternoon." The large, blank canvas in the middle of the poem suggests two ideas: the poet's uncertainty about how he is going to link up the first section of the poem to the last, and his sense that the unwritten section would be long and ambitious. After an incubation period, his first solution to the problem is a section of thirty-eight lines subtitled "Prufrock's Pervigilium," written probably in 1912, after his return to Harvard. Based on the evidence of the "Pervigilium," the young artist seems to have imagined these blank pages as a space where he would explore the full experience of Prufrock's interior suffering and his resistance to inertia, as opposed to "Prufrock among the Women" which primarily explores his social alienation. Thus, the "Pervigilium" itself and the lengthy space left for its drafting reveal that the subsection "Prufrock among the Women" was intended as *introductory* to another problem to be explored in more detail once the artist could summon his nerve or invent the requisite technique.

Vendler has shown how the later section of "Prufrock" recapitulates almost all the themes of the opening section.[7] Yet the two sections are different in atmosphere and character. "Prufrock among the Women" describes an arc that begins in the decorous invitations of Boston social visits and ends in Prufrock's fear mixed with desire for these women. The modes of this section are imperative, interrogative, and indicative. Its scenes are remembered as much as they are imagined; that is to say, "Prufrock among the Women" is rooted in the social realities of Brahmin culture and the squalid poverty of North Cambridge. By contrast, the end of the poem is dominated by the conditional perfect of "would have been." The modes of this section are subjunctive and counterfactual, dominated by the dreamscapes of Lazarus, Hamlet, mermaids, and oceanic reverie. Although the opening and closing sections clearly have themes and other markers in common, it is no wonder that the young artist left himself four blank pages: a lengthy space in which to write from one side to the other.

Two elements that the opening and closing sections have in common is a setting (evening) and a theme (paralysis). The first section opens with the simile of the paralyzed evening, "spread out against the sky / Like a patient etherized upon a table." And the final section begins drowsily, late in the day: "And the afternoon, the evening sleeps so peacefully!" Inevitably, when Eliot turns to draft the "Pervigilium" in 1912, the evening imagery is picked up but with a countertheme: paralysis is actively challenged. The evening "woke and stared into its blindness"; "the evening fought itself awake"; "the midnight turned and writhed."[8] The subtitle of the middle section, "Pervigilium," evokes an eve spent awake, a "vigil" as preparation for a solemnity or important event. As with preparations taken by soldiers and saints, Prufrock's vigil is organized by nocturnal watch points (dusk, evening, night, midnight, dawn) and is filled with mortal and spiritual dangers. He suffers sexual temptation ("Women, spilling out of corsets"), illness ("fever"), hallucination (the darkness "leapt to the floor"), isolation (a "blind old drunken man"), and insanity ("I have heard my Madness chatter").[9] This darkness may be feverish and nauseating, and what Prufrock sees there is hallucinatory madness, but the hero has finally chosen to act, to fight against blindness and unconsciousness, even if the vision he seeks is not forthcoming. The vigil "dissolve[s]," ending inconclusively and abruptly with dawn.

"Prufrock's Pervigilium" might have been an effective addition to the poem, presenting a valiant if doomed struggle to contrast with the paralysis of the outer sections. The problem was in the execution, which created a tonal mismatch. As Vendler describes, the "Pervigilium" unintentionally reproduces 1890s bathos in which elements of the "gothic, paranoid, and melodramatic" combine to produce such awkwardness as "I fumbled to the window to experience the world / And to hear my Madness singing, sitting on the kerbstone."[10] Whereas Laforgue, Baudelaire, and others had given Eliot new models for critiquing social custom and for observing the poor, he has no convincing models for how to construct Prufrock's midnight struggle without veering into the maudlin discourse of decadent poetry. Soon after drafting the "Pervigilium," Eliot realizes that this attempt to describe interior suffering was either artistically impossible or temporarily unfeasible. As Louis

Menand describes the problem, the "Pervigilium" is "much too melodramatic for a poem whose success depends on its handling of the conventional persona of the self-absorbed *flaneur* in a witty and self-mocking spirit."[11] The line "To hear my Madness singing," declares Menand, "is exactly the sort of late-Romantic *Weltschmerz* a line like 'Do I dare to eat a peach?' is meant to send up."[12]

After the "Pervigilium" is drafted, the next datable moment in the history of the poem's composition is February 23, 1913, when Aiken writes to Eliot, "If you have a superfluous copy of the Love Song of J. Alfred Prufrock, any time, here is one who hath an appetite for it."[13] This request suggests two possibilities: either Eliot had already cancelled the "Pervigilium" by 1913, or Aiken's request for a fair copy provoked Eliot to come up with a solution. In this manuscript sent to Aiken—now housed at the University of Maryland—we have what nearly resembles the published text. Eliot has distilled a mere five lines from the lengthy "Pervigilium." However, the author is clearly uncomfortable with this ramshackle fix. He has tried to soft-pedal the awkwardness of the transition by adding larger, double spaces above and below the five lines, with the added space visually signaling the gap in logic.[14] Over a year later, when the poem is being readied for publication in late 1914, Eliot reveals his continuing uncertainty about the gap. In the typescript submitted to *Poetry*, there appears a third solution to the problem—asterisks now surround these orphaned lines from the "Pervigilium." This attempt in turn is abandoned for a fourth solution: Eliot crosses out the asterisks and directs the typesetter to substitute a row of dots instead. All of these permutations reveal Eliot's discomfort with his rickety solutions. They acknowledge that the gap is still too large: the disorienting scene change (from the seabed to a drawing room), the unprepared tense shift (from the perfect progressive to the simple present), and the abrupt tonal change—from sharp regret ("I should have been") to trivial exclamation (the evening "sleeps so peacefully!").

Eliot's attempts to paper over this gap reflect not just an uncertain technique but a deeper, personal crisis—his dream of being a poet fading away. The crisis takes the following form on the page. In Paris and Munich in 1911, the ambitious artist is hard at work on a long masterpiece, drafting two extended sections. Success, of a sort, but he hesitates at a precipice: those four blank pages, a dare to be attempted later. In 1912, the reluctant graduate student has returned to Harvard; a sudden leap is made with the histrionics of "Pervigilium." Almost immediately, a nervous retreat is beaten, and the promise of the blank pages is abandoned. He has tried to extend his bold, poetic experiment of the previous year, but he recognizes his failure to do so "at once."[15] After 1912, no further attempts are made to replace the "Pervigilium" with some other invention. Instead, in 1913–1914, the graduate student toys with formatting: double spaces, asterisks, and dots are arranged and rearranged. Deep into his doctoral courses, he has given up bold gestures, settling for the fussy compromises of a failed apprentice and the future career of a philosophy professor.

With the even bolder fragmentation of *The Waste Land* on the horizon, it is an oddity of modernist history to consider that the most prominent gap in "Prufrock" was haphazardly arrived at and never fully secure in the artist's mind. It was not a eureka moment of artistic resolve nor a deliberate apotheosis of the trope of fragmentation. Rather, it was the result of suffering: the failures and indecisions of the artistic process. With the *Inventions* draft, the "Pervigilium," the Maryland manuscript, and the *Poetry* magazine typescript restored to the poem's compositional history, we can now understand more fully what Aiken meant when he said that Eliot had been "heartlessly indifferent" to the poem's fate.[16] Aiken is only partly right: Eliot was not indifferent to the half-finished poem; he was paralyzed by the artistic problem that would not allow him to finish it. In a telling symmetry, the vocational crisis and the artistic paralysis mirror the indecisions of Prufrock himself, with his brave, if incoherent struggle excised and forgotten.[17] It is a proleptic irony of modernism that the command "do not ask, 'What is it?'" was almost not commanded, that a poem that gestures so compellingly to what cannot be spoken was itself almost undone by its inability to speak.

The surprising story of how "Prufrock" helped to inaugurate a new, modernist sensibility of fragmentation and disruption hinges on two counterintuitive ideas. First, the fragmentation of the published poem was more of an unhappy compromise than a felicitous discovery. Second, and more surprisingly, the poem's earliest readers did not remark on its fragmentation. As discussed below, the early critics of the poem were not interested in justifying or denigrating its technique of fragmentation. Oddly, when "Prufrock" was released into the world, neither the large gap left by the deleted "Pervigilium" nor the smaller gaps were much singled out for comment. Instead, what the initial critics could not compass was the ways the poem handled emotion. This overriding concern placed the problem of the poem's fragmentation in the background. Much later, when the poem came to be accepted, the uneven sutures holding it together had by then blended in with the other, intentional leaps of Prufrock's roving mind.

How It Got Published: The Pound-Monroe Quarrel over "Prufrock"

The reception history of "Prufrock" begins with those friends and editors who read the poem in manuscript. Aiken, Eliot's friend from Harvard, was its earliest fan and respondent. After Eliot had made him a copy on a Blickensderfer italic typewriter sometime in 1913, Aiken took the poem with him to London, intending to hawk their work to publishers. In July 1914, Aiken showed up at Harold Monro's Poetry Bookshop and offered "Prufrock" for Monro's *Poetry and Drama*. After reading the poem, Monro handed it back to Aiken, claiming it was "absolutely insane."[18] Monro was the first but not the last to pass such judgment. Given the drunkenness and madness articulated in the canceled "Pervigilium," there is a kind of intuitive logic in the recurrence of drunkenness, insanity, and pathology in the early lexicon of "Prufrock" criticism. Aiken did not take rejection lightly, however. In the following days, he seized an inopportune moment to press the case for another poem of Eliot's. When this was testily rebuffed, Aiken pursued Monro by letter, only to receive a third rejection. In later years, when Eliot's reputation was assured and Monro had come to admire Eliot, Aiken liked to tease Monro about his rejection of "Prufrock." However, in Aiken's reminiscences of his advocacy, he seems oblivious to how his lack of social tact cost him Monro's goodwill and possibly Eliot's first publication.[19]

Other prepublication readers were divided about the merits of "Prufrock" as well. The famous part of this story is Pound's discovery of Eliot. Arriving in London in August 1914, Eliot called on Pound at Aiken's urging. Eliot sent him "Prufrock" after their meeting, and Pound howled in excitement to Harriet Monroe, the editor of *Poetry*, for whom Pound served as talent scout:

> I was jolly well right about Eliot. He has sent in the best poem I have yet had or seen from an American. PRAY GOD IT BE NOT A SINGLE AND UNIQUE SUCCESS. . . . / He is the only American I know of who has made what I can call adequate preparation for writing. He has actually trained himself *and* modernized himself *on his own*. The rest of the *promising young* have done one or the other but never both (most of the swine have done neither).[20]

Pound's amazement at Eliot's work has been construed in multiple ways, including the mischievous explanation that Pound was astonished that any poets could have modernized themselves without his help.[21] Thereafter, Pound was Eliot's most important ally, and his first task was to get Harriet Monroe to place "Prufrock" in her magazine. In his hectoring manner—hilarious for us to read, though surely irksome to be on its receiving end—Pound repeatedly assailed Monroe regarding what he took to be her foot dragging:

- Sept. 30, 1914: Eliot "has taken ["Prufrock"] back to get it ready for the press and you shall have it in a few days."
- Oct. 1914: "Here is the Eliot poem. The most interesting contribution I've had from an American. / P.S. Hope you'll get it *in* soon."
- Nov. 9, 1914: "Your letter—the long one—to hand is the most dreary and discouraging document that I have been called upon to read for a very long time. / Your objection to Eliot is the climax."
- Nov. 9, 1914 [later the same day]: "No, most emphatically I will not ask Eliot to write down to any audience whatsoever. . . . Neither will I send you Eliot's address in order that he may be insulted."
- Jan. 31, 1915: "Now as to Eliot: 'Mr. Prufrock' does not 'go off at the end.' It is a portrait of failure, or of a character which fails, and it would be false art to make it end on a note of triumph. . . . I will let the unfortunate [poem by Arthur Davison] Ficke pass without complaint if you get on with 'Mr. Prufrock,' in a nice quiet and orderly manner."
- Apr. 10, 1915: "*Do* get on with that Eliot."
- [undated]: "You mark my blossoming word, that young chap will go quite a long way. . . . If you think [Eliot] lacks vigour merely because he happens to have portrayed Mr. Prufrock the unvigorous, vous vous trompez."[22]

The eight-month delay in publication is often read through this lens of Pound's bullying and Monroe's objections. Pound's impatience was motivated by a particular deadline: the limited time Eliot was in London. Pound wanted to secure bona fide publications for the graduate student as a way of encouraging him to abandon his academic plans and to take up a literary career in London. In this version of the narrative, Pound's impatience makes him the champion of groundbreaking art, while Monroe's equivocating makes her the editor caught between her own ambitions and the tetchy nerves of her guarantors. Nevertheless, Monroe's delay in publication probably had little to do with her demurrals about the poem: the simpler explanation is backlog. Many authors of excellent reputation had to wait for longer periods at *Poetry*, Yeats and William Carlos Williams among them.

Ellen Williams offers a subtle reading of the Pound-Monroe spat over "Prufrock," examining how both misconstrue its conclusion. Pound, for example, had written of its final six lines, "The poetic mind leaps the gulf from the exterior world, the trivialities of Mr. Prufrock, diffident, ridiculous, in the drawing room."[23] To later readers of the poem though, there is no escaping the Prufrockian mind that has defined the exterior and interior worlds: "The drawing room world in 'Prufrock' is ugly and trivial enough," Williams points out, "but one wonders how Pound could feel that the poetic mind leaped out of it."[24] Pound's Prufrock is endowed with suspiciously Pound-like energies, remaking the world in his own image. Pound's early reading of "Prufrock" is partly his own understanding and partly an agon with Monroe, who thought Prufrock "unvigorous."

For her part, Monroe projected her own anxieties and concerns onto "Prufrock." As Williams describes her, Monroe would seem to have been the ideal reader for the poem: she had a pessimistic streak, with little faith in civilization.[25] Monroe, in Williams's reading, "had the revolutionary temperament, despite her conventional situation. But the image of 'Prufrock,' of a man denatured by his own civilization but unable to escape from it, is abhorrent to that temperament. The way Eliot's conclusion denies Prufrock any escape from himself, and suggests another level of reality in the sea only to deny it, would be shocking to Harriet Monroe."[26] As a consequence, Monroe's resistance to the poem took the form of biographical simplification, reducing the character's conundrum to the author's psychological struggle with modernity. Monroe later describes the poem as "modern sophistication dealing with the tag ends of overworldly cosmopolitanism"—an evasion of the poem as dubious as Pound's.[27]

Writing to Monroe two years after their quarrel, Pound reminds her that she had at first "loathed and detested Eliot."[28] This accusation is probably exaggerated on Pound's part, but the truth is that she did dislike parts of "Prufrock." In her later life, however, Monroe preferred to remember only her heroic publication of the poem rather than her objections to it. In her autobiography she dissembles about her first encounter with "Prufrock," recalling her impression of "an extraordinarily finished product"—a radical revision of her initial characterization of the poem's "go[ing] off at the end." Her later reminiscence also peevishly erases Pound's role in the affair by reducing him to an anonymous servant: "When 'Prufrock' reached us via our Foreign Correspondent, its opening lines . . . nearly took our breath away. . . . However, we printed the poem in June, 1915, thereby drawing down upon our heads loud protests from shocked critics."[29]

How It Was Understood: The Early Reception History of "Prufrock"

Postpublication Reception: Utterly Stumped

Although Monroe's publication of "Prufrock" set off a round of epistolary complaints, she dampened the flames by declining to publish those negative reactions in the correspondence sections of *Poetry*. In one of those unpublished complaints to Monroe, Louis Untermeyer ascribed the difficulties of "Prufrock" to the pathologies of its author:

> To come back to Eliot for a moment, I confess that his "Love Song" is the first piece of the English Language that utterly stumped me. As a post-impression, the effect was that of the Muse in a psychopathic ward—drinking the stale dregs of revolt. The other Sunday night there was a group at the house—one of those not-too-"arts & crafty" mélanges—a few poets, a lawyer, a couple of musicians & one psychoanalyst. I read it to them quite seriously—& no one, not even James Oppenheim [poet and later editor of *Seven Arts*], who is the most serious person in this thickly populated universe—no one could keep a straight face. No one, that is, except the psychoanalyst who said, "An extremely interesting case. I think a lot could be done for him. It's a muddled case of infantile repressions and inhibitions." Which, as you can imagine, did not clear the air to any perceptible degree. Well, I suppose since it takes all sorts of people to make a world, it takes all sorts of poems to make a magazine of poetry. As a varietist [*sic*] in the arts even an editor sometimes must wander from the sane & narrow paths into the dark alleys of the pathological.[30]

Monroe did receive at least one admiring letter, from Vachel Lindsay, on June 12: "Most of all I liked the Love Song of J. Alfred Prufrock—the best thing you have had for many a day."[31]

On the other side of the Atlantic, Pound reported mystified responses to the poem, with two exceptions. Ford Madox Hueffer "having seen 'Prufrock' came in the other day to find out if Eliot had published a book, as he wanted to write about him. WHICH shows that you can't do a good thing without its being took note of. F. M. H. was just as quick as I to see that Eliot mattered."[32] Another pleased reader was Harold Monro who, like Harriet Monroe, had changed his mind about the poem, perhaps because he could read it in peace without being hounded by Aiken. Apparently unaware that Monro had rejected the poem a year earlier, Pound reports, "Monro discovered 'Prufrock' on his unaided own and asked me about the author when I saw him last night.

I consider Harold is dawning. He was very glad to hear that T. S. E. was in the forefront of our [*Catholic*] *Anthology*."[33]

After the publication of "Prufrock" in the June number, Eliot becomes a regular topic of comment in *Poetry*, signaling Pound's continued support and Monroe's increasing esteem. For every *Poetry* issue from August through December 1915, Monroe and Pound find ways to refer to Eliot's work. In the coterie world of new poetry, Eliot has had a splashy debut, even though, as Ellen Williams has remarked, "in 1914 or 1915 'Prufrock' was accessible on any terms to very few readers."[34] The tangle of initial reactions to its publication had less to do with mapping out coherent interpretations of the poem and more to do with staking out positions on the artist: Did Eliot matter or not?

Another critical judgment, voiced privately by John Gould Fletcher, will ripple outward in public. Writing to Amy Lowell a few months after the publication of "Prufrock," Fletcher remarks, "Harriet [Monroe] is publishing next month some very amusing things by T. S. Eliot, much better than 'Prufrock.' This young scamp is worth watching. . . . [Wallace Stevens] and Eliot seem to be the only new men with anything at all to them. And both suffer from being too damnably clever."[35] This problem of cleverness will cling to early reviews, as will accusations of drunken, crazed pathologies.

Post-collection Reception: Too Clever by Half

The negative reception after the poem's initial publication was muted by Monroe's damage-control tactics: by puffing Eliot in the same magazine and refusing to publish the dissenting voices. This strategy only worked for a few months. By November 1915, Pound had collected Eliot's poems in *Catholic Anthology*, and a year and a half later, *Prufrock and Other Observations* collected even more of them. With this wider distribution in books—and the reviews they invited—the negative responses to "Prufrock" could no longer be ignored, and Eliot's protectors would take to the battlements.

Given the secure place of "Prufrock" in the literary canon today, it would be easy to quote the negative reviews, condescending to their benighted judgments. However, in 1916–1917, with German forces assaulting British troops across the Channel, the war colored the politics of literary battles.[36] Within the island itself, conscientious objectors were seen as threats to national security and patriotic unity. Pacifists such as Bertrand Russell were tried and imprisoned under the Defence of the Realm Act. The resistance to anarchy and revolutionaries, even in matters of literary judgment, was no trivial matter. In addition to this mitigating context of politics, another reason to take seriously those who resisted Eliot is their critical consensus. If the naysayers had disagreed among themselves, then their negative evaluations might be attributed to dyspepsia or contrarianism. But disparate voices were surprisingly in agreement about what they took to be the poet's cleverness and lack of emotion.

One recurrent idea reveals the extent of the hostility: the claim that Eliot's work cannot properly be called poetry. One reviewer complains that Eliot's images "certainly have no relation to 'poetry'," another that "much of what he writes is unrecognizable as poetry at present."[37] The peremptory definition of what constitutes poetry is one indication of the crumbling critical landscape. It is also a neat contradiction, this eagerness of critics to review a poem that most emphatically is not a poem.

Such posturing aside, when the negative reviews turn to the business of explanation, many claim that Eliot manages emotion poorly. The anonymous reviewer in the *Times Literary Supplement* describes Eliot's poetry as "a purely analytical treatment . . . untouched by any genuine rush of feeling."[38] The reviewer in *Literary World* is comparably suspicious: "Mr. Eliot is one of those clever young men who find it amusing to pull the leg of a sober reviewer."[39] All of the reviews that identify Eliot as clever activate a pejorative sense in the word, though the *OED* records no distinctively negative connotation in its current usage, which dates to 1716: "possessing skill or talent; able to use hand or brain readily and effectively; dexterous, skilful; adroit." The missing term—what makes Eliot *merely* clever—is emotion. To these hostile reviewers, Eliot is dexterous at manipulating the forms and cadences of poetry, but this effectiveness precludes the kind of feeling, especially the feeling for beauty, with which they are familiar. Early reviewers sensed—accurately, as it turned out—that Eliot was the leading edge of a destructive tendency; the delicate balance of beauty and strangeness that had heretofore governed poetic communication in the Edwardian and Georgian eras was now a discarded, even despised standard.[40] The rules of the game were changing so drastically that reviewers could not trust the fundamentals on which their critical judgment had rested: emotions and feelings. Eliot's later theorization of impersonality was in part a reaction to these polemics that engulfed his first publication. It must have made a deep impression on an unknown foreigner suddenly to become the center of controversy among respected critics about the management of emotion in art, especially when emotion appears to be absent.

One reason the poem's "cleverness" seemed to block early reviewers from recognizing its emotional seriousness was the surrounding context. Both *Catholic Anthology* and *Prufrock and Other Observations* published "Prufrock" alongside Eliot's short satires: "The Boston Evening Transcript" and "Aunt Helen" were clever indeed. In its book publication, the implicit category of "Prufrock" was one "Observation" among others, and this grouping encouraged readers to see it as another of the portrait satires. Another factor that set conservative reviewers on edge was the venues where Eliot was published. While "Prufrock" had appeared in the progressive if respectable *Poetry*, other poems such as "Rhapsody on a Windy Night" and "Preludes" had appeared in Wyndham Lewis's *Blast*, that snotty, iconoclastic journal of the avant-garde. Similarly, *Catholic Anthology* had been edited by Pound—like Lewis, a loud-mouthed writer of letters to the editor, and an American thorn in the British side to boot. Running with such an unruly mob was almost certain to guarantee Eliot an unfavorable reception among the literary establishment, no matter how traditional his poems had been.

"Cleverness," Arthur Waugh groans with his first word, writing in the conservative *Quarterly Review*. Waugh complains of *Catholic Anthology*, "There are moods and emotions, but no steady current of ideas behind them."[41] Referring to "Prufrock" in particular, Waugh accuses Eliot of "an emotion that settles down into the banality of a premature decrepitude." Waugh ends his review with an aristocratic warning to revolutionaries and anarchists: a parable of a drunken slave displayed to the sons of a household, to shame them from such folly themselves.[42] It was the sort of insult to which Pound thrilled, licensing him to return fire in defense of genius: "If in any land, or upon any floating deck over the ocean, or upon some newly contrapted craft in the aether, genius manifests itself, at once some elderly gentleman has a flux of bile from his liver; at once from the throne or the easy Cowperian sofa, or from the gutter, or from the economical press room there bursts a torrent of elderly words, splenetic, irrelevant, they form themselves instinctively into large phrases denouncing the inordinate product." Preliminary insults out of the way, Pound's praise of Eliot does not at first attend to Waugh's criticism. Instead, Pound simply insists that Eliot has made an advance on Browning, that he has "been an individual in his poems."[43] Two months later, Pound circles back to the problem: "It is complained that Eliot is lacking in emotion"—a complaint that Pound dismisses as "rubbish." He then curiously sets about explaining why Eliot's verse would appear to be lacking in emotion: it is because of Eliot's "unusual intelligence." "There is no intelligence without emotion," Pound asserts, none too helpfully. "The emotion may be anterior or concurrent."[44] Baffled readers are presumably instructed that the emotion is there even if they cannot detect it. Above all, Pound asserts that in Eliot "there is no rhetoric."[45] From his grab bag of defenses, Pound here strikes a note that others will take up: that the newness of Eliot's project is difficult to place because the accepted canons—the "rhetoric," or tired conventions—have been stripped away.

Aiken was likewise shoring up support for his friend, meeting each new publication with an endorsement. In 1916, reviewing *Catholic Anthology*, Aiken describes both "Prufrock" and "Portrait of a Lady" as psychological character studies: "subtle to the verge of insoluble idiosyncrasy, introspective, self-gnawing."[46] The next year, reviewing Eliot's volume, he expands his praise, attempting to ease the resistance with which his friend has been met: Eliot's "temperament is peculiar, it is sometimes, as remarked heretofore, almost bafflingly peculiar, but on the whole it is the average hyper-aesthetic one with a good deal of introspective curiosity; it will puzzle many, it will delight a few."[47]

Pound's and Aiken's continual advocacy had a greater influence on Eliot's reputation in the long run, but the most perceptive early review comes from May Sinclair, writing in the *Little Review* in December 1917. She sensibly addresses the negative press, suggesting that there is more than just "journalistic misadventure" afoot but something deeper, a well-founded fear: "Mr. Eliot's genius is in itself disturbing. It is elusive; it is difficult." What makes Eliot terrifying and unique is his absence of rhetoric: "Reality, stripped naked of all rhetoric, of all ornament, of all confusing and obscuring association, is what he is after."[48] Because conventional minds expect conventional beauty, Eliot's preoccupation with the ugly and the vivid is upsetting. Sinclair's most useful intervention is to connect the management of emotion—a key objection for critics—to the issue of suffering: "The emotion [Eliot] disengages from his ugliest image is unbearably poignant. His poignancy is as unpleasant as his ugliness, disturbing to comfort."[49] By striking out the irrelevant notions of comfort or pleasure, Sinclair reveals the arrow of emotion to be poignancy, which penetrates the reader with the keener sensations of pain and discomfort. Because she has attended so carefully to what has attracted readers and what has repelled them, Sinclair is able to assess the poem in ways that later readers will recognize: "Instead of writing round and round about Prufrock, explaining that his tragedy is the tragedy of submerged passion, Mr. Eliot simply removes the covering from Prufrock's mind: Prufrock's mind, jumping quickly from actuality to memory and back again, like an animal, hunted, tormented, terribly and poignantly alive."[50] The only early critic to grapple with the problem and function of fragmentation—without naming it as such—Sinclair's explanation maps an understanding of the poem, not a mere defense of it. What had seemed drunken, willful, clever, and pathological is instead the dramatization of Prufrock's predicament and the unswerving attention of the author to reality.[51] With the old canons of beauty and order stripped away, what had seemed obscure is instead the fragmentation of the modern mind and the suffering it endures. Nevertheless, Sinclair's compelling interpretation does not become accepted for many years.

Post-1920 Reception: Still Too Clever

For suspicious reviewers, the problem of cleverness continues and is exacerbated by the quatrain poems in Eliot's subsequent volumes: the Hogarth Press *Poems* (1919), and *Ara Vos Prec* and *Poems* (both 1920). Although most reviews of these volumes focus on the new material, the challenges the quatrain poems pose are sometimes reflected backward onto "Prufrock." John Middleton Murry, in an *Athenaeum* review entitled "The Eternal Footman," finds that Eliot's cleverness has only gotten worse since his debut. For Murry, Eliot had first written the "beautiful—we insist, precisely beautiful" poem "Prufrock," which introduced a snickering Footman at a crucial moment. However, with the quatrain poems and "Gerontion," that chortling servant "has grown into a monstrous Moloch. All that Mr. Eliot most deeply feels is cast into his burning belly—or almost all." Thus, the balanced ironies of "Prufrock" are seen retrospectively as a prelude to imbalance, where a corrosive irony will overwhelm Eliot's diagnosis of the modern condition.[52] Murry's review is the first instance of what will be a recurring critical pattern: a shift in Eliot's art, a newly adopted style, will provoke a reassessment of "Prufrock," to fold it back within the changed narrative playing out in Eliot's development. The negative criticism from this two-year period repeats earlier complaints: that Eliot is a "parodist," his disillusioned poems "a species of mordant light verse," or that they represent the decadent end of a cycle of symbolism.[53]

*Post–*Waste Land *Reception: Muddied Waters*

To the wider world, such disagreement among critics was a barely audible skirmish. Eliot's early poetry had been published in small art magazines and limited-run collections. Of his first book, *Prufrock and Other Observations*, only five hundred copies were printed, and sales were slow. Critical response to "Prufrock" was nothing like the sensational aftermath of *The Waste Land*, whose publication made international news. The provocations of *The Waste Land* spilled over from poetry magazines and bled into the popular press, turning Eliot into a household name and prompting in turn new assessments of "Prufrock."

The publication of *The Waste Land* is a signal event in the early reception history of "Prufrock" because the critical terms that had hardened around the poem are dislodged. It is no longer seen as clever or unserious. True, some of the same praise and condemnations perdured: the poem is found to be either erudite and moving, or obscure and uncommunicative. As a consequence of the change in atmosphere, "Prufrock" becomes instrumentalized. When it is mentioned by reviewers, it is often used as a standard, whether negative or positive, whereby *The Waste Land* is condemned or praised. Because of Eliot's newfound notoriety, those critics of *The Waste Land* who until 1922 had never heard of the author looked backward to "Prufrock" as an intimation of later greatness or failed potential—depending on how the critic understood *The Waste Land*. It is instructive, for example, to hear Edmund Wilson struggle to link up the character portraits of *Prufrock and Other Observations* with the cri de coeur of *The Waste Land*:

> Mr. T. S. Eliot's first meager volume of twenty-four poems was dropped into the waters of contemporary verse without stirring more than a few ripples. But when two or three years had passed, it was found to stain the whole sea. . . . His productions, which had originally been received as a sort of glorified *vers de société*, turned out to be unforgettable poems, which everyone was trying to rewrite. . . . [*The Waste Land*] not only recapitulates all his earlier and already familiar motifs, but it sounds for the first time in all their intensity, untempered by irony or disguise, the hunger for beauty and the anguish at living which lie at the bottom of all his work.[54]

In Wilson's telling, "Prufrock" and the other early poems had been memorable, if misunderstood as mere entertainment for the drawing room. Now with the irony stripped away by the seriousness of *The Waste Land*, Eliot's work reveals "the hunger for beauty and the anguish at living" that retrospectively inform even the early poems.

Predictably for Eliot's rocketing reputation, a jump in stock valuation is observed along with the beginnings of myth making. A few months earlier,

Eliot's reputation had still been uncertain. But by late 1922, shortly after the appearance of *The Waste Land*, Gilbert Seldes can describe Eliot's position in the *Nation* as "approaching eminence."[55] The glow of mystique likewise attaches to the *Dial*'s "Comment" announcing its award to *The Waste Land*. There the editors exclaim (or editor—it was probably written by Scofield Thayer): "When *Prufrock* in paper covers first appeared, to become immediately one of the rarest of rare books (somebody stole ours as early as 1919), Mr. Eliot was already redoubtable."[56] Redoubtable, yes, but perhaps not so immediate or rare: Thayer could have easily replaced his copy of *Prufrock and Other Observations* in 1919. The last copy sold in 1921.

As a consequence of these polemics in the wake of *The Waste Land*, critical understanding of "Prufrock" becomes muddied. Because of the author's sudden fame, the early poem is mostly used as a pawn in reviewers' battles over *The Waste Land*. It is not until the 1930s and 1940s, when academic critics step in to assess Eliot's work as a whole, that criticism on "Prufrock" finds richer veins of inquiry. To condense the later reception history: from the 1930s into the next millennium, subsequent criticism took various paths and employed different methodologies, but one constant in this lengthy period is that "Prufrock" is still presented as an "extraordinarily finished product," to use Harriet Monroe's amnesiac praise. The range of methodologies that flourished during this period take as their common starting point the coherence of "Prufrock." Even unsympathetic critics make this assumption, as can be seen in James E. Miller Jr.'s reading of Prufrock as a repressed gay man,[57] or in Sandra M. Gilbert and Susan Gubar's description of the poem as an analysis of "masculine cultural enervation" for which women are blamed.[58] In both cases—Prufrock as self-loathing homosexual or Prufrock as misogynist—the formal properties of the poem are swept aside, and the poem is presented as a coherent ideological statement. While Eliot's politics and poems came in for severe criticism starting in the 1970s, it was his later work that received the most attention, while "Prufrock" remained generally unscathed. That the poem remained popular in the broader culture attests to how its expression of alienation was still able to touch a cultural nerve, regardless of what critics said about it.

To measure the difference between the New Criticism of Cleanth Brooks and Robert Penn Warren in the 1930s and the late-career formalism of Denis Donoghue in the 2000s is to note how much criticism on "Prufrock" has sounded the same themes for much of its later history. Writing in 1938, in the first edition of their long-lived textbook *Understanding Poetry*, Brooks and

Warren argue that the "violent" contrasts of the poem are only superficial: they disappear "as soon as we realize that the relations between the various scenes, ideas, and observations in the poem are determined by a kind of flow of associations which are really based on the fact that they develop and illustrate the fundamental character and situation of Prufrock."[59] The New Critical search for unity and irony solves the main problems of the poem's apparent disunity: its underlying unity takes its cue from the coherence of Prufrock's mind, and the whole poem is held together with "varying shades of irony."[60] Writing more than sixty years later, Denis Donoghue has the advantage of seeing the drafts of the poem in *Inventions of the March Hare*, which allows him to note that the poem had begun "as a bundle of unrelated fragments." Like a latter-day New Critic, though, his sense remains that "Prufrock" is still "a fully achieved poem."[61]

For more than half a century, the popularity of the poem results in a kind of leveling blandness, one sign of which is the coinage of the word "Prufrockian." First appearing in 1946, the neologism is defined by the *OED*: "Resembling or characteristic of Prufrock or his world of middle-class conformity and unfulfilled aspirations." Here, the precisely drawn contours of Boston Brahminism have been flattened out into the broad middle class. (However manifold Prufrock's anxieties, surely being numbered among the bourgeoisie was not one of them.) As an expression of cultural values, Prufrock's exquisite hesitations and moral punctiliousness had once been interpreted as the signs of the rarefied atmosphere of upper-crust New England, with its ethos of pragmatism and reserve. As the *OED*'s definition tracks, though, by midcentury Prufrock has become a generic symbol of conformist suburbia, lumped together with all the other clichés and characters of the postwar malaise.

Of the important midcentury critics, only the subtle antennae of Hugh Kenner detect something amiss in the critical conversation. When he was writing his seminal work of 1959, *The Invisible Poet: T. S. Eliot*, Kenner had not seen drafts of "Prufrock," which had not yet come to light. Nonetheless, his critical eye detects the seams in a hastily sewn-together poem, where others had seen strong coherence:

> Though the poem's skeleton remains complete, a bone suddenly slips out of place:
>
> I should have been a pair of ragged claws
> Scuttling across the floors of silent seas.

> This would seem to be a slight aesthetic error on the poet's part: too good a couplet to sacrifice, but not quite at home in the context of the poem. It is prepared for, by inspired opportunism, with more skill than is always realized.[62]

The image of the crab's claws and scuttle is a "superb epiphany," though Kenner admits that "it appears to belong to another, unwritten, poem." Kenner's is a minority voice, but that he is able to sniff out trouble spots without recourse to the drafts suggests that a closer look at those drafts may help to dislodge a century of criticism and bring us nearer to how its first audiences experienced the poem.

What has been gained in a century of criticism on "Prufrock" is substantial: decades of source criticism have identified the allusions, sources, and echoes. Biographies, historical studies, and cultural theories have illuminated the personal and social contexts of the poem; and ethical criticism and theories of gender and sexuality have explored the political implications of categories that had previously been understood as neutral or natural. Compressing the latter half of the poem's reception history in this way, while it sweeps much of interest under the carpet, has the advantage of emphasizing the early drafts and first reactions, and of reminding us of what has been lost in the beloved and anthologized version of the poem: a sense of how startlingly fragmented it is, how disparate its materials are, and how ingenious the artistry that barely holds it all together.

What "Prufrock" Is Made Of: Intractable Material and Available Discourses

In her admirable chapter on *Inventions of the March Hare*, Helen Vendler describes the notebook as a search for "a set of available discourses through which to present very intractable material."[63] In the trajectory of the notebook, Vendler places "Prufrock" at the end, the poet's first masterpiece that perfectly controls the available discourses and resolves the intractable materials. Those materials include five contradictory attitudes that the poem holds in suspension, like evenly perched seesaws: "a Puritanical suspicion of sex combined with romantic sexual longing; a high sense of the historical tradition of poetry together with a conviction that poetry must belong to its contemporary moment; an intense analytic intellectuality combined with a desire for drama (even melodrama); a pervasive attraction to religion without adult attachment to any church; and a New England propriety struggling with a withering irony."[64] Any one of these paradoxes might have sunk a lesser artist, but with two years of apprentice work under his belt, Eliot has learned the subtle art of balancing.

These conflicting attitudes—managed through techniques discussed below—are matched by a bewildering variety of discourses out of which Eliot builds the poem, each discourse suggesting a different audience and purpose. Vendler identifies a number of them as follows: Dante's theology; the ironic and sophisticated discourse of Laforgue; the urban realism-cum-phantasmagoria of Baudelaire; the "stoic reticence and linguistic formality" specific to Eliot's family and educational culture, including the predictable scripts of social events and courtship rituals;[65] the societal discourses of philosophy and art—that is, the acceptable ways of discussing philosophical questions and artistic works in polite society; the discourse of modernity, including popular culture and the dialect of the poet's own generation; the expressionist bathos of English decadence; the earnest, confessional manner; and, in the closing stanzas of "Prufrock," the discourse of poetic musicality, a "Paterian harmonics" divorced from social function, "self-referential and self-dissolving."[66] The clash and resolution of these discourses—and others—have been tracked throughout this study, but "Prufrock" presents a special challenge for analysis because of the range of discourses mobilized and the consequent complexity of their interactions.

How Prufrock Works: Balances Struck, Modes Contrasted, Rhetoric Forged

The question for the rhetorical critic is how the artist dealt with all these materials and discourses. Whereas source criticism dissolves a poem into the raw materials of its composition, rhetorical criticism points in the opposite direction, asking what holds all these disparate parts together, how are they aimed at an audience, and to what effect?[67] Two of the ways Eliot managed such contrasting materials are through a skillful combination of shifting (gliding between discourses) and pacing (organizing the material to reduce conflict).

In the very beginning of the notebook, we have seen how Eliot struggled to balance Laforgue and Baudelaire, conflicting impulses that had canceled each other out in the unsuccessful "First Caprice in North Cambridge." Now in "Prufrock," there is room for both impulses, separately and together. The ugliness and seriousness of Baudelaire is found in "restless nights in one-night cheap hotels," and the irony of Laforgue is heard: "Is it perfume from a dress / That makes me so digress?" Noting the presence of such disparate materials, however, still requires an explanation of how Eliot shifts between them and molds them into a whole.

One might begin such an explanation with the etherized patient. The third line of the poem marks its most quoted shift, from intimate invitation to deadpan menace. This turns out to be an easy shift for Eliot, who is performing an operation on Romantic sickness. This famous shift is less interesting than a subtler shift that occurs a few lines later, the first magical moment in the poem: "To lead you to an overwhelming question . . . / Oh, do not ask, 'What is it?' / Let us go and make our visit." The portentousness of the question is immediately followed by a Laforguean smirk. Eliot has figured out how to achieve a jazzy evasion that is not sarcastic or destructive. With its Tin Pan Alley double rhyme (is it / visit), this shift slides away from, rather than negates, the seriousness of the question. What Eliot has learned is not how to *blend* voices together but how to *move* between them effortlessly. As a consequence, the cumulative effect of all these shifts is destabilizing rather than wholly disorienting. To take just the opening of the poem, there follows in quick, lithe succession the romance of a love song, the comic banality of "J. Alfred," the high seriousness of Dante, the intimate summons to an unspecified "you," the blank horror of a comatose patient, the scenery souring into urban blight, the moral gravity of a question to be put, and the swerve into ragtime irony—all by the end of the first stanza.

Prufrock can glide from the serious to a smirk, and from the detached mode to the obsessive—also accomplished within the confines of a couplet. Detached intellectual analysis is one of Prufrock's modes—"For I have known them all already"—which is followed immediately by another mode, obsessive sexual longing: "Arms that are braceleted and white and bare / (But in the lamplight downed with light brown hair!)" Here the shift is effected through grammar, with the conjunction "but" accurately signaling a change in logic and tone. There is the dazzle of the parentheses as well: whispered intimately, as if the speaker is leaning in, confessing an obsession, and suggesting a different tone of voice than the dry ratiocinations of what is "known . . . already."

When he cannot glide between them, Eliot keeps distinct modes far apart so that their sharp edges do not jab each other. Most of the poem's stark contrasts, in fact, are noncontiguous. For example, "Prufrock" contains vexed, convoluted rationalization: "And would it have been worthwhile." But this mode does not sit adjacent to its opposite—direct, honest statement: "And in short, I was afraid." Likewise, there is the mode of high, musical lyricism: "I have seen them riding seaward." But this manner is cordoned off from the singsong nursery rhymes: "Time for you and time for me . . . / Before the taking of a toast and tea." Neither the high lyrical nor the singsong mode is contiguous to the prosaic, debunking irony of the poem. And the author contrasts, with due latitude, the emotional outburst—"It is impossible to say just what I mean!"—with cool understatement: "I am no prophet—and here's no great matter." Neither contaminates the other. The quiet, confessional mode—"Shall I say, I have gone at dusk through narrow streets"—is carefully prepared, kept away from the fervent eruptions. As Vendler has shown, moments of blunt agony ("When I am pinned and wriggling") are spaced apart in the poem, which diffuses the melodrama.[68]

Somewhere near the heart of the poem are gestures at the hidden or unspoken, which contrast with the material world of neckties and coffee spoons. What cannot be spoken is gestured to in the unasked "overwhelming question" and in the rhetorical questions that echo it: "how should I presume?" and "would it have been worth it." The tone of those questions seems particularly ambiguous, given the shifts, contrasts, and spacings of the poems' materials. When the speaker asks, "Do I dare / Disturb the universe?" the preceding terrain included modes of deadpan and seriousness, irony and confession. They provide conflicting clues for interpreting the tone: Is a question about the cosmos rhetorical, literal, figurative, evasive, ironic, or serious? Or some of the above?

In additional to modal and tonal contrasts that are carefully balanced in the poem, there are contrasts of themes and materials. For example, in some places time is fluid, stretching forward and backward, and in other places time is hypothetical or already passed. Other sets of contrasting materials include literary and biblical allusions, such as John the Baptist, Hamlet, Dante, Marvell, the Fool, Michelangelo, and mermaids. These fictional and historical allusions swim in the same poem as the real poor of North Cambridge and the social register of Boston elite. The horrific visions of Dante's hell and modern alienation alternate with the trivial and the ridiculous: "so many cakes and ices." The interior, subjective voice has its say—"I have seen them riding seaward on the waves"—as does the exterior, interrupting voice—"How his hair is growing thin!" Is it because we are so familiar with the poem that we have we have ceased to notice that Prufrock's crippling anxiety and self-consciousness are woven into the same texture as his ironic smirking, or is it that the poem has taught us how to feel modern by embracing these contradictions?

Another important contrast in the poem is managed not by setting two equal counterweights against each other but through deliberate lopsidedness. The heavy side of the equation is what pervades the poem: the claims of social expectations and the gritty materiality of contemporary life. Throughout the poem, Prufrock is assailed by the cultural practices and social realities against which he chafes: acceptable feelings, mating rituals, social masks, clichéd responses. Likewise, material culture pervades the poem: sawdust, drains, chimneys, coffee spoons, morning coat, collar, pin, bracelet, platter. Early twentieth-century technology and its by-products are particularly prominent: industrial smog, lamplight, medical ether, sprinkler wagons, a magic lantern. All these technologies are notable for projecting or spreading—smoke curls and slides, lamplight projects, ether spreads the patient out, a water carriage fans water on the dusty streets, a magic lantern spreads a pattern on a screen. (Typographically, the poem itself spreads and slides: the first line of the draft begins with ellipses, oozing into existence; the middle of the poem is peppered with ellipses and rows of dots; the last line of the typescript ends with dots, evaporating. By the time the poem is published, the oozing at the beginning and end is cleaned up with more decisive punctuation.)

Pervading the poem, these social forces and gritty materiality are challenged quietly and briefly by a short, intense section of interiority. Only in the five-line remnant from the "Pervigilium" does Prufrock defy social expectations, asserting the claims of his own experience: "I have . . . watched the smoke that rises from the pipes / Of lonely men in shirt-sleeves, leaning out of windows." There are two other tiny moments of heartbreaking honesty in the poem: "And in short, I was afraid." Here, the businesslike formula of summation—"in short"—contrasts with the emotional content. And of the mermaids, Prufrock confesses, in the only single-line stanza of the poem: "I do not think that they will sing to me." That Prufrock fails even in his sexual fantasies is only part of what makes this line so plaintive. There are also the precisely measured iambics that wring pathos from the line, and the fastidious qualification of "I do not think" contrasted with the bleak admission. However small these interventions, their muted, defiant honesty offsets the preponderant weight of social expectation and Prufrock's own evasions. Part of what we recognize as admirable and interesting in "Prufrock" is this balanced reserve, beneath which lies a sense of panic. This equilibrium is the culmination of Eliot's early aesthetic, a hard-earned balancing of the too indirect, too ironic dismissals of Laforgue and the too direct, too emotional admissions of fear and madness.

The repetitions, variations, and rhymes of the poem constitute another rhetorical strategy, one dealing in line-by-line momentum rather than sectional organization. The words "Let us go" open the poem, and the same phrase is heard again three lines later. The "streets" of line 4 meets the same word of line 8, and the word "time" rings throughout the poem: "Time for you and time for me, / And time yet." In addition to these exact repetitions, linguistic transformations move the reader forward: "Let *fall* upon its back the soot that *falls*"; and "a *formulated* phrase, / And when I am *formulated*, sprawling on a *pin*, / When I am *pinned*." Likewise, the formula "I have *known* X *al*ready, *known* them *all*," aside from being repeated three times, itself restates the word "known" within the line, with "all" repeating the first syllable of "already." This chant-like element suffuses the poem and contributes to its hallucinatory atmosphere and its slow, insistent propulsion. Like the argument of insidious intent, these rhetorical strategies provide their own logic for the poem, starting slowly in the first stanza and reaching their apotheosis in the last two. Their initiating gesture echoes music from earlier in the poem: "I have seen them riding" picks up "I have seen the eternal Footman" while "We have lingered" reaches back to "malingers." Within the stanzas themselves, the linguistic transformations accelerate while the musical rhythms decelerate: "waves" becomes "waves blown" becomes "wind blows"; "chambers of the sea" becomes "sea-girls" becomes "seaweed." These transformations take place at the level of the word, syllable, and consonant.[69]

Although there is no regularly recurring pattern of rhyme in "Prufrock," each verse paragraph is rich in pure, one-syllable rhyme, with the occasional double (visit / is it) and triple rhyme (decisions / revisions) for emphasis. The only section of the poem that does not follow this pattern is the section salvaged from the "Pervigilium." In these five lines, only the last two count as a slant rhyme: claws/sees. There are only 21 lines out of 131 that do not rhyme. Unpredictable and pervasive, the irregularity of its rhyming is part of the destabilizing yet coherence-generating music of "Prufrock."

Whom Prufrock Is Addressing: The Audience of Us, You, and I

Up to this point, the exegesis of the poem's rhetoric—while it attempts to illuminate the materials, strategies, and organization of the poem—has not yet addressed the matter of audience. The most conspicuous place to begin such a discussion is to ask the question that has vexed critics for a hundred years: Who is the "you" to whom Prufrock speaks? Eliot was often asked this question, and he was unnerved by the variety of answers others had concocted for it. Almost fifty years after the poem was composed, Eliot wrote to Kristian Smidt:

> As for "The Love Song of J. Alfred Prufrock," anything I say now must be somewhat conjectural, as it was written so long ago that my memory may deceive me; but I am prepared to assert that the "you" in "The Love Song" is merely some friend or companion, presumably of the male sex, whom the speaker is at that moment addressing, and that it has no emotional content whatsoever. I shall be glad if this simplifies the problem, because I have recently seen some quite astonishing over-interpretation of this poem.[70]

This answer cannot entirely suffice—and not only because of fallacies of intention or memory. Given that generations of readers attest to the pathos of Prufrock's address, Eliot's claim that there is "no emotional content whatsoever" in it smells suspiciously like a red herring.[71]

Identifying this "you" has been a major focus of criticism on the poem. At first blush, it seems like an odd preoccupation. There are thousands of English-language poems that use the second person, and those usages divide into fairly evident categories. Some instances of "you" are clearly identified by the poem as its addressee (such as a beloved), some instances are a historical or fictional character with a distinct identity (as in a Browning monologue), and some are a generic listener who serves as a stand-in for the reader. Yet Prufrock's "you" has been the most talked about second person in literary history. Was Milton ever accosted at market to justify his "thou" to men? Was Yeats repeatedly grabbed by the lapels and interrogated about his various "you"s? Perhaps the insistence of the question begs another: Why are readers so desperate to be reassured that they have experienced such intimacy? I suggest that it is because the intimacy that the poem stages between speaker and reader is both compelling and fraught. "Prufrock" both promises and withholds intimacy. As a consequence, the dissolvent nature of its "you," unmoored to any clear identity, becomes the focus of critical inquiry to explain the uncertain phenomenon.

The century-long debate about Prufrock's "you" focuses narrowly on the issue of identity—whether Prufrock is speaking to a disaggregated part of himself, to a confidant in the poem, or to the reader. But such questions of identity gain more traction when they are connected to the question of rhetorical purpose. For Prufrock, the reason for addressing this "you" is contradictory: to confide and to rationalize—to reveal the self and to protect the self. Thus, the singular "you" rather than the plural "you" serves a psychological function. Prufrock's "you" is singular not merely because invitations in a love song are customarily extended to one person but because it is less risky to attempt such contradictory maneuvers with one person (or oneself) than with a crowd. The tricky thing about intimacy is that it exposes a vulnerable self to the possibility of being fully known or cruelly rejected. Intimacy cannot be achieved without the risk of rejection. (Like Guido da Montefeltro in his machinations with Boniface VIII, Prufrock wants to do away with risk.) Even when intimacy is experienced, it can disappear without warning. "Prufrock" dramatizes these difficult realities: namely, that intimacy is by nature fraught with risk and danger.

There are a number of identities who are writing, speaking, hearing, and overhearing the poem, for whom this fraught intimacy is in play. I use the terms "identity" and "persona" lightly: constructed of other voices, each constitutes a center of gravity itself but is not wholly unitary; each blends with other centers of gravity, making them difficult to separate. To begin with the ethos corner of the rhetorical triangle, there is the authorial persona, one "T. S. Eliot" who signs his name to the work and who exists only for that work. He is distinct from the earlier and later T. S. Eliots, and different as well from the biographical Eliot who was not the author of "Prufrock" but merely a "bundle of accident and incoherence who sits down to breakfast."[72] In the title (which is authorial), there is named another persona, "J. Alfred Prufrock," who speaks the poem that follows, including the revoiced speech of other women.

As for the numerous audiences—the pathos corner of Aristotle's triangle—there is first of all an authorial audience to whom the literary *poem* (as distinct from Prufrock's speech) is addressed. This authorial audience approaches the poem from the widest possible angle, and it includes generations of the poem's real readers and its aspirational readership as constructed by the author. The authorial audience is not the explicit "you" of the speaker's address, but it is not far from it either. Second, there is an anti-audience inside the poem (the women who come and go, who preempt his explanations). Third, there is a skeptical audience outside the range of the authorial audience's notice but inside the speaker's range of worry (those listeners who suspect he is playing at Hamlet) and who shape his utterance. Both the internal anti-audience and the external skeptical audience are listeners who Prufrock presumes will mishear and misunderstand him, and whose judgments he attempts to preempt. Fourth, there is the troublesome "you"—an intimate confidant who is distinct from the critical audiences inside and outside the poem. Named in the first line, this "you" is clearly an audience inside the poem, but it also blends indistinctly with the authorial audience reading the poem. That audience—a singular "thou" rather than a plural mass—hovers between a Browning-like projection of the speaker's imagination and the persona an individual reader dons to become the authorial audience. This "you" is the persona who has been invited into an unsettling intimacy but also blocked from that intimacy by Prufrock's evasions and excuses. Even as the character of Prufrock confesses and equivocates about his anxiety and suffering to a sympathetic listener whom he barely trusts, the poem called "Prufrock" imagines a sympathetic reader who both observes and experiences this dynamic.

The poignancy of the poem resides in the almost-ness of the trust the speaker has for his audience. Given the defensive posturing against hostile and uncomprehending audiences in the earlier stages of the notebook, one might be tempted to conclude that the trajectory of the notebook ends in the author finding an audience in whom he can wholly trust. The more complex reality is that the author did find, or rather create, an audience in whom he could trust, but those hostile audiences who had been defensively preempted in earlier inventions have left their mark in "Prufrock." The speaker still feels the need to forestall a skeptical audience: "No! I am not Prince Hamlet, nor was meant to be." Yet "Prufrock" also addresses a sympathetic audience in league with the speaker: "Let *us* go then, *you* and *I*." These latter pronouns, so distinctly separated in the opening line, melt together in the sonorous cadences of the ending: "*We* have lingered in the chambers of the sea." The complexity of this rhetorical situation is what makes traditional formal categories—is "Prufrock" a lyric or a monologue?—dissolve in the critic's hands.

Robert Crawford captures this ambivalent mixture, how Prufrock's rhetoric both gestures at and confounds intimacy:

> People often say that the poem begins with a buttonholing, vernacular tone: its voice sounds as if it has just sidled up to you. This is only half true. If the poem started by saying "Let's go," it would sound more vernacular: "Let us go" is slower, more stagey. If you say not "Let's go," but "Let us go," you'll sound less urgent, more mannered, more self-conscious. What "The Love Song of J. Alfred Prufrock" introduces into English poetry more intensely than ever before is an acute fusion of modernity and self-consciousness.[73]

The complicated nature of the poem's audience can be tracked not only in its use of personal pronouns but in other, less obvious moments, including its imagery. For example, recall the rhetorical uncertainty of "Second Caprice," whose meddlesome stage managing had the speaker directing the emotional responses of the audience: "This charm of vacant lots! / . . . Demand your Pity." Finally, here in "Prufrock," the images are left to do their work on the reader, without intrusive commentary or arm flapping: "The yellow fog that rubs its back upon the window-panes." Such imagery, then, suggests that the author trusts his audience at one moment, but at other moments he offers a contradictory clue to the poem's rhetorical conception. The epigraph from the *Purgatorio* creates a crisscross effect, like the epigraph to "Marina." The continuity of the epigraph to the poem's content is clear enough: Guido speaks from the hell of his own making, as does Prufrock. The irony of the epigraph, though, is that Guido has found the wrong confidant. He imagines his audience is trustworthy, or at least will not be able to tell his story in the world above. But in reality, Guido's "you" ("*ti* rispondo") is shifty, aligned with forces not in his interests.

Considered as a whole, the *Inventions* notebook reveals many rhetorical problems in various stages of discovery, manipulation, and resolution. One by one, they are resolved by the late Paris poems, especially in "Rhapsody" and "Prufrock." One major rhetorical problem, evident from the juvenilia onward, is the hostile or judging audience. Eliot's initial fear of his audiences had initially been met as decorum in the juvenilia, then explosively released or aggressively curtailed in the early Laforgue inspirations. By the end of the notebook, the relationship between artist and audience has matured into a compound of trust and distrust, an ambivalence that is artistically exploited by the author for the designs he intends in "Prufrock": the harrowing evocation of the risks of intimacy and the dissolvent nature of identity.

By way of conclusion, I turn now to the recollections of three contemporary poets: Carl Phillips, Mark Levine, and Jorie Graham. Contemplating the role that "Prufrock" played in their young lives, each of these poets has described what might be called a conversion narrative. At a lecture in 2000, Carl Phillips described how his tenth-grade teacher taught "Prufrock." As a gay African American, Phillips recalled it as the first time that his experience of alienation had been articulated, and he decided he wanted to achieve something similar to what the poem had helped him understand.[74] Similarly, Mark

Levine has described a seminal encounter with Eliot's early poem: "'Prufrock' would become the poem that lent my adolescent self protection from the wounds of chronic alienation and gave me tart words to wield against the insipidness of the world."[75] Even more dramatically, Jorie Graham recounts the proximate cause of her giving up filmmaking as an undergraduate and turning to poetry:

> One day, I was looking for some new editing room, and I ended up in the wrong hallway and I heard these lines of Eliot's flowing out of this doorway—"I have heard the mermaids singing, each to each. / I do not think that they will sing to me." And I just went into this huge, long classroom and sat and listened. I had never heard poetry in English before. It was like something being played in the key my soul recognized.[76]

It is not often that the expression "soul" is used in critical discourse, unless it is placed in quotation marks. Although my own discourse occupies a different register than Graham's, I hope to have done some justice to the transformational power that these three poets attribute to "Prufrock." That they were not only deeply moved by their experience of "Prufrock" but became poets themselves as a consequence is a fitting homage to the risk and intimacy the poem offers, which its main character can measure with coffee spoons but does not dare to seize.

A century after its composition, with the contexts of the notebook restored, "The Love Song of J. Alfred Prufrock" has a more provisional feel to it. To read it in light of the drafts is to notice how the poem glides and moves, and sometimes jarringly shifts, among modes and styles, its disparate voices straining against one another. The early drafts illuminate how the published poem's jarring lack of transitions is less an artistic choice than an unhappy compromise, the strangest leap in the poem inherited from the unfixable disaster of the "Pervigilium." To note these jagged edges is to restore to the poem its sense of risk, and to its later readers a sense of what a bold and fragile experiment "Prufrock" must have been to its first audiences. When we consider how hard Eliot had to work to construct its audience, it is unsurprising that he neglected the poem, letting it lie in incomplete fragments for years before finally sewing it up into an arbitrary whole and sending it off with Aiken.

By emphasizing in this chapter the disjunctions of "Prufrock," my point is not that the poem is incoherent, only that it is on the verge of being incoherent, and that those formal difficulties cannot be swept aside, to approach straightforwardly the meaning of the poem. Struggling with those local incoherences, the lack of transitions, hearing the way the different discourses clang against one another or slide from one into the next, noticing the gap between the ambitious plan of the first draft and the resulting fragments of the published poem—these are all part of what the poem means. It is not the shellacked and anthologized poem—a poem *about* alienation and suffering—that is a masterpiece. Rather, the imperfections and difficulties are part of how the poem dramatizes the experience of alienation and suffering. Although Prufrock the character can barely stand to look at his fate, the author of the poem is able to do so with an elusive combination of clinical detachment and white-hot fear that scorches and compels whomever its "you" happens to be. The terrifying skill that Eliot develops in the notebook is the ability to gaze without blinking at the real—what May Sinclair and Pound describe as an absence of rhetoric and that is in reality a distinctly modern kind of rhetoric. The shifts and fragmentation of the poem realize the psychology of the hesitant lover who both desires and evades the risks of intimacy: the invitation, the recognition of danger, the swerving away without quite calling the whole thing off. While the poem thematizes this alienation, the rhetoric of the poem partially (and paradoxically) heals that alienation by the very fact of its disclosure: an audience is identified, a community found. "The Love Song of J. Alfred Prufrock," the imperfect and unfinished masterpiece of the notebook, sings in a new register of suffering and alienation, and in so doing mitigates the sting by confiding in an audience that matches its cagey requirements. That the poem struggles imperfectly to dramatize this experience is what makes it such a compelling statement about the modern condition.

CHAPTER EIGHT

Mumbling the Denouement

The Last and Undated Poems of the Notebook, Late 1911–1915

> A personal upheaval of some kind came after Prufrock, & turned him aside from his inclination—to develop in the manner of Henry James. Now he wants to describe externals.
>
> —Virginia Woolf, recording Eliot's conversation in her diary

"The Love Song of J. Alfred Prufrock" is the culmination, though not the termination, of the notebook.[1] The inventions that come after the Paris-Munich draft of "Prufrock" remind us that Eliot is not a poet confidently pursuing an artistic career. He is instead a graduate student in philosophy, and "Prufrock" is still an awkwardly unfinished work. During the preceding two years—from November 1909 to the summer of 1911—the notebook had expanded vigorously with multiple inventions. The completion, or rather, abandonment of "Prufrock" marks the furthest point Eliot can go toward solving the artistic problems on his plate circa 1911–1912. As a consequence, both the resolutions and the irresolutions of the poem take the wind out of his sails. Now in this period—late 1911 to 1915—the notebook dissipates its energies, attempting to launch new trajectories.

The denouement of the notebook begins in the fall of 1911, when Eliot resumes his quondam plans for graduate study in philosophy, a desultory retreat to Harvard. Although he brings back from Paris a cultivated European air, the artist in him recedes upon landing in Cambridge. His liberating experiment in French identity behind him, his handwriting settles back into the rounded script of his undergraduate days, and the poems come at a less pronounced pace. During this time, he complains to friends and family that he fears he is used up. This pattern will recur throughout Eliot's life: a period of composition, followed by a fallow stretch in which he worries whether he will ever write again. From the hindsight of Eliot's long and successful career, such anxieties sound like the unwarranted neuroses of an artist. Experienced from the inside, however, there was no guarantee that the Muse would visit again.

In late life, Eliot could still vividly recall his initial encounter with Laforgue and the circumstances of his first Symbolist creations, but his recollection of the denouement was hazy. In his directions to his executors, written in 1960 and recently released to coincide with the opening of the Hale archive in January 2020, Eliot included an autobiographical statement intended to contextualize the Hale letters from his own perspective. There he defensively describes his poetic output during his work in graduate school: "For three years I had written only one fragment, which was bad (it is, alas, preserved at Harvard). Then in 1914 Conrad Aiken showed *Prufrock* to Ezra Pound."[2] Note that Eliot recalls this one poem as a "fragment"—not even a complete poem, just a part of a poem, and a bad one at that. Eliot is eager to contrast his writer's block in graduate school—when he knew Emily Hale—to the success of his poetry once he moved to England and married Vivienne, his first wife, in 1915.

There are several errors in these two sentences; it was not Aiken who showed "Prufrock" to Pound but Eliot himself. More tellingly, he did not write one bad "fragment" in graduate school. In fact, Eliot wrote many poems during his three years there, including "Portrait of a Lady" III, "Preludes" IV, "La Figlia Che Piange," and "Morning at the Window." Eliot's misremembering is a function of the spin that he is attempting in his statement. What the elderly Eliot wishes posterity to know is that he is happily married to Valerie. Elsewhere in this document, he disparages Hale, downplaying the expressions of love he had given to her and that are soon to be published. As Eliot must have feared, over a thousand letters, many of them ardent expressions of love for Hale, threaten to overshadow his preferred narrative about Valerie.

Besides his agenda for downplaying Hale's role in his life, Eliot has other reasons for misremembering this period of 1911–1915. His output in graduate school was less vigorous than during his undergraduate years and his Paris year. In that period of intense creativity, he had written thirty-eight poems or self-contained sections of poems in less than two years. Furthermore, that earlier period of creativity from 1909 to 1911 was memorable for its clear trajectory: from the explosion of sarcastic, Laforgue-inspired poems, through his empathetic observations in the style of Baudelaire, and his toying with the discourses of slang and popular culture, all of it culminating in "Prufrock." By contrast, the poems of the notebook that follow "Prufrock" reveal an artist very much at sea. So it is not surprising that Eliot would recall this period of his life as a comparatively fallow one. In reality, though, it was a difficult period of retrenchment rather than an extended case of writer's block. The nature of those difficulties—how he tried, mostly ineffectively, to relaunch himself in new directions—is the burden of this chapter.

The poems of the denouement reveal a retrenchment in artistic ambitions, and they have a particular intellectual cast, colored by the questions that Eliot pursued under the discipline of philosophical investigation. Piers Gray offers a quick take on this period of Eliot's intellectual development: "By the completion of 'Prufrock' Eliot had . . . moved towards the end of a period of great creation. The excitement of discovering Laforgue and reading Bergson had transmuted itself into great poetry; but the intellect was becoming dissatisfied, perhaps contemptuous of itself."[3] A major part of that intellectual dissatisfaction was Harvard's philosophy department, which Eliot described as a double misery: its two spheres "the oppression of idealistic philosophy and the oppression of scientific materialism."[4] Although Eliot's graduate papers on Kant and Bradley reveal a student accomplished in the academic discipline, the poems of the denouement reveal an artist unhappy with the hair-splitting nonanswers of philosophy. In his autobiographical statement quoted above, Eliot offered a clear-eyed assessment of his distaste: "I was very immature for my age, very timid, very inexperienced. And I had a gnawing doubt, which I could not conceal from myself, about my choice of profession—that of a university teacher of philosophy. . . . [M]y heart was not in the study, nor had I any confidence in my ability to distinguish myself in this profession. I must still have yearned to write poetry."[5]

Thus, it was not just the dead end of philosophy that oppressed him; it was the sputtering of an artistic vocation that offered no clear way forward. Virginia Woolf recorded in her diary Eliot's description of this in-between time: after "Prufrock," he experienced a "personal upheaval of some kind." The elusive nature of a crisis "of some kind" suggests multiple vectors of the personal, professional, and artistic. All Eliot can say is that the upheaval turned him away from developing "in the manner of Henry James," and that the eventual path he discovered by 1920 (wanting "to describe externals") was not available to him in 1911–1915.[6] Multiple explanations converge as to why the quality and quantity of the notebook poetry fall off.

The question of where and how the notebook ends is a complicated one. On the metaphorical level, the notebook stands for a stage of a young artist's growth, an organic process that does not admit of hard borders. And on the literal level, the notebook is a physical, tactile thing, with later, unrelated poems stuck inside it, seeming to drag the end of the notebook well into the

1920s. Yet another complicating factor is that three poems written during the denouement's time frame are filed in the Berg Collection with *The Waste Land* manuscripts rather than with the notebook. It is unclear why these three poems were placed with *The Waste Land* papers and who did so.[7] To determine where the notebook ends, then, requires not only an assessment of the state of Eliot's technique and the web of his themes, but a consideration of complicated textual and archival matters.

Vendler implies a narrative of the notebook that positions "Prufrock" as its logical endpoint. Since she is concerned with discourses rather than chronology, she describes "Prufrock" as Eliot's first masterpiece, the poem that launched his identity as a major poet. Such an explanation, in turn, suggests that Eliot had gained mastery of his materials, and that he is poised to write more poems with the technique he has forged: "As the social self wanders with the artistic self through the evening streets and the drawing rooms of 'Prufrock,' Eliot at last finds a single rich discourse which can absorb, pattern, and express them all. This discourse—Eliot's newly achieved personal style—is the foundation for *The Waste Land,* where he will complicate it by taking it out of the drawing-room and placing it in larger geographical, historical, and literary contexts."[8] The turn at the end of her essay ignores the fitful nature of the denouement, implying that "Prufrock" directly paves the way for *The Waste Land.* The previous chapter has already complicated our understanding of how polished or finished "Prufrock" ever was. Vendler's terms might instead be recast to suggest that this poem is the last great poem of Eliot's early maturity, and that the denouement represents a hesitant stage of readjustment before he finds new footing.

Although Louis Menand offers a very different explanation for the end of the notebook, he too ignores the chronology of the poems, like Vendler, skipping over the troublesome period of the denouement. But unlike Vendler and other critics who find in the early poetry intimations of Eliot's later style, Menand argues that the notebook does not forecast *The Waste Land* at all. For Menand, there is a stark difference between how Eliot handles allusions in the notebook and what he makes of that technique after the notebook. Whereas the borrowings of the earlier work are unconscious and accidental, Menand claims, the allusions of *The Waste Land* are self-conscious and deliberate: "The notion that a poem could be constructed out of such references was the discovery Eliot made in 1917—which is the year he stopped using the notebook. The notebook isn't continuous with the rest of Eliot's poetry. It is what Eliot left behind in order to write the rest of his poetry."[9]

After 1917, in Menand's telling, "Eliot was now controlling what had seemed to be controlling him. Echo was replaced by allusion."[10] Yet even as he describes an artist not in control of his materials, Menand seems to waver in his theory of a clean break between the notebook and the poems of 1917. He wonders about those earliest poems in the notebook: "How is it that Eliot sounded most like himself by trying to sound like Laforgue?"[11]

As I explain below, Eliot stopped using the notebook as a place of invention long before 1917. This chronology jeopardizes Menand's reading of what motivated Eliot's turn away from the notebook. Another problem with Menand's thesis is that it reduces the notebook's scope to the one technique of allusion. Given the variety of tasks Eliot accomplishes in the notebook, such an explanation cannot satisfy. Contra Menand, I argue that as the notebook progressed Eliot quickly gained control of his materials—including the allusions and impersonations. While his technique and themes would change, these are the constants that Eliot carries with him for the rest of his career: a detachment of tone, a suppleness of rhythm, an intellectual incisiveness, and a self-critical observational stance. It is not merely a set of formalist techniques but a rhetorical pose that he has gained, a sense of how he and his speakers relate to his audiences. This phenomenon used to be described as the modernist "mask," but Eliot's pose is nimbler than that hoary cliché. This pose is how the early, slavish imitations of Laforgue sound like Eliot, and how the later pastiches of Dante sound like Eliot too—what connects the notebook to the later career.

For Eliot, poetry was not primarily a skill to be mastered so as to write at will. Rather than springing from a reliable technique, for Eliot the production of poetry depended upon a shifting set of procedures that solved immediate problems and addressed newly imagined audiences. To offer counterexamples, the technique of both Emily Dickinson and John Ashbery, once it solidified, carried them through the arc of their careers. With a fixed set of tools, and taking the same piercing lyric stance, Dickinson could write hundreds of poems on the same theme, such as the longing for a forbidden heaven. Eliot, by contrast, was a thinker in motion. He could not write the same poem twice, which is why Eliot believed throughout his life that he was always learning how to write, and why his corpus of poetry is relatively small. The interest of the denouement lies in watching the author, who has only recently become "T. S. Eliot," cast about for other Eliots that he might become without discarding the one he has just constructed.

In my reading of the manuscript pages, the denouement of the notebook extends roughly to the middle of 1915, a date that marks a clear biographical turning point: the end of Eliot's graduate work in philosophy and the beginning of his new life as a married expatriate. By 1914, Eliot had already begun to abandon the notebook as a place of invention, turning increasingly to loose leaves for drafts and fair copies. There were plenty of blank pages left in the notebook, so he stops using it not because of practical constraints. The last poems to be written on the leaves of the notebook were drafted in 1914, though poems composed through 1915 were written on loose leaves and kept in the notebook. The neatness of this ending, however, is belied by the published edition of *Inventions of the March Hare*, where numerous poems are printed that were composed much later than 1915. Drafted on loose leaf and laid into the notebook, these poems are not continuous with the trajectories of the notebook.

So how did the manuscript drafts of the quatrain poems (1917–1920) and "Gerontion" (1919) become associated with the notebook and published in Ricks's edition? Menand argues, reasonably enough, that in 1922 as he was negotiating with John Quinn the sale of the notebook, Eliot added loose leaf drafts of more recently published poems to increase the value of the notebook before it was appraised.[12] As a consequence, I do not include in my analysis of the denouement these later poems, since they have no direct bearing on the work of the notebook, which I argue ends in 1915. Nor do I include here the Boston satires—all written in May 1915. As a textual matter, three of these four satires do not appear in the notebook, either on its pages or on loose leaf, which suggests that Eliot considered them distinct from the business of the notebook.[13] Furthermore, as a biographical matter, the Boston satires do not reveal the work of a graduate student in philosophy but the polemics of an expatriate skewering the country he is leaving behind—a starkly different trajectory from the notebook. The satires were most likely written near the end of Eliot's time at Oxford, in May 1915—which is to say, they were composed after Eliot met Vivienne Haigh-Wood but before the June elopement.[14] Given this tight chronology and the short spike of energy associated with drafting four poems so quickly, the Boston satires record not a retrospective rejection of America but a prospective assault, Eliot's turn to mockery as a way of steeling himself to act, to cast his lot with England and literature rather than America and academia. For this reason, the four satires belong to a new phase of Eliot's development.

In a February 25, 1915, letter to Aiken, Eliot offers a clear picture of the frame of mind that provoked him to act. Written before he met Vivienne, the letter is both prescient and explanatory: "I do not know my own plans for the future. Day before yesterday came a telegram from Harvard, notifying me of my renomination to my fellowship. But I do not know what I should do with it if I had it." He dislikes Oxford, and while he prefers London, the war makes life miserable there. But the thought of returning to Harvard is equally distasteful: "On the other hand I dread returning to Cambridge, and the nausea of factory whistles at seven and twelve o'clock . . . and the college bell, and the people in Cambridge whom one fights against and who absorb one all the same." He diagnoses his problem directly:

> The great need is to know one's own mind, and I don't know that: whether I want to get married, and have a family, and live in America all my life, and compromise and conceal my opinions and forfeit my independence for the sake of my children's future; or save my money and retire at fifty to a table on the boulevard, regarding the world placidly through the fumes of an aperitif at 5 p.m.—How thin either life seems![15]

Within a few weeks of writing this letter he meets Vivienne, herself on the rebound from a botched engagement. After a two-month courtship, Eliot marries her, with all the major consequences that decision entailed: disappointing his beloved family; abandoning philosophy as a career; giving up America, Harvard, and academia; settling in a new country for good; cobbling a salary together by teaching and reviewing; and pursuing a literary career under the tutelage of Ezra Pound. Much later in life, Eliot described the self-deceptions that enabled this fateful decision: "I believe that I came to persuade myself that I was in love with [Vivienne] simply because I wanted to burn my boats and commit myself to staying in England."[16] But these regrets come later. In the summer of 1915, a hasty marriage and a new career are all a shock to his system, sending his writing in new directions and signaling the end of the notebook.

The Four Trajectories of the Denouement

There are four identifiable trajectories in the denouement. The first, predictable trajectory is the sunset of the old Laforgue-Baudelaire style, in which Eliot completes his apprenticeship in the French Symbolist manner. This manner is taken up on his return from Paris in late 1911. Of these poems, the successful ones are published, such as "Portrait of a Lady" III and "Preludes" IV. The only unsuccessful experiment in the French style—"Afternoon"—is left in the privacy of the notebook.

In 1912, a second arc begins: a macabre, gothic style with visionary and religious imagery, exploring the novel territory of spiritual crisis. The "Pervigilium" of 1912 is squarely in this mode of grim self-dramatization, but it is not until a year or two later that other poems are attempted in this manner. Three of these poems—"After the turning," "I am the Resurrection," and "So through the evening"—were first published in *The Waste Land Facsimile* in 1971 rather than in *Inventions of the March Hare*; by considering these poems part of the notebook, their relationship to this earlier, gothic style becomes more obvious, as does their distance from the later development of *The Waste Land*. The visionary-religious style provokes many odd experiments, and Eliot declines to publish any of them.

Aside from a few compelling images, the visionary-gothic poems are largely unusable and unpublishable, but the journey that they describe is an extraordinary one. Without a living religious tradition to guide him—which is to say, without mentors, spiritual guides, sacred texts, liturgical practice, or worshipping community—Eliot intuited a spiritual struggle that was more than merely sexual, intellectual, or psychological, though it included all three elements. From a much later, and doctrinally secure position, he would dismiss the religion of his youth as no religion at all: he complained that the moral education given by his parents, and derived from Unitarian principles, meant a system that spoke not of what was "good and evil but of what was 'done' and 'not done.' "[17] (The mercantile class for which nineteenth-century Unitarianism was designed, and the practical ideals of service it enjoined, had no need for, nor any inkling of, metaphysical luster or dark nights of the soul.) As early as the spring of 1914, in an address to the Harvard Philosophical Club, Eliot is making public statements critical of Unitarianism: "I do not plan to deprecate the alcoholic or stimulant value of the idea of Progress. I belong to a church of which one of the tenets refers to the Progress of mankind 'onward and upward forever.' "[18] (However sardonically he views Unitarian notions of progress, he still describes himself as belonging to that church.) The dead ends of philosophy were likewise useless to him. What he had to guide him in this spiritual journey then—aside from his instincts, if those can be separated from social and intellectual influences—was his eclectic reading in mysticism and comparative literature.[19] With little more at his disposal than secondhand schemas and a hodgepodge of literary genres, he attempted to sketch the outlines of a serious spiritual journey. None of these poems can be described as conversion poems, since no converting—to or from—is going on in them. Nor are the poems mere records of what the young Eliot experienced elsewhere, emotions recollected in tranquility. Rather, the act of invention itself constitutes a part of that spiritual journey: the exploration of what might lie Beyond, using the genres, tones, discourses, and poses with which he was familiar.

The artistic rendering of a spiritual journey is still not the same as the journey itself. Of the strengths and weaknesses of the gothic-visionary poems, Vendler notes, "There are two gripping aspects to this writing: one is Eliot's intimidating candour, and the other is his dissatisfaction with the exhibitionistic (and therefore aesthetically distracting) nakedness of that candour."[20] That the poems are artistically unconvincing is only a judgment on their aesthetic quality—their incommunicability to an audience that is commensurate with their ambitions—not on the journey itself, which was undertaken with admirable bravery. In stark contrast to the notebook up to this point, whose trajectories have involved briskly solving rhetorical problems as they are discovered, Eliot's visionary-religious poems show no improvement, even after several years of work. There is no evident way to escape the quandary. As it turns out, life would solve the problem for him. These macabre inventions are aborted in the spring of 1915 as a result of his sudden marriage and changed career plans. These changes propel his mind outward into the practicalities of the real world, and as a result, he lays aside these poems about martyrdom and purgation.

A third trajectory is the newly attempted genre of prose poem. Eliot wrote only three prose poems in his career: "Introspection," "The Engine," and "Hysteria." He turns to the genre of prose poem when he is unmoored by a repetitious pattern—or when a pulsing rhythm suggests an inescapable problem. All three of his speakers respond to these patterns with a nervous, futile urge to control. The interest in these prose poems lies in the contrast between the restless constraint of the speaker's agency and the flat, affectless tone of his voice. The contrast, unfortunately, does not create any interesting tension, and the poems feel ill conceived. "Hysteria" is the only prose poem Eliot publishes, and the sterility of the form never provokes his creative energies again.[21]

The fourth trajectory of the denouement stages the problems of intimacy and eros—a continuation and expansion of the themes of the Paris poems. There are six of these poems, including "Paysage Triste" and "La Figlia Che Piange," and they fit neither in the old French style nor in the new visionary-religious style. These six poems continue the observational strategies of the notebook, but what positions them a step beyond the earlier poetry is that they all describe a tenuous moment of connection with a woman, an object of artistic or erotic interest. While the earlier "Prufrock" and "Rhapsody" had posited erotic encounters, ultimately those women, mermaids, and prostitutes were beyond the reach of their speakers. By contrast, in these six poems of the denouement, the women are not dismissive of the speaker, though neither are they possessed by him. These poems present a speaker looking for romantic intimacy, recording the discomfort and transience of eros even as it is found. Of these six poems, Eliot eventually published two: "La Figlia Che Piange" and "Morning at the Window." The latter is a rare example of a weak poem that is published, while stronger poems, such as "Paysage Triste" and "In the Department Store" are left in the privacy of the notebook. It is likely that these latter two poems are kept private for reasons of decorum: they stage more explicitly a romantic connection between the speaker and a lower-class woman than does "Morning at the Window."

The ghost of Emily Hale lurks somewhere behind these six poems, though as a woman of Eliot's quasi-aristocratic class, she does not figure obviously as any of the women depicted here. Hale was Eliot's first love, to whom he declared himself in 1914 before leaving for Europe. As Valerie Eliot explains, Eliot "had no reason to believe, from the way in which his declaration was received, that his feelings were returned 'in any degree whatever.'"[22] But for Eliot to have fallen in love, and for both of them to have renewed their passionate, if chaste relationship years later, Hale must at least have fondly tolerated his friendship even at first. The forthcoming publication of Eliot's letters to Hale will presumably shed more light on the complexities of their relationship, but whatever the tragedy of their abbreviated romance, the intimacy of their friendship from 1911 to 1914 changes the way that Eliot views women. In the poetry, this manifests itself as a step beyond his Paris poems, in which women had been either unattainable or scornful.

The Poems

Poems spanning late 1911–1914 (Eliot in Cambridge, Massachusetts, aged twenty-three to twenty-five years); then 1914–1915 (Eliot in England, aged twenty-six years)

THE SUNSET OF THE FRENCH STYLE

"Portrait of a Lady" III	drafted late 1911
"Preludes" IV	drafted late 1911
"Afternoon"	drafted by Feb. 25, 1915

THE VISIONARY-GOTHIC STYLE

"In silent corridors of death"	undated, likely post-1910
["Prufrock's Pervigilium"	drafted 1912—discussed in previous chapter]
"Do I know how I feel"	drafted 1912–1913
"After the turning"	drafted 1913–1914
"I am the Resurrection"	drafted 1913–1914
"So through the evening"	drafted 1913–1914
"The Burnt Dancer"	drafted June 1914
"Oh little voices of the throats of men"	drafted by July 1914
"The Love Song of St. Sebastian"	drafted by July 1914
"The Death of Saint Narcissus"	drafted 1915
"Suppressed Complex"	drafted by Feb. 2, 1915

THE PROSE POEMS

"Introspection"	undated
"Hysteria"	drafted early 1915
"The Engine"	drafted mid 1915

THE STAGING OF INTIMACY

"To Helen" ["While you were absent"]	undated, likely post-1910
"La Figlia Che Piange"	drafted late 1911
"Hidden under the heron's wing"	drafted 1912–1913
"Morning at the Window"	drafted Sept. 1914
"In the Department Store"	drafted 1914–1915
"Paysage Triste"	drafted 1914–1915

The Sunset of the French Style

"Portrait of a Lady" III

Drafted Nov. 1911; published with parts I and II in Sept. 1915, Others

In the analyses of the previous two sections of "Portrait of a Lady," it was argued that the section composed first (Feb. 1910) carves a space out between a woman whom the speaker observes and a sympathetic audience whom he addresses. This pose was a rhetorical advance over the November 1909 poems, granting the author significantly more control over his audience. In resuming the poem (Nov. 1910), the author digs himself deeper into an ethical problem: For what reason does he return to this situation of mockery? Two answers are proposed: first, the newly composed section increases the speaker's self-mockery, which complicates the implicit ridicule directed at the woman. Second, the speaker's return to the lady's salon mirrors the author's own inability to free himself of the class obligations of social visitations. But neither of these answers fully resolves the narrative, ethical, and rhetorical issues raised by the first two sections. And so the poet circles back, for a third and final time, to bring closure to this poem.

The draft of this new section begins, as the others did, with an epigraph, this one from Laforgue's *Locutions des pierrots*:

> Je ne suis qu'un viveur Lunaire
> Qui fait des ronds dans les bassins
> – – – – – – – – – – – – – – – –
> Devenez un legendaire
> Au seuil des siècles charlatans![23]
>
> [I'm only a Moon-struck rake / Who makes rings in the basins . . .
> Become a legend / At the threshold of phony ages!]

Staring at the ripples he makes—whether with tears or pebbles—moonstruck Pierrot is aware of his own ridiculousness and of his ambition, even as the times are false. This quotation, while it speaks generally to Eliot's own condition, is not as apposite to the poem as the first epigraph (Feb. 1910), from *The Jew of Malta*. The third section of the poem finally delivers on the promise of that first epigraph, which is why it is retained in the published version of the poem and the other epigraphs are deleted. The Marlowe quotation is an interrupted dialogue, with one speaker inaccurately finishing the speech of another. The lines open with accusations of sex (brazenly confessed) and murder (slyly evaded): " 'Thou hast committed—' / 'Fornication—.' " The epigraph ends with the two solutions of being abroad and the woman's death ("but that was in another country / And besides, the wench is dead"). These are the two solutions the final section explores: the speaker's going abroad and the lady's imagined death.

The final section of "Portrait" begins with the speaker experiencing "a slight sensation of being ill at ease." This foreboding quickly escalates to agony once he ascends the lady's steps, as if on "hands and knees." Mayer has nicely described the stair journey as "a typical Eliot ritual of anguish."[24] This particular ritual in "Portrait" is heightened by the allusion to the pilgrim's gesture: the final ascent of a shrine's steps on hands and knees as a sign of devotion. However, here the added pain and humiliation of walking on one's knees does not coincide with a pilgrim's sense of value. In the notebook, this is where all of Eliot's staircases end: an arrival without meaning.

The endgame of this incessant salon war is near, and the lady seems to be losing her advantage: the speaker's travel abroad means that he can escape from her without the drama of a breakup or the indecency of snubbing her. She recovers from the news of his escape with a slight condescension: "You will find so much to learn," gaining for the moment the upper hand. As always, the audience never hears how the speaker responds to her, only his narrated reaction: "My smile falls heavily among the bric-a-brac." The fake, social smile that he is used to wearing for such occasions nearly falters of its own weight, threatening a breakage of those fragile curios on the shelf. The tension will explode later, but for now, the lady plays another card: "Perhaps you can write to me." Immediately, the speaker recognizes the ploy he had dreaded: "*This* is as I had reckoned"—an epistolary extension of his misery. The lady continues, taking up the theme of friendship from their earlier meeting, "wondering"—but in reality, accusing—"Why we have not developed into friends." Without waiting for an answer, she shuts down the conversation: "You will write, at any rate." Her initial suggestion that he might ("Perhaps") write has now become a command, or at least a presumption of a mutually agreed-upon understanding. The published version of the poem repeats her self-pitying line: "I shall sit here, serving tea to friends." The speaker, trapped by his social graces, can let loose only in his head, turning to vaudeville as a metaphor for his outrage and exasperation. In contrast to the vaudeville references of earlier poems (songs, comedy routines, dance, and masquerades), here Eliot takes up animal acts, vaudevillian turns that raised vexed questions of human nature, posing, empathy, and ethical obligation.

At the height of vaudeville, animal acts had become increasingly popular: they could communicate to an audience without patter or explanation, and they were useful as fillers while scenes were changed or noisy audiences filtered in or out between acts.[25] A contemporary description listing some of the more "incongruous or far-fetched" turns emphasizes the anthropomorphic nature of the animal acts:

> We have bears on roller skates; ponies who ring out a tune on hand-bells; and cats, dogs, rabbits, pigeons, presenting episodes that imitate the doings of the dominant race—sometimes in a manner far from complimentary. We have monkeys who play billiards, ride bicycles, smoke and drink and behave gener-

> ally in a manner so like an extremely ill-bred man that it is a wonder that some of the audiences do not feel affronted.[26]

The general popularity of these acts belied ethical resistance from some quarters. According to Albert F. McLean's account of vaudeville in America, many educated city dwellers feared that animal acts "were *not* mere entertainment but rather affronts to basic values. In part incited by the Darwinian controversy to reevaluate the relationship between man and other members of the animal kingdom, in part merely offended by the utter impracticality and boorishness of highly trained creatures, in part motivated by the high-mindedness of Protestant gentility, these bourgeois reformers created a stir which seems, in retrospect, disproportionate to the number or importance of these acts."[27] In previous decades in America, animals had been part of circus and traveling exhibitions without drawing the ire of reformers.[28] But with vaudeville, a line had been crossed in training animals to act as humans. The evangelical moralists and bourgeois prigs were duty bound to take offense, but even fans of vaudeville felt some ambivalence about what such acts suggested about human nature, entertainment, and empathy. Paradoxically, McLean argues, the very ridiculousness of these animal acts appealed to "the more educated and enlightened" members of the audience, pitting them against the high-minded reformers.[29]

In Boston, the heat of this public moment was highest when Eliot was at Harvard. In 1909–1910, the impresario B. F. Keith had gone to considerable trouble to publicize his most versatile animal, Peter the chimpanzee. Boston periodicals were filled with lengthy articles with such headings as "Many Famous Guests Meet Famous Simian Host," "Noted Monkey Smokes, Dines, Drinks Beer," and "Peter the Great Visits Harvard." One widely circulated photograph was of Peter lighting a cigarette.[30] This vaudevillian context of animal acts is what Eliot calls up in the final section of "Portrait of a Lady":

> And I . . . must borrow every changing shape
> For my expression—dance dance
> Dance like a dancing bear,
> Whistle like a parrot, chatter like an ape;
> Let us take the air, in a tobacco trance—

Eliot's lines are often read as the speaker's exasperation at the wearing of social masks. But by invoking the contemporary anxiety about animal acts—their queasy mixture of entertainment, exploitation, and critique—Eliot has done more than choose a metaphor of alienated playacting. The chattering ape and dancing bear—whose presumed affective lives were dramatized on stage and anthropomorphized by trainers—are caged, like the speaker himself, in the ambivalent system of popular culture. As such, the trained animals occupy a recognizable place in Eliot's moral and emotional universe. For chimpanzees who have been trained to smoke, the speaker's transitional gesture ("Let us take the air, in a tobacco trance") is no escape from the masks demanded by the social system into a life of genuine emotion. It is merely another vaudevillian act, like the hypnotist's trance.

After this climax, the coda begins with a readjustment of the emotional register: "Well!" he begins, suggesting an unruffled resumption of discourse or a more measured expression of irritation. Weighing his obligation to write to her, the speaker wonders, "and what if she should die some afternoon . . . and leave me sitting pen in hand[?]" Hemmed in on every side, the speaker hypothesizes an escape in the lady's death. Before he assesses the consequences of that possibility, the speaker cannot help but add some stage business to her imagined death. Just as the lady has stage-managed her salon with an "atmosphere of Juliet's tomb," the speaker imagines receiving the news of her death on some afternoon "grey and smoky, evening yellow and rose . . . With the smoke coming down across the house-tops." It is a transfixing detail that delays the business of assessing the consequences of writing "tardy or too soon" (his letter arriving after or before her death). Lingering over these decadent details is part of the "music" of the poem; it is "successful with a 'dying fall.'" (Both "Portrait" and "Prufrock," the first two poems in Eliot's debut volume, allude to these lines from *Twelfth Night*.) The speaker, slyly merging with the role of author, admires the effect of his own music, with its heartsick, dying strain, inviting the audience to take the same attitude of admiration. As the portraitist who speaks the satire, making music from this social misery would be the final advantage, if there were one to be had. But the speaker realizes that whether the lady dies or not, whether he writes or not, and whether doing so is "wise or foolish," he would still be caught in the social world whose laws cannot be escaped in time or space. Even if he is "in another country" and "the wench is dead," the lady might still "have the advantage after all."

With the poem's final line, the ethical, rhetorical, and narrative problems raised by the poem reach a precarious resolution, nearly two years in the making: "And should I have the right to smile?" He does not ask whether he should smile but whether he has the *right* to do so. The smile, as always in

Eliot's poetry, connotes falseness, the maintenance of a façade in the game of social custom. Having played this game with the lady to the death, as it were, the speaker wonders whether he has the ethical right to pick up those same conventions he has exposed so ruthlessly, to disappear behind their façade as a way of evading responsibility. Does he—after such a portrait—have the right to resume the game on its own terms? The rhetorical solution is to end on a question; the ethical solution is to admit that he does not know the answer. That the speaker does not seem to know the answer reveals his enslavement to the world he critiques but cannot imagine otherwise.

"Preludes" IV (Abenddämmerung)
Drafted Nov. 1911; published with parts I–III (drafted earlier), in Blast, *July 1915*

As with the feet and hands of earlier "Preludes," here are more depersonalized body parts: the "short square fingers" and "eyes / Assured of certain certainties." This last image of a stranger's glance is a masterly stroke of sinister confidence: to be assured of a certainty is redundant and a "certain certainty" sounds almost tautological, and yet it is Eliot's deft ability with the phrase to suggest a physical image by denoting its emotional value. In the first nine lines, there is no clear syntax, no verb that defines the relations of all these listed things. At first glance, the first line seems to have a defining verb: "His soul stretched tight across the skies." But the phrase is either missing its auxiliary verb ("soul [was] stretched"), making the verb seem to stretch between intransitive and transitive functions, or it is missing a clarifying comma ("His soul, stretched tight"). The draft punctuation is likewise fuzzy: there are two colons suggesting expansion or illustration, and two dashes suggesting an interruption or break, none of which expectations are fulfilled by the order of the words:

> Trampled by the insistent feet
> Of seven and of six o'clock:
> —And short square fingers cramming pipes,
> And evening newspapers—and eyes
> Assured of certain certainties:
> The conscience of a blackened street

When the poem is published, these ambiguous marks are deleted or changed to more straightforward commas and a semicolon.

The last two lines of the stanza bring it to a sinuous close: "The conscience of a blackened street / Impatient to assume the world." Although modifying "street," the adjective "blackened" spreads its malevolent haze backward to "conscience," adding to the air of sordid mystery in these character pieces. As with the preceding six lines, there is no verb governing the subject, but there is an infinitive verb, "to assume," whose meaning seems unclear: in what sense does a conscience or a street "assume" the world? Many of that word's meanings seem to be in play: undertake, seize, usurp, put on, feign, receive.

Whatever the import of this ambiguous close, nothing in that stanza or the previous three preludes sets up the surprising turn: the appearance of the first-person pronoun: "I am wrought by various fancies, curled / Around these images, which cling—." It is not the expression of compassion that is surprising, but the first-person confession that contrasts with the camera's-eye objectivity of the rest of the sequence. The sordid images themselves provoke not the speaker's emotional response but an imaginative projection of "fancies" that are attached to, "curled around," the images. The substance of his response is that even here, where there appears to be no compassion or higher moral order, the speaker senses tenderness and pain: "The notion of some infinitely gentle / Infinitely suffering thing." The supposed biographical genesis of these lines—Eliot claimed to be thinking of his brother—does not aid in reading the poem, as the lines lack specificity.

Whatever the genesis of the image, something has provoked the speaker to a direct expression of compassion, even though he does not allow that expression to stand unqualified. The undercut follows: "Wipe your hand across your mouth, and laugh." This undercutting is of a different sort than the Laforguean dismissals of the earlier poems. It is not a snide laugh but two commands that suggest the audience adopt a pose of weariness (the uncouth gesture of wiping one's mouth suggests weariness, and the consequent laughter is neither snide nor merry). An observation follows: "The worlds revolve like ancient women / Gathering fuel in vacant lots." (Notably, these are not depersonalized body parts, but mythological figures: these are the women who survive war and plague, stoically enduring suffering, too tired for judgment or explanation.) From the surprising expression of compassion, we return to the images of worn-out sordidness, but here, finally, it is invested with a sense of the tragic. It is the most compelling image of the four-poem set because, in the wake of the speaker's outpouring of compassion and its abrupt correction, some residue of compassion still obtains, and that balance of ironic aloofness and intense personal emotion is struck here.

The draft ends with two rhythmically awkward lines: "—And we are moved into these strange opinions / By four-o'clock-in-the-morning thoughts." This apologetic detour, which Eliot wisely deletes before publication, detracts from the starkness of the preceding image and its tonal balance.

"Afternoon"
Drafted by Feb. 25, 1915

In what might seem to be a setup for a satire, ladies arrive at the British Museum on a rainy day, leaving their overshoes in the hall. The ladies' perfume and the steam from their overshoes evaporate in the air, fading, as the women themselves do, "beyond the Roman statuary." The ladies' evaporative quality merges with that indefinable quality they seek in art. Wearing hats with "green and purple feathers," they are compared to Laforgue's entertainers as they move "Like amateur comedians across a lawn / Towards the unconscious, the ineffable, the absolute." If satire is expected, however, the poem never generates the requisite tone for it.[31] Comedians are figures not of mockery but of interest and complexity in Eliot's early work. (Michael Coyle remarks that these bluestockings, not particularly interested in being au courant or concerned about social status, are like *amateur* comedians: revealing the "purposeful gracelessness of physical comedy," they are "not fully in control of their movement.")[32] Likewise, "the ineffable, the absolute" are valued by the author as objects of inquiry or experience. That these women wear "last year's tailor suits," that they come and go, talking of "Assyrian art," are the details that suggest light mockery, but the poem ends in unexpected sympathy. These ladies seek the same things the speaker seeks: intimations of the absolute through art. The extent to which these women merge with their experience of art is accomplished beyond the point of view of the poem, outside of the view of speaker and audience.

Mayer nicely summarizes the interplay of the poem's images and its rhetoric. Noting that the poem begins with images of "intense specificity" (perfume, evaporating steam, vibrant feathers) and ends in the "inclusively abstract" (the unconscious, the ineffable, the absolute), Mayer points to a similar exchange in the poem's point of view: "from that of an implied observer of subjects unconscious of [the speaker], to that of an implied observed artifact, and finally to an observer of another age."[33] This quiet meditation on time and art ends without punctuation, evaporating like the ladies and the speaker's point of view into something beyond—possibly absolute because it is ineffable. In Coyle's reading, this conclusion is a "vision of transformation that implicitly affects the speaker as much as it does the bluestockings to whom he initially condescends."[34]

"In silent corridors of death"
Undated manuscript, likely post-1910

The repetitions, alliterations, and permutations of this poem hark back to Eliot's juvenilia, specifically "Before Morning," with its aura of Edward FitzGerald:

> In silent corridors of death
> Short sighs and stifled breath,
> Short breath and silent sighing

The speaker's relationship to these sighs is unclear—are they his or someone else's?—but the piling up of /s/ sounds lends an air of deflation to the opening. The only explicit indication of emotion is in the verb "crying," yet the soul that cries is offstage: "Somewhere." Other emotions are implied through negation: "There is no moan / Of Souls dying." There is only atmosphere: "the warm / Dry airless sweet scent / Of the alleys of death." At some distance from his suffering, the speaker is lost in his own solitude, with the emotion deliberately obscured. Another poem with a comparable exigence is "Silence." In both poems, a narrator ponders his mortality, bringing on a self-imposed solitude in the midst of other sounds and voices. While in "Silence" the speaker is "terrified" at the prospect of an engulfing peace, in this poem the speaker is detached, "without hope without fear."

With its short lines and arid setting, the repetitions of "In silent corridors" attempt an incantatory quality, while its theme and setting venture a hallucinatory aura. What is missing, however, is an element of internal pressure—a lack that keeps this poem from rising to the level of incantation or hallucination. The author is unhappy with the poem's vagueness, querying himself at the bottom of the page, perhaps for future revision: "Suffused light—light from where? / Stifled scent—scent of what?"

"Do I know how I feel?"
Drafted 1912–1913

In a poem that Vendler has characterized as "ironic doggerel," the speaker begins by acknowledging his dissociated sensibility, admitting not only to a lack of connection between thought and feeling but a lack of understanding of either: "Do I know how I feel? Do I know what I think?"[35] By taking up "ink and paper," the speaker is initially willing to tackle this problem. But the deceleration of ellipses at the end of the second line signals a reluctance, and the writing of a poem is set aside in favor of another option: asking the porter. That the porter might misunderstand the question or be unwilling to engage mirrors Prufrock's hesitance in the face of grand questions. In the imagined first response, the speaker fears that the porter will merely affirm his social identity—a "gentleman" from the second floor—rather than explain "what I think and feel."

As many of Eliot's early poems reveal, encounters with lower-class figures often tear through the fabric of social reserve to reach a different type of self. It is what Eliot's speakers both desire and fear. So it is with "dread" that the speaker imagines another response of the porter. In the first draft, the porter begins, "Sir I have seen . . ." But recalling that the porter is a double for the speaker, giving voice to how the narrator thinks and feels, the author revises the "I" to "we": "Sir we have seen so much beauty spilled on the open street." The anxiety of experiencing the pointless waste of beauty has made the porter/speaker "restless."

In the next stanza, the opening questions reprise the first line, with one variant: the speaker asks "how," rather than "what," he thinks. The object (what) of cognition is replaced by the consciousness (how) of cognition. This meta-consciousness leads imaginatively to an autopsy on the speaker's brain. The audience at his own autopsy, the speaker figures the medical examiner as "A black bag with a pointed beard" who ferrets out with his tools "the cause of death that was also the cause of the life—." Even more menacing than the porter, the medical examiner might possibly "touch the secret" the speaker cannot or will not discover. There is at least the possibility of self-discovery without the contrivances of these projected personae, in which the brain reveals to itself either a "new assertion of the ancient pain" or a "secret which I cannot find." Anthony Cuda argues that the "ancient pain" is "the shameful evidence of his internal corruption and decay" and the secret is "some other, self-revelatory effect."[36]

As the brain drifts toward unconsciousness, the grandest of metaphysical questions poses itself: What happens after death? The response is contradictory and ambiguous: "a blinding light and a little laughter"—the possibility of an ecstatic afterlife offset by the snickering of some eternal Footman, then only "blackness." The speaker abandons his questions in ignorance and feigned apathy: "I do not know what, after, and I do not care either." In Cuda's study of passive suffering in Eliot's work, this poem amounts to another Prufrockian fear, his many speakers' unwillingness "to confront the reality of their own suffering."[37]

"After the turning"
Drafted 1913–1914

This poem and the two that follow are well known as "miscellaneous poems" first published in Valerie Eliot's facsimile edition of *The Waste Land*.[38] Valerie's decision to publish two of these poems in her volume is understandable: "After the turning" and "So through the evening" contain lines reworked much later for *The Waste Land*. The reason for including "I am the Resurrection" in the facsimile is less clear, since no lines from it are reworked for *The Waste Land*; it was presumably included because the handwriting is so similar to the other two poems, or perhaps because the three poems were originally placed with the manuscripts of the later poem.[39] After such a collocation, is it possible, instead of hearing "After the turning" as a precursor to *The Waste Land*—"After the torchlight red on sweaty faces / After the frosty silence in the gardens"—but to hear it as the companion of "Prufrock"? The latter poem's litany of "after"s is concluded by an admission of impotence: "After the sunsets and the dooryards and the sprinkled streets / After the novels, after the teacups . . . / —It is impossible to say just what I mean!" Likewise, "After the turning" ends, as do "Opera" and "Spleen," with a Laforguean sigh:

> After the ending of this inspiration
> And the torches and the faces and the shouting
> The world seemed futile—like a Sunday outing.[40]

The Waste Land, by contrast, expresses a more straightforward despair. Leached of its Laforguean urbanity, stripped even of the pretense of social ritual, the futility of *The Waste Land* is more barren than a Sunday outing: "We who were living are now dying / With a little patience."[41]

The controlling scenario of "After the turning" is the agony in the garden: the prayer, inspiration, betrayal, and judgment that constitute the drama of Christ's passion. The intensity and consequentiality of the past is contrasted to the meaninglessness of the present: the day (Sunday) properly set aside, but the liturgical ritual enacting its remembrance is substituted for an "outing." One reading of the final line was momentarily "The show was ended—." Later deleted, it is a revealing second thought: one effect of "show" is to negate the contrast of past to present, making "show" seem to refer only to the crucifixion drama. Another effect is to present the world of religious conviction as something staged or observed. The original thought ("world," and its ultimate restoration) suggests the opposite. This single crossed out noun—"show"—lays bare the conflict in Eliot's aesthetic and his philosophy: the tension between actors who present an artifice versus the reality of the emotion it produces in the spectator, and the tension between a fictional story that provokes philosophical skepticism versus an impassioned history that elicits an assent of faith. The author has not staked his claim in these debates, but he knows that they matter.

"I am the Resurrection"
Drafted 1913–1914

The previous poem, "After the turning," had relied on a well-known scenario from the passion narratives to elaborate its theme. Likewise, "I am the Resurrection" begins with Jesus's famous declaration from John's Gospel: "I am the Resurrection and the Life." The poem continues, however, not in this scriptural vein but with a series of Heraclitean paradoxes: "I am the things that stop, and those that flow."[42] For Western readers, this contrast and the ones that follow—husband/wife, victim/knife—are not obvious allusions in the manner of the Johannine epithets for Jesus. That such contrasts are untethered to a self-evident context does not necessarily pose a problem for the imagined audience: paradoxes and contrasts are part of the initial Johannine context, as well as a familiar pattern in lyric poetry. The real problem does not assert itself until the final paradox: "I am the fire, and the butter also." Given the domestic banality of butter in American homes, this final image seems to veer into Laforguean irony—the connection between Christian salvation and dairy products is a decidedly underdetermined one. It is not an ironic reference, however; it is a serious allusion to a Hindu scriptural text, the *Bhagavad Gita*, which details the ritual practice of offering oblations with fire and ghee (clarified butter). Editorial notes have explained these facts since the poem's first publication in *The Waste Land Facsimile*, but Eliot's draft has no such apparatus. The authorial manuscript shows no concern with signaling recognition via extratextual notes. And so, in the gap between this tonal uncertainty and the author's intention (is butter funny or serious, trivial or sacred?), a new and vexing rhetorical problem opens up. How does one cue an audience to recognize the import of an obscure allusion?

This is not a problem that needed solving before the fall term of 1911. In Eliot's baccalaureate and masters-level coursework (1906–1910), he had read widely in Western and European philosophy and literature, building on his classics-inflected education at Smith Academy and Milton Academy.[43] The security of this Western canon both enabled and constricted his sense of audience: he assumed that his audiences had either read the same things he had read or could be depended upon to fill in the gaps. Even though Jules Laforgue was as obscure to his earliest audiences as the *Bhagavad Gita*, Eliot was able to adopt the French poet's tones and gestures, to translate them into his American idiom without the need to signal their source, though he chose to do so once, as a self-protective measure, in his subtitle for "Humouresque (After J. Laforgue)"—parentheses that we might identify as Eliot's first footnote. As an example of how Eliot's own education dovetailed with the education he expected of his notebook audiences, consider the line "La lune ne garde aucune rancune" from "Rhapsody on a Windy Night." The original audience would have recognized neither the French author of the line nor the exact poem it paraphrases. Although it does require some rudimentary French—training in several European languages was the currency of a collegiate education—the line does not require knowledge of its source for it to make sense in the English poem.

In the fall of 1911, however, Eliot's mental furniture began to be rearranged, with concepts alien to a Western sensibility, thanks to a series of courses in Indic philology with professors Charles Lanman and James Woods. Much has been made of the connections between Eliot's early poetry and his graduate student reading in Indian philosophy, but this study is concerned with audience rather than sources.[44] The audiences of Eliot's juvenilia and notebook were constructed in the lyric mode. With these 1912–1913 poems in a new, gothic-visionary style, Eliot begins to push against the boundaries of the lyric mode by essaying dramatic and prophetic voices. (Prufrock the character gestures futilely in this direction, but the poem maintains its lyric stance.)

At the same time that Eliot is awkwardly trying out a visionary style with faltering tonal problems, he is also attempting to escape the parochialism of Western sources, leveraging his reading in Eastern philosophy as a potential source of poetic inspiration. In seeking out new sources of wisdom—to sidestep the problems of melodrama in this gothic genre—he unintentionally complicates the problem of audience. Eliot discovers this problem in "I am the Resurrection," but he is unable to solve it right away. The advantage of considering this poem and its two companions with the *Inventions* notebook, instead of with *The Waste Land Facsimile*, is that they remind us not of how close Eliot was to *The Waste Land*, but how far he was from it.

The problem seems to present itself as one of tone—the fragment ends with the phrase "the butter also." Perhaps the tonal complexity of how this image might be understood threw cold water on the poem's progress, keeping it from going any further. The five-line poem sits high on the page; below it is a yawning blank space. Thus far in his poetic development, Eliot has learned to solve problems of tone by modulating his voice and shifting between levels of discourse. But he will discover—or perhaps has just discovered in this poem—that the problem he has stumbled across is of a different sort than a tonal imbalance. It can be solved only by changing the frame and the scope of his poetic ambitions. Those solutions will come later by recourse to the technique of allusion, beginning with the quatrain poems and culminating in *The Waste Land*.

"So through the evening"
Drafted 1913–1914

As with the allusions to Christian and Hindu scriptures in the previous two poems, "So through the evening" presents another gothic journey in which the speaker seeks spiritual meaning. Two of the poem's lines refer obliquely to Christ's injunctions and John the Baptist, but these points of reference are allusions rather than guideposts, vaguely signaling a spiritual journey rather than providing an explanation of the poem. The haunting music and mysterious imagery of this poem make it perhaps the most compelling of the visionary-religious inventions.

Set in the Eliotic "violet air" of evening, the first stanza describes a "tortured meditation" the speaker ultimately cannot follow, as with "Concatenated words" linked by a meaningless syntax.[45] In the midst of this confusion, the speaker hears what might potentially be a revelation: "The This-ye-do-for-my-sake," a hyphenated awkwardness that evokes the Authorized Version without specifying the referent of "This." The speaker acknowledges that there exists the "one essential word that frees" (again failing to specify which word or Word) and an "inspiration that delivers." The problem is that, hearing this word/inspiration in a landscape of wasted dryness, the speaker is neither freed nor delivered. Instead of staking a claim in this (vaguely sketched) religious ground, the poem continues to wander like a "chain of reasoning whereof the thread was gone." That chain gathers only "strange images," two of which are later reworked for *The Waste Land*: a woman who plays "whisper-music" on her hair and a man who crawls down a wall upside down.

The final image is one of disorientation and confusion, and it rhymes with the man crawling upside down: "As a deaf mute swimming deep below the surface / Knowing neither up nor down, swims down and down." The inner ear is connected both to hearing and to balance, and Eliot's description of a "deaf mute" suggests an unintentional disorientation, muddied by the reduced gravity cues in the buoyancy of water. He swims "down and down," going determinedly in what seems to be the wrong direction. It is not exactly an image of drowning, however, a word that does not appear in the poem. Instead, the water is "calm and deep," and the swimmer's strokes are steady. Like the mermaids of "Prufrock," the swimmer's hair is graced with "seaweed purple and brown." The action suggests drowning, but the tone suggests a respite.

The speaker concludes in the plural first person: "So in our fixed confusion we persisted, out from town." Like the swimmer moving away from the surface, the "we" here moves away from town—away from civilization, companionship, and established norms. When one is unsure of where to go, then the only thing to be done is to swim deliberately away from the most obvious answers, the socially acceptable world, even when that divergent path is an oxymoronic one of "fixed confusion."

"The Burnt Dancer"
Drafted June 1914

"The Burnt Dancer" may not have been written in strict sequential order after "So through the evening," but it can be read as a logical extension of that earlier poem. While "So through the evening" articulates the direction of a spiritual journey—away from the civilized world, "down and down"—this poem articulates the dynamic of such a journey, even while the origin and purposes of the struggle remain obscure.

With its epigraph about torment from *The Inferno*, the poem frames the spiritual journey as a struggle whose terms include sacrifice, expiation, death, and the dialectics of desire. As Ricks notes, it is an unmistakably "Dantesque poem."[46] A "black moth" is the burnt dancer of the title, flitting around a flame in "mirthless"—which is to say, deadly serious—revel.[47] The French refrain, "O danse mon papillon noir," points to the idiomatic expression in the plural, "papillons noirs," which translates as "dark thoughts."[48] The moth desires the pain of expiation, a kind of death-seeking self-sacrifice: these are the "golden values" of the flame, as distinct from the ordinary world that clings to life with its "more vital values." The "virtue" of the moth's world is "too strange" even to be named, contrasting with the ordinary world's values of "praise or blame," "good or evil." The moth's sacrificial dance contains some secret, nonhuman meaning. The poem circles, rather than elucidates, that meaning, like a demented catechism posing a series of Blakean questions, each more disturbing than the quatrains of "The Tyger":

> Children's voices in a corner
> Whimper whimper through the night
> Of what disaster do you warn us
> Agony nearest to delight?

The relation of the poet's tortured thoughts and the obsessive path of the moth is made explicit in the third stanza: "Within the circle of my brain / The twisted dance continues." The speaker has associated himself with the moth, admiring it, exhorting it to complete its death dance, but his pronouns muddy the extent of identification: the moth's willing choice to apprentice itself to pain places it beyond "our human sinews," which suggests not only that the moth's commitment is inspired by some nonhuman force, but that the speaker does not share in the mystery, consigned with the rest of us to "our" merely human strength.

Such a poem can end only with the death of the moth. The dynamic has been explored—the contrast of the moth's desires with the ordinary world's values, the gesturing to a liminal world and its mysterious meanings—and now the moth meets the end it has desired: "Losing the end of his desire / Desires completion of his loss." The speaker approves: with a slight variation, the refrain emphatically repeats the command: "O danse danse mon papillon noir!"

"Oh little voices of the throats of men"
Drafted July 1914

Both "Oh little voices of the throats of men" and "The Love Song of St. Sebastian" were originally intended as sections of a longer, never-completed work,

"Descent from the Cross." Sent to Conrad Aiken for commentary, these fragments first appeared in Eliot's published correspondence, and so we have the rare advantage of the poet's contemporary remarks on the poems. Calling the verses "shamefully laboured" by way of preamble, Eliot eventually sends the two poems to Aiken in a subsequent letter. Expressing his disappointment in both, he wonders whether Aiken finds the latter "morbid or forced." By way of postlude, Eliot apologizes in a follow-up letter: "The stuff I sent you is not good, is very forced in execution, though the idea was right, I think."[49] Here we have Eliot's own perceptive analysis of what is wrong with his gothic-visionary style—morbid, forced, and labored indeed—but also why he could not set such poems aside in spite of his multiple and manifest failures: the idea is right. The quandary, as Vendler has described it, is that the genres of gothic and decadent literature enable him to explore with candor the logos, the idea—the dark matters of the soul—but the ethos, the exhibitionistic persona, embarrasses him.

This rhetorical misalignment makes it difficult to assess what the poems are doing and how well they do it. Chinitz has described "O little voices" as a typical mixture of good and bad found in the notebook, the poem's beginning stanzas proceeding "from aesthetic paranoia to clunky metaphysical ramblings." For Chinitz, it is not until, "by a happy narrative stroke, Eliot's harrowed philosopher falls asleep in his armchair" that the poem becomes evocative.[50] However, what Chinitz hears as "clunky metaphysical ramblings," Vendler praises as a style comparable to *Four Quartets*, with its "abstractions, paradoxes, elegiac tone, and philosophical detachment."[51] These are some of the lines that Chinitz and Vendler hear so differently:

> [I] always find the same unvaried
> Intolerable interminable maze.
> Contradiction is the debt you would collect
> And still with contradiction are you paid,
> And while you do not know what else you seek
> You shall have nothing other to expect.[52]

One oddity of the poem is that there are two speakers whose relationship to each other and the audience is unclear. The first implied speaker, found in the opening stanzas, uses a plural ("*our* divers paths," "*we* who seek") that may encompass or exclude the addressee, "you." That the speaker's and addressee's paths are "divers" at first suggests that the speaker finds no commonality: their paths would not likely cross, or only on some "remote frontier of heaven and hell." Yet the speaker then blurs this relationship: "you do well to keep the ways you keep. / And we who seek to balance pleasure and pain / We blow against the wind." If the speaker and the addressee are in league—which "*And* we" seems to suggest—then what is the reader to make of the explicit contrast between "little voices" and the speaker? The first stanza offers a contrast: the speaker, who with others or with "you" futilely attempts to "balance pleasure and pain." This futility is clearly contrasted with the busily destructive, "twisted little hands." Grammatical ambiguities of this type—does "we" mean "you and I," "you and I and others," or "I and others, but not you"?—can normally be sorted out by reference to the context, but the poem offers little help on this score. Even the opening gesture is ambiguous: is "O little voices" an apostrophe or exclamation, subject or object? Are the voices being spoken to or spoken about? The missing definite article ("O [the] little voices") suggests apostrophe, but such a reading is by no means secure.

The problems are compounded in the third stanza, which opens without commas or quotation marks: "Appearances appearances he said." Where did "he" come from? Is a new speaker declaiming about appearances? Or is the previous speaker now to be understood retroactively as a character, with a new narrator taking charge of the point of view? That there are no quotation marks in the entire poem suggests that this confused conception was at least partially deliberate or that the speakers' relationships to each other and the audience were to be sorted out in a later draft.

Whether one sees this poem as confused or evocative, it is covering familiar ground, dramatizing the search for a reality beneath appearances, beyond dialectic. Unsurprisingly, the search yields nothing: only "the same unvaried / Intolerable interminable maze." One telling advance in this insoluble puzzle is the speaker's intuition that his inability to find an answer has less to do with dialectical rigor and more to do with fear and hope: "—of what are you afraid? / Hopeful of what?" Such questions press into new territory, namely the language of gratitude and prayer, though such language is carefully hedged inside a provisional "whether":

whether you keep thanksgiving,
Or pray for earth on tired body and head,
This word is true on all the paths you tread
As true as truth need be, when all is said:
That if you find no truth among the living
You will not find much truth among the dead.

As a statement of philosophy, the most remarkable part of the poem is this assertion about truth. It is not an assertion *of* truth but about where truth must be found if it exists. It is a partial, qualified truism, it is entirely devoid of content, and it is expressed in doggerel rhythms, but the speaker is edging himself away from the dead end of philosophy. It is this arrival, not merely an accidental "narrative stroke," that enables the final stanza, which Chinitz describes as "quite fine."[53] The speaker goes to sleep in an armchair, while all about him shadows leap and crawl around the room and over his body. Although morning light banishes the monster shadows to their lair, the poem ends ambiguously, daybreak bringing no solace, only a "damp dead breeze" that, bustling through the house, makes a noise that might be laughing or weeping.

"The Love Song of St. Sebastian"
Drafted July 1914

This strange poem explores the relationship between the extremes of sadomasochistic fantasy and the extremes of penitential prayer. Mayer describes the poem as "an extraordinary exploration of martyrdom as a kind of madness"; it is a "double fantasy imagined by the saint (as the conditional mood indicates) first of self-abasement and masochistic pleasure, then of ritualistic murder."[54]

The speaker describes a hypothetical narrative in which he comes to a woman's room at night, as if approaching a goddess, and flogging himself until he bleeds all over the floor. This grotesque, bloody scene is contrasted to the woman's white feet and gown. Addressing her, he speculates that she would accept his body "Because I was hideous in your sight."[55] In the second stanza, the speaker becomes fixated on how his beloved's ears "curl back in a certain way." The speaker equates his strangulation of her with a final moment of perfect communion between them as lovers: "I think that at last you would understand. / There would be nothing more to say." As with her acceptance of his hideousness, he in turn would love her "because you were no longer beautiful / To anyone but me."

A useful point of comparison for this poem is the bawdy poetry. Just as the Bolo poems revel in sexual violence, this poem addresses the same impulse, filtered through the genre of gothic and married to an obsession with martyrdom. In the same letter to Aiken that accompanies "St. Sebastian" and that references the Bolo poems, Eliot writes, "what is necessary is a *certain kind* (could one but catch it!) of *tranquillity*, and *sometimes* pain does bring it."[56] If the poem is risible in its sobriety, it is still remarkable that its author dared to venture this far, the furthest extreme from his juvenilia's polite velleities regarding the opposite sex, and to do so not under cover of the masculinist buffoonery of his Bolo sequence but with the seriousness of his poetic ambition.

Critical inquiry on this poem has followed two paths: those who have applied psychological methods to its sadomasochistic content, and those who have plumbed the conceit of St. Sebastian—the martyr who survived being pierced full of arrows—and the artistic representations Eliot had seen of the martyrdom.[57] The poem's rhetorical organization is at first simpler than that of "Prufrock": this is a love song that speaks straightforwardly to the singular beloved. The complication comes with the speaker's conditional narration of how he would murder the beloved. Mayer notes of the speaker's neurotic focus on the beloved's ear: "The obsessive fixing on the ear releases an act of destruction unperformable by the ordinary 'balanced' mind."[58] The poem gains its frisson from the social taboos that it breaks, a boundary violation that implicates the audience. The beloved is assumed to be complicit, or at least submissive to these acts of self-abasement, torture, and murder, and the audience of the poem is likewise asked to consider this extreme psychological state as one worthy of poetic exploration rather than moral judgment.

"The Death of Saint Narcissus"
Drafted 1915

Not much is known of St. Narcissus of Jerusalem—aside from the fact that he was a second-century bishop who died of old age, not martyrdom—and it is likely that Eliot knew nothing of him.[59] The myth of Narcissus, as found in Ovid's *Metamorphoses*, is the more likely source for this poem. This character Eliot then burdens with the unfinished business from "The Love Song of St. Sebastian": the blurring of martyrdom and the sexual impulse, the connection between madness and self-consciousness, the inflicting of violence on the self and others, and a heightened awareness of role-playing.

The speaker begins, like Prufrock, with an off-putting invitation: "Come under the shadow of this grey rock."[60] Later reworked for *The Waste Land*, the familiar lines that follow end not in a "handful of dust" but with the relics of a saint: "his bloody cloth and limbs / And the grey shadow on his lips."

After the invitation of the first stanza, the intimate address ("you") is dropped, and the speaking "I" disappears behind his narration. The rest of the poem is a series of imagined metamorphoses in which the saint first experiences himself as tremblingly alive to physical sensation, making him vulnerable to the temptations of the flesh. In an earlier draft of the poem, the setting is Carthage, the Augustinian city of lust, and the poem's masturbatory reference to "ancient beauty" and "new beauty" blasphemously reworks Augustine's prayer "Late have I loved thee, Beauty so ancient and so new."[61] Continuing the Ovidian metamorphoses, the saint then imagines himself as a tree, as a fish, as a raped girl, and finally as a "dancer to God" who blissfully accepts the "burning arrows" as they pierce him.

Gordon describes the saint as a "caricature of twisted motives and excessive egotism."[62] An attitudinizing figure, he cannot distinguish the fear of his own lusts from the impulse to martyrdom. Because he conflates spiritual conversion with role playing, he is "satisfied" by the staging of his own death, where the blood contrasts theatrically with the whiteness of his skin. The last two lines of the poem do not aim at transcendence or explanation; they simply describe the mutilated, decomposing body, with the "shadow" still lingering in his mouth.

"Suppressed Complex"
Drafted by Feb. 2, 1915

Of this short poem, Eliot admits to Pound, "I know it is not good . . . Burn it."[63] The title calls out, too obviously, for a psychological reading. The woman lying in bed holds her breath "lest she begin to think."[64] She is suppressing not merely a difficult thought but a range of emotionally fraught issues. The speaker identifies himself as a shadow that dances "joyously in the firelight." If this stanza seems sketchy—neither evocative nor effective—the second stanza does little to flesh out the scenario or the relationship of the shadow's delight to the woman's misery: the only change is that the woman is now breathing hard, and dawn dispels the shadow, which goes "joyously out" the window. The dissonance of the shadow's joy is meant to suggest a productive paradox, but it is too shallow to evoke much of anything. The poem seems to be attempting something similar to "Morning at the Window" in a gothic mode, but the flat tone, indicative mood, and declarative statement also recall the prose poems. In the mismatch between the fantastic gothic mode and the sober observational mode lies the failure of the poem's conception.

The Prose Poems

"Introspection"

Undated manuscript

This poem might more properly be called "Solipsism," for it describes not the serene self-analysis of one's mind but a desperate agon from which the mind cannot escape. The poem presents a series of interlinked images describing the tautology of the mind's self-exploration. The first image—"The mind was six feet deep in a cistern"—recalls the depth of the grave, as well as a thick-walled, inescapable circularity.[65] The apparently dry cistern also connotes prophecy, though no singing or communication reaches an audience.[66] The poem continues with a second image: "and a brown snake with a triangular head." The conjunction "and" seems to add something new, the figure of the snake, to the mind in the cistern. Yet, it is clear that the snake, eating its own tail, is both a metaphor for what the introspective mind is like and something that the mind observes. The ouroboros—a snake swallowing its tail—is an ancient symbol for continuity, cyclicality, eternity, or infinity, though here it more simply figures the mind turned in on itself. The process of introspection is further described in a third image, the simile of "two fists interlocked." Circular cistern, the ouroboros, locked fists: the images do not develop, they simply repeat themselves in different forms. Starting from such a brute premise—the impossibility of communication—and with no teleology to drive it elsewhere, the poem can only end, swiftly, at its logical conclusion: the snake's head futilely scraping against the cistern wall.

Although the poem is possibly written around 1914–1915, it is a pity that this poem cannot be dated more precisely. (The only scholar who has hazarded an exact date for it has misinterpreted the evidence.)[67] Given that the notebook has spent much of its energy trying to work around this very problem of how one communicates to an audience, it would be interesting to know at what stage of his development Eliot gave shape to this thought, perhaps his bleakest statement of the problem of solipsism.

Frances Dickey has observed that Eliot's poetic phrase "circle of our thought" (from "On a Portrait") echoes other expressions from his philosophy dissertation (written 1915–1916), such as "finite centers," which he uses to articulate the problem of relating internal realities to an external world. In the sixth chapter of his dissertation, entitled "Solipsism," Eliot wonders, "How do we yoke our divers worlds to draw together? how can we issue from the circle described about each point of view? and since I can know no point of view but my own, how can I know that there are other points of view, or admitting their existence, how can I take any account of them?"[68] Dickey notes of this agglomeration of phrases, "'Circle of thought,' 'finite center,' and 'point of view' all imply a horizon, however broad, that bounds the mind and cuts it off from others. The terms also imply an interior center where self and meaning reside."[69] The circularity of this poem shares intellectual space with the issues Eliot was working on in his graduate philosophy courses.

Solipsism, though, may not be the only problem the author is articulating in this poem. While masturbation is not directly named, as it is in other notebook poems, the images of a snake and fists suggest the action clearly enough, and the struggle and dead-end despair evoked by the poem were associated with masturbation, a practice condemned or proscribed by familial and religious authority. Nineteenth-century medical discussions of masturbation commonly linked solipsism, onanism, and insanity. At the turn of the century, the superintendent of a state-run asylum indicated, in a report submitted to the Massachusetts legislature, that 32 percent of his inmates were institutionalized because of "self-pollution."[70] As we have seen in chapter 3, Eliot's own father angrily condemned "public instruction in Sexual relations" as an introduction to the devil, and his views on masturbation would have been similarly conservative, if widely held, in medical and religious discourse.[71] The hysterical pitch of a "man driven insane by masturbation"—the extreme figure from nineteenth-century imaginings—is not the pitch of this poem, with its desiccated, matter-of-fact tone.[72] However, the poem does worry over inescapable patterns, a solitary exertion, and a quick and brutal end, all of which suggests that the author's intellectual and sexual problems are intimately linked.

"Hysteria"
Drafted early 1915; published Nov. 1915 in Catholic Anthology

Like "Introspection," "Hysteria" is another prose poem that queasily stages compulsive, rhythmic patterns in an atmosphere of sexual dysfunction and futile constraint. The speaker of this poem is in a restaurant in the company of a woman whose embarrassing laughter is unchecked. Unable to contain the woman's spasms of laughter in the measured feet and line length of a poem, the speaker manages to contain his thoughts about them within the typographically square box of a prose poem. (In its original publication in *Catholic Anthology* and in subsequent versions, both the left and right margins of the poem are justified.) Although there is not a regular meter, there is a surfeit of galloping anapests that speed up the poem: "As she *laughed* . . . of be*com*ing in*volved* in her *laugh*ter and *be*ing . . . with a *tal*ent for *squad*- . . . I was *drawn* in by *short* . . ."[73] The enjambed layout of the prose likewise contributes to the poem's feeling of hurried panic. But the meandering, long-limbed sentences act as a counterpoint, bumping against the breathless momentum of the poem. The overall effect of these layered devices is a hectic, jerky rhythm.

Hysteria was originally a term first appearing in medical journals in the early 1800s, superseding older designations for conditions referred to as "vapours" or "hysterical passion." The term purported to describe a pathological condition usually attributed to women: "A functional disturbance of the nervous system, characterized by such disorders as anaesthesia, hyperanaesthesia, convulsions, etc., and usually attended with emotional disturbances and enfeeblement or perversion of the moral and intellectual faculties" (*OED*). By the mid-nineteenth and early twentieth centuries, the term came to have a non-pathological, figurative meaning: "Morbidly excited condition; unhealthy emotion or excitement." While the misogynistic histories of medical practice and hysteria are relevant for understanding the gender politics of this poem, they do not entirely explain which character is the object of satire.[74]

As with "Portrait of a Lady," there is some critical disagreement about whether it is the woman or the speaker who is hysterical.[75] (The waiter might be added to the list: his "trembling hands" rush to spread a tablecloth, and he mechanically repeats his half-finished mantra: "If the lady and gentleman wish to take their tea in the garden, if the lady and gentleman wish to take their tea in the garden"—an "if" clause that never arrives at a "then." While the woman and the male waiter are overtly hysterical, the interest of the poem lies not in their excessive emotion but in the speaker's response to it. Engulfed by the woman's hysteria, the speaker senses his inability to contain his own rising anxieties, and so he works to contain her outburst. In focusing his "attention with careful subtlety" to the object of controlling hysteria, the speaker no doubt will employ the social tools of the well healed to deflect emotional extremes or social gaffs. It is significant that the strategy is not revealed in the prose poem, only the summary of his attempt: "I concentrated my attention." The speaker would presumably need a maneuver more forceful than "That is not what I meant at all / That is not it at all" to salvage this disastrous event. The speaker does not tell the audience whether his maneuvers were effective or not, even though he narrates the event in the past tense. It is an omission that conceals his potential inability to control the situation.

The strangest and most explicit metaphor in the poem likewise reveals the fierce battle for control being waged. Imagining himself swallowed by the woman's open mouth, the speaker perceives her dark orifice as the sky, while her teeth are "accidental stars with a talent for squad-drill." This metaphor of randomly strewn stars forcing themselves into a military lineup betrays the speaker's concern not only with control but with the unlikelihood of its being effective. The woman's hysteria is alarming to the speaker not only because it is a breach of decorum but because it is uncontrollably sexual: her shaking breasts drawing his gaze, her cavernous mouth and dark throat—the figure of the *vagina dentata*—devouring the male speaker.

"The Engine"
Drafted mid-1915

On May 7, 1915, the British ocean liner and passenger ship RMS *Lusitania* was sunk on its regular run from New York to Liverpool by a German submarine. The sinking shocked the world, changing the terms of the war and making civilian travelers fear for their safety: heretofore, it had been understood that only naval vessels would be targets of military operations at sea. Two months later, USMS *St. Louis,* with T. S. Eliot aboard, took the reverse course, from Liverpool to New York. The fear of wartime torpedoing is part of the context of the poem, the speaker thinking drowsily, "And if the ship goes down."[76]

While the possibility of drowning in the Atlantic was a real one, an even more palpable anxiety animates the poem: Eliot's imminent meeting with his parents. The purpose of his hastily arranged voyage was to answer the summons of his mother and father, who were expecting an explanation for his clandestine marriage and changed career plans. Eliot's father was a practical man who ran a successful brickmaking company, and his formidable presence is multiplied in the poem. In cubist fashion, rows of such men appear in all their angular uniformity on deck: "Flat faces of American business men lay along the tiers of chairs in one plane, broken only by the salient of a brown cigar." The impersonal angularity of these men is echoed by the ship's engine, which is "hard, deliberate and alert," though what purpose motivates the engine is unknowable. All that can be said is that the machine is "certain and sufficient as a rose bush"—this last simile a dubious linkage of machine and nature. The oddest detail comes at the end of the first section: the machine is said to be "indifferently justifying the aimless parasite." Businessmen (plural) might depend upon a ship in the way that parasites depend upon a rose bush, but the last word is singular: "parasite." Up to this point in the poem, we have only met rows of businessmen and the self-sufficient machine. The parasite can only be the speaker himself: an organism deriving its life from some other source, such as the businessmen.

Having implicitly identified himself as a parasite, in the second part of the poem the speaker switches to first person, narrating his drowsy experience when the ship's engine is shut off. The pause in the engine signifies the speaker's fugue state as he lies half asleep in bed. As for the engine stopping, not all details in a poem necessarily line up with biographical reality: it is unlikely that the USMS *St. Louis*, a large target on a direct course to New York, would have cut its engine to float idly in submarine-infested waters. (During World War I, before the military advent of sonar and radar, the advantage for military and commercial ships was speed; the general strategy for evading submarines was outrunning them.) By contrast, the stopping of a ship's engine at dock would normally signal a flurry of activity, but here the ship is eerily quiet, with the exception of a "mouth organ from the steerage" that plays the tune the ship's orchestra had been playing earlier. This whiff from steerage reveals the characteristic sympathy the author exhibits for the working class, and as usual, it signals the speaker's romanticized view of the poor in contradistinction to his own misery. As with many other notebook poems, the emotional directness of a tune artlessly sung or played unnerves Eliot's speakers. Unlike those other poems however, in which the interruptive tune is weighted with emotional significance, the flatness of the prose poem betrays little emotion on the surface, even though the ingredients are the same: a miserable speaker, an offstage tune, an evocation of the poor.

The tune provokes the speaker to turn the light on, illuminating a spider. It is "taut as a drumhead"—another strange simile, evoking not only the drumhead of the ship's capstans but the familiar phrase "drumhead court-martial," a quickly arranged military trial on the field of battle. The small spider either evokes or exudes (it is unclear which) the paradoxical emotion of "intense apathy"—a cheap oxymoron. Although the emotional tenor of the poem is confused, the fears of judgment leak through the flat affect, "like a restless scale on the smooth surface." The befuddled speaker is unable to draw any conclusions: the spider will "somehow persist," but the speaker is unable to bring his cloudy thoughts to any conclusion. What brings him back to reality is the returning thought of the businessmen: "But the flat faces . . . ," petering out in unresolved ellipses.

Eliot's biographers have ignored this poem, but its relevance is obvious: the author was an unemployed graduate student (an "aimless parasite"), traveling on a ship to face a verdict and to beg support and forbearance of a disapproving businessman. Read with its biographical contexts restored, the idle speculation—"if the ship goes down"—reads less as a fear of death than as a wish for deliverance from impending judgment. Given the unresolved nature of the poem, with its idle fantasies of death as an escape, it is likely that the poem was written on the passage to America. The anxieties that Eliot faced on his return voyage were of a different kind. Before leaving England for the States, he had agreed to teach at High Wycombe Grammar School. But by August 5, within a week of landing in New York, he was already considering returning to America for the winter, under pressure from his parents to complete his dissertation.[77] Eleven days later, he had changed his plans again, imagining that he would be at Harvard for the fall semester. Writing to his philosophy professor there, J. H. Woods, on August 16, he announced, "I now expect to return to Cambridge in September."[78] He must have cabled this news to Vivienne earlier, because in this same letter to Woods, Eliot tells his correspondent of his wife's canny response: "Unfortunately I have just had word that my wife is very ill in London, so I must go at once, sailing Saturday." He does return to England, deciding during the return voyage or shortly thereafter on a third change of plans; his decision to stay in England required an awkward apology to his father: "I feel that I shall make matters right by returning to my original course."[79] The couple has been married less than two months, and Vivienne's claim of ill health is the first sign of the manipulations and illnesses—real, psychosomatic, and feigned—that would mark their codependent relationship for the rest of the marriage.

The Staging of Intimacy

"To Helen" ["While you were absent in the lavatory"]

Undated draft, likely post-1910

Published in *Inventions of the March Hare* as an untitled lyric, "While you were absent in the lavatory," it has been reproduced in Ricks and McCue's *Poems* with the restored title "To Helen," which Donald Gallup argues should be adopted from the later of two manuscripts.[80]

Although Eliot had reproduced racial stereotypes earlier in his Bolo poems, in "To Helen," he plays those stereotypes in a less vicious key. Certainly, he does not problematize such racial tropes, but he does strike out into new territory, exploring how social discomfort is not always caused by gender or class expectations. This racial anxiety is explored only through the point of view of the white speaker, however. The African Americans remain mute stereotypes, without agency or perspective of their own.

The poem is addressed to a female "you," whose temporary absence provokes the speaker's unease. Into this chasm of anxiety, two "negro" waiters appear, one with "broad flat eyes"—an image recalling racist caricatures. They offer the speaker choices that make him feel "restless" and "a little unhappy." The first waiter bears a tray of tropical fruits, a sign of rich African trade and colonial exploitation, while the second waiter bears a complementary tray of coffee and cigars, whose ingredients of tobacco and coffee beans suggest another route of imperial trade.

Himself the representative of that imperial power, and unnerved by the choices offered by racialized others, the speaker longs for solace in the civilized, white beloved, whose imagined yet momentarily absent "wide mouth" (the smile of social grace) would counterbalance the "broad" eyes of the caricatured African American waiters. The beloved's absence is not merely accidental. That she is "in the lavatory" suggests a tension between civilized charms and more animalistic needs; her absence makes her complicit with the waiters in her partner's unease.

The awkwardness of this tension hangs the speaker upon not a crucifix but a "finger-bowl"—a symbol of refinement whose purpose is removing the stains of primitive appetite and restoring the user to the clinical state of civilization. The unreality of the scene is heightened and resolved by the appearance of a creature from *Alice in Wonderland*. This fantastical "white" rabbit is a projection of the speaker's racial anxiety. Unlike the speaker, the rabbit is not bound by the rules of restraint that must be shown in front of servants. In its whiteness and its animality, this literary rabbit straddles the restrained world of white civilization and the primitive world of appetite: it hops unselfconsciously under the table to feast on the leavings.

Beneath the jangling of its racist stereotypes, the poem is a love song—a real one—in a modernist mode. Prufrock's love song is ironic; his social anxiety causes him to turn away from women and toward the audience for solace. By contrast, in "To Helen," the speaker's mild anxiety is directed at a racial target, while the female addressee is the source of comfort; "my dear" is his affectionate, class-based address to her. That such intimacy is accomplished at the cost of racist discourse shows that Eliot's further explorations of intimacy—a world in which Prufrockian characters are no longer rejected by mermaids—will still be fraught with complications.

"La Figlia Che Piange"
Drafted late 1911; first published Sept. 1916 in Poetry

Before the publication of *Inventions of the March Hare* in 1996, "La Figlia Che Piange" was widely considered to be the last poem Eliot wrote before his pen fell silent for the duration of his graduate work. This belief was bolstered not only by the prevailing chronologies of the poems but by Eliot's placement of "La Figlia" in *Prufrock and Other Observations* as the terminal poem, a positioning that gave the poem a valedictory weight. These misconstruals have had a strong influence on how we understand the poem, as a brief review of some of those readings will show.

As Eliot's first thoroughgoing source critic, Grover Smith believes that the peculiarities of the poem are best sorted out with reference to what extent it is modeling or subverting Laforgue. For example, while the closing gesture of the poem is described as "a Laforguian shrug," what ultimately makes the poem interesting for Smith is that the influence is not overwhelming; the apologetic irony is introduced "where the incidents are not peculiarly Laforguian."[81] In what has come to be a common understanding of the poem, Smith conflates the speaker with the departing lover, the doubling yet another debt to the French poet. Like Smith, Hugh Kenner is enamored of the idea that the speaker and the male lover constitute "a Prufrockian doubling of consciousness," but the rest of his exegesis attends instead to the nuances of paradox: "The lovers feel the pang, the spectator admires the composition. In this impasse between self-sufficiency and art we discern the Laforguian dead end."[82] For Kenner, this dilemma marks "La Figlia" as "the one remaining unwritten poem" Eliot needed to get off his chest; as a consequence, he "wrote no more poems for three years."[83] For both Smith and Kenner, "La Figlia" signals a dropping-off point, when Eliot left Symbolism behind and stopped writing.

Piers Gray also sees the poem as a dead end, but rather than explaining its contexts as Laforguean or Symbolist, he understands it as a record of Eliot's philosophical development. Gray argues that "La Figlia" represents the end of an intellectual stage: "For the fact is, so far as we know, that Eliot stopped writing poetry between 1911 and 1913." Gray argues that a major reason for this paralysis is "a dissatisfaction with Bergsonism."[84] While the mysteries of Bergson had helped to create "Prufrock" and "La Figlia"—dream worlds "devoid of other humans"—their private, visionary worlds paradoxically suggest a common world, "one which men, in their isolation, share."[85] In Gray's reading, since the prison of Bergsonism (and Bergson-inspired poetry) cannot account for that common world, Eliot was forced to leave poetry behind and solve the problem via philosophy, hence his turn to his studies in 1911. As we now know, Eliot did not stop writing poems in graduate school, though his output did slow down. As will be seen when it is restored to its place among five contemporaneous works written in the same vein, "La Figlia" is not a swan song to Symbolism or the dead end of Bergsonian thought, but a poem that stretches earlier notions of intimacy and suffering beyond the stages "Prufrock" was willing to go.

It is understandable that scholarship on "La Figlia" has linked it with what came before. Like the earlier notebook poems, "La Figlia" has an aura of Symbolist longing, and it dramatizes the artificiality of courtship rituals, though here the convention is the sorrowful pose at courtship's end. However, while "La Figlia" and its five companion poems seem to inhale the same air as "Prufrock," they do not exhale the same air. There is nervousness, but not neurosis. There are women whose presence signals danger, but the author does not cordon them off in the conditional perfect. They press upon the speaker and make claims upon him; they will not be dismissed as the eternal enemy of the Absolute, nor feared as haughty gossips, nor romanticized as mermaids. The male speakers are no longer caught inside the prison of a Bergsonian mind; they interact with real women. Contra Gray, poetry is not abandoned in favor of the work of philosophy during this period; rather, the poetry and the philosophy papers are both doing parallel work—attempting to reach beyond the confines of the solitary mind to some external reality. Unfortunately, the gender politics of the notebook's denouement do not become more enlightened as the women become more three dimensional. As a consequence of these forays into the reality of the other, the author has moved beyond some of the crude misogyny and exoticizing of the earlier poems, but the women still obey gendered expectations of passivity, silence, and deference.

Of the twenty-some poems written in the denouement, only "La Figlia Che Piange" is successful on its own terms and as an advance on earlier work.[86] "Preludes" IV and "Portrait of a Lady" III are certainly successful poems, bringing their respective sequences to conclusion, but they resolve only the Symbolist trajectories that had been set up earlier. What is new in "La Figlia" is its stance toward suffering and intimacy. The observation of suffering has been central to the project of the notebook, whether in the speaker's observation of his own suffering or the suffering of humanity. "La Figlia" moves one step further by recording the speaker's observation of someone *else*'s suffering, a specific woman's grief, staged as if for the artistic benefit of an audience. The poem directly tackles an issue only hinted at earlier: is the suffering of another merely an aesthetic spectacle? While "Second Caprice in North Cambridge" had noted the charged relationship between aesthetics and suffering, it did not consider the ethics of such representation.

One difficulty of "La Figlia" involves navigating the shift between the first and second stanzas, a tense shift that seems to present two different realities. In the first stanza, the speaker directly addresses a woman as "you" in a series of present-tense commands. In a role akin to stage manager, the speaker directs a scene of parting lovers. He gives a series of commands to the woman being abandoned: "Stand on the highest pavement of the stair—/Lean on a garden urn—."[87] Of the accustomed gestures required of her, the speaker is concerned less with a pose as an expression of her grief ("Clasp your flowers to you with a pained surprise—") and more with the effect of such a pose on an audience. The theatrics of light are of special concern, the speaker repeating the injunction: "weave, weave the sunlight in your hair." This rhetorical situation collapses in the second stanza, when the speaker turns away from the woman to address a different, listening audience in the conditional perfect: "So I would have had him leave./So I would have had her stand and grieve." This shift troubles the reality of the previous scene. Does it signify that the parting lovers are hypothetical, staged only in the mind of the speaker? Or does the conditional perfect suggest instead that this reality, as witnessed, happens to coincide with the way the speaker "would have" staged it?

To make sense of the relationship between the imperative mode of the first stanza and the conditional mode of the second requires some attention to the rhetoric of speech genres. In the first stanza, the present-tense commands produce the scene as if by speech act: stand, lean, weave, clasp, fling, weave. That these are neither military commands nor the directions of a stage manager is further suggested by their impracticality. An actor might be commanded to stand or to lean, but how can the woman be expected to "weave the sunlight" in her hair? Only someone other than the woman could do this, such as a painter or lighting director. The context suggests then that the speech genre is neither command nor direction but conjuring: the act whereby magicians and artists summon something from nowhere. This conjuring is the key that connects the speaker's reverie to his conditional perfect, where he comments on the ethics of the imagined scenario.

The invented scene of parting absorbs the mind of the speaker, who imagines what the consequences might be had the lovers not parted. As conjuror of the scene, he desires and is complicit in their pain and parting. If they had remained together, he would have lost "a gesture and a pose"—he would have lost the poem, in short. The woman is the speaker's stage prop, which raises the question of how the speaker relates to the male lover. There is a kinship, though still a distinction, between the speaker and the deserting man. They both seek for some appropriate mode of leave taking, a way "incomparably light and deft," a way that avoids grand melodrama, to aestheticize the agony and to keep emotion from spilling over into bad taste. (For the theatricality to remain poignant, rather than disturbing, the woman's anger must be kept offstage. Deft aesthetics require a deferred politics.) Here is why the speaker cannot merely be the double of the male lover: unlike the deserting lover, the speaker creates this scene for no other reason than its effect on an audience. The lover has his reasons for leaving; the poem does not try to imagine them. But the poem must justify the speaker's involvement in this scenario.

Another crucial aspect of the poem's rhetoric and ethic is the specific audience the speaker invokes in the second stanza: "I should find . . . / Some way we both should understand." Edward A. Geary has noted how crucial—and explicitly dual—this "we both" is, but his solution to the problem leads him down the path of perhapses:

> Is it the speaker and his confidant, the implied listener? Or is it the speaker and the lover, or the speaker and the weeping girl? While an artistic understanding among all these parties would be desirable, the emotional crisis of the moment would seem to call most insistently for an understanding between the lovers. But Eliot says "we both" rather than "they both" or "we three." Most commentaries on the poem have rightly interpreted this as an instance of the Laforguian split protagonist. The speaker is also the lover but refers to his active self (or possibly a former self) in the third person—perhaps in an attempt to evade responsibility for the suffering inflicted on the girl, or perhaps simply to mitigate his own pain at the remembered experience.[88]

Because of the theme of the poem—the emotional crisis of lovers parting—Geary is drawn to the idea that "we both" must refer to the woman and her lover, and this conclusion leads him to fall back on the cliché of the speaker and male lover being doubles. However, the rhetoric of the poem pulls in another direction: "we both" most obviously refers to the speaker and the woman, who is the titular character and the only other person in the poem addressed as "you." (A speaker and audience dyad is never ruled out for the "we" of Eliot's notebook poems: "we both" certainly sounds like "you and I," and it is satisfying to think of *Prufrock and Other Observations* as opening and closing with this I-thou intimacy.) It is to the woman that the speaker offers "a smile and a shake of the hand"—small comfort to outsized grief, but it is in proportion to the speaker's relation to this woman, an unnamed stranger. Unlike "Morning at the Window" and "Paysage Triste," the speaker of "La Figlia" claims the woman not as an object of desire but as a fellow sufferer, and the speaker queries his right to stage her suffering for his own artistic purposes. Even the epigraph, added later, models this moral delicacy: "O quam te memorem virgo . . ." (O how should I call thee, virgin?). Virgil's Aeneas does not call out confidently to the woman (his mother, Venus, disguised) but more hesitantly asks how such calling should be done.

The biographical background to the poem, while not necessary for exegesis, does support this reading of "we both" as speaker and woman. In an impromptu explanation of the poem before a public reading, Eliot described its origin, as noted by a collegiate newspaper: "Some one had advised [Eliot] to see a stone stele of Egyptian origin in an Italian museum. The figure was of a woman, and the Italians called it *La Figlia Che Piange*. He never saw the stele, but the title stuck in his head, so that in the end the poem gave his impression of what that piece of sculpture ought to be."[89] Eliot had searched for something that never appeared. This loss provoked a conjuring act to make it appear, and the conjuring act, in turn, provoked a meditation on aesthetics and ethics.

The tone of the conclusion is ambiguous: it is neither sarcastic dismissal nor apologetic qualification but a metanarrative commentary on the poet's predicament: the poet is bewildered by his own "cogitations," which have conjured up this scene. The poem is part fantasy and part aesthetic theory, both hypothetically artificial and ethically consequential. The closing lines point to the moral quandary this division bespeaks: When does the artifice of a staged emotion become manipulative? It is not a question to which the speaker has a clear answer. He is both "troubled" and "amaze[d]" by the possibilities.

By leaving behind the claustrophobia of Prufrock's private neuroses, his tiny world rolled into a ball, "La Figlia" is notable for how it considers the suffering of another. Just as important, it considers the artist's complicated role in depicting another's suffering. In its staging of suffering and intimacy, "La Figlia" signals an expansion of Eliot's moral universe.

"Hidden under the heron's wing"
Drafted 1912–1913

The first six lines of this untitled lyric evoke a romantic relationship at evening.[90] That which is exquisite or unnamable is rendered in a series of oblique grammatical phrases. First, the ineffable is described as being concealed under a bird's wing: the hiddenness connoting secrecy or delicacy, the wing suggesting flight or ecstasy. "Or," the poem continues, it is found in a bird song "before daybreak" or in "Evening whisper of stars together." Grammatically, the phrases pile up but do not coalesce into a clear sentence, ending instead with a question. Without fear of sentimentality, the speaker addresses a woman "Oh my beloved," asking her what she brings to him, ending with an ambiguous dash rather than a grammatically clear question mark. The second quatrain continues this hazy atmosphere: the woman moves toward the speaker, her "fragile arms" suggesting an embrace.

With the last two lines, there is a change of perspective and tone. The speaker is now "broken glass," and the woman is now the housemaid. He is left to be swept up by her "crimson fist." A fist hardened by labor, sweeping up shards of glass—the images suggests fragility, callousness, class anxiety, and shattered romance. The deflationary conclusion and the imagery of detritus and broken glass evoke the Laforguean manner of 1909 and a half-hearted return to earlier themes.

"Morning at the Window"
Drafted 1914–1915; published Sept. 1916 in Poetry

The yellow fog of Prufrock's St. Louis has become London's brown fog in this short lyric. The poem's point of view is likewise foggy: it is hard to know where the speaker is standing with respect to the "level of the roofs." Otherwise, the observational strategy of "Morning at the Window" has the aura of Baudelaire, with its attention to urban drabness. As with the more accomplished "Preludes," the speaker of "Morning at the Window" is slumming, noting in fascinated detail the dreary routines of the working poor. The hallucinatory atmosphere might make it just another city poem were it not for its tenuous erotic connection between the "passer-by" and the speaker. Like "Paysage Triste," this poem narrates a slight incident in which the speaker passes an anonymous woman of lower-class status, making a momentary connection. Here, that connection is only an "aimless smile" that lingers briefly before evaporating.

"In the Department Store"
Drafted 1914–1915

In the late nineteenth and early twentieth centuries, newly created spaces such as department stores, public transit, and parks were sites where upper, middle, and lower classes commingled. Rather than class boundaries becoming blurred within these egalitarian spaces, however, class distinctions were instead reified. As Julia Daniel has argued, within these democratized spaces signals such as dress and behavior enabled individuals to recognize their own kind and subtly to register class difference even as the physical space they occupied seemed to obscure those distinctions.[91] A number of Eliot's notebook poems are set in parks, and two poems of the denouement explicitly stage their moments of erotic connection within other democratized spaces: "Paysage Triste" is set on a bus, and "In the Department Store" is set in a large British department store such as Harrods or Selfridges.

"In the Department Store" narrates a moment of slight connection between the speaker and a "lady" working in the porcelain department or housewares section of a large department store.[92] The difference in their classes and the democratic ground of the department store where they meet are both essential for understanding the ephemeral nature of their connection. The notes to *Poems* offer H. G. Wells's explanation, from 1910, of department stores as "large, rather low-class establishments," but Wells's description is no objective assessment.[93] It is a negative judgment betraying Wells's own English class anxiety. (That his father had been a struggling shopkeeper must also have colored Wells's view of these grand emporia.) While the lower classes were employed on staff and were free to browse and buy as they pleased, the department stores were pitched at the middle and upper classes, with luxury items and dizzying abundance a strategy for educating the desire of those with extra money to spend.

Not only were department stores democratized spaces where many different classes mixed, they were sexualized spaces as well. Department stores and other establishments had begun to employ young, unmarried women—

new to the workforce—as laborers, typists, and clerks. Earning their own money and living alone or with friends in the city, these unchaperoned, liberated women changed not only the dynamics of the workplace but the gender and sexual politics of the wider culture. Because of this disruption of the Victorian social order, such women were often coded as sexually available to men who patronized the establishments where they worked.

At first, the female clerk in this poem is not figured as a sexual object. She and her professional trade—not her feminine sexuality—are firmly connected. She works in a porcelain department, and her most salient feature is her porcelain smile "through a set of false teeth."[94] Even her hair, tightly and demurely tied, is used not to attract men but as a practical aid in her profession: "She is business-like and keeps a pencil in her hair." Her eyes are described as "sharpened," like that pencil of hers. As usually deployed in literary discourse, smiles, hair, and eyes are traditional markers of a woman's sexuality—how she pleases men—but the poem initially emphasizes these details as facets of her competent, formidable exterior.

By the poem's turn, however, she has become sexualized, though less as an object of the speaker's desire, and more as a desiring subject herself. It is not in her eyes—which to the observer appear as sharpened, weaponized, professional—but "behind" her eyes, that is to say, in her imagination, that she dreams of "summer evenings in the park / And heated nights in second-story dance halls." Underneath her businesslike exterior, her erotic imagination comes to life. The speaker, for his part, describes her reveries as remembered facts, not as imaginative projections of his own. How the speaker gains access to the woman's interiority is never explained. Without fuss or signaling, the author simply turns from the limited viewpoint of a man in a department store to the viewpoint of an omniscient narrator. By not drawing attention to the nature of this shift, the poem imbues the woman with a life beyond the limited speaker's own imagining.

Still inhabiting this omniscient viewpoint, the speaker hazards a bleak aphorism on the meaning of life: "Man's life is powerless and brief and dark"—a paraphrase of its source in Bertrand Russell's *The Free Man's Worship* and an echo in phrasing and sentiment of an even bleaker assessment of man's life as "solitary, poor, nasty, brutish, and short."[95] The truism deflates any desire the speaker has for this woman, forcing him back into the limited point of view and cutting short the tercet pattern of the preceding stanzas: "It is not possible for me to make her happy," he concludes. By granting her autonomy and an inner life, he acknowledges her difference from him. The chasms of gender and class separate them, and the bleak reality that their lives are "powerless" to change their terms only affirms these gaps. But the speaker's realization that he could not make her happy is itself a paradoxical, fleeting moment of connection: it suggests that he wishes this state of affairs were not so.

Melita Schaum has described this poem as a "failed human encounter," linking it with the similar failures of communication and courtship in "Prufrock."[96] Rather than an advance on the themes and accomplishments of "Prufrock," Schaum sees this poem as burdened by Eliot's class snobbishness: "There is an implied vulgarity about the saleslady as described through the narrative voice."[97] For Schaum, she has been dehumanized by the speaker's fragmentation of her body into teeth and eyes;[98] the speaker condescends to dance halls and park courtships as "sordid," and his tone betrays an "ambivalence of desire and disdain."[99] In Schaum's reading then, the poem harks backward not only to "Prufrock" but to the earlier poems, where women are feared and dismissed with snide put-downs.

Schaum is right that the poem dramatizes a kind of failure, but when the poem is placed in the chronology of Eliot's development, its advance upon the earlier work is more obvious. The saleslady is fleshed out as an interesting character rather than a mere type, and the failure is attributed to class difference rather than to the woman's vacuity or the speaker's timidity. Whether one reads the description of the saleslady's appearance as condescending depends upon how one understands the rhetorical work those descriptions are doing. For example, where the saleslady is described as smiling through false teeth, the falsity could signal the speaker's negative judgment of the lady's insincerity. However, the falsity might just as well be read as the speaker's acknowledgment of the transactional nature of the retail environment. It is not the woman who is false but the role she must play to sell goods to men: she smiles not "with" her teeth but "through" them.[100] Similarly, the details of her "business-like" exterior and "sharpened" eyes are not obviously condescending; they are instead neutral descriptors, acknowledging the professional armor that prevents the speaker from knowing her. To acknowledge that her professional exterior protects her against sexual objectification is not a disdainful complaint at her unavailability. And far from condescending to working-class entertainment, Eliot's poetry nostalgically renders the sights and sounds of lower-class life, such as street pianos and mandolins that recall lost idylls. The connotations of "summer evenings in the park / And heated nights in second-story dance halls" suggest straightforward romance rather than patronizing superiority. Unlike the fragmented body parts found in earlier poems, this woman is made whole and given an interior life unavailable to the speaker. These are crucial differences that mark this poem as an imaginative advance not only over "First Caprice" but even from "Prufrock," whose women are granted neither interiority nor meaningful agency.

"Paysage Triste"
Drafted 1914–1915

In another democratized and sexualized space, this time a public "omnibus," the speaker remarks a beautiful lower-class "girl" as she steps in. She responds knowingly and casually to the speaker's hungry gaze by ignoring him. That she does so without embarrassment or "surprise" suggests to the speaker that she is used to getting attention for her looks; she carries an "experienced" air. He extends this assumption further, suggesting that she is possibly a woman of easy virtue: it is he who labels her an "almost denizen of Leicester Square"—an upscale entertainment spot where prostitutes found lucrative trade among businessmen and upper-class clientele. Julia Daniels notes that the speaker's use of "almost" in this phrase points in various directions: "The speaker may imply that the girl *looks* like a prostitute, though she isn't one; she *almost* has that Leicester-Square air about her. He may alternately imply that she is a slightly lower class of prostitute; she is a working girl who could *almost* be in Leicester Square."[101] Unlike in "In the Department Store," where a brief flight into an omniscient narration gives the reader access to the lady's interiority, here the girl remains opaque.

The speaker's speculation about her being a prostitute is made *after* she has rejected him; the speaker tries to redeem his rejection in the following stanzas by contrasting his imaginative tryst with this girl to the practical impossibility of their union. Because she is from the lower classes, the speaker notes that she would be unfamiliar with the norms of the mating rituals of his class; she would be uncomfortable in her seat, ignorant of the art of opera, unschooled in the subtle dialectic of reserve and intimacy which govern middle- and upper-class courtship. The working-class girl, the speaker imagines, might easily give her body to him in another situation or for the right price. But because of her class anxiety—again, projected onto her by the speaker—she would be afraid to violate the boundaries of intimacy in the way the speaker's companion at the opera can easily do. That woman, confidently seated in the opera box, leans across the speaker, her elbow on his lap, to claim her opera glasses from a child. The woman prods the boy "impetuously"—

both the prodding and leaning are signs of social equality, gestures that would not translate across class boundaries. The speaker recognizes this easy intimacy as conventional; it does not provoke the censure of a chaperone, nor does it rouse his interest. This physical intimacy does not thrill him as does the vision of the girl's "loosened hair" and "naked feet" in the privacy of her bedroom.

"Paysage Triste" stages not one but two moments of erotic encounter with different women: the lower-class girl who "answer[s]" his stare and the middle- or upper-class "you" who casually brushes his knees with her elbow. Significantly, this latter gesture—the brushing of arms on legs—takes place "when the lights went out." The dimming of lights is a recognizable sign, the theater's signal to the audience that the passion, suicides, and high-decibel lovemaking that is the standard fare of opera are about to begin. This turning down of lights is implicitly contrasted to another recognizable gesture: the turning out of lights before lovemaking. Having recovered from the boy their opera glasses—that device whereby the passion of distant lovers is brought close—the speaker and his female companion, alas, are mere spectators to the passion unfolding on the stage.

Of the six denouement poems that stage erotic intimacy, all make similar assumptions about their audiences. Here there is no fear of a sarcastic reader deriding the speaker's bid for intimacy as sentimental. Two of the poems are more sexually explicit than the others, and their emotional content is more poignant: "Paysage Triste" and "In the Department Store." These are the poems that Eliot declines to publish. By contrast, "Morning at the Window" and "La Figlia Che Piange" are published: the former is more reserved; the latter stages its emotions as an aesthetic problem and a moral quandary rather than a direct invocation of pathos.

The two themes that mark these six poems of the denouement are staging and intimacy. As poems of eros, the intimacy is between speaker and object of desire. But there is also the intimacy between speaker and reader, Eliot's peculiar brand of intimacy that results from verbal staging or rhetoric. In their representation of women, the six poems move beyond the misogynistic fear of earlier poems and beyond the abstractions of unrequited desire. Desire is thwarted in these poems, but not as brutally as in "Prufrock." In staging a tenuous moment of connection, whether erotic or artistic, with a woman and an audience, all six poems strike a tone of intimacy—the direct, lyrical address. As with "Prufrock," the Eliotic manner is assured in these six poems, notable for the unnerving way the speakers worm their way into the reader's confidence.

Conclusion: The Terrible Intimacy of Eliot's Rhetoric

> The miseries that people suffer through their particular abnormalities of temperament are visible on the surface: the deeper design is that of the human misery and bondage which is universal. In normal lives this misery is mostly concealed; often, what is most wretched of all, concealed from the sufferer more effectively than from the observer. The sick man does not know what is wrong with him; he partly wants to know, and mostly wants to conceal the knowledge from himself.
>
> —T. S. Eliot, introduction to Djuna Barnes's *Nightwood*

As we saw in chapter 7, some of the first critical responses to Eliot's publications accused the poetry of being cold or of handling emotion poorly.[102] Fifty years later, Grover Smith picks up the same line of complaint, claiming that compared to Sweeney, the "Prufrockian temperament . . . does not come off well when put alongside the champions of fleshly joy."[103] Smith's summary judgment on the whole oeuvre sounds a note of disappointment: "Apart from poetry by W. B. Yeats, that of Eliot may include the greatest written in the contemporary age; yet his poetry has perhaps failed in essential generosity and good humor, in steady compassion for the human lot. . . . If Eliot's poetic vision falters, it does so because of its peculiar privacy, which admits of no wide sympathies. For Eliot lacks a ready power of empathy, of self-projection into the points of view of others."[104] Similar complaints about Eliot's lack of empathy continued into the 1980s and 1990s, the nadir of Eliot's reputation. A typical example from that era is Kenneth Asher's *T. S. Eliot and Ideology* (1995), which concludes dyspeptically, "There is a systematic lack of generosity, finally, of humanity, in Eliot's work—both prose and poetry—and, in the last analysis, it is this that will exclude him from the classical company to which he devoted so much of his life."[105] And more recently, Marjorie Perloff reviews Ricks and McCue's new edition of *The Poems* in the *Weekly Standard*, finding herself "less than enchanted" with some of the poems and complaining overall that Eliot—a "profoundly elitist poet"—has no sympathy with the lower classes.[106]

As an admirer of Eliot's work, I do not intend this study as an unqualified defense of it. In particular, his various prejudices make assessment of his work a complicated task. While his prejudices were common for many of his time, class, and education, serious scholarship has long grappled with these issues and offered nuanced ways of understanding what can be bracketed or historicized, and what remains to trouble the reception of the work. However, to dismiss the oeuvre for being condescending—when it is most powerful in its sympathy with the lower classes—is to ignore all of these early inventions, published and unpublished. Likewise, to accuse it of lacking humanistic warmth—when the notebook's task has been to construct and then reveal a vulnerable, self-protecting interiority—is to have missed something essential in the rhetoric of his poems.

From early and late in Eliot's work, compassion for human suffering is a key note, starting with "First Caprice in North Cambridge," which attempts to render human suffering metonymically. The choked fear of Prufrock among the mermaids—"I do not think that they will sing to me"—is consonant with *The Hollow Men*'s devastating admission of loneliness:

> Waking alone
> At the hour when we are
> Trembling with tenderness
> Lips that would kiss
> Form prayers to broken stone.[107]

Although the style changes, this theme continues through the bitter regret of *Burnt Norton*: "Down the passage which we did not take / Towards the door we never opened."[108] All of these heartbreaking moments depict suffering—the peculiar, private suffering of one man—in order to articulate a specificity that cannot be contained in the abstract noun "suffering." What invites the audience into the poet's ambit and what robes their suffering in common grief is the very particularity of the suffering—not its sentimental abstraction nor its "self-projection into the points of view of others," which Smith holds up as a model of generosity.

If Eliot's notebook poems do not display steady compassion for the human lot, then it would be difficult to say that any poems do. That such compassion in Eliot's poetry coexists with his snobbery, his prejudices, and his hard edges certainly complicates our response to the work. However, unless our aesthetic principles require that artists be two-dimensional cartoons holding no particular opinions, then for many admirers of Eliot, such problems will not wipe out that compassion entirely. To complain that a philosopher is not a Falstaff, that an anatomist of suffering is no comedian, is to commit a category error against an artist whose gifts are primarily lyrical and introspective rather than dramatic. Chaucer may be more high spirited, and Shakespeare more diverse, but to accept Eliot is to negotiate—not necessarily submit to—the "peculiar privacy" of his vision. That privacy is not an internal quality of a poem, nor is it a summarizable collection of beliefs or attitudes; rather, it is a connection that exists between the poem and its reader, forged in the terrible intimacy of its rhetoric. And though it may lack the dramatic properties of stagecraft, may be of a different kind than Schiller's world-embracing kiss, Eliot's intimacy is a privileged kind of generosity. The genius of Eliot's rhetoric is that it is a whisper, sometimes a horrified one, that creates the illusion of addressing no generic audience but one reader who is already intimately known by the speaker. This phenomenon—a rhetorical finesse that dramatizes the risk of intimacy—is the only way to explain the countless passionate readers who have walked around with lines of "Prufrock" ready on their lips.

While the denouement reveals a sputtering of energies—the completion of Eliot's apprenticeship and clumsy attempts to launch new trajectories—it is not the end of his development as an artist. Soon after his hasty marriage and permanent expatriation in 1915, the expression of his changed realities will require a different rhetoric, calling forth another version of T. S. Eliot. Here in the notebook, even with its inconclusive ending and unfinished "Prufrock," the achievement is already considerable. The poet has learned to rage coldly at the imbecility of social convention, to anatomize the tragic flaw of self-deception, and to sing falteringly of alienation, ennui, and suffering. He has become T. S. Eliot, that rarest of artists who can stare into the abyss and make music from the experience, daring his reader to look with him.

Chronology of Eliot's Work, 1899–1915

All of Eliot's poems and earliest prose pieces are listed here. The undergraduate essays, graduate papers, and philosophical reviews have not been included; their dates of composition and publication can be found in *The Complete Prose*, volume 1. Where a draft date of an early poem or essay is unknown, the earliest publication or recital date is given. As described in chapter 8, I consider most of the poems written in late 1915 to constitute a new phase of development and thus not technically part of the trajectories of the notebook. However, since their composition overlaps with the last poems of the notebook, I include their dating here.

Fireside, nos. 1–14 [9, 10, 12 not extant]	written Jan.–Feb. 1899
Eliot's Floral Magazine	written Feb. 1899
"'The Vision of Sir Launfal,' A Christmas Study" [not extant]	read in Dec. 1904
"A Lyric" ("If Time and Space, as Sages say")	submitted Jan. 24, 1905
"The Birds of Prey"	published Jan. 1905
"A Fable for Feasters"	published Feb. 1905
"A Tale of a Whale"	published Apr. 1905
"The Man Who Was King"	published June 1905
"To the Class of 1905"	recited June 13, 1905
"Song" ("When we came home across the hill")	published May 24, 1907
"Song" ("If space and time, as sages say")	published June 3, 1907
"Before Morning"	published Nov. 13, 1908
"Circe's Palace"	published Nov. 25, 1908
"Song" ("The moonflower opens to the moth")	published Jan. 26, 1909
"On a Portrait"	published Jan. 26, 1909
"Ballade of the Fox Dinner"	recited May 15, 1909
"Nocturne"	published Nov. 1909
"Humouresque"	drafted Nov. 1909
"Conversation Galante"	drafted Nov. 1909
"First Caprice in North Cambridge"	drafted Nov. 1909
"Second Caprice in North Cambridge"	drafted Nov. 1909
"Opera"	drafted Nov. 1909
"Convictions (Curtain Raiser)"	drafted Jan. 1910

"First Debate between the Body and Soul"	drafted Jan. 1910
"Spleen"	published Jan. 26, 1910
"Portrait of a Lady" II	drafted Feb. 1910
"Easter: Sensations of April" I	drafted Apr. 1910
"Easter: Sensations of April" II	drafted May 1910
"Silence"	drafted June 1910
"Ode" [Harvard Class]	published June 24, 1910
"Mandarins" 1–4	drafted Aug. 1910
"Goldfish (Essence of Summer Magazines)" I–IV	drafted Sept. 1910
Hamlet section of "Prufrock"	drafted before Oct. 1910
"Preludes" I–II	drafted Oct. 1910
"Suite Clownesque" I–IV	drafted Oct. 1910
"The Triumph of Bullshit"	drafted Nov. 1910
"Portrait of a Lady" I	drafted Nov. 1910
"Fourth Caprice in Montparnasse"	drafted Dec. 1910
"Fragments"	drafted ca. 1910–1911
Columbo and Bolo verses	drafted ca. 1910–1916
"Inside the gloom"	drafted late 1910 / early 1911
"Entretien dans un parc"	drafted Feb. 1911
"Interlude: in a Bar"	drafted Feb. 1911
"Bacchus and Ariadne"	drafted Feb. 1911
"The smoke that gathers blue and sinks"	drafted Feb. 1911
"The Little Passion"	drafted Feb. 1911–July 1911
"He said: this universe is very clever"	drafted Mar. 1911
"Rhapsody on a Windy Night"	drafted Mar. 1911
"Interlude in London"	drafted Apr. 1911
"Ballade pour la grosse Lulu"	drafted July 1911
"Preludes" III	drafted July 1911
"Ballade pour la grosse Lulu"	drafted July 1911
Paris/Munich draft of "Prufrock"	drafted July–Aug. 1911
"Portrait of a Lady" III	drafted late 1911
"Preludes" IV	drafted late 1911
"La Figlia Che Piange"	drafted late 1911
"Prufrock's Pervigilium"	drafted 1912?
"Do I know how I feel"	drafted 1912–1913
"Hidden under the heron's wing"	drafted 1912–1913
Revised "Prufrock"	drafted 1913–1914
"After the turning"	drafted 1913–1914
"I am the Resurrection"	drafted 1913–1914
"So through the evening"	drafted 1913–1914
"The Burnt Dancer"	drafted June 1914
"Oh little voices of the throats of men"	drafted by July 1914
"The Love Song of St. Sebastian"	drafted by July 1914
"Morning at the Window"	drafted Sept. 1914
"In the Department Store"	drafted 1914–1915
"Paysage Triste"	drafted 1914–1915

"Suppressed Complex"	drafted by Feb. 2, 1915
"Afternoon"	drafted by Feb. 25, 1915
"Hysteria"	drafted early 1915
"The Death of Saint Narcissus"	drafted 1915
"Mr. Apollinax"	drafted May 1915
"The 'Boston Evening Transcript'"	drafted May 1915
"Aunt Helen"	drafted May 1915
"Cousin Nancy"	drafted May 1915
"The Engine"	drafted late 1915
"O lord have patience"	drafted 1915–1916

"In silent corridors of death"	undated, likely post-1910
"Introspection"	undated
"To Helen" ["While you were absent"]	undated, likely post-1910

NOTES

Introduction

1. Thomas Francis Conroy, MD—the husband of John Quinn's niece, the heir to the Quinn estate—has given testimony regarding the transfer of the Quinn letters and the Eliot manuscripts to the Berg Collection at the New York Public Library. Conroy's narrative of the negotiations is not told in chronological order, and so it is not clear exactly when the notebook and *The Waste Land* drafts were handed over. The exchange probably occurred in 1958, after the Conroys had made a microfilm of the manuscripts. The second half of the Berg's payment to the Conroys was made in 1959 (Torrens 64). For the authoritative description of the notebook, see Donald C. Gallup, "The 'Lost' Manuscripts of T. S. Eliot" and *What Mad Pursuits!* For a discussion of how the notebook was acquired by Eliot's patron, John Quinn, and its fate after Quinn's death, see Ricks, preface to *Inventions of the March Hare*; Gallup, *What Mad Pursuits!*; and B. L. Reid, *The Man from New York: John Quinn and His Friends*. For the convoluted story of how the notebook was acquired by the Berg Collection, see James Torrens, SJ, "The Hidden Years of *The Waste Land* Manuscript." For a detailed consideration of the ways in which the draft poems differ among themselves and from the published versions, see Chris Buttram Trumbold, "Earlier Versions of Eliot's Early Verse."

2. In my first article on the notebook poems ("Searching for the Early Eliot"), I concurred with David Chinitz that the arc of Eliot's development was "not a progress upward" (Chinitz, rev. of *Inventions,* 57) but a hodgepodge of successes and failures. However, once the poems are placed back into their order of composition, the stepwise manner of Eliot's development becomes more obvious. With rare exceptions, his mastery and vision expand securely and steadily.

3. *Prose 7* 828.

4. *Prose 7* 14.

5. Booth 71.

6. Eliza Richards has argued that the oral model of voice—that which relies on the metaphor of the speaking voice—and the deconstructive model are mutually exclusive in theoretical approaches to voice. My method does not seek to harmonize the very real differences, but it does offer a model that draws on both theoretical approaches.

7. An important exception is Leonard Diepeveen's "'I Can Have More Than Enough Power': T. S. Eliot's Construction of His Audience." Diepeveen's argument for the

inescapability of intention in literary criticism is also worth careful study (*Modernist Fraud*).

8. Bakhtin 341.
9. *Prose 5* 223.
10. *Letters 8* 12.
11. Ackroyd 39.
12. *Inventions* xii.
13. *Inventions* xv.
14. The leather-bound notebook is still held at the Berg Collection. The Beinecke at Yale University houses the poems excised from the notebook. The Houghton at Harvard University holds *The Fireside* and other juvenilia. King's College, Cambridge, holds some juvenilia as well.
15. Gallup, "'Lost' Manuscripts," 647.

Chapter 1 • Indebted and Well Bred

1. Epigraphs: *Prose 7* 801; *Prose 7* 792–93.
2. *Poems 1* 1067.
3. *Poems 1* 1067.
4. *Letters 1* xviii.
5. Most of the extant juvenilia were originally published in school periodicals, *Smith Academy Record* and *Harvard Advocate*. Later capitalizing on Eliot's fame, the *Harvard Advocate* reprinted in 1938 and again in 1948 the juvenilia that had originally appeared in its pages some decades earlier. It is not likely that Eliot would have had legal grounds for objecting to the *Advocate*'s reprinting. However, it was at the insistence of Eliot, who was a shrewd legal guardian of his own legacy, that action or threat of such was taken against an unauthorized book that was published in 1949 under the title *The Undergraduate Poems of T. S. Eliot*. According to Gallup, of this unauthorized edition, about 750 of the original run (1,000) were officially withdrawn from circulation, though the prohibited copies eventually leaked back into the market. In response to this turn of events, the following year Eliot collected the juvenilia as *Poems Written in Early Youth*, privately printed at the publishing house of Albert Bonnier in Stockholm. That Eliot sought out a foreign publisher, pressed few copies, and prohibited them from sale reveal the author's desire to exercise some control over their copyright rather than his wanting to see the juvenilia republished. Unpublished correspondence in the Hayward Bequest confirms Eliot's strict instructions regarding this edition. Writing to John Hayward on April 5, 1950, Åke Runnquist of Albert Bonnier apologizes for complications that are holding up the private edition of the poems that had been planned for some time. He expresses concern about getting "an assurance of absolute loyalty to Mr. Eliot's wishes from all persons concerned in the project." Then follows some wrangling in which Hayward deems untrustworthy a US contact who had been asked to provide photostats of the original *Advocate* poems. And finally, later that year, on Aug. 29, 1950, Georg Svensson, one of the directors of Bonnier, gives the desired guarantee in unequivocal terms: "I can assure you that the edition will be strictly limited to 12 copies and that no copy shall get into the hands of any unreliable person" (King's).

Because of errors in the unauthorized edition of 1949 and in the Stockholm edition of 1950, and because of general interest in Eliot's minor work, Valerie Eliot oversaw a corrected trade edition of the juvenilia, published under the same title, *Poems Written in Early Youth,* made widely available in 1967. These verses can also be found in the same grouping in British editions (1969 and later) of *The Complete Poems and Plays of T. S. Eliot* (Faber and Faber). In *Poems 1,* all of these verses appear, but they have been interspersed with other poems, in rough chronological order, within the heading "Uncollected Poems."

6. Smith, *Eliot's Poetry,* 9.
7. Moody, *Thomas Stearns Eliot,* 17.
8. Ibid.
9. John T. Mayer 22.
10. Ibid.
11. Ibid. 26
12. Matthews 8.
13. *Prose 7* 796.
14. Cuda, "The Poet and the Pressure Chamber," 4.
15. *Inventions* 397.
16. In a lecture delivered at University College, Dublin in 1936, Eliot remarked that the poets of the 1890s "made it possible for me to discover" the Symbolists (*Prose* 5 303). Bush ("In Pursuit of Wilde Possum") has argued that Baudelaire was mediated for Eliot through the English poets of the 1890s. Schuchard and Sherry have likewise each restored the influence of the decadent tradition to discussion of Eliot's politics and aesthetics.
17. *Poems 1* 302. Ricks and McCue speculate that the poem was written in 1937. They have this line ending with a quotation mark; in Gordon (7), the line ends with a question mark.
18. The source of this anecdote is the same as the more famous incident of the cherry tree: Mason Locke Weems's biography of George Washington, first published in 1800, then in ever-expanding editions. In this influential bestseller, "Parson Weems" as he was known, relates, or more likely fabricates, this story of Washington's obedience to his mother: "At the giddy age of fourteen, when the spirits of youth are all on tiptoe for freedom and adventures, [Washington] felt a strong desire to go to sea: but, very opposite to his wishes, his mother declared that she could not bear to part with him" (226–27).
19. Hall 92–93.
20. See Berlin, *Rhetoric and Reality.*
21. Not extant. This essay takes as its subject James Russell Lowell's long poem on the Grail quest. Eliot's recitation of it, at Smith Academy Christmas Exercises 1904, was announced in the program, but the essay itself has not been found. (See Smith Academy Scrapbook 1904–1905, Series 02, Box 12, Scrapbooks, Letters and Ephemera, Smith Academy Collection, Washington).
22. *Fireside,* Houghton MS Am 1635.5 (1–13). See Crawford (*Savage and the City*) and Soldo for discussions of these domestic productions. March and Tambimuttu's volume includes a reproduction of the title page of *Fireside*'s second issue.
23. Henry Ware Eliot Jr.'s catalog of materials presented to Eliot House at Harvard included "12 issues of *Fireside*" (actually, eleven of *Fireside* and one of *Eliot's Floral*

Magazine) with the notation that "4 others were sent to TSE in 1929 by HWE" (*Poems 2* 150). Nos. 9, 10, and 12 of *Fireside* are absent from the archive and are presumably three of the "4 others" sent to Eliot. The one issue unaccounted for is likely no. 15 of *Fireside* or a second edition of the floral magazine.

24. Twice in *Fireside* no. 1; no. 5; in no. 5 and 6. In the late nineteenth century, "rushing the can" or "working the can" was a new expression that required explanation.

25. *Fireside* no. 3.

26. *Fireside* no. 5.

27. *Fireside* no. 3. In a sublimely sarcastic *New York Times* article about Romulus's methods, the author writes:

> It had been announced beforehand that 'Bob' Fitzsimmons, the fighter, would be referee, but he did not appear, and there was no referee. Romulus and the steer wrestled according to their own notions and without rules. . . . The steer was studying the crowd as if he was calculating the gate money and was giving little of his attention to his supposed antagonist. . . . The second 'bull' was not disturbed or brought out. The one that performed was left in the ring, staring about him in majestic bewilderment, apparently looking for his friend Romulus. ("Romulus and the Steer")

28. *Fireside* no. 4.

29. Internet Broadway Database: http://www.ibdb.com. Mar. 20, 2019.

30. Qtd. in *Poems 2* 151. See Soldo.

31. *Poems 2* 147.

32. As told by Frederick M. Eliot to Harford H. Powel Jr., Dec. 23, 1953; recorded in Powel 27.

33. *Fireside* nos. 4 and 5.

34. *Fireside* no. 8, qtd. in Soldo 33.

35. *Fireside* nos. 1 and 4.

36. *Fireside* no. 2; *Poems 2* 148.

37. *Fireside* no. 2.

38. *Fireside* nos. 3 and 5.

39. *Fireside* no. 4.

40. *Fireside* no. 4, Soldo 33.

41. *Fireside* nos. 4, 6, 7, and 8.

42. *Fireside* no. 13.

43. *Fireside* no. 4.

44. *Fireside* no. 3; *Poems 2* 147; *Fireside* no. 3.

45. *Fireside* no. 4.

46. *Fireside* no. 14.

47. *Fireside* no 8.

48. Ibid.

49. *Fireside* no. 5.

50. *Fireside* no. 13.

51. Ibid.

52. *Fireside* no 7.

53. Crawford, *Savage and the City*, 15.

54. The original MS is among the papers of the Hayward Bequest, King's College, Cambridge (HB P/1). A facsimile is reproduced in March and Tambimuttu. The fair-copy MS bears no title, but when it was published a few months later in the school newspaper, *Smith Academy Record*, it was given the title "A Lyric." Subsequent scholarship often uses this title to distinguish it from its later revision, published at Harvard as "Song."

According to an accompanying letter (Aug. 19, 1943) that Eliot wrote to Hayward, it was the first poem that Eliot had intended others to see. It is written in tidy script on a thick-ruled quarto sheet (Bluestone Mills watermark), a typical exercise paper with two red vertical lines for teaching schoolchildren how to indent on the left and how to gauge the margin on the right. The English master Roger Conant Hatch has given it the mark of "A" on the back and underlined and put question marks above two words ("say" and "vine") whose penmanship is uncertain. "Say" has been later corrected, probably by Eliot, to clarify its final letter. Eliot's sardonic comment on the poem, when handing it over to Hayward's files, is written at the bottom: "(Doggerel License No. 3, 271, 574)" (King's).

55. *Poems 1* 223. Ricks and McCue's edition usefully gathers all the juvenile poetry, so I cite this text as my source in this chapter. To keep intrusive notes to a minimum, I cite only my first quotation from each poem or story.

56. Crawford (*Savage and the City*, 14) has identified the source as the popular children's author Captain Mayne Reid.

57. *Prose 1* 7, 5.

58. Ibid. 3.

59. Grover Smith (1956) first identified this source.

60. *Poems 1* 226.

61. Barham 97, 96. I am grateful to Julia Daniel, who pointed out this similarity between "Fable" and Barham.

62. Lanham 19.

63. *Prose 1* 4.

64. Gordon 12.

65. *Prose 1* 6.

66. Crawford, *Savage and the City*, 19.

67. Unlike the other juvenilia originally published in school periodicals and then reprinted in *Poems Written in Early Youth*, this poem was first published in the 1950 volume. It was given the provisional title in brackets, "At Graduation 1905," since the typescript John Hayward used bore no authorial title. This title is an editorial addition written on another typescript in light pencil, not in Eliot's hand. The text of the poem Hayward edited was taken from a surviving typescript given him by Eliot and now in King's College. The original holograph is not extant, but two different typescripts—with insignificant variations—are preserved. In addition to the provisionally titled and unsigned TS in the Hayward Bequest (HB V/2b) at King's, another TS (untitled, unsigned) is preserved at Washington University, with the addition at the top of the page: "Written by Thomas Stearns Eliot / Class of 1905 / Smith Academy."

In my archival work at Washington University, I discovered the program for the graduating exercises of Smith Academy 1905, which lists the title of the poem as "To the Class of 1905." *Fiftieth Annual Graduating Exercises Smith Academy*, Memorial Hall,

13 June 1905; Smith Academy Scrapbook 1904–1905, Series 02, Box 12, Scrapbooks; Letters and Ephemera, Washington. Ricks and McCue have adopted this corrected title for *Poems*.

68. *Poems I* 227.

69. Ibid. 1071.

70. Something like the Aristotelian four-part arrangement (introduction, argument, counterargument, conclusion/peroration) has been copied by Eliot, adapted for an epideictic occasion, with an exhortation serving as the argument or main point and a digression taking the place of the counterargument.

71. *Prose 7* 792.

72. Qtd. in Howarth 101–2.

73. *Poems 1* 231.

74. John T. Mayer 29.

75. *Poems 1* 223.

76. John T. Mayer 30.

77. Ibid. 31.

78. Qtd. in Howarth 358n101. Assuming that the first *Advocate* poem has been reviewed twice (as both poems are entitled "Song"), Howarth is unaware that "Lyric" has been revised, entitled "Song," and republished ten days after "Song" ("When we came home across the hill").

79. See D'Ambrosio (106–7) for a fuller discussion; she identifies FitzGerald's quatrain IX as the direct source for these images.

80. *Poems 1* 231.

81. John T. Mayer 31.

82. Ibid.

83. *Poems 1* 1073.

84. John T. Mayer 34.

85. *Poems 1* 233. As a consequence of a printer's error or editorial censorship, the *Advocate* version of this line reads "scarlet life," and this error was repeated in all subsequent published versions until corrected by *Poems 1*. Among H. W. H. Powel's correspondence with Haniel Long (Special Collections, Brown University), there appears a photostat of the original manuscript in Eliot's hand. Its final lines clearly read "scarlet lips."

86. John T. Mayer 35.

87. Ibid. 36.

88. The portrait has been in the collection of the Metropolitan Museum of Art in New York since 1889. According to Frances Dickey, the connection of the poem to Manet "was first noted by Harford Powel, Jr. in his unpublished Brown University master's thesis of 1954. It is picked up by John Soldo in *The Tempering of T. S. Eliot* (1983) but not discussed" ("Parrot's Eye," 136n1).

89. Ibid. 114.

90. Ibid.

91. John T. Mayer 47. Mayer places this poem among the post-Laforgue creations, arguing that its pose of indifference is indebted to Laforgue, a conclusion with which I disagree. As Mayer himself has noted, Eliot's juvenilia have been exploring poses of indifference since his first undergraduate poems, in reaction to Harvard irony and

Boston sophistication. Mayer is on stronger ground when he argues that the primary influence on this poem is Symons. But his argument about sources, though illuminating, reveals just how limited that influence is: Eliot is mining Symons's language because he has not yet figured out a way to adopt the philosophy. The ghost of Laforgue is wholly mediated through Symons.

92. Dickey, "Parrot's Eye," 130.

93. The Fox Club was a social club originally founded as the Digamma Club at Harvard in 1898 (see Crawford, *Young Eliot*, 94). Castle's volume was printed for private distribution to Fox Club members.

94. The poem has been wholly ignored by critics. Other than references to its existence, I have not found any critical discussion of it.

95. *Poems 1* 233–34.

96. The term appears in 1859 in John Camden Hotten's *A Dictionary of Modern Slang, Cant, and Vulgar Words*. For its entry on "booze" as an "alcoholic drink, chiefly beer," the *OED* grants T. S. Eliot the last word, its final example citing the term's use in *Sweeney Agonistes*: "We're gona sit here and drink this booze."

97. Ginger ale, incidentally, was a "soft drink" (another expression emerging in the late nineteenth century) sometimes associated with the temperance movement.

In addition to its political valence, Eliot's gleeful partisanship on behalf of intemperance is possibly also a gendered signal. By the turn of the century in the United States, temperance was associated with women's movements for suffrage and other demonstrations of female political clout. The first decade of the century marked the rise of Carry Nation, whose infamous "hatchetations"—in which she attacked saloons and bars—gained her national press. Her provocative actions and speeches made her a prominent, if problematic, spokesperson for temperance. According to one commentator, Nation's "violent actions and bizarre personal behavior lent an unwelcome air of fanaticism and even burlesque to the determined moral activism of American women" (cited in Pegram 111). Thus, in co-opting this particular temperance slogan to demonize female fanaticism, Eliot aligns himself even more squarely with the all-male environment of his club.

98. It is also referred to as the Knickerbocker Trust Panic or the 1907 Banker's Panic.

99. See Robert Sobel's *Panic on Wall Street*; and Robert F. Bruner and Sean D. Carr's *The Panic of 1907*, especially figure 20.1 on p. 144.

100. Castle 12.

101. Harmon and Holman 528.

102. Smith, *Eliot's Poetry*, 30.

103. Some of these Fox Club members are identified in *Poems 2* 565–66; and in Crawford, *Young Eliot*, 94–96.

104. Ibid.

105. Ibid. 23.

106. Howarth 101.

Chapter 2 • The Notebook, Begun

1. Epigraph: *Prose 6* 78.
2. *Prose 5* 603.
3. Epigraph: *Prose 2* 66, emphasis mine.

4. Jewel Spears Brooker has told me that a receipt for the book order bears the date March 1909, but I have been unable to locate this source. Eliot's account, in a letter of 1917, that he sent away to Paris for Laforgue (*Letters 1* 212) is probably more accurate than his later recollection that he found the texts in a foreign book shop in Boston (Hall 65). Various scholars have incorrectly speculated on which volume of Laforgue Eliot owned: it is the two-volume *Oeuvres complètes de Jules Laforgue*, 4th ed. (Paris: Mercure de France, 1909) (*Prose 2* 756n12).

5. Ricks's chronology of the poems (*Inventions*, xxxvii–xlii) inadvertently omits "Conversation Galante" from the November 1909 listing. See also *Inventions*, 346, annotations.

6. Eliot's "Humouresque" had been parenthetically subtitled "(After J. Laforgue)" when it was published in *Harvard Advocate*. But this poem was not included in Eliot's first volume, *Prufrock and Other Observations* (1917). So the first readers of that volume—on the other side of the Atlantic or otherwise outside of Harvard's narrow ambit—would have had no such Laforguean reference to guide them.

7. See Brooker, *The Contemporary Reviews*. René Taupin's *L'Influence du symbolisme français sur la poésie américaine de 1910 à 1920* (1929) was the first extended study of Eliot and Baudelaire. And Edward J. H. Greene was the first to work out the matter of French influence in any systematic way. See his "Jules Laforgue et T. S. Eliot" (1948) and *T. S. Eliot et la France* (1951).

8. Schuchard 77. See also Louis Menand's "How Eliot Became Eliot"; and Anthony Lane's "T. S. Eliot."

9. Epigraph: *Prose 7* 828.

10. Greene notes, "En 1907 ou 1908 il lit Baudelaire, qui le bouleverse" (*T. S. Eliot*, 18).

11. The list of Eliot's Harvard coursework may be found in Jain 252–56.

12. *Inventions* 408–9.

13. *Letters 5* 35.

14. *Prose 7* 483.

15. Epigraph: *Prose 7* 29.

16. Wilson 95.

17. *Poems 1* 56, 42, 239.

18. Ibid. 10.

19. Quoted in Soldo 28.

20. *Inventions* 325.

21. *Poems 1* 234.

22. According to Lighter's *Random House Historical Dictionary of American Slang*, the colloquial meaning of "class" as "elegance of style, behavior, taste, etc." dates to the late nineteenth century. The expression "some class" is identifiable in popular culture by the early twentieth century.

23. Green 1101. Another source, *The Oxford Dictionary of Slang*, dates "snappy" with reference to clothes and dressing to 1881 (Ayto 367).

24. Howarth 106.

25. One exception to this is the non-polemical appearance of the second person: "The kind of face that you forget."

26. Symons 59.

27. *Inventions* 346.

28. Ibid. 13.

29. I am indebted to Jewel Spears Brooker, who pointed out to me the shift from the impersonal camera to the personal voice in this poem.

30. Vendler, "T. S. Eliot: Inventing Prufrock," 91.

31. Ibid.

32. John T. Mayer 71.

33. *Inventions* 15.

34. According to the *OED*, it is an expression that has been in constant use since at least 1583.

35. Reading the poem as a clear psychological record rather than as a garbled rhetorical performance, John T. Mayer sees the artistic intention of the poem as "an escape from engagement": "Momentarily disturbed as the sad scene takes hold, he wriggles out of empathy by focusing on the aesthete yellow and rose sunset and its unexpected charm" (72).

36. *Inventions* 17.

37. See Leblanc.

38. See Dickey's "Musical World" for an extended reading of "Opera" that also focuses on Eliot's ambivalent response to Wagner.

39. Stravinsky 92–93. When Stravinsky republished this short memoir for *Esquire* in his later conversation books, he edited out this story about Wagner.

40. Cf. letters from Verdenal to Eliot and their passionate discussion of Wagner (*Letters 1* 24, 29). These examples of Eliot's emotional reaction to *Tristan und Isolde* may be compared to yet another contradiction: Eliot, writing in 1934, "And I admit that I find the story of Tristram and Isoud is unsatisfactory in its ending; and Matthew Arnold and Richard Wagner have not mended matters. The idea of fatality is there, and provides a fitting under-pattern of Arthur and Guenevere and Launcelot and Elaine and Galahad; but there is a frivolity and inconsequence alien to the central motive" (*Prose 5* 61n12).

41. See the letters to Hale of Jan. 20, 1931, Mar. 16, 1931, and Jan. 15, 1932 (Princeton).

42. Frances Dickey notes that Toscanini's first Boston performance of *Tristan und Isolde* was in January 1910—but this performance is unlikely the one, since the date is two months after the draft of this poem ("Musical World," 105). Crawford speculates that Eliot may have heard the opera on one of his visits to New York (*Young Eliot*, 135). There were two other performances of *Tristan* in Boston before the 1910 date; all three were performed by the Metropolitan Opera on tour: (1) Boston Theatre; Apr. 3, 1907; conductor, Alfred Hertz; (2) Boston Theatre; Apr. 11, 1908 matinee; conductor, Gustav Mahler; (3) Boston, Massachusetts (venue unspecified); Jan. 10, 1910; conductor, Arturo Toscanini (Metropolitan). There were no other Metropolitan Opera touring performances of *Tristan* in Boston between January 1910 and the end of 1914. Dickey claims that the performance of *Tristan* that Eliot attended with Hale was likely a November 1913 performance by the short-lived Boston Opera Company.

43. *Inventions*, 83.

44. "The great danger, for the poet who would write religious verse, is that of setting down what he would like to feel rather than be faithful to the expression of what he really feels." *Prose 8* 514.

45. *Prose 2* 676, 743–46.

Chapter 3 • Clearing the Throat

1. Epigraph: *Prose 2* 213.
2. Ibid.
3. Gammond.
4. See Furia 25–30; and Chinitz, *Eliot and the Cultural Divide.*
5. Furia 49.
6. Ibid. 30.
7. Chinitz, *Eliot and the Cultural Divide,* 39.
8. Ibid. 36. See also my review of Chinitz, "Ambivalence All Around," from which my discussion here is reworked.
9. Chinitz, *Eliot and the Cultural Divide,* 37.
10. Ibid. 38.
11. Chinitz does consider the allusions to popular culture of an even earlier piece, the February 1910 section of "Portrait of a Lady." Although its last stanza does refer to popular culture—"comic strips, drama, boxing (on 'the sporting page'), and sensational murder stories"—Chinitz's critical interest is in how these coarse signs of popular life might provide an alternative reality to the woman's art salon (*Eliot and the Cultural Divide,* 24). He is not claiming that such references infect the rhythm of the poem or duplicate the rhetoric of ragtime.
12. Furia 12.
13. Gershwin 42.
14. Ibid. Another Gilbertian fantasia: "Bellini's *Norma* [is] extravagandized to *The Pretty Druidess; or The Mother, the Maid and the Mistletoe Bough*" (42–43).
15. Chinitz, *Eliot and the Cultural Divide,* 46.
16. Symons 55.
17. Hall 97.
18. *Inventions* 13.
19. Ibid. 328.
20. Ibid. 11.
21. The shortened line and emphatic rhyme appear even earlier in "First Caprice" and "Second Caprice" to uncertain effect—that is to say, the effect does not draw attention to itself in the way that its later usage does, partly because the tone remains the same and the line length is not sufficiently distinguished from what precedes it.
22. *Inventions* 64.
23. Ibid. 329.
24. Ibid. 23.
25. Ibid. 24.
26. Ibid. 18.
27. See his "Reflections on *vers libre*," *Prose 1* 511.
28. *Prose 2* 245.
29. Ibid. 213.
30. *Inventions* 11.
31. "When he put the book together, Eliot paid [Harriet Monroe] a compliment by titling it *Prufrock and Other Observations,* using the group title she supplied for his

third appearance, in *Poetry* (September 1916): 'Conversation Galante,' 'La Figlia che Piange, 'Mr. Apollinax,' and 'Morning at the Window'" (Parisi and Young 171).

32. John T. Mayer 51.

33. Scholarship on Eliot's marionettes dovetails with scholarship on the influence of Laforgue. See Schuchard, "'Our Mad Poetics to Confute': Laforgue and the Personal Voice," in *Eliot's Dark Angel*; and most recently, the psychological account drawn by Cuda, *The Passions of Modernism*.

34. *Inventions* 11.

35. *Letters 1* 11–12.

36. John T. Mayer 52.

37. Woolf 236.

38. *Letters 1* 41.

39. *Poems 1* 233.

40. Later in the poem, the apostrophe appears: "Imagination's / Poor relations."

41. In Eliot's later writings and in other possible sources, Ricks cites various uses of "Absolute" as well as of "supersubtle" and "peasant," though he finds no source for the linkage of the latter two. Not even Tolstoy at his most polemical could have yoked such terms together. Ricks derives "supersubtle" from Henry James. Matthiessen—speaking not of Eliot's use of the term but of the concept of "super-subtlety"—derives it from Babbitt (129).

42. Symons 58, 57.

43. *Poems 1* 196.

44. Brooker (*Eliot's Dialectical Imagination*) reads the poem as a dialectical "mini-drama" (20).

45. *Prose 7* 483.

46. For a fine, if brief, reading of this poem through the lens of musical culture, see Graham 58.

47. *Poems 1* 239.

48. As with "Nocturne," "Spleen" is a poem obviously inspired by Laforgue, but it appears nowhere in the notebook. As described in chapter 1, Eliot reprinted this poem only in the strictly limited edition of *Poems Written in Early Youth*, which was not intended for distribution.

49. John T. Mayer 49.

50. Symons 60.

51. Ibid. 58.

52. This represents the second appearance of a capitalized "Absolute" in the same month, but it is not yet Bradley's Absolute, that "single, all-encompassing consciousness" from which "our individual consciousnesses only appear to be divided" (Beasley 14). Eliot did not begin reading Bradley until 1913 (see Brooker, "Seduction and Disenchantment," 47).

53. Bizley 28.

54. Ibid.

55. *Inventions* 328–29. In Ricks's edition, the two parenthetical lines are placed at the top of a page, making it difficult to tell whether the lines are separated by a space from the preceding four. In the Berg notebook, the six lines constitute a single stanza. The parentheses are indented, as Ricks has set them.

56. It is unclear at what point in the five-year gap between its drafting and its publication in *Others* that Eliot excised these lines. Presumably, the excision occurred later, that is, closer to its publication date, as the lines are not crossed out in the notebook.
57. Aiken, "King Bolo," 21; Southam identifies her as Adelene Moffatt (58).
58. Emphasis mine.
59. *Prose 2* 125.
60. *Inventions* 327.
61. Pondrom 328–29.
62. *Inventions* 23.
63. Symons 32.
64. Gordon 34.
65. Schuchard 121.
66. *Inventions* 18.
67. *Prose 4* 675. Ricks has located the crucial marginalia in Eliot's copy of Pater's *The Renaissance* (which cites the line of Pascal), bringing these two silences together (*Inventions* 126n15).
68. *Poems 1* 196.
69. Gordon, 23–24.
70. Ibid. 49.
71. *Poems 1* 182.
72. *Prose 5* 459.
73. Ackroyd 17.
74. *Poems 1* 242. Ricks and McCue's notes on the poem point to an ambiguity in its public presentation. The ode itself was printed in the program, where Eliot was designated as the class "odist," rather than the class poet, an honor that went to Edward Eyre Hunt. While Hayward notes that Eliot recited the poem at Sanders Theater, the form of the ode was written to be sung to the tune of "Fair Harvard," and at least one newspaper account of the day indicates that the graduating class sang the ode (*Poems 1* 1092–93).

Chapter 4 • Raising the Voice

1. Epigraph: *Prose 2* 66.
2. Gordon 48.
3. *Prose 2* 66.
4. *Letters 1* 12.
5. In later life, Eliot destroyed dozens and perhaps hundreds of his mother's letters, but he kept this one. Perhaps the letter survived serendipitously, but it is also possible that Eliot preserved the letter because it reminded him of the personal cost of his becoming a poet.
6. In my count of fourteen, I do not include the fragments of "Prufrock"—though these too are scraps to be fitted later into a sectionalized whole.
7. "Mandarins," "Goldfish," and "Suite Clownesque" (*Inventions* 19, 26, 32). Elsewhere in the poems of this time frame, the word "complete" appears once in "First Debate between Body and Soul," where the "supersubtle peasant" is described as a "complete idealist" (65). Variations on "complete" appear in the preceding time frame (January–June 1910) in similar usages, especially in "Spleen" and "Portrait" II.

8. "Fourth Caprice in Montparnasse" presents an odd case. See discussion below.

9. *Inventions* 30.

10. Ibid.

11. Aiken, "King Bolo," 21.

12. The earliest instance of a critic making connections between Eliot's published verse and popular culture is Clive Bell's dismissive "Plus de jazz." Most connections between jazz and Eliot tend to emerge after the publication of *The Waste Land* (see Chinitz, *Eliot and the Cultural Divide*, 31–49).

13. *Inventions* 329.

14. Eliot, in letter to John Hayward, cited in Gardner 67.

15. *Inventions* 32.

16. Wayne Booth dismisses the idea of an "ideal reader" as nonexistent, given the inevitable gaps between any reader's ideology and an author's (140). A significant contribution to rhetoric studies in that volume is Booth's idea of an "implied author," a concept that points to how the text presupposes a shaping consciousness separate from its characters and narrators and whose force also responds to and shapes its readership. The implied reader, therefore, is a major and complicated concern of Booth's study, though Booth does not explicitly use this phrase.

17. *Inventions* 329.

18. *Inventions* 176. In this letter, Eliot is presumably describing only the nine lines that in the notebook version begin "No! I am not Hamlet," rather than the succeeding twelve lines that conclude the poem. In correspondence with another critic who had asked about the Hamlet "paragraph," Eliot conceded, "The page in question antedates the rest of the poem by some months"—where Eliot presumably means "paragraph" for "page" (*Letters 7* 825). Elsewhere, Eliot singles out these nine lines, rather than what follows, as predating his trip to France; in John Hayward's copy of *Poems* (1925), Eliot has bracketed only lines 111–19 with the annotation "Cambridge Mass 1909 or 1910?" (*Poems 1* 373).

19. Pound, *Selected Letters*, 50.

20. Fletcher, *Selected Letters*, 19. Coffman's *Imagism* cites this same letter in manuscript, though it is marred by transcription errors (42).

21. Fletcher, *Life Is My Song*, 191.

22. Fletcher, *Selected Letters*, 19.

23. *Inventions* 127.

24. The *OED* dates to 1775 the sense of "mandarin" as a toy or figurine whose head is designed to bob.

25. *Inventions* 19.

26. Mulertt 5.

27. Ibid. 6.

28. Ibid.

29. Ibid. i.

30. *Inventions* 147.

31. Ibid. 26.

32. Before trees grew up around the houses, the harbor of Gloucester could be seen from one side of the Downs, and the Atlantic Ocean from the other.

33. Cuda, *The Passions of Modernism*, 35–36.

34. There are countless character pieces written in the nineteenth century with expressive titles such as Schumann's *Kinderszenen*. But given the neutral content of Chopin's titular "preludes," compare, for example, Liszt's orchestral work *Les Preludes* that supposedly takes its title and meaning from a literary source.

35. *Inventions* 334.

36. While both the "eye" and the "brain" appear in "Second Caprice," they appear not as body parts observed by an authorial audience but as functions of perception or cognition.

37. Smith 21.

38. McLean 20, 44. The material here on the history and form of vaudeville is drawn from McLean, as well as D. Travis Stewart's *No Applause—Just Throw Money*.

39. See McLean.

40. Ibid. 69.

41. Ibid. 68.

42. See McLean's chapter "The New Humor," 106–37.

43. *Inventions* 32. Ricks connects this vaudevillian to Eliot's later writing as a philosophy graduate student: "Solipsism," Eliot writes in his dissertation, "has been one of the dramatic properties of most philosophical entertainers" (*Prose 1* 357). Ricks comments, "The dramatic comedian ('A self-embodied rôle,' . . .) is the supreme solipsist" (*Inventions* 165).

44. For the third section of "Suite Clownesque," readers who rely on Ricks's 1996 edition of *Inventions of the March Hare* will want to note a misplacement of a line in the final stanza. The first seven lines should read:

> If you're walking on the beach
> When the girls are ready for a swim
> You hear everyone remark
> Look at him!
> You will find me looking them over
> Just out of reach
> First born child of the absolute

Ricks claims incorrectly that the line beginning "When the girls" *and* the line "Just out of reach" are both "marked to be moved from their original place" (*Inventions* 36). The MS is a jumble of arrows, deletions, and revisions, but the line arrangement can be determined with accuracy. Ricks and McCue have corrected this error in *Poems 1* 251.

45. *Inventions* 45.

46. Vendler, "T. S. Eliot: Inventing Prufrock," 100.

47. Ibid.

Chapter 5 • Trembling with Pathos

1. Epigraph: *Prose 4* 417–18.

2. *Letters 1* 11–12.

3. Ibid. 11.

4. This identity as an academic star at Harvard is a late development. Eliot was put on probation for poor grades his first semester as an undergraduate, a development that alarmed his parents. Eliot told his second wife that he had "loafed" his first two

years at Harvard (*Letters 1* xxiii). For his solid academic performance as schoolboy, see my article "T. S. Eliot as a Schoolboy."

5. *Prose 6* 512.

6. Hall 72.

7. *Inventions* 14.

8. Quoted in Gordon 53.

9. *Letters 1* 15.

10. In the United States, the concept of culture shock dates to the 1930s but was not fully theorized until the 1950s.

11. *Letters 1* 82.

12. *Inventions* 335.

13. *Letters 1* 82.

14. *Inventions* 327.

15. Ibid. 16.

16. Ibid. 48.

17. Ibid. 53.

18. Ibid. 73.

19. Ibid. 16, 58.

20. Ibid. 328.

21. Ibid. 40.

22. Ibid. 39.

23. *Poems 1* 380. In a remarkable feat of detective work, Frances Dickey has uncovered the domestic and political background of Eliot's smoke and fog. In a conference paper written as part of a forthcoming book project, Dickey has revealed that a major polluter in St. Louis was the Hydraulic Press Brick Company and that one of the groups that led the campaign against smoke was the Wednesday Club. Eliot's father was president of Hydraulic Brick, and Eliot's mother was a member of the Wednesday Club. Dickey reverses the usual reading of these smoky scenes that sees them "as an 'objective correlative' of psychic drama," instead suggesting that they reflect "the historical reality of smoke itself" ("Taking the Air").

24. "To the Class of 1905" (*Poems 1* 229). The source for this image is probably biblical or literary rather than experiential, as Unitarian services are not likely to have included incense. In the doctrinal battles of the nineteenth century, William Greenleaf Eliot's St. Louis congregation leaned toward the Christian rather than the rationalistic branch of Unitarianism, but its liturgy was shorn of medieval practice.

25. *Poems 1* 231.

26. *Inventions* 13.

27. Ibid. 334.

28. Ibid.

29. Ibid. 327.

30. Ibid. 328.

31. Ibid. 51.

32. Ibid. 70.

33. Ibid. 339.

34. Ibid. 39.

35. Ibid.

36. Ibid. 331.
37. Ibid. 43.
38. Ibid. 51.
39. Ibid. 43.
40. Ibid. 68.
41. *Prose 4* 417–18.
42. *Inventions* 328–29.
43. *Letters 1* 20.
44. There is a textual problem with the handwriting that records this date. The final "0" of the year 1910 is imperfectly scrawled by Eliot, and Ricks has suggested a "6" (for 1916) as an alternate reading. Baffled by the indecipherable cipher and taking the viciousness of the poem as a cue, Ricks offers an explanation to support the later 1916 dating. He suggests that if the later date is correct, it is perhaps in response to Harriet Monroe's dithering in her publication of "Prufrock"—negotiations that occurred in 1914–1915. Aside from its illegibility, the skepticism about the 1910 date for "The Triumph of Bullshit" seems to be that the poem's hostility toward "Ladies" might not be invented. See my "Eliot's Culture Shock," which counters this theory.

As a textual matter, other "O"s and "0"s in the notebook betray similar illegibility. At end of "Suite Clownesque" IV, the lightly penciled date "Oct. 1910" has the "9" with the characteristic downward spike. More apposite to this discussion, both the "O" of "Oct." and the "0" of "1910" are wobbly, with the uncertainty most noticeable at the top and right of the letter/digit. This could shed light on the difficulty of the "Triumph" date, whose last digit reads somewhere between a 0 and 6 (thus, 1910 or 1916). This similar wobbliness suggests that the date for "Triumph" is 1910.

45. *Inventions* 307.
46. Ibid. 309.
47. In the original manuscript at the Berg Collection, "Portrait of a Lady" (most of section I) appears on the numbered pages 22–23. Directly preceding these pages is a torn stub, whose excision marks correspond to the tearings on the side of "The Triumph of Bullshit," now in the Ezra Pound Papers at Yale.
48. *Inventions* 327.
49. John T. Mayer 111.
50. *Inventions* 327.
51. Ricks, "T. S. Eliot's Othello."
52. Smith 12.
53. *Inventions* 329.
54. Smith 11.
55. Vendler, "T. S. Eliot: Inventing Prufrock," 100.
56. John T. Mayer 68.
57. *Inventions* 14.
58. Vendler, "T. S. Eliot: Inventing Prufrock," 86.
59. *Inventions* 48.
60. Ibid. 51.
61. Ibid. 68.
62. Ibid. 238.

63. Ibid. 70.

64. Ibid. 73. Ricks lists this poem as undated (xlii), while Gordon (55) dates it to 1910–1911. On the basis of the evolving handwriting of the Paris poems—which makes dating these poems possible—I would narrow the dating to late 1910/early 1911. The script of "Inside the gloom" has migrated away from the rounded hand of Harvard. The "th" and double "tt" of this hand is closest to the manuscripts of December 1910.

65. Gordon dates the later (and shorter) version of the poem, written on the pages of the notebook, to 1914 (60). She notes that the longer version, on a separate leaf laid in, is written in Eliot's Paris hand; I concur with Gordon and further specify that it is written in Eliot's *later* Paris hand and is thus datable to Feb.–July 1911. Ricks lists both versions of this poem as undated (*Inventions* xlii), while Gallup suggests 1915 (*T. S. Eliot and Ezra Pound*, 37).

66. *Inventions* 57.

67. The solitude of the poem's speaker and Eliot's own sexual anxieties in Paris suggest another, complementary reading of these verses. One clue is offered by Ricks, who identifies the "little" of the title as derived from Corbière's "Petit mort pour rire" (*Inventions* 215). Given the French connotations of "petite mort" and the "inevitable" ways in which the poem moves toward the passion, the poem can be read as an oblique reference to masturbation.

68. See Eliot's letters to Hale of Mar. 24, 1931, and Mar. 6, 1933 (Princeton). See further discussions of Prichard in relation to Eliot in Frances Dickey's "'Mandarins' at the Museum of Fine Arts" and John Morgenstern's "The Modern Bacchanal."

69. *Inventions* 17.

70. Ibid. 18.

71. Ibid. 30.

72. Ibid. 329.

73. Ibid. 21.

74. Ibid. 334.

75. Ibid.

76. Ibid. 45–46.

77. Ibid. 71.

78. Still standing, the building has six floors, counting the mezzanine above the *rez-de-chaussée*. How and whether these six floors correspond to "six flights" is unclear, if such details can be turned to the service of biography. In any event, the building is topped off with the requisite garret rooms and dormer windows dictated by the late nineteenth-century Haussmann Plan.

79. Hargrove, 40–41.

80. Hargrove, 42; *Prose 7* 112.

81. *Inventions* 248. Ricks notices a connection between this spider and a brief comment, written almost twenty-five years later, in which Eliot recalls Paris's first decade of the century: "over all swung the spider-like figure of Bergson" (*Inventions* 248).

82. "Bergson makes use of science—biology and psychology—and this use sometimes conceals the incoherence of a multiplicity of points of view, not all philosophic. Has not his exciting promise of immortality a somewhat meretricious captivation?" (*Prose 2* 516). The *Nouvelle Revue Française* version explicitly evokes seduction: "Sa

troublante promesse d'immortalité ('. . . même la mort . . .') ne participe-t-elle d'aucune méthode de séduction?" (*Prose 2* 518).

83. Gray 46.

84. Hall 97.

85. Hugh Kenner's *Invisible Poet* ignores the poem entirely. Only one passing reference to the poem appears in F. O. Matthiessen's *The Achievement of T. S. Eliot*. Northrup Frye's *T. S. Eliot* likewise mentions "Rhapsody" only in passing, even though an entire chapter is devoted to the city poems. And while Helen Gardner devotes a number of pages to "Prufrock" and other early poems, she can summon only the word "disquieting" to describe an image from "Rhapsody" (81). See Smith (24–25) for a general description of the poem that refers to, but is not bogged down by, Bergson. John T. Mayer (79–84) also gives a fine account of the rhetorical force of the poem. See Raffel (32–33) for an opposing view of the poem as unsuccessful. Gordon also describes it as a philosophically failed poem (59).

86. *Inventions* 338; italics mine.

87. See Gray 42.

88. Adding to the complication is the uncertainty of Eliot's punctuation. The notebook version is so faint as to make clear judgment impossible. And even Eliot's published versions betray uncertainties: lines 2–12 of the first stanza (separated as two sentences in draft) have only one period in initial publications (1917, 1920). Not until 1963 was a period added after "precisions." Other changes in punctuation have crept in accidentally, as a result of publishers' positive decisions or negative carelessness, or even at Eliot's whim.

89. *Letters 1* 17.

90. Ibid.

91. *Inventions* 16.

92. In *Inventions*, Ricks notes of the stubs following Eliot's numbered [page] 27: "two leaves excised, one of which is now in the Pound papers" (37). I have compared the stub measurements (and their jagged excisions) of the Berg notebook to the excised pages at Yale, and I can assert that Ricks is too cautious in this instance: both pages are at Yale. "Ballade for Gross Lulu" is the second excised page.

93. *Poems 1* 1130–31.

94. *Inventions* 311.

95. Johnson 19.

96. Villon 106–7.

97. Freeman 80.

98. *Inventions* 334.

99. Ibid.

100. Gray 53.

101. Ibid.

102. *Poems 1* 414.

103. *Inventions* 335.

104. Philippe 76.

105. John T. Mayer 89.

106. See Morgenstern, "The 'Centre of Intensity,'" for an account of how Eliot's engagement with Baudelaire changed during his Paris year.

Chapter 6 • The Short and Surprisingly Private Life of King Bolo

1. "Il y avait une langue là-dedans; ça grasseyait: 'Good night, ladies; good night, sweet ladies! good night, good night!' Ça chantait, et souvent des gravelures" (Laforgue, *Oeuvres complètes*, 391). English translation from *Six Moral Tales from Jules Laforgue*, 176.

2. This chapter is a revision and expansion of my 2017 article of the same title in *The T. S. Eliot Studies Annual.*

3. *Inventions* 311 and 314–15.

4. What to call these dark inventions is yet another trouble that besets discussion (see Poirier; Johnson). Even though some of the verses are mischievously obscene, "naughty verse" as a description is too flippant, and the term does not cover the more troubling moments. Although it risks imprecision, my approach here is ecumenical; I refer to these inventions interchangeably as "blue," "dirty," "obscene," "bawdy," or "scabrous" verse. I use the terms "scatological" or "pornographic" when I wish to convey these more restricted meanings, and I use the term "excised poems" when I am distinguishing the obscene verse published in *Inventions* from obscene verses found elsewhere, such as in the letters or archives. It is likewise imprecise, if occasionally necessary, to distinguish Eliot's obscene poems from his "serious verse."

5. David Chinitz was the first to raise my suspicions on these matters, and this discussion is indebted to several conversations with him. With his permission, I have reworked some of our correspondence. Anthony Cuda and Jim McCue have likewise helped me think through issues of dating and have directed me to pertinent sources, though I take responsibility for the conclusions reached here.

6. In *Modernism, Memory and Desire*, Gabrielle McIntire writes, "Given Eliot's desire to publish these poems, the protracted period of their composition, and the range of issues they invoke, we cannot, though, dismiss them as 'mere' juvenilia" (13).

7. The theory that Eliot intended to publish these poems in *Blast* is also commonly found among Lewis scholars (see Meyers 76; O'Keeffe 168). I know of no critic who has disputed this narrative, one that I have unfortunately repeated in my earlier criticism (see "I Grow Old").

8. *Inventions* 305.

9. *Letters 1* 64.

10. Another obvious joke appears in Eliot's letter to Joyce: "I wish that Miss Beach would bring out a limited edition of my epic ballad on the life of Christopher Columbus and his friend King Bolo" (*Letters 1* 455). In her memoir, *Shakespeare & Company*, Sylvia Beach describes how authors would beg her to publish their own erotica or scandalous fiction. She made clear to all inquirers that Joyce was the only author she would publish. Beach gets a good laugh out of naming the many people who approached her. Unsurprisingly, Eliot is not one of them.

11. In Lewis's account of their early friendship, he is unable to put a date to their first meeting, only confirming that they met sometime between the publications of *Blast* 1 (July 1914) and *Blast* 2 (July 1915) (Lewis, *Blasting*, 285).

12. Neither of the extant versions of "Bullshit" or "Ballade" have words ending in -uck, -unt, or -ugger. Since "Fragments" and the Columbo and Bolo verses do have such words, it is probable that Eliot also sent these to Lewis. This probability strengthens

my case that in their correspondence, Lewis would have understood that there were two operative categories for Eliot's poems: those for Lewis's editorial consideration ("Rhapsody" and "Preludes") and those for his private amusement (the scabrous verse).

13. Pound and Lewis 9.

14. Pound, "T. S. Eliot," 24.

15. Pound and Lewis 13. The exact chronology of these undated letters is unclear. I have relied on Materer's order in *Pound/Lewis*, where he organizes the letters, as best he can, in chronological order.

16. Marshik 3.

17. O'Keeffe 155.

18. It might be argued that Eliot's contributions to *Noctes Binanianae* (1939) vitiates my point that he never sought to publish his scabrous verse. However, the circumstances of that multiauthored collection prove rather than refute Eliot's extreme caution in this regard. Another elaborate in-joke among literary friends (Eliot, Geoffrey Faber, F. V. Morley, John Hayward), this volume of occasional verse commemorated the nights spent at Hayward's flat at Bina Gardens. The poems that had been circulating *entre eux-mêmes* were privately printed in an extremely limited edition of twenty-five copies, not for sale, with coded, semi-anonymous attributions. The assemblage of such verses into a book format does not constitute publication in the normal sense—a work prepared for public sale; rather, it constitutes a memorialization of their friendship, a private keepsake of their homosocial bonds.

Putting aside such secrecy and caution, with the poems of *Noctes Binanianae* finally on view (see *Poems 2* 205–38), it turns out that yet another critical consensus about Eliot's bawdy poems can be exploded. The verses that Eliot contributed to *Noctes*—long suspected of transgressive content—are so inoffensive that they might have been proclaimed from the pulpit of St. Stephen's without raising an eyebrow. Only in "Vers pour la Foulque" does a single, nonsexual reference to "nos culs" (our asses) bring these poems to the brink of bawdy (*Poems 2* 230). And, as the editors describe in their commentary, this very poem was so harmless that Eliot considered publishing it in Pierre Leyris's edition of French translations of Eliot's poems (*Poems 2* 230). For the first scholarly account of the poems in *Noctes*, see Michelle A. Taylor's "(In)discreet Modernism: T. S. Eliot's Coterie Poetics."

19. Valerie Eliot, "Letter."

20. Cheyette 346.

21. Qtd. in Hall 74.

22. McIntire 11. McIntire is more careful elsewhere, when she indicates that Eliot is "most likely" (rather than certainly) composing Bolo poems as late as 1964 (217n9). But this qualification appears in a footnote, while the thrice-repeated claim in her main text is that Eliot wrote these poems "throughout his life" (11, 13, and 15).

23. McIntire 15.

24. Eliot to Clive Bell, Jan. 3, 1941 (cited in *Letters 3* 509n2).

25. *Letters 3* 509.

26. I am indebted to Edward Mendelson for this nice phrase: "the moral urgency of scolding dead people" (44).

27. See Chinitz, "Eliot's Blue Verses." For an overview of the scholarship on the folk

ballad "Christopher Columbo," see Ed Cray, *The Erotic Muse: American Bawdy Songs*, 313–15.

28. Chinitz, "Eliot's Blue Verses," 332; Ricks, "To Keep."

29. The page measures 9 cm. wide by 16 cm. high; hence, this pocketbook, with binding and cover, was about half the size of the *Inventions* notebook (20.5 × 17 cm).

30. Crawford, *Young Eliot*, 140–42.

31. Aiken, "King Bolo," 22.

32. Pound was introduced to Bolo early in their friendship. In an undated letter (likely 1915), Pound writes to Monroe, "If you think [Eliot] lacks vigour merely because he happens to have portrayed Mr. Prufrock the unvigorous, vous vous trompez. His poem of Christopher Columbus is vigorous, and male, not to say coarse. I think however he may produce something both modest and virile before the end of the chapter" (qtd. in Williams 128).

33. Ricks and McCue seem to imply that the pocketbook is from 1915 (*Poems 2* 269), but in my examination of these manuscripts and the related circumstantial evidence (especially the appearance of British spellings), I am led to conclude that the pocketbook dates to the late teens.

34. *Letters 1* 94. The two new stanzas from 1923 explore, with mock prudishness, the queen's pregnancy and the possible paternity of the "embryonic prince" (*Letters 2* 209; *Poems 2* 255). The mock-intellectual aspect that I identify can be traced to as early as 1914, when Eliot imagines various scholars disputing philological niceties within the Bolo poems (*Letters 1* 46–47). Thus, the mock-intellectual and the shockingly ribald elements of the Bolo poems are not mutually exclusive. The point of the chronology offered here is to show how one clearly predominates over the other in different periods.

35. *Letters 3* 509.

36. *Letters 4* 109.

37. The two Bolos addressed to Spencer have been published as stanzas 40 and 41 within *The Columbiad* (see headnote *Poems 2* 270; for the poems, see *Poems 2* 282; or *Letters 6* 514).

38. "One day Columbo and the queen / They fell into a quarrel / Columbo showed his disrespect / By farting in a barrel" (*Inventions* 318).

39. Eliot to Dobrée, Aug. 10, 1930, *Letters 5* 294. The similar quotation appears in the letter to Hayward, Dec. 6, 1940.

40. Eliot to Hayward, Nov. 25, 1940, cited in Stayer, "The Short and Surprisingly Private Life of King Bolo," 17–18.

41. Eliot to Dobrée, Aug. 6, 1941, in *Poems 2* 249. Two seemingly related issues arising in the letters are ultimately red herrings: (1) By 1945 he seems to have acquired a friend, whose last name is Coker and whose nickname is Bolo. It is unclear whether Eliot is the one who has bestowed this nickname, but the conjunction of Bolo and Coker in the same personage is truly odd. (2) One word that had originated in Bolovian mythology but that later floated free of those contexts was the malleable term "Wux" (mainly in "Wux-Ho" and "wuxo"). Used as a farewell, it underwent a resurrection in the early 1940s.

42. *Letters 3* 509n.

43. Eliot to Winthrop Sprague ("Nick") Brooks, July 18, 1956, cited in Stayer, "The Short and Surprisingly Private Life of King Bolo," 18.

44. See Crawford, *Young Eliot*, 95.

45. Huntington Library, Aiken Collection, cited in Stayer, "The Short and Surprisingly Private Life of King Bolo," 19. On November 21, 1963, Eliot wrote to Aiken in a postscript, "Do you remember what happened when the Columbian crew were feasting at the Passover? If not, I will rehearse it to you" (*Poems 2* 283n). This stanza, sent in late 1963 or 1964, is the promised rehearsal. These lines had appeared, in a different arrangement, in a letter (September 29, 1927) to Dobrée (see *Letters 3* 718–19), and the 1964 version as reproduced here appears in a slightly different arrangement in *Poems 2* 283.

46. *Letters 3* 719.

47. "Jewboys," *Letters 3* 718; "bastard jew," *Inventions* 315, and *Poems 2* 271; "feasting at the Passover," *Letters 3* 719, and in Eliot to Aiken, 1964, *Poems 2* 283.

48. *Inventions* 315; and *Poems 2* 271.

49. Chinitz, "Eliot's Blue Verses," 333.

50. Among Eliot's later correspondents (with the exception of Dobrée and Valerie Eliot), the recipients of recycled Bolo stanzas are his Harvard comrades and the friends he made in London ca. 1914–1915: Morris, Nick Brooks, Aiken, Pound, Lewis, and Spencer. (Although they did not matriculate at the same time, Eliot related to Spencer as a Harvard man.)

51. The mildness of Eliot's verse in *Noctes Binanianae* confirms this pattern as well. Although one sonnet in that volume speaks of "crooning like a Harlem coon," the editors are correct in identifying the reference to what were widely described as "coon songs" (*Poems 2* 225–26). The affectionate evocation of jazz culture in the *Noctes* sonnets contrasts with the racial ugliness of "Ballade pour la grosse Lulu." There are two descriptions of rape—in the Bolos sent to Spencer in 1932 (*Poems 2* 282, stanza 41) and in an obscene poem sent to Pound (*Letters 7* 13–14)—but I am arguing for a shift in emphasis, not a complete change.

52. The Bolo poems that I discuss here are found in the published poetry, the published letters, and the unpublished letters. I have also relied on Ricks and McCue for their study of *Valerie's Own Book*, where several Bolo stanzas were copied by Eliot.

Whether more Bolos will be found is an open question. In the first volume of his biography of Pound, A. David Moody describes the "chançons ithyphallique" at the Beinecke and then relates a curious anecdote: "With [the chançons ithyphallique], in the Fall of 1988 . . . was a small black hard-covered notebook, containing a fair copy of the full King Bolo or Columbo epic, written in a very neat small hand, together with a considerable number of other similar verses. I should think it was this fair copy, rather than the miscellaneous drafts and fragments, which EP referred to as 'his earlier EPOS on King Bolo.' In 1994 Donald Gallup told me the notebook was no longer in the Beinecke Pound archive. Ricks did not know of it" (Moody, *Ezra Pound*, 471n321). It is unclear what Moody means by "full King Bolo or Columbo epic." The Bolo pages I have examined at Yale were torn from a smaller notebook, and they do not constitute the "full" Bolo epic as published (and invented) in the Ricks-McCue edition.

I followed up with Moody regarding this odd disappearance. He responded, "It did not occur to me in 1988 that the notebook would vanish from the Beineke, and I was then concerned with the Pound materials. As to what Donald Gallup or anyone else in the Beinecke knew about its disappearance, I can only report that Gallup had no reaction to my asking about it in 1994, beyond confirming that it was not there. There was no suggestion or concern that it had been stolen or lost. It is simply my assumption that since TSE had given it into EP's keeping, Mrs. Eliot reclaimed it" (private correspondence, July 9, 2009). It is unclear whether the pages torn from a smaller notebook that are currently at Yale were originally part of the black notebook Moody recalls.

53. See *Poems 2* 249 and 271, headnote.

54. *Poems 2* 271 and 284.

55. A few decisions do seem inexplicable. Why, for example, is the sexually violent "Fragments" shamed as an "Improper Rhyme" (*Poems 2* 285), while the offensively racist "Ballade pour la grosse Lulu" and obscene "Triumph of Bullshit" are classified neutrally as "Uncollected Poems" (*Poems 1* 260 and 252)—even though all three had been excised from the notebook by Eliot?

56. As a result of the jagged excision marks made when Eliot cut out the obscene verse from the notebook, it is possible to match the stubs in the notebook at the Berg with the corresponding pages at the Beinecke. For those who are interested, I lay out below the order of the excised leaves as they had originally appeared in the notebook. This listing corrects some minor errors and small gaps in *Inventions*. Recall that Eliot numbered the remaining pages of the notebook himself, perhaps to assure Quinn that the excisions were deliberate and that no pages were missing.

(1) Appearing after the notebook's [page] 21 (*Inventions* 30), the first stub corresponds to the page with the end of "Goldfish" IV on the recto and with "Let a tucket be sounded" (*Inventions* 315) on the verso.

(2) Appearing directly after the first stub, the second stub corresponds to the page with "She put the question to the lad" through "Can cure the whistling chancres" (*Inventions* 317–18) on the recto, and "Columbo and his merry men" through "Exeunt the king and queen severally" (*Inventions* 318–19) on the verso.

(3) Appearing before the notebook's [page] 22 (*Inventions* 31, 327–28), the third stub corresponds to the page with "The Triumph of Bullshit."

(4) Appearing after the notebook's [page] 23 (*Inventions* 31), the fourth stub corresponds to the page with the end of "Portrait" I and the aborted beginning of III (beginning "Admire the monuments" [*Inventions* 328] through the deleted epigraph by Laforgue, "Au seuil des siècles charlatans! . . . Pierrots" [*Inventions* 332]) on the recto, and with "King Bolo's swarthy bodyguard" through "And shat upon their sovereign" on the verso (*Inventions* 316).

(5) Appearing before the notebook's [page] 24 (*Inventions* 32), the fifth stub corresponds to the leaf with "One day Columbo and his men / They took and went ashore" through "A-sitting on their bungholes" (*Inventions* 317), with the verso blank.

(6) Appearing after notebook [page] 27 (*Inventions* 37), the sixth stub corresponds to the page with the final line of "Suite Clownesque" III ("Do you think that I'm all right?) and all of IV (*Inventions* 37–38) on the recto, and with "Fragments" on the verso (*Inventions* 314).

(7) Appearing directly after the sixth stub, the seventh stub corresponds to the

page with "Ballade pour la grosse Lulu" on the recto, with the verso blank except for wet ink smudges from the facing recto of [page] 28 (*Inventions* 39), the opening of "Prufrock."

57. Chinitz, "Eliot's Blue Verses," 330; *Inventions* 314.

58. Chinitz, "Eliot's Blue Verses," 332.

59. *Inventions* 314.

60. Townsend 17. I am grateful to Ron Bush, who first drew my attention to this book and suggested the applicability of its categories to my argument about Eliot's bawdy verse.

61. Ibid. 168.

62. Qtd. in ibid. 130.

63. Ibid. 129. Stevens's phrase "much of Tennyson" is as revealing as is his need to assemble a genealogy of non-effeminate poets. Presumably *In Memoriam*, Tennyson's homoerotic love-lament for Arthur Hallam, is what falls outside the bounds acceptable for a man-poet.

64. Townsend 149.

65. *Letters 1* 10–11.

66. Most biographers incorrectly assume that Eliot was a poor student at Smith and Milton (See Stayer, "T. S. Eliot as a Schoolboy").

67. Crawford, *Young Eliot*, 93–94.

68. Ibid. 84.

69. *Prose 1* 20.

70. Crawford, *Young Eliot*, 87.

71. Ibid. 99.

72. See Cray xxv for more on the audience of the bawdy tradition; and Crawford, *Young Eliot*, 79–121, on Eliot's engagement with Harvard social clubs.

73. See *Inventions* 321; and Gill 81n6 for various suggestions about sources for Bolo.

74. Cray 311.

75. See Cray 308–15.

76. Chinitz, "Eliot's Blue Verses," 329–30.

77. One extant version ends with one stanza in Spain, but the bulk of the traditional versions concerns the journey. See Cray 309–12.

78. Gill 71.

79. Ibid.

80. Ibid. 70.

81. McIntire 11.

82. Ibid. 20.

83. See Crawford, *The Savage and the City*, 5–34.

84. *Prose 1* 6.

85. Gill 74.

86. *Inventions* 317.

87. Ibid. 318.

88. *Letters 1* 209.

89. *Inventions* 318.

90. Ibid. 316.

91. McIntire 12.
92. Ibid.
93. Cheyette 336.
94. Ibid. 347.
95. Ibid. 346.
96. McIntire 13.
97. Ibid. 35.
98. *Inventions* xvi.
99. Zwerdling 164.
100. On the topic of form and doggerel, the reader may wish to compare the three bawdy limericks that Eliot wrote out for others: "There was a young lady named Ransome," "There was a young girl of Siberia," and "The Blameless Sister of Publicola" (*Poems 2* 286, 287, and 290). As would be expected of the oral tradition from which they come, these limericks involve some elements of repetition and variation. What matters, then, is not whether they are wholly original to Eliot but to what extent the tight rhythmic and formal constraints of the limerick contrast with the looser, open-ended ballad form in which the Bolo poems were written. The last limerick plays on lines from *Coriolanus* and Valerie's name, and it is more likely original than the first. All three limericks are free of racist or misogynist content and are, in my estimation, more witty and delightfully obscene than all of the Bolo poems and Bolo prose combined.
101. He first appears as "Prof. Dr Krapp (Jena)" in a 1914 letter to Aiken (*Letters 1* 47, and subsequently in *Letters 3* 820 and *Letters 5* 45). He is styled "Herr Dr Krapp of Wien" by Aiken ("King Bolo," 22).

Chapter 7 • "Prufrock," Abandoned

1. Transcribed from audio clip posted with Sara Aridi's "Listen to T. S. Eliot Reflect on Poetry."
2. *Letters 1* 165.
3. Qtd. in Ackroyd 328.
4. *Inventions* 45, emphasis mine.
5. The two leaves (i.e., four pages) on which the "Pervigilium" were written remain in the Berg notebook. A further leaf, originally between pages numbered 34 and 35 of the notebook, was excised before Eliot copied in the final section of "Prufrock." I have measured and plotted the stubs in the Berg notebook against the excised sheets at Yale; none of the latter corresponds to the missing page following the "Pervigilium," which may be presumed lost. It is evident that the excision was made during the drafting of "Prufrock" in Paris 1911, not during the later censoring of the notebook Eliot undertook for Quinn in 1922. At the bottom of the notebook's page 35, the ink (from the lines "To have bitten") has been smudged on the facing verso, page 34. Thus, the resumption of the latter part of "Prufrock"—clearly in Eliot's spiky, Paris hand—happened after the excision. If the missing page was blank, Eliot may have cut it to connect the end of the "Pervigilium" to the latter part of "Prufrock." Or if there was something on the excised page unrelated to "Prufrock," Eliot cut it to ensure that "Prufrock" hung together without extraneous material intervening.
6. Rainey suggests July 1914 as a date for the Maryland manuscript, but neither the watermark of that paper (Falcon Bond) nor Rainey's own measurements of it match the

kinds of paper Eliot was using around that time (198). In a letter to Jane Quinby (Apr. 6, 1948), Eliot dates the Maryland manuscript to a year or two earlier: "I suspect that this is a copy which I gave to Conrad Aiken in 1912 or 1913 to take to London with him and which he unsuccessfully attempted to place at that time on my behalf with several English periodicals" (*Poems 2* 582). In a 1915 letter to Monroe, Aiken suggests an even earlier date: "That poem ['Prufrock'] was written, if I remember rightly, nearly four years ago, and I had a copy of it from the first" (*Selected Letters*, 42). Aiken's bragging to Monroe has a proprietary air and is not reliable as an account of fact. But it does suggest a date much earlier than 1914. Given the uncertainties of memory and other irreconcilable factors, Aiken's Feb. 1913 letter to Eliot requesting a copy is the most reliable piece of evidence; thus, the more likely date for the Maryland manuscript is 1913.

7. Vendler, "T. S. Eliot: Inventing Prufrock," 110–11.

8. *Inventions* 43.

9. Ibid. 43–44.

10. Vendler, "T. S. Eliot: Inventing Prufrock," 93; *Inventions* 43.

11. Menand 26.

12. Ibid. Before the *Inventions* notebook was published 1996, John T. Mayer's *T. S. Eliot's Silent Voices* offered the first extended treatment of "Prufrock's Pervigilium." For Mayer, the "Pervigilium" is the prophetic utterance toward which the outer sections gesture. But after it is drafted, Mayer argues, Eliot senses that the paranoid ranting in the "Pervigilium" would be understood as "the ravings of a lunatic, not the raging of a prophet," and the social element of the poem would be undercut (119). Prufrock would seem like a prophet who had indeed dared however he had been misunderstood.

13. Aiken, *Selected Letters*, 26.

14. The double space is obvious after the five-line passage, whereas the double space before is implicit: the section begins at the top of a page, and the preceding page has plenty of space for three lines. There are other moments in this typescript separated by double spaces.

15. In later life, Eliot recalled, "I did, I think, in 1912, make some additions to the poem and I am grateful to Mr. Aiken for having perceived at once that the additions were of inferior quality" (*Inventions* 176).

16. Sept. 4, 1915, Aiken to Harriet Monroe, *Selected Letters*, 42.

17. Another extended study of "Prufrock's Pervigilium" can be found in Nicholas B. Mayer's "Catalyzing Prufrock," which describes the deleted section as the backstory to the poem, representing the poem's conception even though it was written last. In attempting to explain why the section was deleted, Mayer offers interesting insights into how the "Pervigilium" is too conscious, conflicting with the subterranean mood and inarticulacy of the published sections.

18. Qtd. in Grant 101.

19. Later in Aiken's visit, after Monro had already rejected "Prufrock," Monro and F. S. Flint were discussing Symbolism. Aiken, who had a copy of Eliot's "La Figlia Che Piange" in his pocket, offered it to Monro. As Aiken remembers the story, Monro "thrust it back at me, with the remark 'O I can't be bothered with this.' He so obviously thought I was seizing the opportunity for showing something of *my own* that I put things right the next day by sending it to him, with Eliot's address in Germany and—of course that

too was rejected" (Grant 101–2). The self-incriminating detail here is that Aiken imagines he is "put[ting] things right" with his continuous badgering.

20. Pound, *Selected Letters*, 40.

21. In his review of Helen Carr's *The Verse Revolutionaries*, Christopher Reid reads Pound's astonishment as his admission of how difficult it had been to modernize himself:

> Pound's remark that Eliot had 'actually trained and modernized himself on his own' . . . is often quoted, and taken to signify astonishment that his personal services as converter had not, in this unique case, been required. When you read the words again on page 691 of *The Verse Revolutionaries,* however, you realize that they mean something different. By this stage of the book, the slowness, reluctance, and muddle of Pound's own progress towards a modern, or Modernist, position has been thoroughly documented, as well as the amount of help he needed from more far-sighted associates like T. E. Hulme and F. S. Flint. (7)

22. Pound, *Selected Letters* 40, 41, 45, 50, 57; the undated letter is quoted in Williams 128.

23. Pound, "Drunken Helots and Mr. Eliot," in Brooker, *The Contemporary Reviews*, 6.

24. Williams 126.

25. Ibid. 123–29.

26. Ibid. 127.

27. Ibid.

28. Pound, *Selected Letters*, 110.

29. Monroe 394.

30. Qtd. in Parisi and Young 170.

31. Qtd. in Williams 128.

32. Pound's letter to Monroe, dated July 1915 by her, qtd. in Williams 127.

33. Pound, *Selected Letters*, 63.

34. Williams 127.

35. Fletcher, Sept. 20, 1915, *Selected Letters*, 29.

36. Brooker makes the same point in her introduction to *T. S. Eliot: The Contemporary Reviews* (xv).

37. Qtd. in Brooker, *The Contemporary Reviews*, 6, 9.

38. Ibid. 6.

39. Ibid.

40. See "Recent Verse" in Brooker, *The Contemporary Reviews*, 7.

41. Waugh, qtd. in Brooker, *The Contemporary Reviews*, 3.

42. Ibid. 4.

43. Pound, qtd. in Brooker, *The Contemporary Reviews*, 4–5.

44. Ibid. 8.

45. Ibid. 7.

46. Aiken, qtd. in Brooker, *The Contemporary Reviews*, 3.

47. Ibid. 9.

48. Sinclair, qtd. in ibid. 12.

49. Ibid. 11.

50. Ibid. 13.

51. Marianne Moore's early review calls this quality "honesty" (qtd. in ibid. 15). The peculiar relationship of fragmented consciousness to language had been theorized well before Sinclair, most famously in William James's essay "Stream of Consciousness" in *Principles of Psychology* (1890) and *Briefer Course* (1892).

52. Murry, qtd. in Brooker, *The Contemporary Reviews*, 25–26.

53. Ibid. 47, 46, 49.

54. Wilson, qtd. in ibid. 83. Wilson's description of Eliot's "first meager volume of twenty-four poems" is technically inaccurate: the twenty-four poems of *Ara Vos Prec* constitute his third volume of poetry.

55. Qtd. in Brooker, *Contemporary Reviews* 87.

56. Ibid. 82.

57. Miller 66.

58. Gilbert and Gubar 97.

59. Brooks and Warren 591.

60. Ibid. 590.

61. Donoghue 5, 3.

62. Kenner 35.

63. Vendler, "T. S. Eliot: Inventing Prufrock," 83.

64. Ibid. 83–84.

65. Ibid. 85–87.

66. Ibid. 111. In spite of the fact that Eliot was well versed in the discourse of academic philosophy, Vendler argues that this discourse was not a productive one, because Eliot is able only to parody it in the notebook poems (93). I have declined to list here a discourse that Vendler identifies as "oblique," a middle discourse between the Scylla of corrosive irony and the Charybdis of maudlin expressionism. According to Vendler, this middle discourse, which is expressed in a variety of ways, is "serious but not propositional. It neither assents nor dissents" (94). It is unclear to me how this functions as a discourse, since this middle discourse in Vendler's telling can include a wide range of expression: suggestive imagery, exclamatory statement, the "swerve from irony to inwardness" (94). It seems as if Vendler is not identifying a discourse—a system of language with ideological boundaries—but a series of modes that call upon varied discourses.

67. In the paragraphs that follow, my argument is indebted to Vendler's chapter, especially her discussion of discourses, and I cite her when the ideas are clearly derived from her work. However, I add some categories of my own, I do not use all of her categories for the same ends for which she has designated them, nor do I follow her distinction that sees the lyric voice as the true or honest voice of "Prufrock."

68. Vendler, "T. S. Eliot: Inventing Prufrock," 109.

69. Vendler spells out this "reduplicative semiosis" of the final stanzas ("T. S. Eliot: Inventing Prufrock," 111).

70. *Poems 1* 376.

71. In 1953, six years before writing this letter to Smidt, Eliot had begun a correspondence with his solicitors regarding John Peter's article "A New Interpretation of *The Waste Land*," in which Eliot suggested legal action if the article were disseminated any further. At issue was the interpretation of "homosexual passion" in the poem. Given the unsettling intimacy that "Prufrock" evokes, it is possible that Eliot's explanation—a

male “companion” whose relationship bears “no emotional content whatsoever”—may be seen as an attempt to shut down any suggestion of a homoerotic subtext.

72. Yeats 379.

73. Crawford, “T. S. Eliot: The Poet Who Conquered.”

74. International T. S. Eliot Society Memorial Lecture, 2000. Phillips made these impromptu remarks after the lecture, and he was kind enough to confirm these details to me by email.

75. Levine.

76. Qtd. in Schiff 64.

Chapter 8 • Mumbling the Denouement

1. Epigraph: Woolf 68.

2. Eliot, “Statement.”

3. Gray 84.

4. *Prose 1* 582.

5. Eliot, “Statement”; *Letters I* xix.

6. Woolf 68.

7. Three poems written in 1913–1914—“So through the evening,” “After the turning,” and “I am the Resurrection”—as well as “The Death of Saint Narcissus” (1915) were published not in *Inventions of the March Hare* but in Valerie Eliot’s facsimile of *The Waste Land*. According to Ricks, it was Valerie Eliot, conferring with Gallup, who judged them to belong with *The Waste Land* drafts, a judgment that guided her decisions in the facsimile edition (*Inventions* xiv). But whether she physically removed the three poems from the notebook and placed them with the leaves of *The Waste Land* is unclear.

8. Vendler, “T. S. Eliot: Inventing Prufrock,” 113.

9. Menand 27.

10. Ibid.

11. Ibid. 28.

12. Ibid. 26.

13. The Boston satires might seem to be part of the notebook’s energies insofar as they run on its exhausted fumes. A draft of “Mr. Apollinax” (1915) does appear on loose leaf inserted into the notebook, but the presence of this poem seems to follow the same rule as the later poems such as “Gerontion” and the quatrain poems—all probably added at the last minute to the notebook before Eliot sent it to Quinn. I have also excluded “O lord have patience” from consideration; though undated, this poem most likely dates to 1915–1916, when Eliot began to think seriously about Hulme’s politico-theological categories of classicism and romanticism.

14. Eliot later dated all four satires to “Oxford 1915,” a place that points to the first half of 1915. (In the latter half of 1915, Eliot was living in London and High Wycombe.) That Pound, who kept close tabs on Eliot’s output, seems to refer to the satires as “a few amusing poems” (*Poems 1* 426) in a letter of May 31 seems to indicate that the poems were written at Oxford in May 1915.

15. *Letters 1* 95–96.

16. Eliot, “Statement”; *Letters1* xix.

17. Cited in Gordon 18; Levy and Scherle 121.

18. *Prose 1* 95.

19. Eliot read Evelyn Underhill's *Mysticism* (1911) in 1913–1914. Eliot's dissertation (1914–1916) betrays knowledge of William James's *The Varieties of Religious Experience* (1902).

20. Vendler, "Writhing and Crawling," 8.

21. Eliot uses the form for *Anabasis* in the 1930s, but this is a translation of St.-John Perse's French prose poem.

22. *Letters 1* xix.

23. *Inventions* 332.

24. John T. Mayer 83. Other poems that call up this tortured stair-journey include "He said: this universe," "Rhapsody on a Windy Night," "Prufrock," "Boston Evening Transcript," and *The Waste Land*. It is only with *Ash-Wednesday* and *Burnt Norton*'s "figure of the ten stairs" that unredeemed agony gives way to purgation.

25. McLean 140.

26. Caffin 217.

27. McLean 142.

28. In European countries, and in Russia and Slavic countries especially, the tradition of dancing bears stretched back to the Middle Ages.

29. McLean 141.

30. Ibid. 152.

31. I disagree, but see Coyle for a description of the poem's tone as one of "scorn and envy" (36).

32. Ibid. 47.

33. John T. Mayer 167. My discussion of "Afternoon" is generally indebted to Mayer.

34. Coyle 39.

35. Vendler, "T. S. Eliot: Inventing Prufrock," 101; *Inventions* 80. Rainey (198) dates the manuscript of "Do I know how I feel?" to Jan.–Apr. 1915. I have dated it to 1912–1913, following Gordon, who dates "Hidden under the heron's wing" to 1912 or "the same period" (81): the post-Paris handwriting, in pencil, is identical for both poems, and they appear on the same leaf.

36. Cuda, *The Passions of Modernism*, 38.

37. Ibid.

38. *Facsimile* v.

39. Ibid. 130.

40. *Poems 1* 272.

41. *Poems 1* 68.

42. *Facsimile* 110.

43. The curriculum at Smith was modeled on Harvard's, which had jettisoned its classical program in the late nineteenth century under the leadership of Charles Eliot Norton. The newly implemented elective system gave students more freedom to choose courses and resulted in a deemphasis of Greek and Latin. But the curriculum at Smith was still emphatically humanistic rather than technical, and Eliot studied many foreign languages while there, including Latin, Greek, German, and French. (See my article "T. S. Eliot as a Schoolboy.")

44. See the concise note in *Poems 1* (1159); P. S. Sri's *T. S. Eliot: Vedanta and Buddhism*; and Cleo McNelly Kearns's *T. S. Eliot and Indic Traditions*.

45. *Facsimile* 112.

46. *Inventions* 220.
47. Ibid. 62.
48. Ibid. 222.
49. *Letters 1* 46, 48, 63.
50. Chinitz, rev. of *Inventions*, 57–58.
51. Vendler, "Writhing," 9.
52. *Inventions* 75.
53. Chinitz, rev. of *Inventions*, 58.
54. John T. Mayer 149–50.
55. *Inventions* 78.
56. *Letters 1* 46.
57. See Kaye for a reading of the poem in light of the "homosexual cult" of St. Sebastian.
58. John T. Mayer 152.
59. Eliot to Anne Ridler, Sept. 30, 1952: "St. Ishmael is a charming name (like St. Narcissus, of whom I know nothing" (*Poems 1* 1156). See headnote to "The Death of Saint Narcissus" in *Poems 1* (1154–56), which offers a clear discussion of various attempts to date the poem. Ricks and McCue suggest 1915 as the most probable date (*Poems 2* 585).
60. *Poems 1* 270.
61. Augustine X.27.
62. Gordon 92.
63. *Letters 1* 94.
64. *Inventions* 54.
65. *Inventions* 60.
66. In Wilde's *Salome* (1891) and Strauss's opera (1905), the prophet sings from an empty cistern.
67. From the manuscript evidence, I have not been able to draw any conclusions on the basis of handwriting. Of the many scholars who have essayed dates for the notebook poems, only Rainey suggests a date for "Introspection": the specific time frame of July–Aug. 1915. However, the evidence he uses to adduce this conclusion has been misinterpreted (Rainey 198–99). In his impressive table collating the types of paper Eliot used, the only bit of evidence for this dating seems to be the Waldorf Club watermark of the paper on which "Introspection" is written. Rainey connects this ostensibly American detail to Eliot's few weeks in America in July–Aug. 1915, where he was summoned to explain his marriage to his parents. While Waldorf Clubs were a fixture of Americana in the early part of the century, Rainey has misinterpreted the clue: it is a British paper company's watermark. In a column advertising British stationery, the Times Book Club is described as having displayed in its window ("fronting Oxford street") Welch & Co.'s new line of stationery, Waldorf Club ("'All British' Week").
68. *Prose 1* 357.
69. Dickey, "Parrot's Eye," 125.
70. Cited in Townsend 53.
71. *Letters 1* 41.
72. Townsend 52.
73. *Poems 1* 26.

74. For commentary on the gendered history of hysteria, see the discussion of the poem's title in *Poems 1* (446); and the numerous references to "Hysteria" throughout Laity and Gish's volume.

75. Smith, for example, argues that it is the speaker, not the woman, who is hysterical (33). Indeed, the speaker's paranoia at being engulfed by the woman and his focused struggle to arrest her laughter can be read in the very psychological terms evoked by the title and apparently directed toward the woman.

76. *Inventions* 90. Rainey (198) claims April 1915 as a draft date for "The Engine." The poem is written on notepaper from USMS *St. Louis*, on which ship Eliot sailed to America from July 24 to Aug. 1, 1915 (*Poems 1* 1162; the editors explain the acronym as United States Maritime Service, but it refers instead to United States Mail Steamship). Although it is possible that Eliot obtained the ship's notepaper from a ticketing office in April, given the poem's content as discussed below, it is more likely that Eliot drafted the poem en route in July or later.

77. *Letters 1* 121. My account of Eliot's trip to America is indebted to Crawford (*Young Eliot*, 238–39).

78. *Letters 1* 123.

79. Ibid. 125. On Aug. 16 (a Monday), Eliot reports that he sails on Saturday (Aug. 21). The eight-day trip would have placed him in London around Aug. 29, 1915. In a letter sent to Scofield Thayer six days later (Sept. 4), he invited Thayer to visit him in London, revealing no intention to return to the States.

80. *Inventions* 61; *Poems 1* 271.

81. Smith 28.

82. Kenner 39.

83. Ibid.

84. Gray 86.

85. Ibid. 87.

86. No draft version of "La Figlia" appears in the pages of the notebook.

87. *Poems 1* 28.

88. Geary 28.

89. *Poems 1* 451.

90. "The same period" or 1912 is Gordon's dating (81).

91. My reading of this poem and "Paysage Triste" is indebted to Julia Daniel's unpublished paper "Looking, Class, and Social Space in *Inventions of the March Hare*," from which I cite below specific ideas. Rainey also describes class and gender issues through the figure of the typist in *Revisiting "The Waste Land."*

92. *Inventions* 56.

93. Qtd. in *Poems 1* 1150.

94. By the early twentieth century, porcelain teeth had long been set in dentures as prosthetic devices.

95. Hobbes XIII.

96. Schaum 336.

97. Ibid. 338.

98. Ibid. 339.

99. Ibid. 338, 336.

100. I am indebted to Daniel for this detail (17).

101. Daniel 9.
102. Epigraph: *Prose 5* 459.
103. Smith 29.
104. Smith 289.
105. Asher 165.
106. Perloff.
107. *Poems 1* 82.
108. Ibid. 179.

WORKS CITED

Ackroyd, Peter. *T. S. Eliot*. New York: Penguin, 1984.

Aiken, Conrad. "King Bolo and Others." *T. S. Eliot: A Symposium*. Ed. Richard March and Tambimuttu. New York: Tambimuttu and Mass, 1965. 20–23.

——. *Selected Letters of Conrad Aiken*. Ed. Joseph Killorin. New Haven: Yale UP, 1978.

——. *Ushant*. New York: Duell, Sloan and Pearce, 1952.

"'All British' Week." *American Stationer* 69 (1911): 22.

Aridi, Sara. "Listen to T. S. Eliot Reflect on Poetry." *New York Times* Mar. 11, 2019.

Asher, Kenneth. *T. S. Eliot and Ideology*. Cambridge: Cambridge UP, 1995.

Augustine of Hippo. *Confessions*. Trans. F. J. Sheed. Indianapolis, IN: Hackett, 1993.

Ayto, John, ed. *The Oxford Dictionary of Slang*. Oxford UP, 1998.

Bakhtin, Mikhail. *The Dialogic Imagination: Four Essays*. Trans. Caryl Emerson and Michael Holquist. Ed. Michael Holquist. Austin: U of Texas P, 1981.

Barham, Richard Harris [pseud. Thomas Ingoldsby]. "The Ghost." *The Ingoldsby Legends; or, Mirth and Marvels*. London: Richard Bentley, 1840. 95–104.

Beach, Sylvia. *Shakespeare & Company*. New ed. Intro. by James Laughlin. Lincoln: U of Nebraska P, 1991.

Beasley, Rebecca. *Theorists of Modernist Poetry: T. S. Eliot, T. E. Hulme, Ezra Pound*. Abingdon: Routledge, 2007.

Berlin, James A. *Rhetoric and Reality: Writing Instruction in American Colleges, 1900–1985*. Carbondale: Southern Illinois UP, 1987.

Bizley, W. H. "The Decadent Metropolis as Frontier: Eliot, Laforgue, Baudelaire." *Theoria* 68 (1986): 25–35.

Booth, Wayne. *Rhetoric of Fiction*. 2nd ed. Chicago: U of Chicago, 1983.

Brooker, Jewel Spears. "Seduction and Disenchantment: Eliot in the Bergsonian World." *T. S. Eliot, France, and the Mind of Europe*. Ed. Jayme Stayer. Newcastle upon Tyne, UK: Cambridge Scholars, 2015. 24–38.

——, ed. *T. S. Eliot: The Contemporary Reviews*. Cambridge: Cambridge UP, 2004.

——. *T. S. Eliot's Dialectical Imagination*. Baltimore: Johns Hopkins UP, 2018.

Brooks, Cleanth, and Robert Penn Warren. *Understanding Poetry*. New York: Henry Holt, 1938.

Bruner, Robert F., and Sean D. Carr. *The Panic of 1907*. Hoboken: Wiley & Sons, 2007.

Bush, Ronald. "In Pursuit of Wilde Possum: Reflections on Eliot, Modernism, and the Nineties." *Modernism/modernity* 11 (2004): 469–85.

Buttram Trumbold, Chris. "Earlier Versions of Eliot's Early Verse: The Newly Published Drafts in the Berg Collection." *Journal of Modern Literature* 21.1 (1997): 89–108.

Caffin, Caroline. *Vaudeville*. New York: Mitchell Kennerley, 1914.

Castle, William R. *Fifty Years*. Cambridge, MA: private printing, 1949.

Cheyette, Bryan. "Eliot and 'Race': Jews, Irish, and Blacks." *A Companion to T. S. Eliot*. Ed. David E. Chinitz. Malden, MA: Wiley-Blackwell, 2009. 335–49.

Chinitz, David. E., ed. *A Companion to T. S. Eliot*. Malden, MA: Wiley-Blackwell, 2009.

——. Rev. of *Inventions of the March Hare*, by T. S. Eliot. *ANQ* 11.3 (1998): 56–63.

——. *T. S. Eliot and the Cultural Divide*. Chicago: U of Chicago P, 2003.

——. "T. S. Eliot's Blue Verses and Their Sources in the Folk Tradition." *Journal of Modern Literature* 23.2 (1999): 329–33.

Coffman, Stanley K., Jr. *Imagism: A Chapter for the History of Modern Poetry*. Norman: U of Oklahoma P, 1951.

Coyle, Michael. "'Afternoon' at the British Museum." *The Edinburgh Companion to T. S. Eliot and the Arts*. Ed. Frances Dickey and John Morgenstern. Edinburgh: Edinburgh UP, 2016. 36–50.

Crawford, Robert. *The Savage and the City*. Oxford: Oxford UP, 1987.

——. "T. S. Eliot: The Poet Who Conquered the World, 50 Years On." *Guardian* Jan. 10, 2015.

——. *The Young Eliot: From St. Louis to "The Waste Land."* New York: Farrar, Straus and Giroux, 2015.

Cray, Ed. *The Erotic Muse: American Bawdy Songs*. 2nd ed. Urbana: U of Illinois P, 1999.

Cuda, Anthony. *The Passions of Modernism*. Columbia: U of Southern Carolina, 2010.

——. "The Poet and the Pressure Chamber: Eliot's Life." *A Companion to T. S. Eliot*. Ed. David E. Chinitz. Malden, MA: Wiley-Blackwell, 2009.

——. "T. S. Eliot's Etherized Patient." *Twentieth Century Literature* 50.4 (2004): 394–420.

D'Ambrosio, Vinnie-Marie. *Eliot Possessed*. New York: New York UP, 1989.

Daniel, Julia. "Looking, Class, and Social Space in *Inventions of the March Hare*." Draft essay in manuscript, 2019.

Davenport-Hines, Richard. *Auden*. New York: Pantheon, 1995.

Dickey, Frances. "'Mandarins' at the Museum of Fine Arts." *The Edinburgh Companion to T. S. Eliot and the Arts*. Ed. Frances Dickey and John Morgenstern. Edinburgh: Edinburgh UP, 2016. 9–24.

——. "The Musical World of Eliot's *Inventions*." *The Edinburgh Companion to T. S. Eliot and the Arts*. Ed. Frances Dickey and John Morgenstern. Edinburgh: Edinburgh UP, 2016. 101–20.

——. "Parrot's Eye: A Portrait by Manet and Two by Eliot." *Twentieth-Century Literature* 52.2 (2006): 111–44.

——. "Taking the Air: Eliot and the Smoke of St. Louis." Paper delivered at the International T. S. Eliot Society Meeting, St. Louis, MO. Sept. 29, 2019.

Diepeveen, Leonard. "'I Can Have More Than Enough Power': T. S. Eliot's Construction of His Audience." *Marketing Modernisms: Self-Promotion, Canonization, and*

Rereading. Ed. Kevin J. H. Dettmar and Stephen Watt. Ann Arbor: U of Michigan P, 1996. 37–60.

——. *Modernist Fraud: Hoax, Parody, Deception*. Oxford: Oxford UP 2019.

Donoghue, Denis. *Words Alone: The Poet T. S. Eliot*. New Haven: Yale UP, 2000.

Eliot, T. S. *The Complete Prose of T. S. Eliot: The Critical Edition*. Vols. 1–8: 1905–1965. Ed. Ronald Schuchard et al. Baltimore: Johns Hopkins UP, 2014–2019.

——. *Inventions of the March Hare*. Ed. Christopher Ricks. New York: Harcourt Brace, 1996.

——. *The Letters of T. S. Eliot*. Vols. 1–8: 1898–1937. Ed. Valerie Eliot et al. London: Faber, 2009–2019.

——. *The Poems*. Vols. 1–2. Ed. Christopher Ricks and Jim McCue. London/Baltimore: Faber and Faber / Johns Hopkins UP, 2015.

——. *Poèmes, 1910–1930*. Ed. and trans. Pierre Leyris. Paris: Éditions du Seuil, 1947.

——. "Statement by T. S. Eliot on the Opening of the Emily Hale Letters at Princeton." [1960/1963] Jan. 2, 2020. T. S. Eliot Foundation. https://tseliot.com/foundation /statement-by-t-s-eliot-on-the-opening-of-the-emily-hale-letters-at-princeton/.

——. *The Waste Land: A Facsimile and Transcript of the Original Drafts*. Ed. Valerie Eliot. San Diego: Harcourt Brace Jovanovich, 1971.

Eliot, Valerie. "Letter." *Times Literary Supplement* Feb. 17, 1984.

Fletcher, John Gould. *Life Is My Song: The Autobiography of John Gould Fletcher*. New York: Farrar and Rinehart, 1937.

——. *Selected Letters of John Gould Fletcher*. Ed. Leighton Rudolph et al. Fayetteville: U of Arkansas P, 1996.

Freeman, Michael. *François Villon in His Works: The Villain's Tale*. Atlanta: Rodopi, 2000.

Frye, Northrup. *T. S. Eliot*. New York: Capricorn, 1972.

Furia, Philip. *The Poets of Tin Pan Alley*. Oxford: Oxford UP, 1990.

Gallup, Donald. "The 'Lost' Manuscripts of T. S. Eliot." *Times Literary Supplement* Nov. 7, 1968: 1237–43. Rpt. with some alterations in *Bulletin of the New York Public Library* 72 (1968): 641–52.

——. *T. S. Eliot: A Bibliography*. Rev. and extended ed. New York: Harcourt, Brace and World 1969.

——. *T. S. Eliot and Ezra Pound: Collaborators in Letters*. New Haven: Henry W. Wenning/C. A. Stonehill, 1970.

——. *What Mad Pursuits! More Memories of a Yale Librarian*. New Haven: Yale UP, 1998.

Gammond, Peter. "Ragtime." *The Oxford Companion to Music*. Ed. Alison Latham. Oxford University Press, 2002. *Oxford Reference Online*. Oxford University Press. www.oxfordreference.com. Jan. 15, 2010.

Gardner, Helen. *The Art of T. S. Eliot*. London: Faber, 1968.

Geary, Edward A. "T. S. Eliot and the *Fin de Siècle*." *Rocky Mountain Review of Language and Literature* 40.1/2 (1986): 21–33.

Gershwin, Ira. *Lyrics on Several Occasions*. New York: Knopf, 1959.

Gilbert, Sandra M., and Susan Gubar. *No Man's Land: The Place of the Woman Writer in the Twentieth Century*. Vol. 3: *Letters from the Front*. New Haven: Yale UP 1996.

Gill, Jonathan. "Protective Coloring: Modernism and Blackface Minstrelsy in the Bolo

Poems." *T. S. Eliot's Orchestra: Critical Essays on Poetry and Music*. Ed John Xiros Cooper. New York: Garland, 2000. 65–84.

Gish, Nancy K. "Disincarnate Desire: T. S. Eliot and the Poetics of Dissociation." *Gender, Desire, Sexuality in T. S. Eliot*. Ed. Cassandra Laity and Nancy K. Gish. Cambridge: Cambridge UP, 2004. 107–29.

Gordon, Lyndall. *T. S. Eliot: An Imperfect Life*. New York: Norton, 1999.

Graham, T. Austin. *The Great American Songbooks: Musical Texts, Modernism, and the Value of Popular Culture*. Oxford: Oxford UP, 2013.

Grant, Joy. *Harold Monro and the Poetry Bookshop*. Berkeley: U of California P, 1967.

Gray, Piers. *T. S. Eliot's Intellectual and Poetic Development 1909–1922*. Atlantic Highlands, NJ: Humanities Press, 1982.

Green, Jonathon, ed. *The Cassell Dictionary of Slang*. London: Cassell, 1998.

Greene, Edward J. H. "Jules Laforgue et T. S. Eliot." *Revue de Littérature Comparée* 22 (1948): 363–97.

——. *T. S. Eliot et la France*. Paris: Éditions contemporaines, 1951.

Hall, Donald. "T. S. Eliot: The Art of Poetry." *Writers at Work: The "Paris Review" Interviews*. 2nd ser. New York: Viking Press, 1963. 89–110.

Hargrove, Nancy Duvall. *T. S. Eliot's Parisian Year*. Gainesville: UP of Florida, 2010.

Harmon, William, and Hugh Holman. *A Handbook to Literature*. 9th ed. Upper Saddle River, NJ: Prentice Hall, 2003.

Hobbes, Thomas. *Leviathan*. Ed. C. B. Macpherson. New York: Penguin, 1985.

Hotten, John Camden. *A Dictionary of Modern Slang, Cant, and Vulgar Words*. London: John Camden Hotton, 1859.

Howarth, Herbert. *Notes on Some Figures behind T. S. Eliot*. Boston: Houghton Mifflin, 1964.

Internet Broadway Database. http://www.ibdb.com. Mar. 20, 2019.

Jain, Manju. *T. S. Eliot and American Philosophy*. Cambridge: Cambridge UP, 1992.

Johnson, Loretta. "T. S. Eliot's Bawdy Verse: Lulu, Bolo and More Ties." *Journal of Modern Literature* 27.1/2 (2003): 14–25.

Kaye, Richard A. "'A Splendid Readiness for Death': T. S. Eliot, the Homosexual Cult of St. Sebastian, and World War I." *Modernism/modernity* 6.2 (1999): 107–34.

Kearns, Cleo McNelly. *T. S. Eliot and Indic Traditions: A Study in Poetry and Belief*. Cambridge: Cambridge UP, 1987.

Keller, Mark, and Mairi McCormick. *A Dictionary of Words about Alcohol*. New Brunswick: Rutgers Center of Alcohol Studies, 1968.

Kenner, Hugh. *The Invisible Poet: T. S. Eliot*. New York: Harcourt, Brace & World, 1959.

Laforgue, Jules. *Oeuvres complète*. Vol. 2: *1884–1887*. Ed. Maryke de Courten et al. Lausanne: Editions L'Age d'Homme, 1995.

——. *Six Moral Tales from Jules Laforgue*. Ed. and trans. Frances Newman. New York: Horace Liveright, 1928.

Laity, Cassandra, and Nancy K. Gish, eds. *Gender, Desire, Sexuality in T. S. Eliot*. Cambridge: Cambridge UP, 2004.

Lane, Anthony. Rev. of *Inventions of the March Hare*, by T. S. Eliot. *New Yorker* Mar. 10, 1997: 86–92. Rpt. as "T. S. Eliot" in *Nobody's Perfect*. New York: Vintage, 2003. 438–48.

Lanham, Richard A. *A Handlist of Rhetorical Terms*. 2nd ed. Berkeley: U of California P, 1991.

Leblanc, Cécile. *Proust écrivain de la musique*. Turnhout, Belgium: Brepols, 2017.

Levine, Mark. "Letter of Recommendation: 'The Love Song of J. Alfred Prufrock.'" *New York Times Magazine* Aug. 6, 2015.

Levy, William Turner, and Victor Scherle. *Affectionately, T. S. Eliot: The Story of a Friendship 1947–1965*. London: J. M. Dent and Sons, 1968.

Lewis, Wyndham. *Blasting and Bombardiering*. 2nd ed. Berkeley: U of California P, 1967.

Lighter, J. E., ed. *Random House Historical Dictionary of American Slang*. New York: Random House, 1994.

March, Richard, and Tambimuttu. *T. S. Eliot: A Symposium*. Chicago: Henry Regnery, 1949.

Marshik, Celia. *British Modernism and Censorship*. Cambridge: Cambridge UP, 2006.

Matthews, T. S. *Great Tom: Notes towards the Definition of T. S. Eliot*. New York: Harper & Row, 1974.

Matthiessen, F. O. *The Achievement of T. S. Eliot*. 3rd ed. London: Oxford UP, 1958.

Mayer, John T. *T. S. Eliot's Silent Voices*. Oxford: Oxford UP, 1989.

Mayer, Nicholas B. "Catalyzing Prufrock." *Journal of Modern Literature* 34 (2011): 182–98.

McCue, Jim. "Editing Eliot." Rev. of *The Annotated Waste Land with Eliot's Contemporary Prose*, ed. Lawrence Rainey. *Essays in Criticism* 56.1 (2006): 1–27.

McIntire, Gabrielle. *Modernism, Memory and Desire*. Cambridge: Cambridge UP, 2008.

——. "An Unexpected Beginning: Sex, Race, and History in T. S. Eliot's Columbo and Bolo Poems." *Modernism/modernity* 9.2 (2002): 283–301.

McLean, Albert F., Jr. *American Vaudeville as Ritual*. Lexington: UP of Kentucky, 1965.

Menand, Louis. "How Eliot Became Eliot." Rev. of *Inventions*. *New York Review of Books* 44.8 (1997): 26–29.

Mendelson, Edward. "A Different T. S. Eliot." *New York Review of Books* Feb. 22, 2016: 43–45.

Meyers, Jeffrey. *The Enemy: A Biography of Wyndham Lewis*. London: Routledge, Kegan, and Paul, 1982.

Miller, James E., Jr. *T. S. Eliot's Personal Waste Land: Exorcism of the Demons*. University Park: Pennsylvania State UP, [1977] 1978.

Monroe, Harriet. *A Poet's Life: Seventy Years in a Changing World*. New York: Macmillan, 1938.

Moody, A. David. *Ezra Pound: Poet; A Portrait of the Man and His Work*. Vol. 1: *The Young Genius, 1885–1920*. Oxford: Oxford UP, 2007.

——. *Thomas Stearns Eliot: Poet*. 2nd ed. Cambridge: Cambridge UP, 1994.

Morgenstern, John. "The 'Centre of Intensity': T. S. Eliot's Reassessment of Baudelaire in 1910–1911 Paris." *Religion & Literature* 44.1 (2012): 159–67.

——. "The Modern Bacchanal: Eliot and Matisse." *The Edinburgh Companion to T. S. Eliot and the Arts*. Ed. Frances Dickey and John Morgenstern. Edinburgh: Edinburgh UP, 2016. 51–68.

Mulertt, Hugo. *The Goldfish and Its Systematic Culture with a View to Profit*. Cincinnati: McDonald and Eick, 1883.

O'Keeffe, Paul. *Some Sort of Genius: A Life of Wyndham Lewis*. Berkeley: Counterpoint, 2000.

Parisi, Joseph, and Stephen Young, eds. *Dear Editor: A History of "Poetry" in Letters.* New York: Norton, 2002.

Pegram, Thomas R. *Battling Demon Rum: The Struggle for a Dry America, 1800–1933*. Chicago: Ivan R. Dee, 1998.

Perloff, Marjorie. "Old Possum's Nest." *Weekly Standard* June 6, 2016. www.weekly standard.com/old-possums-nest/article/2002569.

Peter, John. "A New Interpretation of *The Waste Land*." *Essays in Criticism* 2 (1952): 242–66; rev. and rpt. *Essays in Criticism* 19 (1969): 140–75.

Philippe, Charles-Louis. *Bubu de Montparnasse* [1905]. Lausanne: Éditions du Grand-Chêne, 1946.

Phillips, Carl. "Poetry, Consciousness, Gift: The Model of T. S. Eliot." International T. S. Eliot Society Memorial Lecture. St. Louis, MO, September 2000. Published under the same title in *Coin of the Realm: Essays in the Life and Art of Poetry*. St. Paul, MN: Graywolf, 2004: 75–92.

Poirier, Richard. "The Waste Sad Time." *New Republic* Apr. 28, 1997: 36–45.

Pondrom, Cyrena. "Conflict and Concealment: Eliot's Approach to Women and Gender." *A Companion to T. S. Eliot*. Ed. David E. Chinitz. Malden, MA: Wiley-Blackwell, 2009. 323–34.

Pound, Ezra. *Collected Early Poems of Ezra Pound*. Ed. Michael John King. New York: New Directions, 1976.

——. *The Selected Letters of Ezra Pound: 1907–1941*. Ed. D. D. Paige. New York: New Directions, 1971.

——. "T. S. Eliot." *We Moderns*. New York: Gotham Book Mart, 1940. 24–25.

Pound, Ezra, and Wyndham Lewis. *Pound/Lewis: The Letters of Ezra Pound and Wyndham Lewis*. Ed. Timothy Materer. New York: New Directions, 1985.

Powel, Harford Willing Hare, Jr. "Notes on the Life of T. S. Eliot, 1888–1910." MA Thesis. Brown University, 1954.

Quinion, Michael. "Rush the Growler." World Wide Words: Investigating the English Language across the Globe. Aug. 2, 2003. http://www.worldwidewords.org/qa/qa-rus1.htm.

Raffel, Burton. *T. S. Eliot*. New York: Continuum, 1991.

Rainey, Lawrence. *Revisiting "The Waste Land."* New Haven: Yale UP: 2005

Reid, B. L. *The Man from New York: John Quinn and His Friends*. Oxford: Oxford UP, 1968.

Reid, Christopher. "After Halloween." Rev. of *The Verse Revolutionaries*, by Helen Carr. *TLS* Oct. 30, 2009: 7–8.

Richards, Eliza. "Voice." *The Princeton Encyclopedia of Poetry and Poetics*. 4th ed. Ed. Roland Greene, Stephen Cushman, et al. Princeton: Princeton UP, 2012.

Ricks, Christopher. *Allusion to the Poets*. Oxford: Oxford UP, 2002.

——. "Crabby." *New Republic* June 9, 1997: 48.

——. "To Keep the Ball Rolling." *Times Literary Supplement* June 6, 1997: 17–18.

——. "T. S. Eliot's Othello" (lecture). T. S. Eliot International Summer School, University of London, Institute of English Studies, June 30, 2009.

"Romulus and the Steer." *New York Times* May 27, 1899: 14.

Schaum, Melita. "'Just Looking': Class, Desire, and the Consuming Vision in T. S. Eliot's 'In the Department Store.'" *Journal of Modern Literature* 23.2 (1999–2000): 335–50.

Schiff, Stephen. "Big Poetry." *New Yorker* July 14, 1997: 60–67.

Schuchard, Ronald. *Eliot's Dark Angel: Intersections of Life and Art*. Oxford: Oxford UP, 1999.

Sherry, Vincent. *Modernism and the Reinvention of Decadence*. Cambridge: Cambridge UP, 2015.

Smith, Grover. "Charles-Louis Philippe and T. S. Eliot." *American Literature* 22.3 (1950): 254–59.

——. *T. S. Eliot's Poetry and Plays: A Study in Sources and Meaning*. Phoenix. Chicago: U of Chicago P, 1960.

Sobel, Robert. *Panic on Wall Street*. New York: Macmillan, 1968.

Soldo, John J. "Jovial Juvenilia: T. S. Eliot's First Magazine." *Biography* 5.1 (1982): 25–37.

Southam, B. C. *A Guide to the Selected Poems of T. S. Eliot*. 6th ed. New York: Harcourt Brace, 1996.

Sri, P. S. *T. S. Eliot: Vedanta and Buddhism*. Vancouver: U of British Columbia P, 1985.

Stayer, Jayme. "Ambivalence All Around." *Twentieth-Century Literature* 51.4 (2005): 504–11.

——. "Eliot's Culture Shock: Imagining an Audience for the Paris Poems." *T. S. Eliot, France, and the Idea of Europe*. Ed. Jayme Stayer. Newcastle upon Tyne, UK: Cambridge Scholars, 2015.

——. "I Grow Old: T. S. Eliot's 'The Love Song of J. Alfred Prufrock' and *Inventions of the March Hare* 100 Years On." *Literature Compass* 9.4 (2012): 317–25.

——. "Searching for the Early Eliot: *Inventions of the March Hare*." *A Companion to T. S. Eliot*. Ed. David E. Chinitz. Malden, MA: Wiley-Blackwell, 2009. 107–19.

——. "The Short and Surprisingly Private Life of King Bolo: Eliot's Bawdy Poems and Their Audiences." *The T. S. Eliot Studies Annual*. Ed. John Morgenstern. Clemson: Clemson UP, 2017. 3–30.

——, ed. *T. S. Eliot, France, and the Mind of Europe*. Newcastle upon Tyne, UK: Cambridge Scholars, 2015.

——. "T. S. Eliot as a Schoolboy: The Lockwood School, Smith Academy, and Milton Academy." *Twentieth-Century Literature* 59.4 (2013): 619–56.

Stewart, D. Travis. *No Applause—Just Throw Money*. New York: Faber, 2005.

Stravinsky, Igor. "Memories of T. S. Eliot." *Esquire* 64.2 (1965): 92–93.

Symons, Arthur. *The Symbolist Movement in Literature*. Ed. Matthew Creasy. Manchester: Carcanet, 2014.

Taupin, René. *L'Influence du symbolisme français sur la poésie américaine (de 1910 à 1920)*. Repr. Paris ed. Geneva: Slatkine Reprints, [1929] 1975.

Taylor, Michelle A. "(In)discreet Modernism: T. S. Eliot's Coterie Poetics." *College Literature* 47.1 (2020): 34–64.

Torrens, James, SJ. "The Hidden Years of *The Waste Land* Manuscript." *Santa Clara Review* 76 (1989): 36–42. Rpt. in Lois A. Cuddy and David H. Hirsch, eds. *Critical Essays on T. S. Eliot's "The Waste Land."* Boston: G. K. Hall, 1991. 60–65.

Townsend, Kim. *Manhood at Harvard: William James and Others*. Cambridge, MA: Harvard UP, 1996.

Vendler, Helen. "T. S. Eliot: Inventing Prufrock." *Coming of Age as a Poet*. Cambridge, MA: Harvard, 2003. 81–113.

——. "Writhing and Crawling and Leaping and Darting and Flattening and Stretching." Rev. of *Inventions of the March Hare*. *London Review of Books* Oct. 31, 1996: 8–9.

Villon, François. *The Complete Works of François Villon*. Trans. Anthony Bonner. New York: David McKay, 1960.

Weems, Mason Locke. *A History of the Life and Death, Virtues and Exploits of General George Washington*. Mount Vernon ed. Philadelphia: J. B. Lippincott, 1918.

Williams, Ellen. *Harriet Monroe and the Poetry Renaissance*. Urbana: U of Illinois P, 1977.

Wilson, Edmund. *Axel's Castle*. New York: Charles Scribner's Sons, 1931.

Woolf, Virginia. *The Diary of Virginia Woolf*. Vol. 2: *1920–24*. Ed. Anne Olivier Bell. New York: Penguin, 1984.

Yeats, W. B. "A General Introduction for My Work." *W. B. Yeats: The Major Works*. Ed. Edward Larrissy. Oxford: Oxford UP, 1997. 379–89.

Zwerdling, Alex. Rev. of *Inventions of the March Hare*, by T. S. Eliot. *Modernism/modernity* 5.2 (1998): 163–65.

INDEX